SHOW NO FEAR

SHOW NO FEAR

Daring Actions in Canadian Military History

Edited by Colonel Bernd Horn
Foreword by Lieutenant-Colonel Omer Lavoie

DUNDURN PRESS
TORONTO

Editor: Michael Carroll
Copy-editor: Shannon Whibbs
Designer: Jennifer Scott
Printer: Marquis

Library and Archives Canada Cataloguing in Publication

Show no fear : daring actions in Canadian military history / edited by Bernd Horn.

Includes index.
ISBN 978-1-55002-816-4

1. Canada--History, Military. 2. Battles--Canada. 3. Soldiers--Canada--History. I. Horn, Bernd, 1959-

FC226.H67 2008   355.00971   C2008-900718-2

1   2   3   4   5   12   11   10   09   08

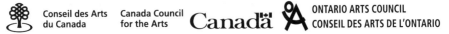

Conseil des Arts du Canada   Canada Council for the Arts   Canadä   ONTARIO ARTS COUNCIL CONSEIL DES ARTS DE L'ONTARIO

We acknowledge the support of the **Canada Council for the Arts** and the **Ontario Arts Council** for our publishing program. We also acknowledge the financial support of the **Government of Canada** through the **Book Publishing Industry Development Program** and **The Association for the Export of Canadian Books**, and the **Government of Ontario** through the **Ontario Book Publishers Tax Credit** program and the **Ontario Media Development Corporation**.

Care has been taken to trace the ownership of copyright material used in this book. The author and the publisher welcome any information enabling them to rectify any references or credits in subsequent editions.

J. Kirk Howard, President

Printed and bound in Canada
www.dundurn.com

Dundurn Press
3 Church Street, Suite 500
Toronto, Ontario, Canada
M5E 1M2

Gazelle Book Services Limited
White Cross Mills
High Town, Lancaster, England
LA1 4XS

Dundurn Press
2250 Military Road
Tonawanda, NY U.S.A.
14150

CONTENTS

FOREWORD

Initially I was surprised when I was asked to write the foreword to *Show No Fear: Daring Actions in Canadian Military History*. After all, I am neither a historian, nor a scholar. I am an infantry officer. But, as I began to work my way through this volume, I quickly realized the connection. I was the commanding officer of Task Force (TF) 3-06, which was based on the 1st Battalion, The Royal Canadian Regiment Battle Group, from August 2006 to February 2007, and deployed to Afghanistan during a very critical time in Kandahar Province. Our tour was a very difficult and costly rotation. Our many successes, including NATO's first combat action as an alliance, came at a great cost in human lives and suffering. Often undermanned, short of the enablers necessary to prosecute operations and always in a very complex, chaotic, and lethal environment, the men and women of TF 3-06 persevered and accomplished tasks and missions that, in the final analysis, no one had a right to expect them to do.

This is where the link comes in with this book. *Show No Fear* captures the indomitable spirit of Canadians who throughout our military history have gone into harm's way to serve their nation and fellow Canadians. This book demonstrates the bold, courageous, and unconquerable spirit of the average Canadian soldier, sailor, and airmen/women. It speaks to our military heritage as capable warriors, dependable allies, and a dreaded foe.

I was given the privilege of leading our contemporary soldiers in combat. Their unrelenting professionalism, sense of humanity, and tenacity to accomplish the mission was humbling. In constant combat from the moment they arrived on the ground until they left the theatre, they never wavered or faltered. In the true Canadian military tradition, when the chips were down, whether forced to go it alone or with allied support, they got the mission done. I can see now that what in fact they accomplished was to write another chapter in our proud military history of being a nation of warfighters.

In the end, I highly recommend this book to all Canadians, whether military or civilian. It captures the essence of our rich and colourful Canadian military history. It also speaks to the warrior ethos and warfighting tradition of our nation's military.

Lieutenant-Colonel Omer Lavoie
Commanding Officer TF 3-06

ACKNOWLEDGEMENTS

Assembling a book, whether alone or in concert with others, is always a huge undertaking. As such, it is never really the work of one individual. Many hands play their part, some more obvious than others. In that vein, I wish to acknowledge, both on my own account, but also on behalf of all contributors, the assistance of others. Initially, I wish to specifically thank all the contributors for taking the time and enormous effort in putting together their essays that appear in this book. Your knowledge of the subject and continued enthusiasm in sharing that knowledge is always inspiring.

In addition, I would like to thank Paramount Press, Susan Surgeson, and Parks Canada, as well as Robert Flacke Sr. and the Fort William Henry Corporation, who made possible the use of many of the graphics that are used in the first four chapters of the book. Similarly, I would also like to thank Craig Mantle, who ably assisted in sourcing many of the photographs that appear on the pages in this volume.

Collectively, we would also like to thank a number of individuals and organizations for their expertise and invaluable assistance. We owe a debt of gratitude to the staff of the Fortress of Louisbourg, National Historic Sites of Canada, specifically, Ken Donovan, Sandy Balcom, Ruby Powell, Brain Harpell, Rebecca Duggan, and Judith Romard, as well as George Vandervlugt of CRM Collections Management, Parks Canada. Additionally, our gratitude is also extended to the Royal Military College of Canada, Library and Archives Canada, and the Department of National Defence Directorate of History and Heritage.

I must also acknowledge the assistance of Dundurn editorial director Michael Carroll, whose efforts ensured a rough manuscript was massaged into the book you see before you, and assistant editor Shannon

Whibbs, whose contribution put a fine polish on the manuscript. Finally, I must thank my wife Kim and my girls, Calli and Katie, who have always indulged my self-imposed exile in my office to work on my projects.

INTRODUCTION

Canada is presently at war with a brutal and unrelenting enemy. The casualties suffered in Afghanistan, which in early summer of 2007 numbered 66 dead and well over 300 wounded, are testimony to the scale of battle that we are experiencing in that southwest Asian location. In fact, Canada currently has suffered the second-highest number of combat casualties of all NATO troop-contributing nations. However, Canadians still have difficulty accepting this reality. Understandably, they lament the loss and suffering of their soldiers, as well as that of the Afghan people. They proudly support their military, but are strongly opposed to the involvement of the Canadian Forces (CF) in Afghanistan. At the heart of the Canadian philosophical and political discord is the peacekeeper mythology.

Quite simply, Canadians do not believe that their military is a warfighting force. Rather, they wish to maintain an illusion of a nation of peacekeepers who venture forth in the turbulent violent world and do good. They wish to hang on to images of soldiers delivering humanitarian supplies, providing aid and infrastructure, and passing out teddy bears to children in impoverished war-torn or disaster-inflicted areas around the world. This expectation and myth grew out of the Cold War when Canada in many ways made its name in the United Nations (UN) as a reliable and effective peacekeeping force.

However, the reality is much different. Throughout this nation's history, Canadians have proven to be formidable warriors — dreaded foes and cherished allies. Although not a militaristic society or people, we have continually been capable soldiers — second to none. From Canada's first expeditionary force in the Boer War, through the two World Wars, Korea, and then the myriad peacekeeping missions during the Cold War, through the turbulent 1990s in the post Cold War era in such places as Somalia, Bosnia-Hercegovina, East Timor, Cambodia and now Afghanistan, this nation's soldiers have always shown courage, daring, and tenacity. Its allies, as well as the international community as a whole, have long realized that Canada's soldiers, sailors, and airmen/women would get the job done.

And accomplish the mission is exactly what our military has always done — often, showing a distinctive, daring attitude in the process. Exactly what is meant by *daring?* In essence, our military forces have always had the courage to oppose and defy the odds of success, to boldly venture forth to accomplish the mission, no matter how dangerous. They have always been prepared to take risks and display the necessary fearlessness to take on even the hardest tasks. In the end, our nation's military has always shown daring — whether in thought, planning, or execution.

Clearly, daring applies to actions and deeds — for instance, the storming of an impregnable stronghold or position; an attack or spirited defence against insurmountable odds; or the conduct of an individual, group, or organization. However, daring can also extend to planning or a continual mindset, one that operates on the fringes and constantly pushes the proverbial envelope of safe or conventionally accepted reasoned action.

The book begins with an examination of the adventurous and audacious practice of ranging and the use of *la petite guerre* during the struggle for North America by partisans, rangers, and Natives. The struggle to survive, and later control, the wilderness of the New World thrust the Europeans into a theatre where their conventional and cultural understanding of war was alien and not entirely effective. As a result, techniques borrowed from the Native way of war were adopted and proved to be a demanding and challenging method of warfare that taxed the intrepid practitioners. In the end, the gruelling, desperate life-and-death struggle in the hinterlands of the continent dramatically impacted the strategy and campaigns of the European protagonists in their battle for control of North America.

Chapter 2 provides a dramatic and illustrative example of the theme explored in the book's opening chapter. It is the account of a desperate fight for survival between the legendary Robert Rogers and his Rangers and their French-Canadian nemesis, Charles Langlade. Set against the backdrop of the harsh winter environment of Lake Champlain, it characterizes both the daring nature of the raids on the frontier, particularly in the context of the unforgiving terrain, as well as the savagery that marked these ongoing skirmishes in the wilderness.

The next chapter continues the theme of the Seven Years' War in North America. In chapter 3 Michel Wyczynski recounts the dramatic events surrounding the siege of the strategic Fortress of Louisbourg in 1758. Specifically, he focuses on the daring raid by British sailors to capture and destroy two French warships anchored in the Louisbourg harbour. This intrepid act, supported by an elaborate deception plan and carried out with extreme stealth in the dead of night, was designed to open the way for the British fleet to penetrate the harbour. Like most high-risk missions, the payoff was of extremely high value. The successful destruction and capture of the ships allowed the British to enter the harbour and increase exponentially the firepower available to relentlessly hammer the fortress, triggering an almost immediate French capitulation.

The next story, in chapter 4 by John Grodzinski, is another tale of daring frontier soldiering. Undermanned, facing imminent invasion, and potentially overwhelmed by the resource capability of the Americans, who had just declared war on Great Britain, General Isaac Brock was left with little recourse but to boldly strike out, and, using the offensive as the best form of defense, attack the United States to preempt, disrupt, and dislocate American forces from pouring into Canada. In this chapter, Grodzinski reveals the bold manoeuvres that Brock, his subordinates, and Native allies conducted to capture Fort Mackinac and Fort Detroit in 1812.

The next recount by John Bell changes the pace. In chapter 5, Canada becomes a backdrop for intrigue and intrepid plans in the American Civil War. It chronicles the attempts of Confederate naval officers, conspirators, and potential commandos to prosecute bold raids and attacks on Union ships, shipping, and facilities, including a prisoner-of-war camp. Throughout, the cat-and-mouse game of planning, equipping, and executing the missions while trying to avoid Union spies and Canadian authorities makes the chapter resonate with subterfuge and daring. In all, the chapter sheds light on a very exciting, yet, little-known period of Canadian military history.

The Boer War provides the setting for Chapter 6 and the next action. Overconfident in a conflict pitting British Regulars against a nation of "farmers," the Empire was quickly sent reeling after a series of defeats by the Boer irregulars. Into this tempest, Canada sent approximately 1,039 largely inexperienced Canadian volunteers, which formed the 2nd Special Service Battalion of The Royal Canadian Regiment (RCR). Itching for action, the colonials quickly learned the reality of modern war in a deadly battle at Paardeberg Drift. Although repulsed at first, the Canadians were fed into battle roughly a week later in a daring night attack. Although the second assault against the Boer position at Paardeberg was a success, in fact the first British victory of the war, the nature of the battle raises the question of whether the saviours of Paardeberg were accidental heroes. However, in the end it is difficult to argue with the fact that the success and the victory at Paardeberg by the Royal Canadians boosted the stature of the Canadian soldiers and the nation itself.

In Chapter 7, Andrew Godefroy examines the daring trench raids that became the hallmark of the Canadian Army in the First World War. Bold and innovative in their own right, Godefroy points out that doctrine and tactics evolved considerably due to the knowledge and experience gained from these audacious raids against the German lines. At first they were designed to simply harass the enemy and cause attrition and damage, but by 1917 raids were being used as "on the job training" for new troops, as well as to hone skills of the more veteran soldiers and refine tactics techniques and procedures. Raids also grew in size, from a few dozen men of a single infantry battalion to almost a thousand troops from all arms. Godefroy explains how combined arms warfare solidified itself in Canadian doctrine through these raids and became an example for all other armies to follow. In the end, he argues that the implementation of these successful raids actually enabled the Canadian Corps to seize Vimy Ridge, the muddy heights of Passchendaele in 1917, and to break the German lines of defence in 1918.

The book then moves on to the Second World War. In Chapter 8, Tony Balasevicius tells the story of one of Canada's most controversial battles. Surrounded by heroism and daring feats of arms, it is also cloaked with criticism and accusations of military incompetence. The author analyzes the genesis of the raid, the reasons for its failure but also the bold execution by the combat troops. In the end, Balasevicius underlines how the actions of Canada's soldiers on the bloody beaches of Dieppe in many ways epitomized the courageous persona of this nation's warriors. Eager to join the fray, the Canadians representing all regions of the country fought a tenacious battle against overwhelming odds and wrote another chapter of Canada's proud military heritage with their blood.

A co-authored piece by Bernd Horn and Michel Wyczynksi continues the Second World War theme. No story carries more excitement or hazard than the daring drop of Allied paratroopers into occupied Europe on the eve of the great Normandy landings. Intended to secure flanks, destroy some bridges to delay German reinforcements, while holding others to allow for Allied advances, the Canadian, British, and American paratroopers who stormed Hitler's Festung Europa jumped into a devil's cauldron that forced them all, initially as individuals and small groups, and later as larger formed units, to fight for their very lives. In essence, Chapter 9 tells the story of the fight for survival that Canada's paratroopers experienced in the first 24 hours of D-Day.

The book ends with a very contemporary action. In Chapter 10, Bernd Horn recounts his eye-witness account of a stiff action in defence of Strong Point Centre against a concerted Taliban attack. This story highlights the bold scheme of manoeuvre undertaken by Canadian troops in the volatile Panjawyi district in the Kanadahar Province of Southern Afghanistan. On 14 August 2006, a platoon from "C" Company, of the 1st Battalion, The Royal Canadian Regiment, was heavily attacked as it was guarding a key position on a vital road being built in the heartland of the Taliban in Pashmul, near Kandahar City. Stretched thin, the Canadian troops courageously drew a line in the sand and imposed their presence on behalf of the Afghan government and NATO coalition. The chapter recounts a very dramatic and personal account of the desperate struggle that ensued.

In sum, the collection of essays in this volume captures the richness of Canadian military history. Although Canadians see their nation as a peaceable kingdom and themselves as an unmilitary people, the truth is that our nation has a proud military heritage. Moreover, its citizens and their descendents share a legacy of courage, tenacity, and warfighting prowess. It showcases our rich and distinct national military experience while capturing the indomitable spirit of the Canadian soldier.

CHAPTER 1

Only for the Strong of Heart:
Ranging and the Practice of *la Petite Guerre*
During the Struggle for North America

BERND HORN

Arguably, nothing embodies the idea of daring action more than the practice of *la petite guerre,* or in simpler terms, the frontier scouts, ambushes, and raids that were conducted by the French and English, as well as their Native allies, during the struggle for North America in the 17th and 18th centuries. Facing a harsh climate, unforgiving terrain, and intractable and savage enemies, the intrepid practitioners of *la petite guerre* personified boldness, courage, cunning, and tenacity. Their fearless forays and daring raids behind enemy lines struck terror in the hearts of colonists and soldiers and, actually, for an extended period of time, these tactical actions had a strategic effect on the bitter struggle.

Paradoxically, popular perception, based on adventure novels, Hollywood epics, and other media, have created a frontier myth that depicts the colonial settler as a savvy frontiersman who was as comfortable on his homestead as he was clutching a musket and tomahawk in pursuit of his wily foes in the depths of the harsh North American wilderness. Not surprisingly, this perception is not entirely accurate. The Europeans who came to the New World imported their cultural bias, disease, technology, as well as their methods of warfare. Unfortunately for them, their manner of waging war was unsuited for the wilderness environment. Their reliance on close order drill, discipline, and the overwhelming firepower born from massed volley fire, although effective on the European battlefields against opponents who recognized and practiced this style of combat, was ineffectual against an elusive, devious enemy who waged war in a completely different manner.

In North America, individualism, camouflage, stealth, surprise, and tactical acumen were of paramount importance. Needless casualties were abhorred and cover and concealment were always utilized. In fact, combat was only engaged when victory was assured. As such, ambuscades and raids were the favored approach. Although this manner of war was initially ridiculed by Europeans, its devastating effect on their settlements and economies necessitated a recognition of the North American manner of fighting, commonly referred to as *la petite guerre*.[1] More importantly, the Europeans had to adapt their warfighting methodology to counter it. Although slow in coming, ranging companies were eventually adopted, manned by frontiersmen who were familiar with the forests of North America, and, more importantly, with the Native way of war.

The creation of the ranging companies was a critical evolutionary step. Rather than suffer war — always on the defensive, never knowing when, or where, the next attack by a Native war party would strike, these "rangers" now represented a shift in initiative — they could make war by ranging far and wide to take the fight to the enemy in his own territory. With time, many colonials developed abilities and skills equal to that of the Natives in fighting in the trackless forests of North America. Of greater consequence, the superior organization and discipline of the whites, as well as their ready access to technology and larger infrastructure and support, eventually marginalized the impact of Natives in North American conflict. Nonetheless, the ranger tradition in North America was born from the necessity to bridge the cultural and philosophical gap between Old World and New, specifically the tactical disadvantage regular forces encountered when fighting a foe who simply did not follow the "recognized" conventions of war. Regardless, it was a tradition that would embody daring, resilience, and tenacity.

Predictably, the Europeans arrived in North America with cultural and experiential biases, as well as their preconceived notions of how affairs, particularly warfighting, were conducted. The relative ineffectiveness of the Europeans on the North American battlefields was largely a result of their arrogance, as well as their deep-rooted cultural understanding of war. Armies consisted mainly of conscripts and social outcasts led chiefly by the country's aristocracy. There was little binding these two groups together. While the officer corps may have had a reason to fight for King and country, as a result of their position and stake in the respective society, their soldiery did not. Their allegiance was to themselves. They did not fight, nor did they wish to die, for an ideological, political, or philosophical cause. Their primary focus was on making a living.

Not surprisingly, soldiers were not expected, nor trusted, to operate as individuals or small groups because of their commanders' justifiable fear that they would desert or create havoc within the countryside, regardless of whether they were in friendly or enemy territory. "I have a very mean opinion of the infantry in general," wrote James Wolfe to his father in 1755. "I know their discipline to be bad, & their valour precarious. They are easily put into disorder & hard to recover out of it; they frequently kill their Officers thro' fear, & murder one another in their confusion."[2] This reality was one reason that commanders utilized only large formations in combat to ensure that the troops remained in their place of duty and fought. This lack of cohesion within an army, in addition to the absence of a clear purpose that the soldiers could identify with, also necessitated a reliance on iron discipline to create a unified, effective fighting force.

The exigency for harsh discipline also extended to the type of combat that the soldiers conducted. This was also another driving force behind the use of large formations. The weaponry of the day, particularly the fourteen-pound .75 calibre smoothbore flintlock Long Land Pattern Musket, affectionately called the "Brown Bess," was usually 46 inches in length and had limited effectiveness. It was inaccurate and capable of only short-range engagements. Although capable of firing up to 300 yards, it proved primarily effective from ranges of less than 100 yards. Reloading lasted about 30–40 seconds and the average soldier could reload approximately two to three times per minute. However, a musket would typically misfire 3–4 times out of every 25 loadings. Furthermore, after 50–100 loadings it would be useless unless the firer carefully cleaned out the vent, swabbed the barrel, and inserted new flints.[3]

During combat, battalions stood elbow to elbow in a solid line, three ranks deep, facing a mirror image of themselves no more than 30–80 meters away. On a given command, volleys would be exchanged with devastating effect on the closely packed formations. Soldiers in the ranks rarely took specific aim, which explains the contemporary adage stating that it took a man's weight in bullets to kill him. Victory lay with the side that could deliver the most volleys in the shortest possible time and not break and run.[4] At 80 paces, there was little time to reload, therefore, the failure to ensure the volley struck home could lead to the necessity to withstand a bayonet charge by the enemy. As a result, repetitive training to turn the uninspired levy of reluctant combatants into an efficient mechanical fighting force was critical. Loading and firing a musket required approximately 12 movements, all of which were coordinated by drum beat or on word of command by an officer. Normally, it took at least 18 months on the drill square to train the raw recruit, who normally represented the offal of society, to manoeuvre and perform effectively on the battlefield.[5]

But equally important, severe discipline was also necessary for combat performance to ensure that soldiers maintained the advance under murderous fire or simply remained in position to deliver their volleys and accept the enemy's bayonet charge. Frederick the Great's dictum that a soldier "must be more afraid of his officers than of the dangers to which he is exposed," was not an idle rumination.[6] It was not uncommon for regulations to specifically emphasize that "if a soldier during an action looks about as if to flee, or so much as sets foot outside the line, the non-commissioned officer standing behind him will run him through with his bayonet and kill him on the spot."[7]

Battle, therefore, in the European model, became an elaborate set-piece manoeuvre. Formations of artillery, cavalry, and infantry were carefully deployed and repositioned to gain the maximum amount of advantage over the enemy. Tactics relied almost exclusively on heavy infantry and cavalry. The courage of the soldiers to withstand the murderous volleys of the enemy was maintained by an iron discipline. The ability to pour a withering fire into the opponents' ranks was honed by constant drilling and training. The soldier was in many ways seen by his commanders as nothing more than an expendable automaton, albeit an expensive one to train.

As such, virtually all European commanders shared a distinct contempt for the concept of light infantry fighting on their own, relying on their initiative and utilizing cover from which to engage the enemy. Light troops according to most British officers were "for the most part young and insolent puppies, whose worthlessness was apparently their recommendation for a service which placed them in the post of danger, in the way of becoming food for powder, their most appropriate destination next to that of the gallows."[8]

But the European manner of war went beyond mere tactics. It also included specific expectations in regard to behaviour during and after a battle. Elaborate protocols for the conduct of sieges, surrenders, and honours of war were stringently followed. Courage and gallantry were respected. To honour one's word, to treat prisoners in a merciful manner, and to protect the civilian population, by the mid-18th century were considered by most European commanders, under most circumstances, to be the accepted manner of waging war. Arguably, in many ways, the peace treaty was the actual goal of the conflict. In essence, battle was designed not to destroy nations, religions, or ideology, but rather to secure a strong bargaining position and a favourable settlement of the dispute.

However, the European paradigm was shattered in North America. The Natives practiced a way of war that was diametrically opposed to the European model in both philosophy and physical execution. The Native way of war was fundamental to the practice of *la petite guerre* in North America, but it carried a distinct New World nuance that the Europeans soon contemptuously titled the "skulking way of war." Key to its success was the selection of limited objectives that could be easily overcome. Stealth and surprise were of the utmost importance. As such, ambushes and raids that enabled them to achieve maximum shock and surprise against their unsuspecting victims were the preferred methods of attack. Lightning strikes were always succeeded by immediate withdrawals. Moreover, the Natives would never fight if they were outnumbered, or if they could not achieve a decisive advantage.

The Natives placed great reliance on guile, stealth, the use of cover, and especially marksmanship. This is not surprising. Traditionally, these attributes were required to be successful on the hunt. The rudimentary weapons available to the Natives necessitated exceptional fieldcraft skills if a hunter was to kill game. The more clever and stealthy the hunter, the greater were his chances of triumph. Firearms provided a more efficient and lethal weapons technology with which to kill, giving the Natives an added advantage.

But understandably, all of the skills associated with a successful hunt were transferable to war-making — especially their marksmanship ability. Some contemporary writers felt that it was the unerring fire of the Natives that made them such a threat.[9] As a point of principle, they aimed at single targets, specifically at officers who were easy to identify by their dress and position on the battlefield.[10] Captain Pierre Pouchot, a member of the French Béarn Regiment that fought with distinction in North America, wrote in his memoirs that the Natives were excellent marksmen who "very rarely fail to shoot their man down."[11]

The Native manner of warfare also took full advantage of the Natives' innate mobility and knowledge of the terrain and forests. "The woods," wrote Jesuit missionary Pierre Roubaud, "are the element of the Savages; they run through them with the swiftness of a deer."[12] They used cover to its fullest benefit, deliberately choosing not to make themselves an obvious target. "They seldom expose themselves to danger, and depend entirely on their dexterity in concealing themselves during an engagement, never appearing openly, unless they have struck their enemies with terror, and have thereby rendered incapable of defence."[13]

According to the Natives themselves, they gained great advantage because they "always took care in their marches and fights not to come too thick together; but the English always kept in a heap together [so] that it was as easy to hit them, as to hit a house."[14] Similarly, prisoners released from Native capture reported that "their [Native] young men from their past observations express no very respectable opinion of our manner of fighting them, as, by our close order, we present a large object to their fire, and our platoons do little execution as the Indians are thinly scattered, and concealed behind bushes or trees."[15]

In essence, warfare to the Natives was irregular in nature. "The art of war," declared Tecaughretanego, a Kahnawake chief, "consists in ambushing and surprising our enemies, and in preventing them from ambushing and surprising us."[16] Similarly, Jesuit Missionary Father Nau, observed that "Their [Native] mode of warfare is but stratagem and surprise."[17] One Jesuit Missionary noted that the Natives were "so stealthy in their approach, so swift in their execution, and so expeditious in their retreat, that one commonly learns of their departure before being aware of their arrival."[18]

Other European concepts, such as holding terrain regardless of the cost in lives, were anathema to the Natives. Abbe H.R. Casgrain, the prominent 19th-century French Canadian chronicler of the Seven Years' War, explained that "for them, withdrawal was not a flight, nor a disgrace, it was a means of falling back to occupy a better position."[19]

The Native way of war also deviated substantially from the European practice because of its emphasis on individualism. This was a deep-rooted cultural and philosophical component that was not always understood by Europeans. For the Native warriors "taking up the hatchet" or more simply put, going to war, was largely a personal endeavour. It was meant to prove a warrior's courage and skill and to obtain prestige through achievement in combat. The individual warrior was subordinate to no other. They saw neither shame, nor dishonour, in abandoning the field if the odds of easy success were against them.[20] Moreover, if individuals tired of the campaign or simply failed to support a plan of action, their departure was seldom condemned by their peers.[21] "The Savage," observed Missionary Father Pierre Roubaud, "is his own Master and his own King, and he takes with him everywhere his independence."[22] Not surprisingly, Native leaders could not always control their warriors.

This reality created a philosophical divergence in warfighting techniques, based specifically on the issue of desired outcomes. The Native's definition of success diverged substantially from that of the white man. A victorious campaign was determined by the accumulation of prisoners, scalps, and plunder. The Natives deemed a campaign successfully completed when a victory, regardless of how inconsequential, was won.[23] Moreover, as already noted, casualties were totally unacceptable. In the eyes of the Native, "a victory bought with blood," explained Jesuit Priest Pierre de Charlevoix, "is not victory."[24]

From the Native perspective, the quintessential triumph was that which was won with the most minimal of casualties. The capture of territory, forcing an enemy to abandon a strategic fortification or to postpone an offensive simply did not resonate with the Natives. It was only through tangible actions such as the accumulation of valuable commodities, such as prisoners, scalps, or plunder, which also carried a significant economic benefit, that individual warriors could show their achievement in battle. Once this was accomplished, the Natives were satisfied to end the campaign lest they push their luck.[25]

As such, the Natives were not interested in a fair fight, but only one in which they could achieve their aims with a minimum of casualties. Therefore, camouflage, concealment, and marksmanship were used to great effect. Moreover, ambush, raid, and terror were the preferred methods of conducting war. Tactical surprise was of the utmost importance and guile and deceit were utilized to the greatest degree possible. In short, the Natives practised the "skulking way of war."[26]

And so, overwhelmingly, European arrogance and its subsequent unwillingness to acknowledge the ability of the "savages," or to recognize the effectiveness of their manner of fighting, created a paradoxical situation. On one hand, the Europeans condemned the Natives and their manner of war-making in the most contemptuous terms. "None are more courageous when no resistance is offered them, and none are more cowardly when they encounter opposition," recorded one Jesuit Missionary.[27] "It is not people in army's that Indians will ever daringly attack," noted Edward Abbot, a Lieutenant-Governor of Vincennes during the colonial period, "but the poor inoffensive families ... who are inhumanely butchered sparing neither woman or children."[28] Another early colonist agreed. "The Indians, notwithstanding their Subtility and Cruelty," asserted Reverend William Hubbard, "durst not look an Englishman in the Face in open Field, nor even yet were known to kill any Man with their guns, unless they could lie in wait for him in an ambush, or behind some Shelter, taking aim undiscovered."[29]

Almost universally, the Natives were seen as cowards and a race unable to fight with honour. "Consider the bloody villains," wrote one Virginian, "thievishly lurking about a man's plantation, and where they dare not attack like men, basely like vermin, stealing and carrying away the helpless infant, that happened to wander, tho' but a little distance from his Father's threshold."[30] Major-General Jeffery Amherst, who was known for his utter disdain of the Natives, confided in his journal that "The cowardice of these barbarians is so great & their little arts in war so easily prevented from taking place ... Their whole dependance is upon a tree or a bush." He admonished, "you have nothing to do but to advance, & they will fly. They never stand an open fire or an attack."[31] Similarly, the memoirs of one French soldier revealed, "Of them [Iroquois] it has been said, they came like foxes, attacked like hares, and fled like birds."[32]

But there is a paradox. Despite the disdain and contempt, the Natives achieved a high degree of success. Their methods were clearly effective. Most colonists feared the Natives and felt they were almost defenceless against the savages in the trackless forests of North America. Native war parties consistently forced the colonists to remain barricaded in cramped stockades and only venture out to tend their fields in large armed groups, which even then were no guarantee of survival. "The Iroquois used to keep us closely confined," conceded one Jesuit missionary, "that we did not even dare till the lands that were under the cannon of the forts."[33] The Iroquois control over the French for much of the 17th century was such that one Sachem boasted, "We plied the French homes in the war with them that they were not able to go out a door to piss."[34] His taunt was no idle bluster. "The Iroquois," decried King Louis the XIV, "through massacres and inhumanities, have prevented the country's population from growing."[35]

The English experience was no different. One letter revealed, "We are under the utmost fear and consternation, upon accounts of the Natives having again began their murders and massacres in the province of Pennsylvania, upon the River Delaware adjoining to this province ... These fresh depredations have so terrified us that we dare not go out to our daily labour, for fear of being surprized and murdered by the Indians."[36] A British officer wrote, "Nothing is to be seen but desolation and murder, heightened with every barbarous circumstance, and new instances of cruelty." He added, "They [Natives] ... burn up the plantations, the smoke of which darkens the day and hides the mountains from our sight."[37] Claude-Godefroy Coquart, a French priest, wrote his brother, "Our Indians have waged the most cruel war against the English ... Georgia, Carolina, Marrelande, Pensilvania, are wholly laid waste. The farmers have been forced to quit their abodes and to retire into the town. They have neither plowed nor planted."[38]

The field of battle witnessed the same Native success. "In all the time," recounted one lucky survivor of Major-General Edward Braddock's defeated force at the Monongahela on 9 July 1755, "I never saw one nor could I on Enquiry find any one who saw ten [Natives] together." He added, "If we saw five or six at one time [it] was a great sight."[39] Another soldier at the same battle reported, "The Indians ... kept an incessant fire on the Guns & killed ye Men very fast. These Indians from their irregular method of fighting by running from one place to another obliges us to wheel from right to left, to desert ye Guns and then hastily to return & cover them."[40]

But this one battle was not an anomaly. On countless occasions a small force of Natives consistently inflicted disproportionate casualties on larger white forces. For example, during a small skirmish, an English captain conceded that "It is estimated that though they [Natives] were but five, they killed about 20, not counting the wounded."[41] Overall, as one British officer revealed, "Our troops yielded ground, chiefly owing to the consternation the Indian method of fighting."[42]

In the end, those versed in the ways of war in North America discerned the challenge. Colonel Henry Bouquet, a recognized expert on light infantry tactics and Native fighting during the 18th century concluded that Native warriors were "physically active, fierce in manner, skillful in the use of weapons, and capable of great guile and stealth in combat."[43] He considered them formidable opponents. Similarly, Colonel Isaac Barre, another officer who served in colonial North America, felt that the Natives were as enemies "the most subtile and the most formidable of any people upon the face of God's earth."[44]

In sum, despite the contemptuous opinion of the Natives and the very divergent cultural and philosophical understanding and practice of war, the European refusal to recognize and adapt to the North American reality led to a prolonged period of suffering. Daring Native raids and ambushes deep in enemy territory killed and captured hundreds of civilians and soldiers alike. Furthermore, they devastated homesteads, farms, and entire regional colonial economies.

However, not all accepted the status quo. There were some who recognized the advantage in "ranging," that is, to scout at a distance from stockades and towns to determine the enemy intentions and provide early warning and intelligence on their movements. More importantly, ranging allowed for offensive action. Rather than suffer war, the whites could practise the offensive as the best method of defence. It returned to them the initiative.

The French-Canadians in New France were quicker to adapt than their Anglo-American counterparts in the English colonies. In many ways this was due to their greater tolerance, acceptance of, and assimilation with, the Natives.[45] To survive, the French colonists very early entered into cultural, economic, political, and social alliances with a number of Northern Native tribes (e.g. Abenakis, Algonquin, Huron, Montagnais, and Outaouais). They quickly became apprentices under the tutelage of the friendly Natives and learned how to dress, fish, hunt, travel, navigate, and flourish in the North American wilderness. Of equal importance, survival necessitated that they also learn the Native manner of fighting.

Although they derived great benefit from their Native alliances, their choice of friends also earned them the enmity of others, namely the Five

Nations of the aggressive Iroquois Confederacy.[46] Participation in operations with their newfound allies against the Iroquois in 1609 exacerbated the antagonism and eventually led to a century of virtual continual conflict that at times threatened the very existence of New France.[47]

Amazingly, it was not until 1666 that the French finally resolved to attack the Iroquois in their own territory. This was based on the infusion of a large number of French regular troops and the establishment of a number of forts located strategically on the frontiers. These forts became important as economic, political, and social centres that cemented Native alliances. Equally significant, they also provided a secure forward operating position that enabled offensive strikes deep into the territory of their enemies.

With their initial bold expedition began a tradition that would be ruthlessly practised by the succeeding leaders in New France. However, this initial foray was not without risk. It was launched at the height of the vicious North American winter. Ironically, although the professional soldiers brought confidence to the Canadians and provided the belief that offensive action could now transpire — they were not the key to success. Predictably, the 300 regular French troops were not inured to the difficulty of operating in the hostile winter environment. However, the approximately 200 Canadians and a number of friendly Natives who accompanied them were. In fact, Daniel de Rémy de Courcelle, the Governor of New France and leader of the risky expedition, became deeply impressed by the abilities and fortitude of the Canadians. He quickly realized that they were at home in the woods and capable of the Native method of war.[48] He made great use of them, notably as the vanguard during the approach and as the rearguard during the return to French territory. In subsequent expeditions, as a point of principle, large contingents of Canadians were always included.

In the end, the expedition did not attain the optimistic goals that were set. In short, it failed to destroy or humble the Iroquois.[49] Its brief and inconclusive encounter with Mohawk warriors actually occurred on the outskirts of the Dutch-Anglo settlement of Schenectady, the sovereign territory of another European power. In addition, French casualties were quite heavy due to the severe winter conditions and they were exacerbated by the poorly equipped regular troops who did not have adequate clothing, shoes, or supplies, and who were not versed in survival in the bitterly cold North American wilderness.

Nonetheless, the excursion represented a turning point. It demonstrated that expeditions, even at the worst time of the year when operations were normally never conducted by either side, were possible. Moreover, elements of the French expedition, namely the Canadians, proved to the French leaders and regulars, as well as the Natives, a mastery of travelling, surviving, and fighting in the trackless forest.

The next French foray took place in the autumn of the same year. Peace overtures were suspended when a continuing series of Iroquois raids in the spring and summer of 1666 killed a number of French soldiers. The French were now intent on another expedition. The inclusion of Canadians necessitated a fall operation since the harvest was of primary importance and no one could be spared until this critical task was completed. This time, the force was substantially larger — made up of approximately 600 regulars, an equal number of Canadian volunteers, and about 100 Natives.[50]

It was also more successful. Although the two-month operation failed to bring the Mohawks to decisive battle, a large force did march with impunity deep into Mohawk territory and destroy four villages, their crops and stored foodstuffs estimated at sufficient quantities "to nourish all Canada for two entire years."[51] The French action condemned their enemies to a possible slow death by starvation and exposure over the winter, or the humiliating prospect of begging for subsistence from other tribes, or their English allies. Importantly, the net effect was achieved — the bold strikes brought their enemies to the peace table and allowed for an era of prolonged peace.[52]

Overall, the expeditions had an important psychological effect on the Iroquois and the French. Both realized the initiative had irrevocably changed. Their larger resources, string of fortifications, discipline, firepower, and willingness and ability to fight in the wilderness now made the French and Canadians a more imposing foe. The expeditions also underlined to the Canadians the importance and effectiveness of offensive action. They also inculcated volunteers with military experience and regulars with wilderness indoctrination.[53]

But, of greatest consequence, the expeditions highlighted the inherent strength of utilizing experienced woodsmen who were adept at living, travelling, and fighting in the Native fashion in North America. The Canadians themselves now realized that it was within their power to prosecute war. It buoyed their confidence and ingrained in them a powerful war-making methodology. Jacques de Meulles, the Intendant of New France in 1683 wrote, "They [Iroquois] have two thousand six hundred good soldiers, and are well seasoned for war. But our youth is hardened and quite used to the woods." He added, "Besides, we make war better than they do."[54]

This capability was increasingly demonstrated, much to the misery of the English and, to some degree, their Iroquois allies to the south. As the two competing European powers increasingly fought for control of North America, the French consistently relied on the outnumbered Canadians to hold on to French territory through their proficient execution of the Native way of war, specifically small parties of experienced *coureur de bois* and partisans who conducted dangerous scouts, ambushes, and raids in English territory.[55] As such, raids against the English in Hudson's Bay in 1686, the Seneca in New York in 1687, the Iroquois in 1693 and 1696, and a number of devastating strikes against English settlements such as Casco, Deersfield, Haverhill, Salmon Falls, and Schenectady during a succession of wars from 1688 to 1748 refined the French Canadian practice of *la petite guerre*.[56]

The Taking of Mary Jemison by Robert Griffing, Paramount Press.

French-Canadian and Native raiding parties proved to be the scourge of the frontier. They laid waste to homes and crops, killing settlers and livestock, and taking many as captives.

Many French and Canadian leaders, particularly those with extended exposure to the North American manner of war, or those born and raised in Canada, came to believe that the optimum warfighting technique was achieved by a mixed force that included the military strengths of regulars (e.g. courage, discipline, tactical acumen) with those of the volunteers and Natives (e.g. endurance, familiarity with wilderness navigation and travel, marksmanship) who relied more on initiative, independent action, and small unit tactics than on rigid military practices and drills. The Canadians very ably practised the Indian way of war and adopted many of the cultural and philosophical aspects as well. During the contest for North America between the French and the English the practice of the Natives way of war became as much associated with the Canadians with the Natives. In fact, their very successful and brutal practice of *la petite guerre* demanded an English countermeasure.

Experienced at traversing the inhospitable North American wilderness, a Canadian volunteer and soldier of *les Companies Franches de la Marine* conduct a winter raid against the New England frontier.

Reconstitution by Francis Back, © Parks Canada.

Conversely, the English were slower to adapt, and in the end found themselves at a great disadvantage. This is somewhat surprising. The term "ranger" originated in England as far back as the 13th century. It was used to describe far-ranging foresters or borderers, as well as keepers of the Royal forest. By the 1600s, the term was also used to refer to such unique irregular military organizations such as the "Border Rangers," who policed the troubled frontier region between England and Scotland.[57]

The concept migrated to the New World as well. As early as 1622, faced with conflict against hostile Natives, towns, villages, and isolated plantations and stockades employed bold adventurous armed men to "range" the countryside for signs of enemy activity, as well as possible targets of opportunity. These individuals also escorted surveyors and hunted down escaped slaves. By 1648, a list of conditions by which "raingers and scouts" were to be regulated were drawn up by the General Assembly of Maryland.[58]

Nonetheless, scant overall importance seems to have been placed on these introverted individuals or organizations. Whenever military operations were undertaken, they generally followed the European model of close order drill and volley fire. Despite the European lack of success, resistance to adopting the Native method of warfare was still overwhelming. It was only during King Philip's War (1675–1678), as a result of frustration with the inability to defeat the Indians and run down the elusive Wampanoag chieftain King Philip, that Benjamin Church was finally able to convince others that a company of rangers specially organized to fight on the same terms as the Natives was necessary.[59]

In July 1676, Captain Benjamin Church was authorized to raise what is considered the first ranger company in North America. Governor Josiah Winslow commissioned Church to "raise a company of volunteers of about 200 men, English and Indians; the English not exceeding the number of 60." He further charged Church and his rangers "to discover, pursue, fight, surprise, destroy, or subdue our Indian enemies."[60] Church quickly showed the sagacity of the decision. He employed Native tactics — ranging the woods, tracking, laying ambushes, and conducting lightning-swift raids that carried the shock of speed and surprise. In these successful forays he captured prisoners and obtained further intelligence.

Within months he had made his reputation. Church and his mixed company were extremely successful. He matched the ruthlessness of the

Natives and chased their raiding parties, and the enemy in general, to their own homes, haunts, and hiding places in the deepest swamps and forests. He captured and killed their warriors and families. He burnt their homes and foodstuffs. He was relentless in his pursuit. Less than a month after establishing the company, on 12 August 1676, Church tracked down and killed the insurgent Native leader King Philip.

But, Benjamin Church's ranger service was not over with the end of Native resistance in New England. The growing confrontations between France and England in North America required his services again in 1689, 1696, and 1704. During these frontier wars he plied his lethal trade in the same fashion as the French and Natives. He was once again charged with "discovering, pursuing, subduing and destroying the said common enemy, by all opportunities you are capable of; always intending the preserving of any of the near towns from incursions, and destruction of the enemy; yet chiefly improving your men for the finding and following the said enemy abroad, and if possible to find out and attack their head quarters and principal rendezvous."[61]

Church proved himself an able guerilla leader. He firmly believed that rangers should be "men of known judgment" who know how to use arms "in shooting right, at a mark, and that they be men of good reason and sense to know how to manage themselves in so difficult a piece of service as this Indian hunting is."[62] Of note, his forces ravaged Beaubassin in 1696, and Penobscot, Passamaquoddy, as well as the settlements of Minas and Beaubassin again, all in Acadia, in 1704.[63] Nonetheless, at the termination of each conflict, Church's command was dissolved and the importance, if not the whole concept of rangers, largely forgotten.

The success of Church's mixed company of rangers was not the only early British North American experience. Due to the incessant menace of the Abenaki and Micmac Natives and their constant attacks against the English garrison at Port Royal, Nova Scotia, the British raised, in 1712, a company of Iroquois rangers, which consisted of 56 Mohawk warriors commanded by two white officers. They camped outside the fort, were given a blanket and a musket and operated practically independently of the other troops. They proved to be very effective at countering the French and Natives, as well as capturing deserters. In May 1713, a number of the Mohawks deserted to go home and the remainder were deployed to Boston and disbanded.[64]

In addition, in 1734, a small and mobile organization called the Georgia Rangers was also established to defend the hostile frontier region between the border garrisons of the two-year-old colony from which they took their name. Reaching a peak of 15 officers and 122 men in 1746, the Georgia Rangers were disbanded as a cost-cutting measure a few years later once the war with Spain had ended.

In 1744, during the War of the Austrian Succession (1740–1748), the Abenakis and Micmac threat resurfaced once again. As a result, an "independent corps of rangers," also known as the corps of Nova Scotia Rangers, was raised in New England. Two companies were recruited and deployed to Annapolis in July to reinforce the garrison. In September, a third company arrived, led by Captain John Goreham, whose father apprenticed under Benjamin Church.[65] Goreham's command comprised 60 Mohawks and Métis. Familiar with the Native way of war, they swiftly engaged the French and their Native allies. Massachusetts Governor William Shirley commended Goreham and his rangers for their success, stating that "the garrison is now entirely free from alarms."[66] The majority of the companies later returned to Massachusetts where they originated, leaving Captain Goreham and his company to patrol Nova Scotia alone from 1746 to 1748.[67] Their success was such that Shirley wrote "the great service which Lieut. Colonel Gorham's Company of Rangers has been of to the Garrison at Annapolis Royal, is a demonstration of the Usefulness of such a Corps."[68]

It became apparent that ranging was a family endeavour. John's brother, Joseph, was appointed a lieutenant in Goreham's ranger company. By 1752, he was promoted captain and as a result of the death of his brother to smallpox the year prior, became the commanding officer of the company. The rangers were used to protect the British settlements in Nova Scotia against Native raids until the outbreak of the Seven Years' War, at which time they became increasingly involved in military operations specifically because of their expertise in irregular warfare.[69] "They have most assuredly been of great utility," confided Governor Peregrine Thomas Hopson, "such as protecting the out settlers, ranging the Country, and marching upon services the regulars would not be spared for."[70]

And so, despite this apparent knowledge and experience with "ranging" — the English were still caught flat-footed. It was during

Painting by Ted Zuber.

"It was from this place [Fort St. Frederic]," wrote Major-General William Shirley, a former commander-in-chief of British forces in North America, "that all those parties which during the late war ravaged and laid waste to many towns and settlements upon the Frontiers of New York and the Massachusetts Bay were fitted out; and so great was the influence which the French had over the Five Nations of Indians by means of this fort, so great were their apprehensions of the mischief, which it was in the power of the French to do them, that it was not till late in the war and not even without great difficulty and still greater expense that they were prevailed upon to take up the Hatchet."

"Remarks on the Fort built by the French at Crown Point in North America," Library and Archives Canada, Colonial Office (CO), Microfilm B-25, Vol 13, 157.

the Seven Years' War (1754–1760 in North America)[71] that the English failure to better integrate ranging reached its zenith. Two attempts by the British to expel the French from the Ohio valley, the first by Major George Washington in 1754, and the second the following year, in July 1755 by Major-General Edward Braddock, both ended in failure. More importantly, Braddock's foray against Fort Duquesne underlined a major British weakness in its struggle in North America, namely a deficiency of Natives or rangers versed in forest combat in the New World.

Braddock's defeat proved to be a fatal lesson on warfare in North America. His 45 years of service had, predictably, endowed him with a deep-rooted comprehension of warfare that was reinforced by his own experience. He accepted as truth that the more disciplined and well-drilled force would normally emerge victorious. In fact, Benjamin Franklin, writing 15 years after the event, recorded that Braddock dismissed the threat posed by irregular troops or Natives. "These savages may, indeed, be a formidable enemy to your raw American militia," declared Braddock, "but upon the King's regulars, it is impossible they should make any impression."[72]

He was sadly mistaken. Lieutenant William Dunbar recounted the harrowing slaughter of Braddock's forces. "We had not marched above 800 yards from the River," he wrote, "when we were allarmed by the Indian Hollow [battle cry], & in an instant, found ourselves attacked on all sides, their methods, they immediately seize a Tree, & are certain of their Aim, so that before the Genl [General] came to our assistance, most of our advanced Party were laid sprawling on the ground." Dunbar revealed:

> Our Men unaccustomed to that way of fighting, were quite confounded, & behaved like Poltrons, nor could the examples, nor the Intreaties of their officers prevail with them, to do any one what was ordered. This they denied them, when we begged of them not to throw away their fire, but to follow us with fixed Bayonets, to drive them from the hill & trees, they never minded us, but threw their fire away in the most confused manner, some in the air, others in the ground, & a great many destroyed their own Men & officers. When the General came up to our assistance, men were seized with the same Pannic, & went into as much disorder, some Part of them being 20 deep. The officers in order to remedy this, advanced into the front, & soon became the mark of the Enemy, who scarce left one that was not killed or wounded.[73]

Another British officer conceded that "By the particular disposition of the French and Indians it was impossible to judge of the numbers they had in the field that day."[74] Conversely, the French forces had excellent fields of observation and fire and they continued to pour an unrelenting fire that mercilessly cut swaths into the British ranks.

Braddock's failure, or inability, to adjust his European mode of combat resulted in the destruction of his army. In the end, Braddock's courage and steadfast belief that inevitably the undisciplined, motley opponents that faced his troops would break, combined with the training and discipline of his regulars to stand their ground regardless of the chaos that engulfed them, led to their ruin. Once ambushed, the closely packed troops were impossible to miss and they suffered horrendous casualties.

Ironically, the provincials, particularly the Virginians, immediately sought cover and began to return fire against their phantom antagonists. Their actions provided some hope of staving off defeat. However, Braddock, incensed at this lack of courage and discipline, ordered them back into line using both oaths and the flat of his saber.[75] But it was for naught. The contrast in dialectic between the European and Native way of war was never sharper. Tom Faucett, a bitter veteran, who served with the Provincials, scathingly reminisced, "We was cowards, was we, because we knowed better than to fight Injuns like you red-backed ijits across the ocean is used to fight: because we wouldn't stand up rubbin' shoulders like a passel o' sheep and let the red-skins made sieves outen us!"[76]

And so, despite the exhortations of the officers and the discipline of the regulars, as the ranks were continually thinned by a steady and deadly fire, from an antagonist that could not be seen, the regulars lost their steadiness and eventually succumbed to an uncontrollable panic. "And when we endeavored to rally them," recounted George Washington, then a young officer assigned to Braddock's staff, "it was with as much success as if we had attempted to stop the wild bears of the mountains."[77] The cost of the debacle was enormous. The French lost approximately five percent of their engaged force. The British lost 70 percent of theirs, including 60 out of 86 officers.[78]

The subsequent success of French arms over the British reinforced the Native proclivity to support the French. In fact, after Braddock's defeat, the Natives rejected British overtures to remain neutral and replied, "It is not in our power to comply with it, for the French & we are one blood, & where they are to dye we must dye also."[79] The Native attitude heightened concerns arising from the British defeats. Lord John

Campbell Loudoun, who would become the commander-in-chief of British forces in North America two years later, questioned how British troops would execute "the Bush fight in which the [French] have so great an advantage by their Canadians and Indians."[80] Similarly, Washington asserted that "without Indians we shall never be able to cope with those cruel foes to our country."[81] John Askin, an experienced American frontiersman, declared that in the forests, one Native warrior was equal to three white men.[82] The feeling was generally universal. "Here in the forests of America," wrote one journalist, "we can no more do with out them [Natives] than without cavalry on the plain."[83]

Added to the threat of the Natives was that of those who actually led them, the Canadians, who were by now well versed in ranging. Major-General James Wolfe felt that "Every man in Canada is a soldier."[84] Other contemporary English accounts echoed with the lament that the Canadian woodsmen and *coureur de bois* "are well known to be the most dangerous enemy of any … reckoned equal, if not superior in that part of the world to veteran troops."[85] Even the French regulars, who despised the Canadians and Natives, had to concede that they contributed distinct skills and capabilities to campaigns. "God knows," wrote Colonel Louis Antoine de Bougainville, "we do not wish to disparage the value of the Canadians … In the woods, behind trees, no troops are comparable to the natives of this country."[86] The renowned Canadian colonial historian Abbe H.R. Casgrain described them as "the elite Canadians and Indians," who "glide from tree to tree, stump to stump," from which they maintain an accurate and incessant fire.[87] The official journals kept by Lieutenant-General Louis-Joseph De Montcalm's army also revealed that "The Canadians … certainly surpass all the troops in the universe, owing to their skill as marksmen."[88]

Together, the Canadian woodsmen and their Natives allies controlled the forests, denying the British intelligence and secure communications. "It is not possible to conceive the situation and danger of this miserable country," deplored Washington, "such numbers of French and Indians are all around that no road is safe."[89] One British colonel confided, "I am ashamed that they have succeeded in all their scouting parties and that we never have any success in ours."[90] This state of affairs continually blinded the British command and deprived them of intelligence of French preparations or plans. Understandably, this often led to poor and

Photo-Art by Silvia Pecota.

The French-Canadian leader of a Native war party halts to discuss the continued participation of his allies.

untimely decisions laden with unfortunate consequences, whether the ambush of a British column or the loss of a strategic fort.[91]

Moreover, the constant depredations, ambushes, and raids of the Canadians and their Native allies caused a constant material and economic drain on the British. But equally important, they created an overwhelming psychological and moral blow against the Anglo-American colonies. The British forces seemed unable to strike back. It was a constant series of defeats, thwarted campaigns and offensives, and devastated colonies. Everywhere, the Canadians and Natives would appear as phantoms in hit-and-run attacks, leaving in their wake smoldering ruins and the mutilated bodies of the dead and dying. Despite their small numbers, they consistently inflicted an unproportionally high number of casualties on the enemy. The end result was an utterly paralyzing effect on the English combatants and colonists alike.[92]

The need to strike back was evident — as was the need for rangers. Luckily, in this instance, the initial solution to both problems was close at hand in the form of a charismatic, bold individual. Once again, a personality emerged to galvanize the ranger concept. Robert Rogers was initially a captain of "Company One" of the New Hampshire Regiment. At first Rogers and his men escorted supply wagons between Albany and Fort Edward. However, Rogers's knowledge and experience with the "haunts and passes of the enemy and the Indian method of fighting" soon brought him to the attention of his superior, Major-General William Johnson.[93] By the fall of 1755, Rogers was conducting dangerous scouts deep behind enemy lines.

Rogers's efforts soon earned him a overwhelming reputation. "Captain Rogers whose bravery and veracity," wrote Johnson, "stands very clear in my opinion and of all who know him … is the most active man in our Army."[94] These efforts also led Major-General William Shirley, then the commander-in-chief of the British Army in North America, to argue that "It is absolutely necessary for his Majesty's Service, that one Company at least of Rangers should be constantly employ'd in different Parties upon Lake George and Lake Iroquois [Lake Champlain], and the Wood Creek and Lands adjacent … to make Discoveries of the proper Routes for our own Troops, procure Intelligence of the Enemy's Strength and Motions,

destroy their out Magazines and Settlements, pick up small Parties of their Battoes upon the Lakes, and keep them under continual Alarm."[95] This outlook is not surprising. After all, Shirley was an early supporter of Goreham and the ranger concept in Nova Scotia.

The creation of Rogers's Rangers was a direct result of the British attempt to increase their ability to gain intelligence and provide a scouting capability in the wilderness, as well as counter the French raiding parties.

By the winter of 1756, Rogers's bold forays with his small band of unofficial rangers behind enemy French lines were regularly reported in newspapers throughout the colonies. They provided a tonic to a beleaguered English frontier. In March 1756, Major-General Shirley ordered Rogers to raise a 60-man independent ranger company that was separate from both the provincial and regular units. As such, it was titled His Majesty's Independent Company (later Companies) of American Rangers. His unit was directed to scout and gain intelligence in the Lake Champlain theatre, as well as "distress the French and their allies by sacking, burning and destroying their houses, barns, barracks, canoes, battoes … to way-lay, attack, and destroying their convoys of provisions by land and water."[96]

British commanders soon called for the establishment of an additional ten companies. These companies were expected to maintain open lines of communications between towns and advanced forts, procure intelligence, surprise and cut off the enemy's convoys, and "harass them in Canada by scouting parties in every way they can."[97] In fact, Rogers's commission specifically made mention of the need of a "number of men employed in obtaining intelligence of the strength, situation, and motions of the enemy, as well as other services, for which Rangers, or men acquainted with the woods, only are fit."[98] In the end, they conducted the myriad tasks with a vicious regularity.[99]

The reputation and accomplishments of the rangers soon had an impact on British officers. All wanted rangers to accompany their expeditions as a foil against the enemy's Canadians and Natives, as well as the rangers' ability to navigate and survive in the merciless wilderness. In the course of the war, the rangers participated in virtually every campaign. Lord Loudoun went so far as to consider turning two companies of every regiment of a thousand men into ranging companies. Some British officers, such as George Augustus Viscount Howe, and Lieutenant-Colonel Thomas Gage agreed and recommended regular light infantry units as a permanent part of the British Army.

Without doubt, "Rogers's Rangers," as they became universally known, brought to life the ranger tradition in North America and ensured it would forever endure. Their deeds and prowess have with time become legendary, even if not fully deserved.[100] Nonetheless, the Rangers, led by the very adventurous, courageous, and exceptionally tough

Robert Rogers, created a very romantic image that seemed to both symbolize, as well as define, the strength of the American Ranger. In essence, the established tradition depicted an adventurous, if not daring, attitude that was overly aggressive and always offensively minded. The ranger tradition that was created also embodied the concept of individuals who were seen as mavericks to the conventional military institution and mentality — men who were adaptable, robust, and unconventional in their thinking and warfighting. But above all else, the tradition captured the frontier spirit, if not myth, of the independent fearless fighter, with an eagle eye and steady aim, who was at home in the woods and had no peer in bush combat. What is without dispute, is the fact that the rangers filled a void. They provided capability, largely due to the lack of Native allies, which allowed the British to contest control of the forests in North America.[101]

Painting *Sergeant Beubien* by John Buxton courtesy Paramount Press.

A scouting party of Rogers's Rangers discuss their mission with a British officer on Lake George.

Ironically, despite the apparent utility and arguable success of rangers, as well as the constant calls for their employment, they never became fully accepted by their professional counterparts. During the war they were never taken on to the official strength of the British Army. Moreover, their lax discipline, disheveled if not unruly appearance, as well as their manner of war making was simply unacceptable to most British officers. "I am afraid," lamented Lord Loudoun, "[that] I shall be blamed for the ranging companies."[102]

Major-General Wolfe was clear in his scorn. "The American Rangers," he excoriated, "are for the most part, lazy cowardly people — the best men they get upon the Continent for that Service, are Irish Vagabonds, & Convicts, the Inhabitants are a poor Spirited Race."[103] He later wrote the British secretary of state that "The four new companies of Rangers are so very bad that I expect no service from them, unless mixed with the light infantry." Gage agreed. He was of the opinion that all rangers on the continent should be replaced. "When you are better acquainted with them you will find them not very alert in obeying orders, especially when at a distance and at home," he wrote, "They have never been on a proper footing and want to be new modeled."[104]

Despite the enmity, the need for rangers or troops capable of providing a similar service was clear. In essence, the need for troops capable of fighting in the Native manner in North America became accepted. The rangers provided the stopgap measure required, but their lack of discipline and existence outside the regular army necessitated another solution. As such, Rogers was directed to train regular officers in "ranging." Lord Loudoun sent 56 gentlemen volunteers from his regular regiments to Rogers for intensive training on all aspects of irregular warfare. Specifically, Loudoun ordered him to instruct them "in the ranging discipline, our methods of marching, retreating, ambushing and fighting."[105] To expedite the process he wrote up his twenty-eight rules of ranging, which some historians label the first manual on North American fighting techniques.[106]

Throughout this period, Captain John Goreham and his ranger company in Nova Scotia were also active. In 1757, Lord Loudoun tasked Goreham and a number of his rangers with conducting a reconnaissance to gather intelligence on the Fortress of Louisbourg. The following year, his company of rangers participated in the successful siege and capture of that strategic sentinel. In 1759, they accompanied the expedition against Quebec and assisted in quelling the hostile actions of Canadians. In August 1760, he was promoted to major in the British Army. In the end, Goreham's company was the most highly rated ranger organization employed during the war by the British high command.[107]

Nonetheless, despite the existing ranger companies, or perhaps as a result of them, British commanders still wanted to establish a corps of light infantry that would provide the necessary bush-fighting expertise, but with the requisite discipline and control that was integral to a regular infantry organization. Therefore, in 1758, Lieutenant-Colonel Thomas Gage's battalion emerged as the "80th Regiment of Light Foot," or more commonly referred to as "Gage's Light Infantry." Their muskets were cut shorter and made lighter. Uniforms were modified by cropping the tricorne hat into a cap and shortening the coat, as well as removing the lace.[108] A number of the officers posted to this unit were actually trained in "Rogers's methods." Clearly, the intent was to provide a more disciplined version of the existing American rangers.[109]

The initiative went even farther. That same year, in preparation for the expedition against the Fortress of Louisbourg, Amherst's force evolved its own plan for a body of light infantry to act as irregulars. Each regular battalion was to furnish 30–40 men — those accustomed to the woods and with good marksmanship abilities. They were also to be alert, good-spirited, and "able to endure fatigue."[110] The following year the experiment was advanced even more and each regular battalion of line infantry serving in North America formed a light company whose training emphasized skirmishing and marksmanship. In addition, the 60th (Royal American) Regiment of Foot also raised a light infantry company in each of its four battalions.[111]

But the light companies, much like the rangers, were seen as a necessary evil. They were not fully accepted. This became evident once the original threat, that is, the inability to contest the forests and operate in the wilderness of North America, receded. At the end of the war, Rogers was dispatched, with two ranger companies, to occupy the French trading forts in the west. Once hostilities officially ceased in North America, not surprisingly, the ranger companies were disbanded.[112] Goreham's company, however, was taken on to the regular establishment in September 1761. But they, too, were disbanded two years later when peace was declared between England and France in 1763.[113] At this time, Gage's Light Infantry battalion, as well as all the light infantry companies were also disbanded.[114] Only the Royal Americans survived and they became the principal guardians of the frontier, although they, too, were dispersed in small groups to numerous isolated wilderness posts where they were largely forgotten.[115]

In the end, ranging and the practice of *la petite guerre*, although not strategically decisive to the final victory, was nonetheless an important component of virtually all campaigns. Moreover, the intrepid individuals who conducted the scouts, raids, and ambushes in the untamed and hostile North American wilderness established a legend of daring and tenacity. Conducting operations in the remote wilderness against a merciless foe required courage, perseverance, and stamina and most men were unable to survive. Travelling long distances through virgin wilderness, often behind enemy lines, surviving on meagre rations and always on the alert, took its toll. Nonetheless, brave, daring men answered the call and established the legends that continue to this day.[116]

Notes

1. *La petite guerre* was in essence small-scale irregular warfare. The European understanding of *petite guerre* is "carried on by a light party, commanded by an expert partisan ... separated from the army, to secure the camp or a march; to reconnoiter the enemy or the country; to seize their posts, convoys and escorts; to plant ambuscades, and to put in practice every stratagem for surprising or disturbing the enemy." M. Pouchot, *Memoirs on the Late War in North America between France and England* (originally Yverdon, 1781; reprint, Youngstown, NY: Old Fort Niagara Association, Inc., 1994), 242. See also Hew Strachan, *European Armies and the Conduct of War* (New York: Routledge, 1983), 30–37; and Ian McCulloch, "Within Ourselves ... The Development of British Light Infantry in North America During the Seven Years' War," *Canadian Military History*, Vol. 7, No. 2 (Spring 1998): 44–45.
2. Richard Holmes, *Acts of War. The Behaviour of Men in Battle* (New York: The Free Press, 1985), 316.
3. A.J. Barker, *Redcoats* (London: Gordon & Cremonesi, 1978), 10–11; and William R. Nester, *The Great Frontier War* (Westport: Praeger, 2000), 126. A Prussian experiment in late 18th century that consisted of a battalion of infantry firing at a target 100 feet long by 6 feet high, representing an enemy unit, resulted in: 25 percent hits at 225 yards, 40 percent hits at 150 yards and 60 percent hits at 75 yards. However, under the stress of combat there would be invariably a different proportion. One consistent problem was the fact that soldiers would constantly fire prematurely, thereby wasting the effectiveness of their shot. John Keegan and Richard Holmes, *Soldiers* (New York: Konecky & Konecky, 1985), 66. The other variable was the musket that remained inaccurate. "The burning of the black powder caused the barrel to foul and, to avoid having to clean the barrel during battle, the ball had a very loose fit, usually one-twentieth of an inch smaller than the bore. This sacrificed muzzle velocity and accuracy but sped up loading and deferred the need to ream out barrels." Archer Jones, *The Art of War in the Western World* (New York: Oxford University Press, 1987), 271.
4. Emphasis in training was placed on speed and not accuracy of firing. As one subject matter expert has written, "Loading and firing was done in precision by word of command with as many as twelve separate motions required to accomplish this. With bayonets fixed, the attacking force would advance to beat of drum, if necessary the alignment of its ranks kept straight or evenly spaced by the sergeants'

halberds. On account of the inaccuracy of the smooth-bore musket, the attackers were relatively free of casualties until they reached a point eighty to a hundred yards from their objective. Now came the first crucial test of the foot soldier: the ability to hold his fire for the next fifteen seconds or so needed to negotiate the advance to a point fifty yards or less from the enemy. Here, at point-blank range, the order to fire was given. Then, as one synchronized machine and without breaking stride, the men reloaded and delivered a second volley, and if the distance allowed, a third. At the moment of impact, as it closed in upon its opponent, the attacking force turned to the bayonet. In this manner of warfare, rate of fire became more valuable than accuracy; speed and precision had to be combined with iron discipline, factors necessary for the soldiers to continue loading and firing among the heaped-up bodies of their motionless or writhing comrades. Precision and discipline had become as important elements of linear tactics as the rapidity of fire." Anthony D. Darling, *Red Coat and Brown Bess* (Ottawa: Museum Restoration Service, 1970), 10–11. See also Strachan, 16–25; Robert Leckie, *A Few Acres of Snow — The Saga of the French and Indian Wars* (Toronto: John Wiley & Sons, 1999), 52–3, 280; Geoffrey Parker, ed., *Warfare* (Cambridge: Cambridge University Press, 1995), 176–8, 185; R.R. Palmer, "Frederick the Great, Guibert, Bülow: From Dynastic to National War," in *Makers of Modern Strategy*, ed. Peter Paret (Princeton, NJ: University of Princeton Press, 1986), 93–94; Carl Benn, *The Iroquois in the War of 1812* (Toronto: University of Toronto Press, 1998), 68; and Patrick M. Malone, *The Skulking Way of War* (Lanham, MD: Madison Books, 1991), 56–58.

5.   On the eve of the Seven Years' War, the typical British battalion of ten companies was divided into 18 of "platoons," which in turn were grouped into three firings to ensure the maintenance of a rippling barrage — a virtually continuous fire. Nonetheless, as mentioned earlier, soldiers tended to fire prematurely. See Stephen Brumwell, *Redcoats: British Soldiers and War in the Americas, 1755–63* (Cambridge: University of Cambridge, 2002), 195; and W.J. Eccles, "The French Forces in North America during the Seven Years' War," in *Dictionary of Canadian Biography* [henceforth *DCB*], *Vol. III, 1741 to 1770* (Toronto: University of Toronto Press, 1974), xvi.

6.   Parker, 178.

7.   Palmer, 99–100. The regimental commander of the 20th Foot at Canterbury in 1755 issued regimental orders clearly directing that "A soldier who quits his rank, or offers to flag, is instantly to be put to death by the officer or sergeant who commands that platoon, or the officer or sergeant in the rear of that platoon." Richard Holmes, *Redcoat: The British Soldier in the Age of Horse and Musket* (London: HarperCollins, 2002), 34; and Holmes, *Acts of War*, 336.

8.   Holmes, *Redcoat*, 42.

9.   Benn, 71; and Malone, 59–60.

10.   The Natives often carved grooves into the stocks of their weapons so that they could take better aim by being able to align their eyes along the barrel of their musket and in line with their target. This was because neither the French Charleville .69 calibre musket, nor the British .75 calibre "Brown Bess" musket had rear sights,

as the Europeans felt this was unnecessary due to the perceived inaccuracy of the smoothbore musket and the reliance on volley fire. The North Americans believed otherwise. A Native veteran observed that in combat "the right men [Native leaders] concealed themselves, and are worst clothed than the others." Leroy V. Eid, "American Indian Military Leadership: St. Clair's 1791 Defeat," *Journal of Military History,* Vol. 57 (January 1993): 81.

11. Pouchot, 160, 476.

12. Letter, Father Pierre Roubaud, Missionary, 21 October 1757, in *The Jesuit Relations and Allied Documents. Travels and Explorations of the Jesuit Missionaries in New France, 1610–1791, Vol. 60,* ed. Reuben Gold Thwaites (New York: Pageant Book Company, 1959), 121.

13. *Warfare on the Colonial American Frontier: The Journals of Major Robert Rogers* [henceforth *Journals of Major Robert Rogers*] *& An Historical Account of the Expedition Against the Ohio Indians in the year 1764, Under the Command of Henry Bouquet, Esq.* (1769; reprint, Bargersville, IN: Dreslar Publishing, 2001), Bouquet's Account 52.

14. Thomas Church, *The History of Philip's War* (Exeter, NH: J & B Williams, 1829; Bowie, MD: Heritage Books Inc., 1989), 108–109. One survivor of Braddock's defeat reported "They continually made us Retreat, they haveing always a large marke to shoute [shoot] at and we having only to shoute at them behind trees or on their Bellies." Charles Hamilton, ed., *Braddock's Defeat: The Journal of Captain Robert Cholmley's Batman; The Journal of a British Officer; Halkett's Orderly Book* (Norman, OK: University of Oklahoma Press, 1959), 28–29.

15. Jeremy Black, *War: Past, Present & Future* (New York: St. Martin's Press, 2000), 127. The Natives did acknowledge "our troops thereby show they are not afraid, and that our numbers would be formidable in open ground, where they will never give us an opportunity of engaging them."

16. D.P. MacLeod, *The Canadian Iroquois and the Seven Years' War* (Toronto: Dundurn Press, 1996), 34–35.

17. He added, "Their encounters are mere attempts at assassination. They fight bravely then only when they know that the sole alternative lies between victory or death." Letter from Father Nau, missionary, in Thwaites, Vol. 68, 275.

18. K.L. Macpherson, *Scenic Sieges and Battlefields of French Canada* (Montreal: The Valentine & Sons Publishing Company, 1957), 4.

19. H.R. Casgrain, *Montcalm et Lévis : Les Français au Canada* (Québec: Maison Alfred Mame et Fils, undated), 43.

20. Colonel Bouquet observed that "They seldom expose themselves to danger, and depend entirely on their dexterity in concealing themselves during an engagement, never appearing openly, unless they have struck their enemies with terror, and have thereby rendered them incapable of defence." *Warfare on the Colonial American Frontier,* Bouquet's Account 52.

21. See Robert F. Berkhofer, "The French and Indians at Carillon," *The Bulletin of the Fort Ticonderoga Museum,* Vol. 9, No. 6 (1956): 137–138, 147; D.P. MacLeod, *The*

Canadian Iroquois and the Seven Years' War (Toronto: Dundurn Press, 1996), 21; William M. Osborn, *The Wild Frontier* (New York: Random House, 2000), 45; Benn, 82; Eid, 81; and Martin L. Nicolai, "A Different Kind of Courage: The French Military and the Canadian Irregular Soldier during the Seven Years' War," *Canadian Historical Review,* Vol. 70, No. 1 (1989): 60.

22. Letter, Father Pierre Roubaud, Missionary, 21 October 1757, in Thwaites, Vol. 60, 137. See also Osborn, 45.

23. Pouchot writes in his journal that "… even if there are three hundred of them & they were to take only one or two scalps, they would not begin another operation, even were they capable of devastating an entire territory and killing other men." Pouchot, 477. See also Nicolai, 59; and Benn, 53.

24. Quoted in Memoirs of John Johnson, given in A. Doughty, *The Siege of Quebec and the Battle of the Plains of Abraham, Vol. I–VI* (Quebec: Dussault & Proulx, 1901), 117. See also Brumwell, 204.

25. For example, a group of Natives having successfully executed an ambush that yielded both supplies and prisoners without incurring any casualties. They then decided to return home. "The Master of Life has favoured us," they explained to the French commander, "here is the food, here are the prisoners, let's return." MacLeod, 35–36.

26. For example, Lieutenant-General Jeffrey Amherst described them as "These little skulking men …" Jeffrey Amherst, *Journal of William Amherst in America, 1758-1760* (London: Butler & Tanner Ltd., 1927), 20. Captain John Knox described them as "these skulking wretches," although he did include that they "are so hardy, that scarce pass one day [in February 1758] without scouring the environs of this fortress." Captain John Knox, *An Historical Journal of the Campaigns in North-America for the Years 1757, 1758, 1759, and 1760,* Vol. 1 (London: 1769), 102. See also Malone, *The Skulking Way of War.*

27. William Wier, *Fatal Victories* (Hamden, CT: Archon Books, 1993), 112.

28. Jack M. Sosin, "The Use of Indians in the War of the American Revolution: A Re-assessment of Responsibility," *The Canadian Historical Review,* Vol. 42, No. 2 (June 1965): 120.

29. Ross Brian Snyder, "Algonquin Warfare in Canada and Southern New England 1600–1680" (master's thesis, University of Ottawa, 1972), 157.

30. Letter, gentleman in Virginia to friend in Annapolis, 16 January 1754, quoted in Lucier, ed., *French and Indian War Notices,* Vol. 1, 3.

31. Amherst, *Journal of William Amherst in America,* 15–16.

32. Sylvester K. Stevens, Donald H. Kent and Emma E. Woods, *Travels in New France by J.C.B.* (Harrisburg, PA: The Pennsylvania Historical Commission, 1941), 25.

33. W.J. Eccles, *Canada Under Louis XIV* (Toronto: McCelland and Stewart, 1964), 46. From 1633 until the end of the century, the Canadians realized less than 15 years of peace. One hundred ninety-one settlers were killed by the Iroquois between 1608 and 1666 — out of a population that numbered 675 in 1650 and 3,035 in 1663. W.J. Eccles, *The French in North America 1500–1783* (Markham, Ont.: Fitzheny & Whiteside, 1998), 40–41.

34.   Quoted documents, display (Chambly, Que.: Fort Chambly National Historic Site of Canada, accessed 23 August 2001).

35.   *Ibid.*

36.   Extract from a letter dated 28 April 1757, quoted in Armand Francis Lucier, ed., *French and Indian War Notices Abstracted from Colonial Newspapers, Vol. 2: 1756–1757* (Bowie, MD: Heritage Books, 1999), 233.

37.   Letter from an officer, dated Fort Cumberland, 6 October 1755, in Lucier, ed., *French and Indian War Notices, Vol. 1*, 329. Another account revealed "The barbarous and bloody scene which is now opened in the upper parts of Northamton County, is the most lamentable that perhaps ever appeared … There may be seen horror and desolation; populous settlements deserted; villages laid to ashes; men, women and children cruelly mangled and massacred." Letter from Virginia, 11 December 1755, in *ibid.*, 353.

38.   Robert C. Alberts, *The Most Extraordinary Adventures of Major Robert Stobo* (Boston: Houghton Mifflin, 1965), 152. Similarly, a French officer observed, "people of the country [English colonies] have great fear of the savages, to the extent that they do not harvest their crops — as a result they lose their grain because it is overripe." H.R. Casgrain, ed., *Lettres du Chevalier De Lévis concernant La Guerre du Canada (1756–1760)* (Montreal: C.O. Beauchemin & Fils, 1889), 75.

39.   Hamilton, *Braddock's Defeat*, 29; and Fred Anderson, *Crucible of War* (New York: Vintage Books, 2001), 100. The veteran also recalled that "… they Either on their Bellies or Behind trees or Running from one tree to another almost by the ground." At the battle at Lake George, in early September 1755, Baron Dieskau's French regular officers and men, who remained in the open, suffered horrendous casualties against the New England men who fired from behind logs. They lost nearly all their officers and approximately half of their soldiers. Conversely, the French Canadians and Natives on their part remained behind cover and suffered negligible losses. Anderson, 158–159.

40.   Hamilton, *Braddock's Defeat*, 50.

41.   Canada Archives, *The Northcliffe Collection* (Ottawa: King's Printer, 1926), 216.

42.   Letter from an officer fighting in the Ohio, 25 August 1755, in Lucier, ed., *French and Indian War Notices, Vol. 1*, 278.

43.   Charles E. Brodine, "Henry Bouquet and British Infantry Tactics on the Ohio Frontier, 1758–1764," in *The Sixty Years' War for the Great Lakes, 1754–1814*, eds. David Curtis Skaggs and Larry L. Nelson (East Lansing: University of Michigan, 2001), 46. Another contemporary officer wrote, "They are an active hardy People, capable of fatigue, hunger, and cold and know perfectly the use of arms. And tho' their number nor their valour may not make them a formidable enemy, their little wood skirmishing, and bush fighting will always make them a very troublesome one." *The Northcliffe Collection*, 70.

44.   Quoted in *The Conquest of Canada, Vol. II* (New York: Harper & Brothers, Publishers, 1850), 18.

45. The Indians tended to prefer French to English because of attitude and cheerfulness. The French were more accepting of their culture and stature. In fact, many *coureur de bois* and soldiers living in frontier outposts actually lived with the First Nations people and took Native wives. In 1667, the secretary of state for the colonies, Jean-Baptiste Colbert, instructed the intendant of New France, "You must try to draw these [Native] peoples, and especially those who have embraced Christianity, into the neighborhood of our settlements and, if possible, intermingle them there so that, with the passage of time, having but one law and the same master [King] they will form thereby a single people of the same blood." Quoted in Peter N. Moogk, *La Nouvelle France: The Making of French Canada — A Cultural History* (East Lansing: University of Michigan Press, 2000), 21. The English were less tolerant and generally saw the Natives as simply savages. "To the English the Indians were irrelevant except as obstacles to achieving God's will." C.E.S. Franks, "In Search of the Savage *Sauvage*: An Exploration into North America's Political Cultures," *The American Review of Canadian Studies* (Winter 2002): 559. One historian noted that "The Indians were always at disadvantage with the English, in all the arts of civilized life. The English paid no heed to Indian laws or customs or traditions; and ruthlessly imposed their own laws, customs, and religious ideas with no apparent thought of their intolerance and injustice…. In brief the pilgrims and Puritans mostly looked upon the Indians as heathen …" George M. Bodge, *Soldiers in King Philips War* (Boston: The Rockwell and Churchill Press, 1906), 25, 189.

46. Bruce G. Trigger, "The French Presence in Huronia: The Structure of Franco-Huron Relations in the First Half of the Seventeenth Century," *The Canadian Historical Review*, Vol. 49, No. 2 (June 1968): 118. The Iroquois confederacy (Five Nations) consisted of the Cayuga, Oneida, Onondaga, Mohawk, and Seneca tribes. The Tuscarora joined the confederacy (now Six Nations) approximately in 1715. The Huron viewed the Iroquois as "devil men, who needed nothing, and were hard to kill." George T. Hunt, *The Wars of the Iroquois: A Study of Intertribal Trade Relations* (Milwaukee: The University of Wisconsin Press, 1967), 93. See also Nester, *The Great Frontier War*, 96.

47. On 20 July 1609, Champlain led the first combined French, Algonquin, and Huron force against the Iroquois at a site near present-day Ticonderoga, New York. Armed with an arquebus, Champlain felled two Iroquois chiefs and injured a third warrior with his first shot. His two French companions, also equipped with firearms, then opened fire from the flank. This onslaught, particularly because of the new weaponry involved, caused panic among the Iroquois and they fled the field of battle. In June of the following year, Champlain accompanied another expedition that expelled an Iroquois war party from the Richelieu Valley. These humiliating defeats inflicted on the Iroquois were not soon forgotten and led to an extended period of conflict that lasted almost 100 years. Eccles, *The French in North America*, 21–23; and Marcel Trudel, "Samuel de Champlain," in *Dictionary of Canadian Biography, Vol. 1*, ed. George Brown (Toronto: University of Toronto

Press, 1966), 186–199. See also W.J. Eccles, *France in America* (Markham, Ont.: Fitzhenry & Whiteside, 1990), 103.

48.   See Jack Verney, *The Good Regiment: The Carigan-Sali res Regiment in Canada, 1665–1668* (Montreal: McGill-Queen's University Press, 1991), 42–43; René Chartrand, *Canadian Military Heritage, Vol. 1, 1000–1754* (Montreal: Art Global Inc., 1993), 68; and Michel Wyczynski, "New Horizons — New Challenges: The Carignan-Sali res Regiment in New France, 1665-1667," in *Forging a Nation: Perspectives on the Canadian Military Experience*, ed. Bernd Horn (St. Catharines: Vanwell Publishers, 2002), 31.

49.   They failed to locate any Mohawk villages and only destroyed a few outlying cabins. Furthermore, they only killed four warriors and wounded six others at the cost of approximately 400 of their own. An approximate casualty count is given as 400 by Verney. Most of these are attributed to hypothermia and starvation. Only seven French were killed and four wounded in the skirmish with the Mohawks. Verney, 50, 52; Wyczynski, 32.

50.   Thwaites, Vol. 50, 140; Verney, 43, 72; and Dennis, 217.

51.   Thwaites, Vol. 50, 143; Dennis, 217; and Verney, 79. For a detailed account of the expedition see Verney, 71–84 and Wyczynski, 33–36.

52.   *Conquest of Canada, Vol. II*, 290; Hunt, 135; Verney, 90; and Edward P. Hamilton, *Fort Ticonderoga: Key to a Continent* (Ticonderoga, NY: Fort Ticonderoga, 1995), 33.

53.   Of note, a core of regulars chose to remain in Canada. Of the 1,200 members of the Carignan-Salieres Regiment that landed in 1665, 446 settled in Canada and 200 returned to France. Intendant Jean Talon stated, "integrate the soldiers and the settlers so that they can teach each other how to farm and help defend themselves in times of need." The benefit was enormous. It provided a nucleus of military experience, which when added to exposure and knowledge of the Native way of war created unrivaled irregular fighters for *la petite guerre*. Letter, Talon au ministre, 27 October 1667, National Archives, MG 1, Series C11A, Vol. 2, folio 308, microfilm F-2. See also Wyczynski, 37.

54.   Letter, De Meulles to Seignelay, 1683, in Richard A. Preston and Leopold Lamontagne, *Royal Fort Frontenac* (Toronto: University of Toronto Press, 1958), 147; and Eccles, *France in America*, 95. One French regular officer observed, "The Canadians are well built, very robust & active, with an admirable capacity to endure hard work & fatigue, to which they are accustomed through long & arduous journeys connected with their trading activities, in which a great deal of skill & patience are required. As a result of their travels, they are habitually rather idle because of the type of life they lead during them. They are brave, fond of war and very patriotic." Pouchot, 321. See Bernd Horn, "Langy and Marin: Master Practitioners of *la petite guerre*," in B. Horn and R. Legault, *Loyal Service* (Toronto: CDA Press/Dundurn, 2007), 53–86.

55.   With a population of only 60,000, New France faced the danger of being engulfed by its larger neighbor to the south, namely the English colonies that numbered

approximately 1,500,000. Stanley, 61; Eccles, "French Forces," xx; Leckie, 103; Doughty, Vol. I., 158; Nester, *The Great Frontier War*, 54; and Thomas Fleming, "Braddock's Defeat," *Military History Quarterly*, Vol. 3, No. 1 (Autumn 1990): 87. The scale of the threat was enormous. During the French and Indian War, the English colonies outnumbered New France in manpower by nearly 25 to one. The supply of foodstuffs appeared limitless. In 1755, the Governor of Pennsylvania asserted that he alone could produce food for an army of 100,00 men. In addition, the colonial iron industry was able to compete effectively with that of Britain. See Ian K. Steele, *Guerillas and Grenadiers* (Toronto: Ryerson Press, 1969), 74.

56. Notably — King William's War (War of the Grand Alliance), 1688–1697; Queen Anne's War (War of the Austrian Succession), 1740–1748; and King George's War (War of the Austrian Succession), 1740–1748. See Robert Leckie, *A Few Acres of Snow* (New York: John Wiley & Sons, 1999) and Ian K. Steele, *Guerillas and Grenadiers* (Toronto: Ryerson Press, 1969). For example, on 25 January 1693, 100 Troupes de la Marine, 200 Natives, and 325 Canadians left Montreal to strike at the Mohawk. They torched three villages, destroyed their winter food supply, and took 300 prisoners. W.J. Eccles, "Frontenac's Military Policies, 1689–1698: A Reassessment," *The Canadian Historical Review*, Vol. 37, no. 3 (September 1956): 208. The infamous attack on Deerfield, Massachusetts, on 16 March 1704 by 200 Natives and 50 Canadians destroyed the town, killed 47 inhabitants, and resulted in 111 others being carried away as captives. Dale Miquelon, *New France, 1701–1744* (Toronto: McClelland & Stewart, 1989), 40.

57. David Hogan, *Raiders or Elite Infantry? The Changing Role of the U.S. Army Rangers from Dieppe to Grenada* (Westport, CT: Greenwood Press, 1992), 2; John D. Lock, *To Fight with Intrepidity: The Complete History of the U.S. Army Rangers 1622 to Present* (New York: Pocket Books, 1998), 1.

58. Lock, 2.

59. King Philip's War began in the summer of 1675. At its root was conflict over land ownership between settlers and Natives. During the dispute, King Philip, the Wampanoag tribe chief, was fined for conspiracy and ordered to disarm his tribe. Extremely humiliated, war broke out between a number of Native tribes and the three colonies of Plymouth, Massachusetts Bay, and Connecticut. It lasted almost three years. When peace was finally achieved in 1678, all Native resistance in New England had collapsed. The conflict cost the colonies £90,000, 500 settlers captured or killed, and the destruction and/or desertion of approximately 20 towns.

60. Church, 93; and Malone, 91–92.

61. Church, 158. His rangers were given an added incentive. They were entitled to keep all of their captives and lawful plunder, as well as the reward of £8 per head for every fighting Native man slain by them over and above their stated wages.

62. *Ibid.*, 247. He believed that "bad men are but a clog and hindrance to an army, being trouble and vexation to good commanders, and so many mouths to devour the country's provision, and an hindrance to all good actions."

63.   Miquelon, 40. Church was eventually retired as a colonel.

64.   Chartrand, *Canadian Military Heritage, Vol. 1,* 166.

65.   Church, 219 and 247; and Lock, 4. John Goreham (also spelled Gorham at times), the senior, was Major Church's second-in-command in 1696.

66.   *DCB, Vol. III,* 260.

67.   Chartrand, *Canadian Military Heritage, Vol. 1,* 171.

68.   *DCB, Vol. III,* 261.

69.   *Dictionary of Canadian Biography, Vol. IV, 1771–1800* (Toronto: University of Toronto, 1979), 308. John Goreham died in England of smallpox in 1751.

70.   Quoted in John E. Grenier, "'Of Great Utility': The Public Identity of Early American Rangers and Its Impact on American Society," *War & Society*, Vol. 21, no. 1 (May 2003): 1–2. Hopson wrote the report, which assessed the contributions of the Anglo-American Rangers in late 1752 and sent it to the Lords of Trade in England.

71.   The Sevens Years' War, 1756–1763, was arguably the first global conflict. It was fought in Europe, North America, and India, with maritime operations reaching out over the Atlantic and Indian Oceans, as well as the Mediterranean and Caribbean Seas. At its core, Austria, France, Russia, Sweden, and Saxony, deeply concerned over Prussia's growing strength and territorial expansion under Frederick the Great, formed a coalition designed to defeat Prussia. Not surprisingly, England, already involved in a colonial and maritime struggle with France, entered into an alliance with Prussia. In North America, the conflict (often termed the French and Indian War) actually began two years earlier in the late spring of 1754. The growing competition for the rich lands of the Ohio Valley proved to be the catalyst for the latest round of conflict between the French and English colonies. Robert Dinwiddie, the Governor of Virginia, concerned with the news that the French and Canadians were solidifying their claim to the Ohio by means of constructing a series of forts, dispatched Lieutenant-Colonel George Washington and a detachment of militia to build a fort of their own on the forks of the Ohio River. A confrontation soon ensued. Washington and his party were subsequently defeated by the French at Great Meadows (Fort Necessity) and pushed back over the Allegheny Mountains. A second attempt by Major-General Braddock was made the following summer, but his force was ambushed near Fort Duquesne and virtually annihilated. The North American theatre eventually became part of the greater conflict. Initial French victories and English setbacks in the early years of the war were reversed by 1758, due to the British decision to focus their strategy and resources on the wilderness campaign. A virtual naval blockade, in concert with an infusion of more than 20,000 British regulars, turned the tide. The capture of the Fortress of Louisbourg and Fort Frontenac in 1758, forced the French to adopt a defensive posture centred around Quebec and Montreal. The deteriorating French condition also resulted in the defection of a large number of their Native allies. In 1759, the British began to roll up the remaining French forts on the frontier. One army captured Fort Niagara, and another marched up

the Lake Champlain/Richelieu River corridor, while a third invested Quebec. The siege ended in September 1759, with the British victory on the Plains of Abraham. The remnants of the French Army and their Canadian militia and remaining Native allies withdrew to Montreal in hopes of recapturing Quebec in the spring. Although almost successful, as a result of their victory in the Battle at Ste. Foy and subsequent siege of Quebec in April 1760, the appearance of the Royal Navy forced the French to return to Montreal, where they later surrendered on 8 September 1760. The war was formally ended by the Treaty of Paris, which ceded virtually all of New France to the British.

72. Benjamin Franklin, *The Autobiography of Benjamin Franklin* (New York: E.P. Dutton & Co. Inc, 1937 ed.), 168. See also Anderson, 95; Fleming, 90; and Nicolai, 60. The French force consisted of 36 officers and cadets, 72 colonial regulars, 146 Canadian militia, and 637 Natives commanded by Captain de Beaujeu, a colonial officer of the Troupes de la Marine. The British force numbered approximately 1,200 British regulars and 800 provincials. Paul E. Kopperman, *Braddock at the Monongahela* (Pittsburg: University of Pittsburg Press, 1977), 30; George F. Stanley, *Canada's Soldiers: The Military History of an Unmilitary People* (Toronto: The Macmillan Company of Canada Limited, 1960), 65; Noel St. John Williams, *Redcoats Along the Hudson: The Struggle for North America 1754–63* (London: Brassey's Classics, 1998), 76; Anderson, 96–97; and Strachan, 28. Brumwell gives the British strength at 1,469. Brumwell, 16.

73. John Keegan, *The Book of War* (London: Penguin Books, 1996), 92–93.

74. Letter from an officer, dated Fort Cumberland, 18 July 1755, in Lucier, Vol. 1, 251.

75. Francis Parkman, *Montcalm and Wolfe* (New York: The Modern Library, 1999), 111, 117–118; Leckie, 284–285; Anderson, 102–103; and Kopperman, 79. Tragically, as the provincials moved forward to take cover and engage the enemy in the woods, they were cut down by volleys from the British regulars, who mistook them for enemies upon seeing the smoke of discharges coming from the brush at the side of the road.

76. Kopperman, 139 and Annex E. See also Hamilton, *Braddock's Defeat*, xvii.

77. Stanley, 66; and Kopperman, 70.

78. Strachan, 28; Anderson, 105; and Stanley, 66. Actual numbers vary. Pouchot recorded in his journal that the casualties were approximately 1,300 for the English and 11 killed and 29 wounded for the French. Pouchot, 82–83. A more accurate count of the English casualties is given at 977 men, 500 of which were killed. French losses were 23 dead (3 officers, 2 men, 3 militiamen, and 15 Natives) and 16 wounded. Chartrand, *Canadian Military Heritage*, Vol. II (Montreal: Art Global, 1993), 20. Benjamin Franklin gave the English casualties as 63 out of 86 officers killed or wounded, and 714 men killed out of 1100. Franklin, 170. Brumwell states that two thirds of the 1,469 British troops or approximately 979 were either killed or wounded. Brumwell, 16. William Weir places them at 456 killed and 421 wounded of 1,459 engaged for the English and 8 French or Canadians killed, 6 wounded, and 27 Natives killed or wounded. Wier, 111.

79. Theodore Burnham Lewis, Jr., "The Crown Point Campaign 1755," *The Bulletin of the Fort Ticonderoga Museum*, Vol. 13, No. 1 (December 1970): 37. See also Walter O'Meara, *Guns at the Forks* (Pittsburg: University of Pittsburg Press, 1965), 114; and Louis de Courville, *Mémoires sur le Canada depuis 1749 Jusqu'à 1760* (Quebec: Imprimerie de Middleton and Dawson, 1873), 90.

80. Quoted in Ian McCulloch, "'Within Ourselves': The Development of British Light Infantry in North America During the Seven Years' War," *Canadian Military History*, Vol. 7, No. 2 (Spring 1998): 46.

81. Major James H. Silcox, "Rogers and Bouquet: The Origins of American Light Infantry," *Military Review*, Vol. 65, No. 12 (1985): 65.

82. Benn, 64.

83. Parkman, 241; and Anderson, 189.

84. Letter, Major-General James Wolfe to William Pitt, quoted in Doughty, *The Siege of Quebec*, 65.

85. Impartial Hand [John Mitchell], *The Contest in America Between Great Britain and France with Its Consequences and Importance* (London: *Strand*, 1757), 128. The writer also notes that the Natives and Canadians who travel without baggage, support themselves with stores and magazines and who maintain themselves in the woods "do more execution ... than four or fives time their number of our men." *Ibid.*, 138. See also Eccles, *French in North America*, 208. The English often referred to their opponents as "... our cruel and crafty enemy the French ..." Letter to *Boston Gazette*, 13 June 1757, quoted in Lucier, ed., *French and Indian War Notices, Vol. 2*, 256. During King William's War, a Canadian scouting party ran into English troops and fought like Natives. The "New England men taunted them as cowards who would never fight except under cover." Journal extract quoted in Steele, *Guerillas and Grenadiers*, 30. One American summed up the sentiment of many when he wrote, "Canadians delight in blood; and in barbarity exceeding if possible, the very savages themselves." Quoted documents, display (Chambly, Que.: Fort Chambly National Historic Site of Canada), accessed 23 August 2001.

86. Edward P. Hamilton, ed., *Adventures in the Wilderness. The American Journals of Louis-Antoine de Bougainville, 1756–1760* (Norman, OK: University of Oklahoma Press, 1990), 333. Even Lieutenant-General Montcalm, who particularly disliked the Canadians, wrote after his victory at Fort Ticonderoga in July 1758, "The colonial troops and Canadians have caused us to regret that there were not in greater number. Chevalier Lévis under whose eyes they fought speaks highly of them." Quoted in Andrew Gallup and Donald F. Shaffer, *La Marine. The French Colonial Soldier in Canada, 1745–1761* (Bowie, MD: Heritage Books, 1992), 42. Captain Pouchot noted that "They [Canadians] had always imaged that one Canadian could put ten Englishmen to flight, a prejudice that unexpected success had rooted more and more deeply in them." Pouchot, 76.

87. Casgrain, *Les Français au Canada*, 87.

88. Quoted in Abbé H.R. Casgrain, *Wolfe and Montcalm* (Toronto: University of Toronto Press, 1964), 196–197. Casgrain, a renowned expert on this period of

North American history wrote: "These Canadians seasoned and skillful hunters, do not waste a single bullet and create gaps in the ranks of the enemy." *Ibid.*, 60.

89.   Parkman, 168. See also Extract of a letter from Sir William Johnson to General Shirley, 10 May 1756, PRO, War Office 1/4, Correspondence, 1755–1763. See also O'Meara, 84; Doughty, Vol. I, 167; Le Comte Gabriél de Maurès de Malartic, *Journal des Campagnes au Canada de 1755 à 1760* (Paris: Librairie Plon, 1902), 217; and Pouchot 136.

90.   O'Meara, 85.

91.   "Memoir on the Defense of the Fort of Carillon," *The Bulletin of the Fort Ticonderoga Museum*, Vol. 13, No. 3 (1972): 200–1; Ian K. Steele, *Betrayals: Fort William Henry & the Massacre* (New York: Oxford University Press, 1990), 96; and Anderson, 187.

92.   For instance, after a brief but bloody engagement with Natives, recalled a frontier veteran, "… at night there was a Hundred men upon gard or more for feare of there [Natives] coming a Gain in the Night…." Quite simply, soldiers hated to go into the woods for reconnaissance or foraging because of the fear of being killed and scalped by the Natives. "Amos Richardson's Journal, 1758," *The Bulletin of the Fort Ticonderoga Museum,* Vol. 12, No. 4 (September 1968): 278; and *Governor Murray's Journal of the Siege of Quebec, from 18th September, 1759 to 25th May, 1760* (Toronto: Rous & Mann Ltd, 1939), 14. See also H.R. Casgrain, ed., *Journal du Marquis De Montcalm Durant ses Campagnes en Canada de 1756–1759* (Québec: L.J. Demers & Frère, 1895), 252; "Fragments of a Journal in the Handwriting of General Wolfe, 1759 (Wolfe's Journal 19 June–16 August 1759). Held in Royal Military College of Canada Library, Rare Book Collection, 17, 25, and 27 July 1979; *The Northcliffe Collection,* 216; Thomas Haynes, "Memorandum of Colonial French War A.D. 1758," *The Bulletin of the Fort Ticonderoga Museum*, Vol. 12, No. 3 (October 1967): 8; Casgrain, *Wolfe and Montcalm*, 40; Pouchot, 118; and Doughty, Appendix, Part I, 261.

93.   Rogers was a smuggler prior to the war. On Robert Rogers and his Rangers the definitive work is Burt G. Loescher, *The History of Rogers' Rangers: Volume I — The Beginnings Jan 1755–6 April 1758* (1946; reprint, Bowie, MD: Heritage Books, Inc., 2001) and *Genesis Rogers' Rangers: Volume II — The First Green Berets* (1969; reprint, Bowie, MD: Heritage Books, Inc., 2000). See also Russell P. Bellico, *Chronicles of Lake Champlain: Journeys in War and Peace* (New York: Fleischmanns, 1999), 143–147; John R. Cuneo, *Robert Rogers of the Rangers* (New York: Oxford University Press, 1959); *DCB, Vol. IV, 1771–1800*, 679–682; Lock, 8–130; Timothy J. Todish, *The Annotated and Illustrated Journals of Major Robert Rogers* (Fleischmanns, NY: Purple Mountain Press, 2002); and *Warfare on the Colonial American Frontier: The Journals of Major Robert Rogers & An Historical Account of the Expedition Against the Ohio Indians in the year 1764, Under the Command of Henry Bouquet, Esq.* (1769; reprint, Bargersville, In: Dreslar Publishing, 2001).

94.   Loescher, Vol. 1, 32; and Bellico, 144.

95.   Cuneo, 33.

96. This company was unofficially called Rogers's Rangers. They were paid and fed by the King but they were not part of the regular army. As such, they enjoyed more freedom and laxness than the regulars, but they did not share the permanency of regular units. Moreover, their pay was higher. A Ranger received two shillings and sixpence New York currency per day. This was more than double the wage received by a British soldier. This was one inducement to join the Rangers, and unfortunately, it did not always draw the right type of recruit. Amherst later set a restriction that those joining the Rangers had to be between the ages of 18 and 30 and experienced in the woods to impede the recruitment of those seeking the higher rates of pay without actually being capable of performing the task. Rogers was given a permanent regular commission at the rank of captain. He would end the war as a regular major. See *Rogers' Journal*, 13–14; Loescher, Vol. 1, 63–64 and 87; Brumwell, 213; and Cuneo, 32–33.

97. See "At a council of war held at the camp at Albany, 25 May 1756." PRO, WO 1/4.

98. *Journals of Major Robert Rogers,* 93.

99. See Letters, Abercromby to Pitt, April–May 1758. NA, CO 5/50, Microfilm reel B-2113. Johnson wrote, "Major Rogers is doing very well on the farther end of Lake Champlain, keeps the enemy in constant alarm for the more we can force them to assemble, by which they must consume their provisions is hastening them so much sooner to their fall." Letter, Amherst to Sir William Johnson, 21 June 1760. PRO, WO 34/38. Amherst Papers. The French also noticed a difference. Major-General Montcalm noted in his journal (July 1757) that the enemy is very alert and they continually have scouts in the field. He attributed the lack of success of the Native detachments sent out and their distaste for "*la petite guerre*" to the English efforts. Casgrain, ed., *Journal du Marquis De Montcalm*, 235–236. Another French senior officer, Bougainville, made similar observations during the same time frame. He wrote, "The enemy is very alert. They have scouting parties out all the time. The poor success of most of these detachments and the great number of our Indians do not discourage them in this petty warfare; advantage to them of having companies of volunteers, an example we should follow." Hamilton, *Adventure in the Wilderness*, 131. Montcalm referred to Rogers as the "famous partisan"and to his "elite troops." Casgrain, ed., *Journal du Marquis De Montcalm*, 339–340. Captain Pouchot called them "elite volunteers, who were called 'rangers.'" Pouchot, 131.

100. Rogers was repeatedly bested by the Canadians and suffered horrendous casualties. General Jeffrey Amherst considered the Canadians, owing to their skill and discipline, superior to the American Rangers. Quoted in Chartrand, *Canadian Military Heritage*, Vol. II, 49. Gage agreed. For example, he revealed, "But I despair of this being done [chase-raiding Natives] by the Rangers only. Judging from many pursuits of those people after Indians during my service in this country in which they have never once come up with them. The light infantry of the Regiment headed by a brisk officer with some of the boldest Rangers mixed with them, to prevent them being lost in the woods will be the most likely people

to effect this service." Letter, Thomas Gage to Amherst, Albany, 18 February 1759. PRO, WO 34/46A, Amherst Papers.

101. That is not to say that Native allies did not come with their own problems. Alliances with the Natives came at a price. European commanders characterized the Natives as an unwanted burden, if not a nuisance. "They drive us crazy from morning to night," exclaimed one senior French officer. "There is no end to their demands," he added, finally concluding that "in short one needs the patience of an angel with these devils, and yet one must always force himself to seem pleased with them." A. Doughty, *The Siege of Quebec*, Vol. II, 202; *The Northcliffe Collection*, 138; and Berkhofer, 146. Bougainville bemoaned, "One must be the slave to these savages, listen to them day and night, in council and in private, whenever the fancy takes them, or whenever a dream or a fit of vapors, or their perpetual craving for brandy, gets possession of them; besides which they are always wanting something for their equipment, arms, or toilet." Hamilton, *Adventure in the Wilderness,* 133. In an attempt not to aggrieve the Natives, the most wanton outrages were often accepted. One French officer decried the tolerance shown to their Native allies. "You could see them running throughout Montreal," he recorded, "knife in hand, threatening and insulting everyone." Courville, 97; Doughty, 202–203; and Benn, 136. Governors of New France, particularly Vaudreuil, were constantly criticized for their leniency towards the Natives. Of 76 Natives accused of disorderly conduct, assault, or murder in the Montreal District alone from 1669 to 1760, only one was actually prosecuted. The rest were released without charge. The rationale was simple, albeit unpalatable for the French and Canadians — the authorities feared that the application of the harsh justice demanded by the French criminal code would alienate the Natives and cause them to defect to their enemies. See Moogk, 43–45; and Gallup, 142. Their behaviour on campaigns was little better. Montcalm confided to his journal that "[the Natives] feeling the need we have of them, are extremely insolent; they wish our fowls this evening. They took with force some barrels of wine, killed some cattle, and it is necessary to endure all." Casgrain, *Journal du Marquis De Montcalm*, 385. French officers claimed that it proved very expensive to maintain their Native allies because they "exhausted so much provisions" and "could not be stinted to allowance taking everything at pleasure and destroying three times the Quantity of Provisions they could eat." The Natives had no sense of rationing and would consume a week's allocation of provisions in three days and demand additional replenishment. Consistently, the Europeans denounced the Natives as disruptive to their campaigns and a drain on valuable resources. Steele, *Betrayals*, 132–133; Parkman, 238; Berkhofer, 156; and Robert S. Allen, *His Majesty's Indian Allies* (Toronto: Dundurn Press, 1992), 144. "One is a slave to Indians in this country," lamented Bougainville, but he also added that, "they are a necessary evil." Hamilton, *Adventure in the Wilderness*, 171. In the end, both French and English regular officers preferred a disciplined force of Europeans capable of ranging duties instead of Natives, Canadians, or American rangers.

102. Loudoun did add, "… but as really in effect we have no Indians, it is impossible for an Army to act in this country without Rangers; and there ought to be a considerable body of them, and the breeding them up to that, will be a great advantage to the country, for they will be able to deal with Indians in their own way; and from all I can see, are much stronger and hardier fellows than the Indians, who are many of them tall, as most of the People here are, but have a small febble arm, and are a loose-made indolent set of People; and hardly any of them, have the least degree of Faith or honesty; and I doubt a good deal of their Courage; better times may show them in a different light." Quoted in Loescher, Vol. 1, 164.

103. *The Northcliffe Collection*, 110.

104. Letter, Thomas Gage to Amherst, Albany, 18 February 1759; and Letter, Amherst to Brigadier-General Gage, New York, 26 February 1759. PRO, WO 34/46A, Amherst Papers.

105. *Journals of Major Robert Rogers*, 52.

106. The following rules are taken from Rogers's journal as reprinted in: *Warfare on the Colonial American Frontier: The Journals of Major Robert Rogers & An Historical Account of the Expedition Against the Ohio Indians in the year 1764, Under the Command of Henry Bouquet, Esq.* (1769; reprint, Bargersville, IN: Dreslar Publishing, 2001), 55–64; and Timothy J. Todish, *The Annotated and Illustrated Journals of Major Robert Rogers* (Fleischmanns, NY: Purple Mountain Press, 2002), 72–78. The spelling is left as found in the journal:

ROBERT ROGERS "RULES OR PLAN OF DISCIPLINE"

I. All Rangers are to be subject to the rules and articles of war; to appear at roll-call every evening on their own parade, equipped, each with a firelock, sixty rounds of powder and ball, and a hatchet, at which time an officer from each company is to inspect the same, to see they are in order, so as to be ready on any emergency to march at a minute's warning; and before they are dismissed the necessary guards are to be draughted, and scouts for the next day appointed.

II. Whenever you are ordered out to the enemies forts or frontiers for discoveries, if your number be small, march in single filed, keeping at such a distance from each other as to prevent one shot from killing two men, sending one man, or more, forward, and the like on each side, at the distance of twenty yards from the main body, if the ground you march over will admit of it, to give the signal to the officer of the approach of an enemy, and of their number, & c.

III. If you march over marshes or soft ground change your position, and march abreast of each other to prevent the enemy from tracking you (as they would do if you marched in a single file) till you get over such ground, and then resume your former order, and march till it is quite dark before you encamp, which do, if possible, on a piece of ground that may afford your centries the advantage of seeing or hearing the enemy some considerable distance, keeping one half of your whole party awake alternately through the night.

IV.   Some time before you come to the place you would reconnoitre, make a stand, and send one or two men in whom you can confide, to look out the best ground for making your observations.

V.   If you have the good fortune to take any prisoners, keep them separate, till they are examined, and in your return take a different route from that in which you went out, that you may the better discover any party in your rear, and have an opportunity, if their strength be superior to yours to alter your course, or disperse, as circumstances may require.

VI.   If you march in a large body of three or four hundred, with a design to attack the enemy, divide your party into three columns, each headed by a proper officer, and let those columns march in single files, the columns to the right and left keeping at twenty yards distance or more from that of the center, if the ground will admit, and let proper guards be kept in the front and rear, and suitable flanking parties at a due distance as before directed, with orders to halt on all eminences, to take a view of the surrounding ground, to prevent your being ambuscaded, and to notify the approach or retreat of the enemy, that proper dispositions may be made for attacking, defending, & c. And if the enemy approach in your front on level ground form a front of your three columns or main body with the advanced guard, keeping out your flanking parties, as if you were marching under the command of trusty officers, to prevent the enemy from pressing hard on either of your wings, or surrounding you, which is the usual method of the savages, if their number will admit of it, and be careful likewise to support and strengthen your rear-guard.

VII.   If you are obliged to receive the enemy's fire, fall, or squat down, till it is over, then rise and discharge at them. If their main body is equal to yours, extend yourself occasionally; but if superior, be careful to support and strengthen your flanking parties, to make them equal to theirs, that if possible you may repulse them to their main body, in which case push upon them with the greatest resolution with equal force in each flank and in the center, observing to keep at a due distance from each other, and advance from tree to tree with one half of the party before the other then or twelve yards. If the enemy push upon you, let your front fire and fall down, and then let your rear advance thro' them and do the like, by which time those who before were in front will be ready to discharge again, and repeat the same alternately, as occasion shall require; by this means you will keep up such a constant fire, that the enemy will not be able easily to break your order, or gain your ground.

VIII. If you oblige the enemy to retreat, be careful, in your pursuit of them, to keep out your flanking parties, and prevent them from gaining eminences, or rising grounds, in which case they would perhaps be able to rally and repulse you in turn.

IX. If you are obliged to retreat, let the front of your whole party fire and fall back, till the rear hath done the same, making for the best ground you can; by this means you will oblige the enemy to pursue you, if they do it at all, in the face of a constant fire.

X. If the enemy is so superior that you are in danger of being surrounded by them, let the whole body disperse, and every one take a different road to the place of rendezvous appointed for that evening, which must every morning be altered and fixed for the evening ensuing, in order to bring the whole party, or as many of them as possible, together after any separation that may happen in the day; but if you should happen to be actually surrounded, form yourselves into a square, or if in the woods, a circle is best, and if possible, make a stand till the darkness of the night favours your escape.

XI. If your rear is attacked, the main body and flankers must face about to the right and left, as occasion shall require, and form themselves to oppose the enemy, as before directed; and the same method must be observed, if attacked in either of your flanks, by which means you will always make a rear of one of your flank-guards.

XII. In general, when pushed upon by the enemy, reserve your fire till they approach very near, which will then put them into the greatest surprize and consternation, and give you an opportunity of rushing upon them with your hatchets and cutlasses to the better advantage.

XIII. When you encamp at night, fix your centries in such a manner as not to be relieved from main body till morning, profound secrecy and silence being often of the last importance in these cases. Each centry therefore should consist of six men, two of whom must be constantly alert, and when relieved by their fellows, it should be done without noise; and in case those on duty see or hear anything, which alarms them, they are not to speak, but one of them is silently to retreat, and acquaint the commanding officer thereof, that proper dispositions may be made; and all occasional centries should be fixed in like manner.

XIV. At the first dawn of day, awake your whole detachment; that being the time when the savages chuse to fall upon their enemies, you should by all means be in readiness to receive them.

XV. If the enemy should be discovered by your detachments in the morning, and their numbers are superior to yours, and a victory doubtful, you should not attack them till the evening, as then they will not know your numbers, and if you are repulsed, your retreat will be favoured by the darkness of the night.

XVI. Before you leave your encampment, send out small parties to scout round it, to see if there be any appearance or track of an enemy that might have been near you during the night.

XVII. When you stop for refreshment, chuse some spring or rivulet if you can, and dispose your party so as not to be surprised, posting proper guards and centries at a due distance, and let a small party waylay the path you came in, lest the enemy should be pursuing.

XVIII. If, in your return, you have to cross rivers, avoid the usual fords as much as possible, lest the enemy should have discovered, and be there expecting you.

XIX. If you have to pass by lakes, keep at some distance from the edge of the water, lest, in case of an ambuscade or an attack from the enemy, when in that situation, your retreat should be cut off.

XX. If the enemy pursues your rear, take a circle till you come to your own tracks, and there form an ambush to receive them, and give them the first fire.

XXI.   When you return from a scout, and come near our forts, avoid the usual roads, and avenues thereto, lest the enemy should have headed you and lay in ambush to receive you, when almost exhausted with fatigues.

XXII.   When you pursue any party that has been near our forts or encampments, follow not directly in their tracks, lest they should be discovered by their rear-guards, who, at such a time, would be most alert; but endeavour, by a different route, to head and meet them in some narrow pass, or lay in ambush to receive them when and where they least expect it.

XXIII.   If you are to embark in canoes, battoes, or otherwise, by water, chuse the evening for the time of our embarkation, as you will then have the whole night before you, to pass undiscovered by any parties of the enemy, on hills, or other places, which command a prospect of the lake or river you are upon.

XXIV.   In padling or rowing, give orders that the boat or canoe next the sternmost, wait for her, and the third for the second, and the fourth for the third, and so on, to prevent separation, and that you may be ready to assist each other on any of emergency.

XXV.   Appoint one man in each boat to look out for fires, on the adjacent shores, from the numbers and size of which you may form some judgement of the number that kindled them, and whether you are able to attack them or not.

XXVI.   If you find the enemy encamped near the banks of a river or lake, which you imagine they will attempt to cross for their security upon being attacked, leave a detachment of your party on the opposite shore to receive them, while, with the remainder, you surprize them, having them between you and the lake or river.

XXVII.   If you cannot satisfy yourself as to the enemy's number and strength, from their fire, & c. conceal our boats at some distance, and ascertain their number by a reconnoitring party, when they embark, or march, in the morning, marking the course they steer, & c. When you may pursue, ambush, and attack them, or let them pass, as prudence shall direct you. In general, however, that you many not be discovered by the enemy on the lakes and rivers at a great distance, it is safest to lay by, with your boats and party concealed all day, without noise or shew, and to pursue your intended route by night; and whether you go by

> land or water, give out parole and countersigns, in order to know one another in the dark, and likewise appoint a stations for every man to repair to, in case of any accident that may separate you.

107. See *DCB, Vol. IV*, 308; and Chartrand, *Canadian Military Heritage*, Vol. II, 49.

108. A contemporary directive stated, "The Commanding Officers will order their leggins of what colour they please. The Barrells of the Firelocks of the Light infantry must all be made blue or brown, to take off the glittering; And the Coats of the light Infantry may be quite plain, or with the Facing of the Regt., as the Commanding Officers like best. The less they are seen in the Woods the better." Moneypenny Orderly Book, 26 February 1759. Reproduced in *The Bulletin of the Fort Ticonderoga Museum*, Vol. 13, No. 2 (June 1971): 170.

109. Brumwell, 228–233. Wolfe wrote, "We have establish'd a Corps of Light Foot, that might be infinitely usefull, tho' at present they are not so, from particular causes. They are cloath'd and Arm'd a la Legere — commanded by officers adapted to that service; & the Volunteers are mix'd amongst them, at the head of Divisions & Squads." "Some Unpublished Wolfe Letters, 1755–1758," *Society for Army Historical Research Journal*, Vol. 53 (1975): 85.

110. Brumwell, 229–231.

111. The Royal Americans were recruited in the colonies, largely from Swiss and German immigrants. Many of the officers were Europeans with local commissions.

112. Rogers was given command of an independent company of regulars in South Carolina. Rogers reached his zenith during the French and Indian War. Financial problems and intrigues resulted in Rogers's incarceration in both North America and England. During the American War of Independence, Rogers seemingly wavered between sides. However, his British commission was viewed with suspicion by the Americans, who eventually imprisoned him as a spy. He subsequently escaped and offered his services to the British. In August 1776, he was appointed to the rank of lieutenant-colonel and directed to raise a battalion that was called the Queen's American Rangers. Rogers's age and years of hard campaigning, however, began to show and he was retired on half-pay early in 1777. He eventually returned to England where he died penniless and alone on 18 May 1795.

113. In 1762, after having performed garrison duties in a number of locations, Goreham's Rangers were sent to Havana, Cuba, to participate in the siege of that city.

114. Holmes, *Redcoat*, 40–41. By 1770 a light company was established in every battalion of the British infantry but was often used as regular infantry (e.g. Battle of Bunker Hill 1775). The idea that light infantry companies should have a distinct role was resisted. Strachan, 28.

115. See McCulloch, "Within Ourselves," 52; and Hogan, 3. In 1771, a company of light infantry was reintroduced to every battalion throughout the line regiments (some which had unofficially maintained a flank/skirmish company). Nonetheless, most

were seen as "penal colonies," filled with the worst characters of the battalion. In 1774, the state of the light companies was so bad that a training camp was established on Salisbury Plain by General William Howe to instruct them in the necessary manoeuvres and skills.

116. The end of the Seven Years' War did not entirely mark the end of ranging or the practice of *la petite guerre* in North America. Pontiac's Rebellion in 1763, constant skirmishing against the Natives as whites expanded their quest for land, as well as the American War of Independence all encompassed the successful tactical usage of ranging and *la petite guerre*, however, it never reached the zenith achieved during the French and Indian War.

CHAPTER 2

Hollow of Death:
The Desperate Fight for Survival by Rogers's Rangers
21 January 1757

BERND HORN

Despite the cold January rain, Captain Robert Rogers was sweating profusely.[1] He knew time was of the essence. He and his men were in a precarious position — caught between two major French garrisons at Fort St. Frederic and Fort Ticonderoga.[2] Their survival lay in evading the French before they could muster a pursuing force capable of destroying the Rangers.

Rogers set a gruelling pace and his Rangers made good time. However, his instincts, which never betrayed him before, gnawed at him incessantly. "Keep spread out," he cautioned his men. Then, a thunderclap of muskets shattered the damp winter air. Rogers felt a sting of pain as a shot glanced across his forehead. His worst fear was now realized.

The "scout" gone bad had initially promised to be not only an adventure but yet another daring raid by the intrepid Robert Rogers and his Rangers. Ordered to conduct a scout by Major Sparks, the commanding officer of Fort Edward, Captain Rogers assembled a hand-picked team of experienced woodsmen comprised entirely of volunteers.[3] On 15 January 1757, Rogers, Lieutenant Stark, Ensign Page, as well as 50 Rangers departed Fort Edward for Fort William Henry at the head of Lake George, New York. There they prepared supplies and constructed snowshoes while they waited for reinforcements.

Two days later they were joined by Captain Speakman,[4] his officers — Lieutenant Kennedy, Ensign Brewer — and 14 of his men, as well as Ensign James Rogers and 14 men from Captain Hobbs's ranger company. The men were issued rations for two weeks (consisting of dried beef, sugar, rice, and dried peas and cornmeal held in a shoulder knapsack slung over the shoulder and diluted rum in their canteen), 60 rounds of ammunition (ball and powder) and blankets, which they draped over their heads and fastened to their waist belts.

Prior to sunset, that same day, they set off on their mission. They were tasked, as per normal, to reconnoitre to gain intelligence on the French garrison, specifically their strength and intentions, as well as cause as much "mischief" as possible — to disrupt, harass, and destroy enemy forces, equipment, and morale. Rogers chose to travel on the ice of Lake George to avoid the rugged, trackless mountainous terrain that framed the Lake George/Lake Champlain corridor. Travelling in Indian file, they made good

Courtesy The Fort William Henry Corporation.

Rogers's Rangers were in essence the British response to the effective French employment of Canadians and Natives in the scouting and raiding role.

time despite the adverse weather conditions and halted for the night on the east side of the first narrows. The next morning Rogers discovered that 11 men had been injured because of the strenuous march. He immediately sent them back to Fort William Henry. His war party was now only 74 strong.

They continued 12 miles down the lake, hugging the shoreline to avoid detection and encamped on the west side. The following day, after a final three miles on the lake, Rogers decided it was too dangerous to stay in the open and led his group off the ice. Strapping on snowshoes, they then took to the frozen forest. Progress was slow as they trudged through the deep snow and forced their way through the pines overburdened with snow. By 20 January, Rogers was parallel to the western side of Lake Champlain, about three miles inland. Well behind enemy lines, the Rangers were on

A member of Rogers's Rangers in winter dress.

their guard as they penetrated even farther into French-dominated territory.

The next morning was ushered in on an ominous note. It was raining steadily. The Rangers dried their muskets under covered fires in pits dug out of the snow about three feet deep. Once this was accomplished, they set off. They now changed course and stealthily marched due east under the dripping trees until they reached the ice of Lake Champlain. They were now approximately halfway between the French strong points of Fort Ticonderoga and Fort St. Frederic (known as Crown Point by the English). It appeared as if good fortune was once again favouring the intrepid bush-fighter and his men. Upon reaching the lake, as if on cue, the French were seemingly delivering a huge bounty to their antagonists.

Earlier, Sieur de Lusignan, the commandant of Fort Ticonderoga, dispatched a sergeant and 15 men to escort a group of empty sleighs to Fort St. Frederic to pick up badly needed supplies, namely fodder and rum. As the French soldiers bundled up against the wet cold and whipped their horses to begin their task, few, if any, had any idea of the danger that lurked ahead. The sleighs lumbered through the deep, wet snow and quickly began to spread out as each team and driver settled into a comfortable pace.

Back at the edge of the lake, the Rangers immediately spied the lead sleds. Rogers quickly determined a plan of action. He ordered Lieutenant Stark, with 20 men, to cut off the lead sled, while he personally led another group to backtrack and act as a blockade should the sleighs try to retreat. He left Captain Speakman in the centre with the remainder of the party.

As Rogers hastened to get into position his heart suddenly sank — they had miscalculated their prey. There was an additional 8–10 more sleds than they had at first realized! Rogers quickly sent word to Stark to stay hidden. But, would word reach his subordinate commander in time?

The horses were the first to sense the intruders. The driver, buried in his blankets and furs, squinted into the distance as the cold rain lashed at his face. He noticed the threat too late. Although he tried to stop the sled and turn it around in time, the Rangers that poured onto the ice proved to be too agile, too quick, and too many.

Rogers witnessed Stark and his group dash from the trees across the slippery snow to intercept the first sled. It became obvious that he had not received the warning. They were now committed. There was no turning back. Rogers reacted instantly and personally led his group into the fray. In fact, he captured the first prisoner as the lead sleigh tried to avoid Stark's men. Despite the frantic efforts of the Rangers, the rearmost sleds careened wildly away and back to the safety of Fort Ticonderoga. Pursuit was hopeless. In all, the Rangers captured three sleds, six horses, and seven prisoners.

Their apparent dilemma did not elude Rogers or his men. However, not prone to panic, Rogers calmly interrogated his prisoners. The news, although not surprising, was unsettling. It appeared that 200 Canadians and 45 Natives, all experienced in wilderness warfare — in the art of *la petite guerre* (ambuscades, raids, scouting, and individual forest combat), had just arrived in Ticonderoga. An additional 50 Natives were also expected from Fort St. Frederic any day. All this added to an existing garrison of 600 French regular troops at Fort St. Frederic and 350 at Fort Ticonderoga. Further to the distressing news was the admission by the prisoners that the magazines at the forts were well stocked in preparation for a spring offensive against the English forts. But the most disturbing revelation was the fact that the newly arrived reinforcements were well equipped and "in a condition to march upon any emergency at the least notice."

Having learned everything he needed to know, Rogers wasted no time. He knew that it was now a race for survival. He ordered his group to assemble and expeditiously marched through the wet, dripping pines to his camp from the previous night. This was a calculated risk. Although Rogers himself preached and adhered to the principle that one must never use the same route twice, particularly to return home after a sortie in enemy territory, he concluded in this instant that it was unavoidable. It was necessary first to return to their last campsite to rekindle their fires and dry their guns in anticipation of combat with the French. Furthermore, as speed was now critical, he also believed that following a beaten path would expedite their escape, particularly in the wet snow and driving rain. It was not lost on any of the Rangers that the hunters had now become the hunted.

Meanwhile, back at Fort Ticonderoga, the Rangers' worst fears were quickly realized. As the first sleds came back into sight, the alarm was raised. The most inexperienced French soldier knew that there was only one reason for the unexpected return of the obviously terrorized sleigh teams — Rogers! Lusignan immediately sent off approximately 100 regular soldiers and colonial troops under the command of Captain Basserode. He was also fortuitous enough to have with him the experienced Ensign of Les Troupes de la Marine, Charles de Langlade, who led the Natives and Canadian volunteers, which numbered about ninety.[5] Together they hoped to intercept the English on their return to Fort William Henry.

As the Rangers dried their muskets, Rogers quickly assembled his officers. Although many disagreed with Rogers's decision to retrace their steps, he overruled them and ordered them to prepare their soldiers for the march. As the rain continued to fall, the Rangers, with their muskets and powder carefully tucked under their blankets, which they wore as overcoats, set out in single file. Rogers and Lieutenant Kennedy were at the front, Captain Speakman in the centre and the reliable Lieutenant Stark at the back. Sergeant Walker commanded the rear guard. The Rangers advanced approximately half a mile over broken ground in this formation until they reached a deep valley. The terrain was unforgiving and Rogers was extremely apprehensive.

Most of the other Rangers, however, were less preoccupied. Fatigued, wet and cold, they trudged along, trying to keep up with the pace Rogers was setting. Most stared at the ground directly to their front. Knowing Rogers was at the lead brought a sense of security and confidence. His reputation as a bush-fighter was only surpassed by his innate ability at navigating through the forbidding wilderness.

But the Rangers were not the only soldiers marching expeditiously in the rain. The French sortie quickly departed the relative comfort of Fort Ticonderoga and boldly struck out to intercept the insolent English troops. Langlade and his Canadians and Natives broke trail as they were the sole personnel with snowshoes. Moreover, this was their type of war — one at which they excelled.

Langlade quickly deduced the route Rogers had taken. The rugged, inhospitable terrain narrowed the options of approach and passage through the Adirondacks. He was soon rewarded as they came upon the Rangers' earlier path. The French followed it until they came to a suitable ambush site. The constant rain and wetness made their flintlocks unreliable. Therefore, they needed a spot where they could quickly fall upon and overwhelm the English interlopers.

By mid-afternoon, after marching only approximately a mile and a half, as the lead elements reached the top of the west side of yet another ravine, the sudden solitary roar of a musket discharging was quickly drowned out by a thunderclap of explosions as the nearly 200 Frenchmen, Canadians, and Natives deployed in a semicircle around the valley, unleashing their fire on the unsuspecting Rangers. Luckily, the volley was less than effective due to the wetness of the muskets. However, the French, arrayed a mere 5–30 yards from the ranger column, now fell upon them with tomahawks and bayonets.

Soldier dressed for winter campaign by Francis Back © Parks Canada.

The French-Canadian militiamen were unrivalled at traversing and surviving in the harsh North American environment. After years of warring with the Iroquois, they became extremely proficient at *la petite guerre*.

Despite the obvious disadvantage, the Rangers reacted quickly. The opening volley killed two and wounded several others, including

Rogers, but instinct, as well as an ingrained sense of survival, took over. Rogers, known for his courage and coolness in combat, ordered his men to return fire and withdraw to the ridge on the far side. Lieutenant Stark and Sergeant Brewer, seeing the crisis unfolding, immediately formed up the rear of the column, comprised of approximately 40 men, into a defensive posture on the high ground and prepared to cover the retreat of their comrades.

The struggle was desperate. The forward-most Rangers became embroiled in savage hand-to-hand combat. Not all could break away — those who could were hotly pursued and only reached the safety of the far hill as a result of the brisk fire from Stark's group, which beat the French pursuers back. Not before, however, several others were killed or taken captive.

Rogers now deployed his remaining force. Lieutenant Stark and Baker held the centre. Ensign Rogers and Sergeants Walter and Phillips were moved into a position in reserve to watch the enemy's movement and prevent the Rangers from being flanked. Both sides continued to exchange fire. Darkness was now the Rangers' only hope. Outnumbered, inundated with wounded, and low on ammunition, the Rangers were in a precarious position. Moreover, Rogers was unsure if French reinforcements were at this moment moving towards the battlefield.

The Rangers, however, were not the only ones in a precarious situation. Their seven prisoners faced an uncertain future. Unbeknownst to them, their escort was ordered by Rogers to "knock them on the head" and kill them should the Rangers come in contact with the enemy in order to avoid having potential foes lurking amongst them if the situation became untenable. At the back of the column, the prisoners could not see what was happening, but by the volume of gunfire they rightly surmised that a French rescue party had arrived. Their good fortune was short-lived. The Ranger guards quickly went about dispatching their charges so that they could move forward and assist unencumbered with the battle. For some unexplainable reason, only three of the captives were actually killed, the other four in the end were recovered by their French comrades.[6]

But that was only one small drama of many that played itself out in the depth of the North American wilderness on that sodden January afternoon. No sooner had Rogers completed positioning his troops when the cry went up that the French were attempting to flank them on the right. Ensign Rogers and Sergeants Walter and Phillips quickly led the reserve in a quick counterattack and delivered a volley that beat back the French sortie. However, the French were not to be cheated of their prize and pressed an attack on the centre. Fortunately for the Rangers, sheltered by large trees, they were able to keep up a steady, accurate fire that inflicted substantial casualties on their antagonists, forcing them to retire once again.

Tenaciously, the French attempted to flank the Rangers yet again, but were unable to do so because of the swift and effective response of Rogers's reserve force. This final defeat broke the spirit of the French. The regulars with no snowshoes were limited in their ability to manoeuvre — floundering in the knee-deep wet snow. Furthermore, they were un-accustomed to this type of individualist combat. As a result, the French now settled into exchanging a steady, and not altogether ineffective, fire with the Rangers. Mr. Baker was one of several who was killed and Rogers himself sustained another wound — taking a musket ball through his wrist, which disabled him to such an extent that he was unable to load

his musket. Fearing the im-pact on morale as a result of his latest wound, Rogers sent word by runner to his officers that he was fine and that all should keep up a diligent fire and hold their positions.

Rogers was not the only individual to sustain multiple wounds. Thomas Brown, a sixteen-year-old Ranger private, was one of those wounded in the initial dis-charge with Rogers. Although he was able to make it back to the centre of the Ranger posi-tion and join in the firefight, his musket was soon disabled

French-Canadian militiaman.

LAC, C-6217.

by an enemy ball that cut it off at the lock. He then took a ball in the knee, and, as he tried to withdraw to the rear of the position, took another ball in the shoulder.

As the woods echoed with the clap of constant fire, darkness started to seep into the already overcast sky. Sensing their chance of capturing the "forest runners" was slipping away, the French attempted various stratagems to try and induce the Rangers to surrender. First, they threatened them with dire consequences if they refused to submit, warning that a large number of reinforcements were on the way, which would "cut" the Rangers "to pieces without mercy." Other times, they flattered and cajoled them, "declaring it was a pity so many brave men should be lost." This was always followed by a guarantee that upon surrender they would "be treated with the greatest compassion and kindness." Rogers, particularly, was singled out by name and given "the strongest assurances of their [French] esteem and friendship."

As the light finally disappeared, both sides stopped firing. The cloak of darkness could not have come sooner. The Rangers had a large number of severely wounded who could not travel without assistance and their ammunition was almost exhausted. Moreover, their proximity to Fort Ticonderoga gave the enemy a distinct advantage. They could

Photo courtesy B. Horn.

Sentinel in the wilderness. Fort Ticonderoga guarded the southern approach to Lake Champlain. It was also an important staging point for incursions behind English lines.

easily deploy additional forces and simply overwhelm the hard-pressed Rangers during night, or at first light. As a result, Rogers decided to use the night to make his escape. He issued his orders expeditiously and those capable of marching set off.

The French stayed on the battlefield throughout the night attempting to track down the Rangers. During this period they received a reinforcement of 25 men, a convoy of food and munitions, as well as a surgeon and chaplain.[7] Although unable to come to grips with Rogers and his main body, the French were able to capture several of those too wounded to escape.

As such, for the seriously wounded, the night harboured no safety. Brown later explained that Captain Speakman, Baker, and himself, all badly wounded, had withdrawn to the rear of the position and built a small fire to keep warm. In the dark, they suddenly realized they could no longer see or hear any of their men. Speakman called out to Rogers but received no reply. They now realized that those Rangers capable of flight had departed. Thomas could barely walk and the other two "could scarcely move." Therefore, the three decided to surrender to the French.

Their plan was not to be. Thomas spied a Native coming towards the small group huddled around the fire. He crawled away from the fire so that he could not be seen, although he was able to witness the horror that was about to unfold. "The Indian came to Captain Spikeman, who was not able to resist," explained Brown, "and stripped him and scalped him alive." Baker, who was lying next to Speakman, pulled out his knife and tried to kill himself, but the Native stopped him and carried him away.

Witnessing this atrocity, Brown decided to attempt to escape as best he could. As he crept along, he passed a corpse of a Ranger. Not having shoes or leggings any longer, he stopped long enough to pull off the stockings, the individual had no shoes, to protect his own legs. By now the French had become aware of the Ranger withdrawal and had made a fire and deployed large numbers of sentries on the Rangers' path. Brown, without shoes and with great loss of blood, despite his pain and agony, was able to elude capture until the next day.

At about noon, he heard shouts of Natives behind him and within minutes four of them came running towards him. Struck with fear, he threw off his blanket and quickened his pace. Suddenly he heard the cocking of muskets. The Natives told Brown to stop. He refused,

This map depicts the Lake George/Lake Champlain theatre of operations. It also shows Rogers's route and place of battle at La Barbue Creek.

Author's collection.

hoping for a quick death by being shot rather than the fate that befell Captain Speakman. The Natives soon overtook him, but, surprisingly, did not kill him. They quickly rifled through his pockets and took his money. They then took some dry leaves and put them in his wounds before turning about and ordering Brown to follow them into captivity.[8]

That same morning the other surviving Rangers reached Lake George approximately six miles south of the French pickets. Once on the lake, travel was somewhat easier. Rogers immediately dispatched Lieutenant Stark with two men to make best speed to Fort William Henry to arrange sleigh transport for the wounded.

Remarkably, Sergeant Joshua Martin, another one of the seriously wounded who was left behind because of a shattered hip and a stomach wound, refused to die. Dragging his crippled body through the freezing-cold snow, he limped and crawled in pursuit of the Ranger main body. On the morning after the battle, unlike Brown, he caught up with the others on the ice of Lake George. Martin actually recovered and went on to serve with the Rangers for the remainder of the war.

The following morning, 23 January 1757, a party of 15 men and a sled under command of Lieutenant Buckley of Hobbs' Company of Rangers met the ragged column at the first narrows. That night, the survivors, 45 effective, and 9 wounded, arrived at Fort William Henry.

The grim, bitter wilderness struggle was exceedingly costly. The Rangers suffered 14 killed, 6 wounded, and 6 captured — a total of 26 out of 74 participants, or a casualty rate of 35 percent. Rogers's estimates of French dead, which he claimed to be 40 in his report to General Abercrombie and 116 in his later published journal, were both overly optimistic. French accounts revealed a toll of 14 killed and 24 wounded.[9]

Not unusual, both sides claimed a victory. However, each side interpreted the actions of their commanders in a different light. Rogers and his Rangers received praise for their bold strike at the French. At this juncture of the war, and particularly in this region, the Rangers represented the only real successful offensive strikes at the enemy. Their feats proved good for public morale. The high casualty toll was accepted by Rogers's superiors as the inevitable cost of such ventures.

As for the French, although the courage and efforts of the soldiery were commended, Lusignan, the commandant of Fort Ticonderoga, actually earned censure from Louis-Antoine Comte de Bougainville, an aide to Lieutenant-General Montcalm. Despite the relative success of the French sortie, Bougainville criticized Lusignan for "having weakened his garrison considerably and thus running the risk of being taken [Fort Ticonderoga] by a surprise attack."

The savage struggle at La Barbue Creek on that wet January afternoon never proved to be a critical tactical engagement of the war. Rather, it represented just another of a continuing series of "cat and mouse" engagements that framed much of how conflict in the North American wilderness was waged during the early years of the Seven Years' War (commonly referred to as the French and Indian War). Nonetheless, the contest was important. Constant scouts and raids served many important functions. They provided intelligence and attacked the enemy, thus, depleting his physical and material strength, as well as his morale.

Rogers's strike behind enemy lines, despite his close escape, proved important if for no other reason then to let the French and their Native allies know that they no longer owned the forests. Nonetheless, for the Rangers, the nondescript ravine in the Adirondacks became a hollow of death where they fought savagely for their survival.

NOTES

1. Robert Rogers remains one of the legendary colonial heroes to emerge from the French and Indian War. Born in Methuen, Massachusetts, on 18 November 1731, Rogers moved to New Hampshire near present-day Concord with his family in 1739. He spent his youth exploring the wilderness and the proximity of his hometown on the frontier made him familiar with Natives and their ruthless raids in time of war. At the age of only 14 he served in the militia during the War of the Austrian Succession. From 1743 to 1755, some historians suggest that Rogers was engaged in smuggling. In April 1754, he signed up 50 recruits and became a captain of "Company One" of the New Hampshire Regiment. At first Rogers and his men escorted supply wagons between Albany and Fort Edward. However, Rogers's knowledge and experience with the "haunts and passes of the enemy and the Indian method of fighting" soon brought him to the attention of his superior, Major-General William Johnson. By the fall of 1755 he was conducting scouts behind enemy lines. By the winter of 1756 the bold forays behind enemy French lines were regularly reported in newspapers throughout the colonies and, in March 1756, Major-General Shirley, commander-in-chief of the British forces in North America, ordered Rogers to raise a 60-man independent Ranger company that was separate from both the provincial and regular units.

2. The Seven Years' War (1756–1763) was arguably one of the first global conflicts. It was fought in Europe, North America, and India, with maritime operations reaching out over the Atlantic and Indian Oceans, as well as the Mediterranean and Caribbean Seas. In North America, the conflict (often termed the French and Indian War) actually began two years earlier in the late spring of 1754. The growing competition for the rich lands of the Ohio Valley proved the catalyst for the latest round of conflict between the French and English colonies.

3. The following sources were used to prepare this text: Russell P. Bellico, *Chronicles of Lake Champlain. Journeys in War and Peace* (New York: Fleischmanns, 1999), 143–147; Louis-Antoine de Bougainville, *Adventure in the Wilderness*, edited and translated by Edward P. Hamilton. (Norman, OK: University of Oklahoma Press, 1964), 81–82; H.R. Casgrain, ed., *Journal du Marquis De Montcalm durant ses Campagnes en Canada de 1756–1759* (Québec: L.J. Demers & Frère, 1895), 147–148; John R. Cuneo, *Robert Rogers of the Rangers* (New York: Oxford University Press, 1959), 45–51; *Dictionary of Canadian Biography, Vol. IV, 1771–1800* (Toronto: University of Toronto Press, 1979), 679–682; John D. Lock, *To Fight with Intrepidity … The Complete History of the U.S. Army Rangers 1622 to Present* (New York: Pocket Books, 1998), 31–40; Burt G. Loescher, *The History of Rogers Rangers. Volume I — The Beginnings* [Jan 1755–6 April 1758] (1946; reprint, Bowie, MD: Heritage Books, Inc., 2001), 111–140, 325–350; Francis Parkman, *Montcalm and Wolfe* (New York: The Modern Library, 1999), 222; Timothy J. Todish, *The Annotated and Illustrated Journals of Major Robert Rogers* (Fleischmanns, NY: Purple Mountain Press, 2002), 57–64; and *Warfare on the*

Colonial American Frontier: The Journals of Major Robert Rogers & An Historical Account of the Expedition Against the Ohio Indians in the Year 1764, Under the Command of Henry Bouquet, Esq. (1769; reprint, Bargersville, IN: Dreslar Publishing, 2001), 35–41.

4. Captain Speakman is often misspelled as Spikeman in contemporary accounts.

5. The exact numbers are difficult to ascertain. Rogers gives a figure of 250 French in his journals, although it is largely agreed that this number is somewhat inflated. Bougainville states that 100 French regulars were dispatched but does not quantify the number of Natives or Canadians. Parkman quotes the Governor of New France, Philippe de Rigaud de Vaudreuil, as stating that the French sortie against Rogers totaled 89 regulars and 90 Canadians and Natives. Loescher gives the number as 115 (inclusive of Regulars, Canadians, and Natives) at one point, but later states the number could be anywhere from 145 to 250.

6. The fate of the prisoners is also contentious. Rogers does not mention his orders to kill the prisoners, nor does he state what happened with them. Nonetheless, the Rangers did not return to Fort William Henry with prisoners or scalps. Cuneo and Loescher state that the prisoners were killed. Bougainville states that four were recovered.

7. At 2000 hours, two Canadians arrived at Fort Ticonderoga with a message that the French forces were low on ammunition. As a result, a detachment of 25 men to carry powder and rations (biscuits), as well as a surgeon and priest were dispatched. "Relation de L'action lancé contre les anglois ce les frontier, 21 Janvier 1757 (Carillon)." National Archives of Canada [NA], Microfilm C-362, Bourlamaque Collection, Vol. IV, 11 March 1756–18 April 1760), 310.

8. See Cuneo, 49 and Loescher, 331–340 for a description of Brown's subsequent captivity.

9. Again, exact numbers are difficult to nail down. Bougainville gives the French total at 11 killed, 27 wounded, of which 3 later died. Lieutenant-General Montcalm's account concedes only 9 killed and 18 wounded (some of which he states later died of wounds). Parkman quotes Vaudreuil as giving total casualties at 37. Bellico states that French casualties amounted to 19 killed and 27 wounded, of which 23 later died, and Loescher puts them at 18 and 27. Bougainville and Montcalm assigned to the Rangers 42 dead and 8 captured.

CHAPTER 3

A Particular Gallant Action:
The Capture of the *Prudent* and *Bienfaisant*
During the Second Siege of Louisbourg, 1758

MICHAEL WYCZYNSKI

Since 1713, with the foundation of Louisbourg, in Île Royale (Cape Breton), the strategic location of this French fortress, and its seaport had always presented a serious economic, military, and naval threat to the British colonies and to England's aspiration for expansion in North America. Quite simply, if the British were to conduct successful combined ground and naval operations to control the continent they knew that Louisbourg had to be neutralized, if not captured. For whoever controlled Louisbourg, controlled all the adjoining coastal naval routes, the approaches to the sea lanes, and, more importantly, the access to the Gulf of the St. Lawrence River.

Conversely, in the event that Louisbourg fell to the British, the effectiveness of the French squadrons in the North American naval theatre would be seriously compromised. The captains of French warships needed this protected harbour to assemble their squadrons after long and gruelling sea voyages, as well as to refit their vessels, carry out necessary repairs, rest their sick or wounded sailors, and use the seaport as an operational base to plan, launch and maintain blockades, patrols, and raiding operations.

In addition, Louisbourg was also critical for the continual control and resupply of New France. As the years passed and tensions between the two empires grew, the British became increasingly apprehensive of the threat this fortress posed. As a result, between 1713 and 1758 they launched three major operations (1745, 1757, and 1758, specifically) to capture this highly valued strategic military objective.

The first siege commenced on 11 May 1745. Sir Admiral Peter Warren commanded a British naval squadron, which totalled 12

Courtesy Parks Canada.

Louisbourg Harbour as depicted in Lewis Parker's *View from a Warship.*

warships.[1] Though a difficult and stressful campaign, Warren nevertheless successfully protected the invasion forces' supply vessels, and manned a naval blockade off Louisbourg while providing continual support to Sir William Pepperell, commander of the land component, which comprised 3,000 New Englanders.[2] Despite having isolated the French defenders to the confines of their fortifications, the concerned admiral feared, throughout the course of the siege, that his small squadron could fall prey to a larger French relief naval force. Finally, on 28 June 1745, after seven weeks of artillery bombardments and siege works, Louis Du Pont Duchambon, commanding officer of the fortress, capitulated. However, the British occupation of Louisbourg was short-lived.

Three years later, in 1748, the fortress was returned to the French, in accordance with the agreed conditions of the Treaty of Aix-la-Chapelle.[3] Upon their return to Louisbourg, the French immediately set out to repair and expand the existing fortifications, increase their artillery and garrison, as well as ensure a regular presence of warships in the harbour and adjoining costal areas. In 1749, to compensate for the loss of Louisbourg the British founded the city and port of Halifax. This new naval base provided the British with a much-needed harbour, as well as excellent facilities required to assemble and launch large expeditions against various parts of the French colonies. As both belligerents consolidated their various fortifications and reinforced their contingents in North America, it became evident that it was only a matter of time before the two expanding powers clashed once again.

This prophecy soon came to pass. Between 1754 and early 1756, British regular troops and colonial militias went on the offensive, which resulted in a series of unsuccessful operations against French forts and outposts on Lake Champlain, at the Niagara frontier, the Ohio Valley, and in the Maritimes. Their only successful venture resulted in the capture of Fort Beauséjour, located on the Nova Scotia border. Anticipating a new series of enemy incursions, the French Minister of Colonies dispatched two regular force infantry battalions to bolster Louisbourg's garrison.[4]

Tensions between the two countries continued to mount and finally, on 18 March 1756, England declared war on France, thus initiating the long and gruelling Seven Years' War. A month later, Pierre De Rigaud de Vaudreuil de Cavagnial, the governor general and commander-in-chief of New France, ordered his newly arrived military commander, Major-General Louis-Joseph de Montcalm, to attack the British fort at Oswego on Lake Ontario. In concert with these operations, the French mounted a successful raiding campaign on the frontier, which struck terror into the colonies. The following year, in August 1757, French forces captured Fort William Henry on Lake George.[5] These important French victories left the British colonies in a precarious position.

If the British were to successfully pursue the war in North America, they had to devise a series of well-planned military operations, under the direction of competent, experienced senior officers, and be willing to commit vast numbers of regular-force ground troops, supported by numerous vessels of the Royal Navy. That same year, the British Secretary of State, William Pitt, Earl of Chatham, acknowledged the urgency of resolving the contest for North America. Among his top priorities was the capture of the fortress of Louisbourg.

The planning of a second operation against Louisbourg commenced in early 1757. Pitt selected Vice-Admiral Francis Holburne to command the British naval forces and support the ground troops led by Lord Loudoun, the commander-in-chief in America.[6] From the outset, the planning and preparations for this large campaign proved to be challenging and difficult. The French were not going to relinquish Louisbourg without a fight. British intelligence confirmed that between January and April 1757, one French squadron had already left from Toulon, while two others had sailed from Brest. The last squadron reached Louisbourg safely on 21 June 1757. Under the command of Emmanuel-

Auguste de Cahideuc, Comte Dubois de La Motte, this impressive armada totalled 24 warships comprising an impressive combined firepower of 1,380 guns.[7] Concurrently, the French garrison, under the command of its governor, Augustin De Boschenry De Drucour, worked feverishly to consolidate the fortress's structures and further strengthen the surrounding coastal defensive positions and gun emplacements built to counter beach assault landings.

The unexpected arrival of these three French squadrons coupled with the British ground forces' long, drawn-out preparations now prompted Loudoun to re-evaluate his plan. The concerned commander-in-chief wrote to Holburne, on 4 August 1757, seeking the vice-admiral's advice on the feasibility of still conducting a successful operation. "In the view of the intelligence received from Louisbourg," explained Loudoun, "is there any chance of success in its attempted reduction?" A skeptical Holburne replied, "the season was too far advanced, and the enemy too strong for an attempt to be successful."[8] The vice-admiral's correct assessment of the foredoomed campaign would come back to haunt him. Nevertheless, the frustrated vice-admiral sailed from Halifax in August 1757 for Louisbourg, hoping to draw out and engage some of the French warships. By 19 August 1757, Holburne's vessels patrolled off the coast of Louisbourg. Dubois de la Motte observed his adversary's movements, but opted, for the moment, to remain in the harbour. As the weeks passed, the weather worsened.

A hurricane suddenly ravaged the coast off Louisbourg during the night of 25 September 1757. Over the course of the next few hours, high winds and waves tested the British sailors' resolve while violently dispersing Holburne's battered squadron. As the sun rose, the distressed vice-admiral surveyed his crippled fleet. Of his 21 vessels, 13 had sustained various degrees of damage, and one ship of the line had been smashed against the rocky coastline near St-Esprit.[9] Not wanting his damaged vessels to fall prey to the French squadron, Holburne quickly signalled all his captains to return immediately to Halifax. Thus ended the second attempt to capture Louisbourg. Both Loudoun and Holburne sent letters to Pitt apprising him of this tragic outcome. Upon reading these dispatches, a furious Pitt immediately set forth to devise a new plan to launch the next year, in 1758, a series of military and naval operations to conquer North America.

Unhappy with the previous lack of aggressive planning and leadership, Pitt relieved Lord Loudoun of his duties and appointed Major-General James Abercromby as the new commander-in-chief in North America. Then, in a lengthy directive dated 30 December 1757, Pitt emphasized to Abercromby that it was the King's intention "to repair the losses and disappointments of the last inactive and unhappy campaign."[10]

Despite this 1757 debacle, the British high command drew upon the lessons learned. Firstly, it was imperative to assemble, in Halifax, a large army composed of regular force personnel supported by experienced personnel drawn from the Royal Engineer and Royal Artillery Corps. The King agreed with this recommendation and ordered that upwards of 14,000 men be committed to the upcoming siege of Louisbourg.[11] Second, the planners were to ensure that the requisite siege equipment was inspected and repaired. Third, this campaign was to commence no later than 20 April 1758, so that the ground troops and sailors could operate in favorable climatic conditions. Thus, all the commanding officers of the selected British army regiments and corps, as well as the Royal Navy ships of the line and support vessels currently in Britain and in North America were ordered to spare no efforts or expenses to prepare in earnest for this campaign.[12] Last, it was imperative the Royal Navy gain and retain total control of the European and North American coastal waters, as well as all the major shipping lanes. This was to be achieved by isolating and destroying all French warships operating in the North American waters while blockading all other French relief squadrons sailing from various seaports on the French Atlantic, in the Mediterranean, and Caribbean seaports from interfering with this operation.[13] Efficient planning, extensive preparations, solid leadership, and a large well-trained, equipped, and supported invasion force were the key elements that were required to capture Louisbourg once and for all.

During the months of January and February 1758, Pitt carefully selected and assembled senior army officers who would take part in and lead the upcoming operations against Louisbourg. Colonel Jeffery Amherst was appointed the commander of all the British ground forces, and was promoted to the rank of "Major-General in America." Brigadiers James Wolfe, Charles Lawrence, and Edward Whitemore would serve under his command.[14] Admiral Edward Boscawen, recently promoted to Admiral of the Blue, was designated to command the large invasion fleet.

Furthermore, Boscawen was to ensure and provide quick and efficient logistical support to the ground forces. Moreover, when required, the admiral would make available additional manpower drawn from his vessels in order to expedite the construction of Amherst's numerous siege works and gun emplacements. Assisting Boscawen with the defensive naval operations would be Sir Charles Hardy, the admiral's second in command. As the various components of this large invasion force were being assembled, Pitt strongly encouraged Boscawen to assault the harbour when the opportune moment presented itself. He stated, "His Majesty relying on your zeal for his service, is persuaded, tho' no particular order is given, by your instructions to that purpose, that you will not omit to force the harbour of Louisbourg, in case you shall judge the same to be practicable, as the success of that operation will greatly tend to shorten and facilitate the Reduction of that Place."[15]

Keeping this suggestion in mind, Boscawen continued to oversee the preparations of his vessels. Concurrently, his counterpart, the Commodore Marquis Jean-Antoine Charry Desgouttes, commanding officer of Le Prudent (74 guns), had been selected by the King to escort six frigates and supply ships to Louisbourg.[16] The commodore was informed that he would then be joined by two other squadrons hailing from the ports of Brest and Rochefort. Upon their arrival in Louisbourg, the naval officers were directed to report to Desgouttes, and serve under his command.[17] The commodore's role while at Louisbourg was simple. "The first objective," ordered the King, was to collaborate with the governor Augustin De Boschenry De Drucour "in defending the fortress in the event of an attack."[18] As Desgouttes was finalizing his preparations, Boscawen weighed anchor on 19 February 1758, and sailed with eight warships and three transports. After an uneventful voyage the admiral arrived in Halifax on 10 May 1758.[19]

Desgouttes's voyage, on the other hand, was marred by a series of neverending problems. Certain vessels under his command were forced to break away from the convoy and returned to France in need of urgent repairs. To further complicate matters, another ship was in such bad shape that it had to be burnt at sea. As the commodore finally approached the Grand Bank, the final leg of his escort mission was further complicated by the sudden appearance of increasing treacherous ice floes, and severe weather conditions.[20] The sudden cold temperatures caused additional hardships to his already sickly crew. "A part of my crew," lamented Desgouttes, "was staffed by sailors who had just been released from hospital, with death on their lips."[21] Of the seven vessels initially under his command, only two dropped anchor in Louisbourg harbour on 24 April 1758.[22]

Four days later, the much-awaited reinforcements, consisting of 660 men of the Second Battalion of the Volontaires Étrangers transported by Louis-Joseph Beaussier de Lisle, arrived without incident from Brest aboard four warships and a frigate. Among these vessels was *Le Bienfaisant* (64 guns), commanded by Chevalier De Courserac.[23] When all personnel and supplies were unloaded, the commodore ordered that all the ships of the line be immediately positioned in a defensive horseshoe formation extending from Lighthouse Point to Battery Island, thus sealing off the harbour's entrance.[24] Due to an increasing number of British warships cruising in the vicinity of Louisbourg, Comte Du Chauffault de Besné, commanding officer of the third squadron, opted not to risk joining up with Desgouttes. Instead, he moored his vessels in St. Anne's Bay, on 29 May 1758.[25] Waiting impatiently aboard these ships of the line were 685 members of the Second Battalion of the Régiment de Cambis. During the course of the next few days, the soldiers disembarked, and were loaded with supplies. They then conducted a forced march to Louisbourg and reached the fortress on 6 and 8 of June respectively.

While the newly arrived troops received a warm welcome by Louisbourg's inhabitants, Desgouttes hoped that this sudden influx of manpower would alleviate some of his sailors' heavy workloads. Throughout the month of May, Governor Drucour requested, on numerous occasions, that the commodore and his captains provide manpower and supplies from their vessels to consolidate and man the coastal defensive positions along Gabarus Bay. These extended from White Point to Cormorandière Point. Additionally, the governor ordered Desgouttes to regularly patrol the terrain surrounding the harbour, set up guard details to ensure the safety of his vessels, man defensive positions around the harbour, and provide sailors to form a harbour patrol force.[26] Furthermore, extra sailors were requested and organized into work parties used to haul additional artillery pieces and equipment to the costal positions. Last, when required, the admiral was to provide gun crews to man these coastal canons.[27]

Amid this flurry of activities, Desgouttes became increasing skeptical as to the operational role and value of his 10 ships of the line and frigates during the upcoming defense of Louisbourg. Moreover, the numerous strenuous physical activities exhausted his crews, who were already wracked by illness and disease. In fact, a total of 400 sick and dying sailors of the commodore's 530-man crew were put ashore for treatment and recuperation since his arrival to Louisbourg.[28]

Additionally, Desgouttes's vessel was in need of major repairs. The commodore reported that his main mast, topsail, and main yard had been severely damaged during his voyage. To further complicate his dire situation, the required spare parts were not available in Louisbourg.[29] From his deck, an apprehensive commodore reflected on his current predicament while observing the British blockade manned by Sir Charles Hardy's squadron.[30] Despite the inclement weather, Hardy patrolled aggressively on the outskirts of Louisbourg. From 5 April to 8 June 1758, he captured French supply ships, and, more importantly, diverted much-needed French naval reinforcements from entering Louisbourg.[31]

Whereas Desgouttes's efforts were plagued by a series of neverending problems, Boscawen, on the other hand, diligently assembled his vessels and vast quantities of supplies during May 1758. Moreover, the admiral also focused his efforts on training both his soldiers and sailors by devising and conducting a series of combined amphibious assault landing exercises. Extensive preparations, attention to detail, and speedy execution were imperative in ensuring a successful landing and an aggressive, positive beginning to a possibly long, drawn-out siege. Satisfied by the performance of his troops, Boscawen ordered his captains to prepare to sail.

Concurrently, as Major-General Jeffery Amherst reached the outskirts of Halifax on 29 May 1758, he met up with Boscawen's squadron and immediately transferred onto the *Namur* (90 guns), Boscawen's flagship. Without delay, Amherst briefed the admiral, and Brigadiers Lawrence and Wolfe as to the respective upcoming roles. While the senior officers focused their attentions on the logistics and preparations of the assault landing the impressive British armada consisting of 185 vessels approached Louisbourg.[32]

To protect the arrival of Boscawen's flotilla, Sir Charles Hardy ordered his captains to cruise closer to Louisbourg. This sudden increase in British activity prompted Desgouttes to reposition his warships and form a line extending from Lighthouse Point to Island Battery. Thus, their broadsides now provided welcomed additional firepower to the batteries defending the harbour's entrance.[33] As Boscawen sailed past the fortress, on 2 June, he did not seem overly concerned by this manoeuvre or by the number of French warships.[34] The following day, the British invasion fleet dropped anchor in Gabarus Bay.[35]

When all vessels were securely positioned and moored, the admiral selected, on 4 June, a few frigates and ordered their captains to cruise as close as possible to the coastline located between Pointe Platte (Simon's Point) and l'Anse à la Cormorandière (Fresh Water Cove). This was, in fact, the area where the invasion force was to storm ashore. Boscawen hoped that this manoeuvre, plus speculative fire, would incite the well-entrenched enemy gunners to fire back, thus enabling the British planners to assess the capabilities of the coastal defences.

The ruse was successful. Over the course of the next five days, the French gunners fired upon these targets of opportunity.[36] During this action, a cautious Boscawen ordered Hardy to position himself closer to the harbour's entrance and be ready to counter any possible sorties attempted by the French ships of the line.[37] Despite the garrison's upbeat morale, Drucour and his senior officers knew that it was now only a matter of days before the British would storm the coastline.

Under the cover of darkness, at 0400 hours, on 8 June 1758, the landing embarkations transporting the British assault force formed up into three divisions. Commanded by Brigadiers Wolfe, Lawrence, and Whitemore, the groups left their transport ships and rowed quietly towards their respective assembly areas. Upon the given signal, the rowing cadence was accelerated and the three groups simultaneously headed to their predetermined landing sites. The vigilant French gunners opened fire on these defenseless crafts. To minimize losses, the sailors were ordered to conduct evasive manoeuvres. However, high winds, and rough surf hampered their efforts while complicating their final approaches towards the inhospitable shoreline.[38] If these inclement conditions persisted the assault landing could be compromised.

Nevertheless, Wolfe patiently surveyed the coastline and uncovered an alternative landing site at the Anse-aux-Sables. As the longboats approached closer to the shore, the eager infantrymen prepared to disembark. As the orders to land were being screamed out, the soldiers, clutching their muskets, jumped into the rough cold surf and waded ashore with great difficulty. Witnessing this successful manoeuvre, the two other assault groups rowed in earnest to Wolfe's location. In the next hour, hundreds of infantrymen were landing unopposed. Time was now of the essence. Officers rallied their men, barked out orders, and formed them up without delay. Weapons at the ready, the invaders quickly marched towards the French coastal positions.

A view of the town and harbour of Louisbourg from British positions at Lighthouse Battery, during the siege, June–July 1758. Drawn by Captain Charles Ince of the 35th Regiment and engraved by P. Canot.

As the British soldiers approached the enemy entrenchments their vessels continued to lay down supporting fire. This sudden turn of events disheartened the alarmed defenders. Fearing that their escape routes would soon be cut off, the French soldiers and gunners, after a series of brief skirmishes, were ordered to spike their cannons and retreat in all haste to Louisbourg. Within an hour of the initial landing the coastline had fallen to the invading British forces. Seeing that the coastline and the terrain adjacent to the fortress were lost, Drucour dispatched small groups of soldiers, during the latter part of the day, with orders to burn buildings and houses located around the harbour. The governor did not want these structures and, more importantly their lumber, to be used by the enemy's engineers.[39]

As the British infantrymen occupied and consolidated their positions within the abandoned French costal emplacements, Desgouttes and his captains were on high alert and maintained their defensive formation at the harbour entrance. Furthermore, the French commodore dispatched rowboats to pick up the last contingent of soldiers of the Régiment de Cambis, who arrived that same day at the bottom of inland portion of the harbour. Desgouttes's sailors were also called upon to assist in the hasty evacuation of a coastal hospital camp, located outside the fortress's walls. Over 1,000 sick soldiers, sailors, and civilians were temporarily sent onto merchants ships that were then relocated to the bottom part of the harbour.[40] This swift and successful landing did not bode well for the future of the French garrison and squadron. "It was a fatal day for France," lamented a dejected François-Claude-Victor Grillot de Poilly, one of the fortress's engineers.[41]

As the disheartened defenders helplessly watched the subsequent landings of hundreds of additional British troops, Desgouttes met with his captains to deliberate the squadron's options and upcoming role. All agreed that it was imperative to save the vessels. Additionally, the crumbling facings of the fortifications' outer walls, as well as the British-controlled high ground that overlooked the fortress, which would inevitably provide ideal artillery positions, reduced any chance of prolonged resistance and inevitably meant the fall of the fortress and the loss or capture of the French squadron.[42]

The concerned French commodore met with Governor Drucour and the members of his war council the following day, on 9 June 1758. Desgouttes vehemently pleaded his case, hoping that his arguments would sway the Council to grant him permission to leave.[43] During these deliberations the commodore explained that if authorized, this would be the opportune moment to set sail for France. Or, if ordered, some of his vessels could attack and inflict considerable damage to the British supply vessels sailing to and from Halifax.[44] Jean-Mascle de Saint-Julien, commanding officer of the Second Battalion of the Régiment d'Artois, remarked that if such an order were given, "the British would take the harbour, and destroy the town in less than a day."[45] Moreover, the governor reminded the commodore of the King's orders, stipulating that he should to do all in his power to assist in the defense of the fortress. The war council then voted on this proposal. The majority of the members rejected Desgouttes's request.[46] Word of the commodore's intentions got out quickly, and infuriated both the inhabitants and the garrison. From that moment on, they placed little faith and confidence in the squadron's role and support. Upon leaving the governor's residence, Desgouttes realized that the fate of his isolated squadron had been sealed.[47]

During the days following the landing, Boscawen's sailors continued to stubbornly battle inclement weather, a rough sea, and a difficult coastline surf to deliver much-needed camp supplies, rations, engineering equipment, and ammunition.[48] As men and supplies landed hourly, Amherst deployed them without delay to further consolidate and protect his expanding bridgehead against possible counterattacks from Drucour's soldiers and raids by guerilla forces reported to be operating in the vicinity.[49] More importantly, the British general wanted to occupy and secure, as quickly as possible, the terrain and high ground surrounding Louisbourg and the harbour, thus ensuring that Desgouttes's squadron remained trapped within the harbour.[50]

Amherst knew that speedy execution, aggressive artillery bombardments, and maintaining a strong naval blockade were the key elements to bring the siege to a rapid conclusion. On 12 June, the commander ordered Brigadier Wolfe to take 1,400 men and make his way by land around the harbour and identify positions favorable to set up numerous artillery and mortar emplacements. Wolfe was assigned two very important objectives: first, to destroy the French squadron, and second, to neutralize Island Battery defending the harbour's entrance.[51] Once the terrain was secured, Wolfe's engineers and labourers commenced their work immediately.

To impede the brigadier's movements and fieldworks, Desgouttes initiated a series of offensive naval manoeuvres. He ordered Jean Vauquelin, captain of the frigate L'Aréthuse (36 guns), to position his vessel in the Barachois and engage the enemy's work parties. The commodore then dispatched a sloop armed with two 24-pounders to engage new British earthworks unveiled at the end of the harbour.[52] Simultaneously, the French gunners on Battery Island opened fired on Wolfe's personnel operating in the vicinity of Lighthouse Point. To ensure the operational readiness of Wolfe's batteries, Boscawen loaded the required guns, accessories, and supplies, and had them delivered by small boats to l'Anse à Gauthier. From this protected beachhead, guns and mortars were dragged to their designated locations.[53] Furthermore, Boscawen passed along information to Wolfe, confirming that Desgouttes's warships were ordered to remain and defend the fortress.[54] Thus, the confident brigadier now knew that he would require numerous batteries to continually harass and ultimately destroy this squadron.

The engineers surveyed the terrain overlooking the harbour and confirmed the best locations upon which to position Wolfe's guns, howitzers, and mortars. Once these artillery emplacements were completed the British gunners could engage the French warships, regardless of their locations within the harbour's confines. Each gun crew was issued with specific orders as to their upcoming roles. Some would concentrate their fire on the rigging and masts, while others would target the vessels' lower masts and hulls.[55] Wolfe's immediate objectives were to inflict heavy structural damages to the warships, and silence both Battery Island, and the Horseshoe Battery located on Rochefort Point. The brigadier hoped that his sustained artillery barrage would negate the French commodore's offensive and defensive options. Thus, Desgouttes's ships could not leave the harbour to attack Boscawen's fleet, nor be able

Courtesy B. Horn.

This photograph of a replica tall ship provides a graphic example of a gun deck that would have been similar to the ships used during the siege.

to position themselves to repulse the British vessels when they attempted to force their way into the harbour. In order to cripple the French ships of the line as quickly as possible, Wolfe instructed his gunners to fire around the clock so that "the Enemy may have no rest nor time to repair their damages."[56]

Three British batteries commenced firing against the French ships on 19 June.[57] As the rounds fell on and around the vessels, Wolfe observed the initial reactions of the French sailors and qualified them "as being in a confounded scrape."[58] Throughout the course of that very clear night, Grillot de Poilly reported that approximately 100 shells were fired in the direction of the Island Battery and the warships.[59] Even Desgouttes did not escape the intensity of this initial barrage. The commodore sustained a slight thigh injury while overseeing operations aboard *Le Prudent*.[60] "The vessels suffered greatly during the night," commented the concerned naval officer.[61] Nevertheless, the French naval gunners and artillery gunners of Battery Island also returned a heavy fire.

Wolfe, however, rated their effectiveness as poor. "They have thrown away a vast quantity of shot," remarked the very pleased brigadier, further adding that, "their confusion last night, when we began, was inexpressible."[62] Whereas some damage had been inflicted onto the French vessels, the British gunners were still attempting to find and confirm their range. Additionally, Wolfe could not obtain the full firepower from his mortars and guns due a series of breakdowns and malfunctions. Moreover, certain guns that were being transported to their positions were badly bogged down and additional men had to be brought in to extricate them.[63] Hoping that these problems could be rectified quickly, and with the unveiling of new batteries, the brigadier also wanted to reassure General Amherst that there would be an improvement in the marksmanship of his gunners. "Now I have got their distance better," explained Wolfe, "I hope the firing will be more effectual."[64]

For his part, Boscawen was not impressed by the efficiency of Wolfe's initial bombardments. The admiral feared that this could be interpreted by the enemy naval officers as a sign of weakness. This might prompt them to conclude that this would be the opportune time to slip away.[65]

Having survived the initial barrage, Desgouttes knew that if his ships maintained their current position, the situation would deteriorate rapidly. To spare the vessels from any unnecessary hardships the governor authorized the captains to relocate their vessels closer to the docks, providing they continued to lay down covering fire for the Island Battery and engage the enemy batteries located around the harbour.[67] One unidentified French army officer criticized this decision. "The more distance a shell travels," explained the officer, "the more altitude it gains, and thus easier to aim."[67]

On the other hand, Wolfe observed with some apprehension the repositioning of the French ships of the line, as well as the crews' work to improve their defensive positions aboard the vessels. Moreover, Wolfe was now not quite sure as to Desgouttes's intentions. All this movement and work confused the brigadier. "Their ships are certainly lumbered," observed Wolfe, "and prepared I suppose to sail. They cleared and made ready, and are now altering their position to bring all their broadsides to bear against the hill."[68]

However, this new location provided only temporary relief and cover to the French warships. To limit casualties, Desgouttes ordered his captains to evacuate all wounded personnel and unload food supplies. Furthermore, great quantities of gunpowder were removed, and sent ashore so as to minimize the possibility of explosions and fires aboard the vessels. Additional lumber and tobacco barrels were delivered to the crews. These were positioned throughout the vessels to provide additional protection for the sailors against incoming British shells and bombs.[69] Despite firing back briskly at the elevated and well-concealed British batteries, Desgouttes knew that the efforts of his gun crews were ineffective. "The guns aboard these vessels," lamented the disheartened Commodore, "can only fire up to a certain elevation."[70] With the warships now so close to the wharfs, the harbour's entrance became increasingly vulnerable to a possible forced entry by Boscawen's vessels.

Since the French warships could no longer position themselves to block off the harbour's entrance, Desgouttes proposed that four smaller vessels, *L'Apollon*, *La Fidèle*, *La Chèvre*, and *La Ville de Saint-Malo*, currently serving as hospital ships be stripped down, loaded with ballast, and scuttled in the pass of the harbour's entrance.[71] From the 22 to 29 June, great quantities of stones were hauled to the docks and loaded aboard the four designated vessels. Moreover, the commodore ordered Captains Beaussier de L'Isle and Chevalier de Marolles to prepare their vessels *L'Entreprenant* and *Le Célèbre* and be ready, at a moment's notice, to set sail for France. However, unfavorable winds dashed this escape attempt.[72] It was also during this time that the sailors' intensity and sense of urgency to complete their various tasks waned.

Grillot de Poilly and French Army officers who oversaw this urgent scuttling operation were disgusted by the lack of sustained effort displayed by Desgouttes's sailors. Additionally, those who remained on board the ships of the line also displayed little interest and energy regarding their gunnery and guard duties. They preferred to seek refuge behind their makeshift wooden barricades erected to protect them against shrapnel and flying wood splinters.[73] To further add to the mayhem and plummeting morale, a British soldier, captured on 25 June, revealed to the French high command that Admiral Boscawen was preparing to force his way into the harbour.[74] This latest news fuelled the rumor mill. Not wanting his ships to fall into enemy hands, an alarmed Desgouttes instructed his captains to be ready to initiate scuttling procedures aboard their ships of the line. Concurrently, the final preparations to scuttle the four smaller vessels were finally completed.

Mercifully, on 29 June, at 0300 hours, this operation was successfully conducted without incident under the cover of a thick fog. Unaware of this action, the British gunners did not engage the enemy. As day broke, the governor was very disappointed in the manner the scuttled ships were positioned. "*La Fidèle* had not been aligned properly," criticized Drucour, "and *L'Apollon* had not been sunk close enough to the entrance. Thus, another vessel had to be scuttled."[75] Chevalier de Tourville, Captain of *Le Capricieux*, became very concerned when he noted that the mast tops protruded the surface. These could be used as indicators by the British sailors, and guide their entry to assault the harbour. More importantly, Tourville was worried that the continual motion of the waves would eventually rock the vessels onto their sides, thus rendering the harbour's entrance vulnerable once again.[76] The masts were cut down by Desgouttes' carpenters the following night.[77]

Apprised of this latest development, both Amherst and Boscawen were unimpressed by this feeble defensive manoeuvre. These sunken vessels, "cannot stop up the entrance by that method," explained the British admiral, "nor any other that can be contrived, perhaps they may have laid a kind of boom."[78] The desperation of this latest operation, however, confirmed to Boscawen, that the French naval officers, "were now determined in the ships to share the fate of the town. Indeed I have thought so for sometime."[79] However, the British admiral knew that this was still not the favourable moment to force the harbour. The presence of these five large enemy warships within a confined area worried him. Further damage had to be inflicted upon the cornered enemy squadron before Boscawen would entertain the planning of such a bold attempt.

Despite Wolfe's continual artillery barrage, only a small percentage of rounds actually hit the French warships. These nevertheless created the desired effects causing damages to the masts, hulls, sails, and rigging of the ships. Furthermore, casualties were mounting daily, and fires broke out regularly aboard the vessels. Wolfe's Lighthouse Point Battery, which had come into action on 25 June, also hammered unmercifully both the Island Battery and the Rochefort Point Battery. This increased bombardment seriously weakened the French defence of the harbour's entrance.[80] In an attempt to relieve the increased pressure applied on these two batteries, Drucour ordered Desgouttes to engage Wolfe's well-concealed gun position. The commodore's tentative attempts to do so were foiled due to shallow waters and heavy enemy fire. Furthermore, to get a direct line of fire against this eight-gun battery, meant that Desgouttes had to exit the harbour.[81] Regrettably, this endeavour proved unsuccessful. As the vessel pulled away, Wolfe's gunners were now confident that the Lighthouse Point Battery could not be challenged by the French warships.

During the first 12 days of operations, from 19 to 30 June 1758, the effect of the British artillery had improved daily, causing increased structural damage to the enemy vessels. More importantly, it caused significant psychological and physical hardships for the exhausted crews.[82] The constant bombardment and the perpetual fear of a sudden explosion strained the sailors' nerves. One such shell hit *Le Capricieux* on 29 June, and set her on fire. As the sailors desperately fought to contain the blaze, even Grillot de Poilly, the squadron's harshest critic, acknowledged, "such events intimidated the sailors aboard these ships."[83] The efficiency of Wolfe's gunners had improved notably.

Desgouttes's vessels had now become floating targets. "The vessels were riddled by shot," observed the commodore, "and my vessel was now taking on water."[84] The disheartened commodore and his captains met with the Governor on 5 July to reassess the hopelessness of their current situation.

During these deliberations, Desgouttes reported, "the shots fired from his ships into the mountains were ineffective, and it was now preferable to leave a small guard on each vessel to service the guns."[85] To avoid any further unnecessary casualties, Desgouttes recommended that his vessels be manned by skeleton crews. Moreover, many sailors were still in poor health. Prolonged guard shifts under stressful conditions weakened them even more. Drucour agreed and ordered that all ship captains and the majority of their crews be put ashore on 5 and 6 July 1758.[86]

Upon reaching the wharfs, the sailors were divided into small groups and sent to assist the soldiers and the gunners along the various bastions. Meanwhile, the skeleton crews continued to man their guns. Regrettably, the dejected Desgouttes rated their efforts as "very brisk but fruitless. The damage done during the day was repaired at night."[87] During the first week of July, the French warships were now taking an increasing number of hits. "The masts and hulls," bemoaned Desgouttes, "were being slashed to pieces."[88] Additionally, many guns aboard the warships had sustained various degrees of damage and were no longer serviceable. It also became progressively more difficult to find volunteers to relieve the skeleton crews.[89] The ever-increasing damages inflicted upon the French vessels as well as their reduced activities were noted by Boscawen. Seeing that Desgouttes's ships were now showing visible evidence of daily deterioration, the confident British admiral concluded that these vessels were no longer seaworthy and reduced the number of men of war blocking the harbour, tasking them for other duties.[90]

Whereas the French commodore's remaining warships continued to play an elusive cat-and-mouse game with the British batteries, the only vessel that successfully engaged the invaders from the outset of the siege was the frigate L'Aréthuse (36 guns). Since 12 June, its captain, Jean Vauquelin, had positioned his frigate as close as possible to the shoreline in the Barachois and fired daily upon British earthworks constructed in the vicinity of Green Hill. From the outset, Amherst noted Vauquelin's smart fire, stating that his troops in that area were forced to continue their works under difficult conditions and had to "approach [the fortress] with the greatest security."[91] David Gordon, an officer with a Highland regiment also attested to the French captain's aggressive actions. "The work on the *Epaulement* much interrupted by the Enemy's fire particularly from *L'Aréthuse.*" The officer added that Vauquelin became very familiar with their operations in that area. The French naval officer aimed his broadside efficiently, "towards a low pass by which the troops were obliged to advance."[92] Nevertheless, this continual action exhausted Vauquelin's gunners to the point where they requested to be relieved.

In order to maintain a constant pressure on the enemy's positions in front of the main landward fortifications, Drucour sent in a new group of gunners on 4 July.[93] Despite their heroic actions, the increased enemy fire during the course of the next five days proved too much for Vauquelin's valiant crew. "The frigate," observed a relieved General Amherst, "was so hurt that she was hauled in near the town."[94] The governor ordered Vauquelin to immediately repair his frigate. Under the cover of darkness he sailed out of the harbour on 15 July. The captain successfully eluded Admiral Hardy's blockade and set course for France. Desgouttes's squadron was now reduced to five ships of the line manned by tentative skeleton crews.[95]

Encouraged by their recent success against the diminishing numbers of French warships, the British increased their artillery barrages against the vessels and Island Battery. Moreover, they began targeting buildings within the town as well as the hospital.[96] This new bombardment technique prompted Drucour to send a note to Amherst requesting that the hospital be spared. General Amherst and Admiral Boscawen viewed the governor's request as an ideal opportunity to further restrain Desgouttes's activities. They proposed that injured personnel be relocated to Island Battery and that they be visited regularly by a British officer. Alternatively, the sick and injured could be moved aboard one of the remaining ships. This designated floating hospital would then be separated from the other ships of the line, or sent out of the harbour, where it would remain under the protection of Admiral Hardy's blockading vessels.[97]

This counter-proposal was rejected by Drucour, thus placing the town, the inhabitants, and Desgouttes's vessels in further danger. The defenders' overall position was now deteriorating rapidly. Desgouttes obtained status reports on 19 July detailing the conditions of his vessels. They were in such poor shape that even if ordered to set sail for France, they could no longer even consider attempting such a long and demanding voyage. Not wanting his ships to fall into enemy hands, the commodore requested the governor's authorization to scuttle his remaining vessels.[98] "It is not yet the time," retorted Drucour. "The vessels defending our docks provide much needed fire power."[99] Desgouttes complied with the governor's order.

At half past two in the afternoon on 21 July, combustible shells fired from the Marine Battery, located between the Hauteurs de Martissans and the abandoned French Royal Battery, hit *Le Célèbre*, setting the ship of the line ablaze. The reduced crew could not contain the large fire. The flames spread rapidly to the adjoining *Le Capricieux* and *L'Entreprenant*, causing a chaotic scene.[100] Chevalier de Tourville, wanting to save his vessel, quickly returned to *Le Capricieux*. His efforts to reposition his ship were hindered by the low tide and an adjoining sandbar. Meanwhile, *L'Entreprenant* was now also burning uncontrollably. Furthermore, the flames had burnt her moorings, and now this floating inferno drifted slowly towards Tourville's vessel. "The burning *Entreprenant* closed in on us," reported the panic-stricken captain. "The heat became so unbearable, that I ordered my men to leave the ship and embark in the rowboats."[101] Desgouttes helplessly watched from his flagship the unfolding of this tragic incident. "I watched three beautiful ships burn," reported the dejected commodore.[102] Witnessing this incredible scene encouraged the British gunners to fire upon all incoming rowboats carrying sailors sent to extinguish the fires. As the skies over the harbour filled with thick, billowing clouds of black smoke, an irate Desgouttes met with the governor, deploring this terrible event. "Since the navy was navy," expounded the incensed commodore, "it was unheard of to subject war vessels to bear a siege in a closed harbour which now resembled to a mouse trap, where the vessels were positioned so close together that they were nearly touching each other."[103]

The British officer David Gordon pitied the French sailors, "in short to humanity tho' an enemy, the scene was very shocking."[104] This dramatic turn of events left the harbour virtually defenseless. More importantly, this unforeseen tragedy forced the governor to cancel a large raid, which was planned for that evening against British trenches facing the main French land fortifications. Desgouttes was to provide covering fire during the raiding party's withdrawal.[105] This setback was now compounded by the news that the bastions and connecting walls facing the main invasion force were deteriorating rapidly.

General Amherst's troops had made significant progress with their siege works during the first three weeks of July. Furthermore, increased artillery fire inflicted heavy damages on the fortress's outer walls, gun positions, and bastions. They were now well beyond repair. Moreover, the buildings inside the town continued to be subjected to relentless day and night bombardments that caused many hardships to the population and wounded personnel. During the following day, 22 July, new British batteries augmented the deadly bombardment. Shells hit the large wooden army barracks, setting them ablaze.[106] These structures burned uncontrollably throughout the entire day. This latest disaster dampened the garrison's will to fight. For the past four weeks, Drucour's soldiers, gunners, and sailors had been seriously deprived of sleep. The continual bombardment and enemy advances on all fronts forced them to live next to their guns and defensive positions along the fortification walls. Regardless of their weakened state, their commanding officers fully expected them to carry out all daily duties, and, when required, serve as emergency firemen, stretcher bearers, and labourers.

Boscawen closely monitored this increasingly chaotic scene. His assessment of the defenders' deteriorating situation was confirmed by daily updates sent by to him by Amherst. The two most noticeable developments were that the French guns located on Island Battery were no longer returning fire.[107] Second, and more importantly, was the fact that the last two battered French ships of the line were now non-factors in the harbour's defence. In fact, they were themselves in a very vulnerable position. "The enemy's fire much decreased," confirmed David Gordon, "a shot now and then from the remaining ships."[108] The admiral judged that it was an opportune moment to seize the harbour. However, Boscawen was still unwilling to risk his ships of the line to force the harbour. As an alternative, he proposed to organize a raid to seize the two remaining vessels and bring the time-consuming siege to an end.

To ensure its successful outcome, it was imperative to gather and analyze the latest data regarding the state of the harbour. On 24 July 1758, Boscawen ordered Captain George Balfour of the *Aetna* to go ashore and conduct a reconnaissance mission. The officer was to report the inner harbour's overall condition, assess the operational status of the French ships, and present a series of recommendations to be used for the planning of the raid.[109] To assist Balfour with this upcoming operation, Boscawen selected Captain John Laforey of the *Hunter*. Both officers joined up at the Lighthouse Point Battery. Together they surveyed the harbour, noted the exact positions of the enemy vessels, and paid particular attention to the harbour's inner shoreline. One positive factor was that both enemy ships of the line were moored at a large distance from one another. This was due to the fact that the harbour was now cluttered with burnt-out hulls and vast quantities of floating debris from the other destroyed warships.

Manned by only 60 sailors and located the farthest from the town was *Le Bienfaisant*. The vessel was located between the Barachois and the abandoned structure of the Royal Battery. *Le Prudent*, manned by 100 sailors, was anchored closer to the town. In case of an attack, the crews were instructed by Commodore Desgouttes to burn the ships and abandon them.[110] As the unsuspecting French sentries patrolled the decks of these vessels, the two British naval officers confirmed their point of entry into the harbour as well as their approach routes towards their respective objectives.[111] Meanwhile, the activities aboard these two warships were now limited to guard duties. The sailors' continued unwillingness to provide covering fire frustrated the French soldiers. "We are not getting any support fire from these vessels," critiqued a frustrated Grillot de Poilly. "They let themselves be fired upon without helping us, or even defending themselves. It is truly pitiful."[112] Satisfied with the information gained, Balfour and Laforey quietly withdrew and returned to Hardy's squadron to commence their preparations.

Upon their arrival, Boscawen immediately informed Amherst that the arrangements for the upcoming raid were now underway. Barges, pinnaces, cutters, and sailors were drawn from vessels anchored in Gabarus Bay. This small assault fleet assembled at Boscawen's ship at 1500 hours.[113] The vessels were then dispatched in small groups to Hardy's squadron, so as not to alert the French defenders.[114] The groups then formed up and joined another group armed and manned by personnel taken from Hardy's blockading vessels. The raiding party now comprised 600 men loaded aboard 51 rowboats, each commanded by a lieutenant. When all vessels reached Hardy's position, Boscawen instructed his vice-admiral to divide the raiders into two groups: one under command of Captain Laforey and the other under command of Captain Balfour.[115] As their lieutenants received orders, the sailors concurrently carried out their final preparations, verified their weaponry, and greased all the oarlocks with spruce gum.[116] All participants concurred that the operation's success depended on the personal discipline and stealth of each individual raider, and, above all else, the maintenance of total silence.

To assist with ensuring success, Boscawen sent a message requesting Amherst to lay down a heavy barrage during the evening and night. This much-needed diversion was essential in facilitating the raiding party's entry into the harbour. The British gunners were requested to provide "a constant fire from the guns and mortars all the Forepart of the night. It will much contribute to the success of this enterprise." Underlined Boscawen, "As it will greatly prevent so good a look out, as they would otherwise keep, and fix their attention to the land attack."[117]

Amherst complied. On 25 July, all batteries fired briskly throughout the entire day and night. "To keep the Enemy's attention to the land," confirmed the general.[118] As British gunners engaged their targets, infantrymen huddled in their trenches at the ready. During the previous days, they received scaling ladders and awaited orders to launch a general frontal assault at a moment's notice.[119] Around midnight, under the cover of darkness and a very thick fog, the raiding party rowed silently. "Abreast from each other, and in a line, in one large group," described Captain Balfour, as he passed by the Lighthouse Point Battery.[120] Without a sound, the raiders closely followed the shoreline. They then arrived upon, and passed without difficulty, the scuttled French vessels in the harbour's entrance. Staying close to the shore the small vessels then awaited the pre-arranged signal, rapidly cut across the harbour, and headed towards the abandoned French Royal Battery located on the opposite shoreline. As the last rowboat reached the assembly point, the group then split up into two divisions.

Luckily, the anxious raiders had still not been detected.[121] Captain Balfour and his group commenced the final leg of their approach. Hugging the shoreline, they rowed towards *Le Bienfaisant*. However, Captain Laforey's route to his objective was far more risky. In order to reach *Le Prudent*, his group had to row from the Royal Battery through the widest part of the harbour without the benefit of any cover. Fortunately, the gun blasts from Amherst's batteries covered any unintentional noises, and forced the French garrison to focus all their attention towards the main British siege works. During that evening, Amherst's himself went into the trenches. However, by 0100 hours the general became increasingly worried that the raid would not take place.[122]

Meanwhile, the British sailors were within a few yards of their respective objectives. As these ghostly figures approached *Le Prudent*, one of the leading rowboats was suddenly hailed by a sentry. A quick-thinking British officer immediately replied in French that he had come from the town and he was coming aboard. Satisfied, the unsuspecting sentry continued his rounds.[123]

Moments later, the raiders armed with bayonets, cutlasses, muskets, and pistols let out a series of loud cheers and rapidly climbed over the sides. They stormed aboard the lightly defended ships, and quickly subdued the guards.[124] During this initial action, the main French guard parties were sleeping below deck and did not have a chance to counter the attack.[125] After a brief firefight both warships were captured within minutes. Fortuitously, the casualties of the raiding parties had been limited to seven killed and nine wounded.[126] The French losses on *Le Prudent* totalled one soldier killed and two officers wounded.[127] Meanwhile, all the French sailors aboard *Le Prudent* were rounded up and sent below.

Alerted by the gunfire, noise, and screams aboard *Le Prudent*, Drucour and all available soldiers rushed to the wharfs. There they helplessly witnessed the final moments of the capture of Desgouttes's vessel. Moreover, the fog was so thick that the French defenders could only hear the fighting and screams aboard the more distant *Le Bienfaisant*.[128] As a last resort, the French soldiers and gunners posted along the wharfs were ordered to open fire on the vessels, hoping to repulse the raiders. A British officer report that the French had lain down "a most furious fire" on *Le Prudent*.[129] Drucour hoped that this action would dissuade the enemy raiders from towing the vessel to the northeastern part of the harbour. While under heavy enemy fire, Captain Laforey's team remained calm, cut the moorings of their captured prize, and attempted to manoeuvre her towards the end of the harbour. Their efforts were nullified due to the fact that Desgouttes's vessel had several feet of water in her hold and had run aground during low tide.[130] Seeing that his prize could not be saved, and not wanting the vessel to be recaptured, Laforey ordered his raiders to free the prisoners and set fire to the immobilized flagship.[131] The disgruntled British sailors abandoned the burning ship and rowed in earnest towards *Le Bienfaisant*, where they joined up with Captain Balfour's group.

LAC, C-007111.

The burning of *Le Prudent* and the capture of *Le Bienfaisant* by British sailors at 0100 hours, 26 July 1758, in Louisbourg harbour. Drawn by Richard Paton, engraved by P.C. Canot.

The majority of this vessel's guard detail had also been surprised sleeping below deck. The towering flames and billowing black smoke rising from *Le Prudent* now shielded the actions of the British raiders. They were determined not to lose *Le Bienfaisant*. However, this ship of the line was in very bad shape, which greatly hampered the efforts of the British sailors to move her to safety. Luckily, a breeze suddenly came up, enabling the sailors to unfurl what a bystander reported as "what ragged sails, yards, and rigging she had left after the constant fire she had so long received from our batteries."[132] "The masts were so shattered," added Captain John Montresor of the Royal Engineers, "that her mainmast, and mizzen were carried away when they took her away."[133] Another anonymous observer noted that the very poor state of this warship gave her the "horrid appearance of a wrecked, as well as a conquered ship."[134]

As the last French ship of the line was towed to the end of the harbour, out of the range of the French gunners, Amherst sent soldiers to meet and provide cover to the jubilant raiding party. Once the raiders were safely on shore, Boscawen requested that Amherst provide an armed escort to remove 80 prisoners, and send surgeons to take care of the injured.[135] As exuberant sailors exchanged stories and boasted of their exploits, a relieved

Captain George Balfour commended his raiders for their efforts and professionalism. "They behaved with the utmost resolution," commented the pleased naval officer, "calmness and intrepidity without the least disturbance or confusion."[136] Patience, hard work, daring initiatives, and careful planning had paid off.

For the first time since 16 June 1758, British personnel had the opportunity to view, firsthand, the extent of damages inflicted by their batteries upon the French warships. The post-operation inspection of *Le Bienfaisant* as well as observations made during the actions aboard *Le Prudent* revealed a grim picture of these once magnificent ships of the line:

> Their decks were strewed about a foot high with tobacco leaves, and large pieces of junk, as a precaution to lessen the violent effects of our smaller shells that might accidentally alight them. And, that all their sides within, were nailed over with thick netting, to prevent some of the mischiefs from splinters occasioned by shots through the sides. They had much greater experience of the real use of the latter expedient, than of the former during the course of this siege. For, you have seldom seen ships more shattered by shot-holes, especially on one side, with their masts standing, that the two were, at the time they fell into our possession. Shells indeed none of the ships received many of; and what happened to hit them, were none of the largest sort, and but by accident could have done them mischiefs they suffered.[137]

Regardless of the current condition of *Le Bienfaisant*, the senior British officers were both very pleased and relieved that the daring operation had resulted in a resounding success.

A total of 40 days, from 16 June to 26 July, had passed before the overly cautious Boscawen had been willing to consider and execute this raid. As the siege unfolded, both Amherst and Boscawen did not seem pressed for time. Knowing full well that the besieged garrison would not be rescued, the senior British officer preferred to proceed with great caution, and wanted to avoid any unnecessary casualties, or loss of vessels during the capture of the harbour.[138] Even though Boscawen had been urged by William Pitt, "to force the harbour of Louisbourg ... to shorten and facilitate the reduction of that place," the admiral elected to patiently wait for the opportune moment.[139]

However, the young and impatient Brigadier Wolfe critiqued the time it took to destroy the French squadron and assault the harbour. "Our next operations were exceedingly slow and injudicious, owing partly to the difficulty of landing our stores and artillery, and partly to the ignorance and inexperience of the engineers."[140] Furthermore, Wolfe decried that the invaders had been falsely intimidated by Desgouttes's squadron's perceived firepower. "The opinion of most people here, sea and land," reported Wolfe, "had a terrible notion of their broadsides."[141]

Nevertheless, there were also positive elements that were used for the raid. Wolfe provided some insights regarding the value of intelligence gathered during the siege to plan this raid. "This coup was quite unexpected and astonishing," wrote the young brigadier, "and indeed, if we had not been very well informed of their [French ships' crews] negligence and security, would have appear to be a rash attempt."[142] Moreover, Wolfe complimented the deportment of the raiders, stating that they carried out the operation, "with incredible audacity and conduct."[143] Nevertheless, the he lamented the fact that it was regrettable that Duchauffault de Besné's squadron had not been able to join up with Desgouttes's squadron, for "they would have shared, the fate of those that did, which must have given an irretrievable blow to the marine de France."[144]

"We had gone on slow and sure," revealed Wolfe, regarding the manner in which the overall operations were conducted, "and at great length have brought things to a very good conclusion with little loss."[145] Regardless of the time it took to plan and execute the raid, Boscawen was nonetheless particularly pleased when he reported its successful outcome to William Pitt. The proud admiral qualified the raid as "a particular gallant action."[146] An unidentified observer further described this exploit as a "memorable occasion, as it must be a lasting, indelible honour to the vigilance and activity of those who projected, and to the bravery and conduct of those who executed, the bold design will also be a new, and perhaps a seasonable conviction to the whole world, that, however arduous, however apparently impracticable any prospect of difficulty or danger, but will exert themselves as far as men can do, and at least deserve success, when led on to it by such as are worthy to command them."[147]

This unexpected and daring accomplishment devastated what remained of the fighting spirit of the French defenders. As the sun rose above the horizon on the morning of 26 July, a disheartened Drucour and staff stared at the smoldering remains of *Le Prudent*, still flying the French colours.[148] The French high command was now very concerned that Boscawen's warships would soon force their way into undefended harbour and open fire into the town. An unidentified French infantry officer lamented the loss of the remaining warships. "I must confess, Sir, that this action did as much honour to the English as damage to us. And, indeed so long as our as our ships remained in the harbour, it would have been difficult for them to make a general assault. Here then was our *coup de grace*."[149]

Grillot de Poilly, who had severely criticized Desgouttes and his captains, was bitterly disappointed by the sailors' lack of fighting spirit during the raid. "We were relying on their vigilance," commented the engineer, "however was our confidence in them well founded?"[150] Poisson de Londes, a French officer, described the loss of these vessels as, "humiliating for the nation and disgraceful for the navy."[151] Another anonymous French officer added that regardless of the tasks conferred to Desgouttes's personnel, they could not be trusted. "The batteries facing the harbour were turned over to the sailors," explained the officer. However, when the raid took place, "these batteries had been abandoned, their conduct caused a bitter deception of being witness to such pitiful conduct."[152] Whereas the ground forces had fought valiantly, they nevertheless felt that they had been let down by their naval counterparts. Adding to their woes, their brave resistance was now hampered by the desolate state of the fortifications.

Louis Franquet, chief engineer of the fortress of Louisbourg, reported that the main fortifications works and gun positions were in very poor shape, and for the most part were beyond repair. Certain sections of the walls had collapsed and filled the outer ditches. Wide, unprotected breaches could now be easily climbed and exploited by enemy infantry during a full frontal assault. Moreover, the vault in which muskets and other weaponry were stored had been hit by a shell, and severely reduced the number of firearms. Additionally, for the past weeks, soldiers and civilians had been forced to live and sleep in the streets under makeshift shelters. The wounded fared no better and were lodged along the fortress's inner walls and in the few remaining undamaged houses and buildings.[153] The town and harbour were now vulnerable to a two-sided attack.

As for Amherst and Boscawen, the successful raid presented them with a new series of operational options to end the siege. On the morning of 26 July, Boscawen met with Amherst and proposed to force the unprotected harbour with six ships of the line.[154] Both agreed that a simultaneous coordinated naval and ground attack would crush the defenders. The next morning, at 1000 hours, Drucour sent a messenger to the British general requesting that his garrison be granted the "honors of war," similar to those granted to the British garrison in Minorca. The governor hoped that Amherst and Boscawen would agree that his officers and soldiers be permitted to retain their personal weapons, battalion colors, and be immediately transported to France. His request was rejected outright.

In turn, the two senior officers quickly drafted their own capitulation terms. These comprised six articles. The first being that the entire French garrison be taken as prisoners of war, and not be granted the requested "honors of war."[155] Upon reception of these humiliating conditions,

LAC, C-561.

Drucour briefly entertained the possibility of organizing a last stand against the impending general assault. However, re-evaluating all his options, he opted to spare the innocent inhabitants from the horrors and hardships of such an assault. With no other options, the governor and

Sir Jeffrey Amherst, victor at Louisbourg, 1758. He would be appointed commander-in-chief in North America the following year.

his council reluctantly agreed to the terms. Louisbourg capitulated on 26 July 1758.

Three days later, Sir Charles Hardy, accompanied by a few ships of the line, sailed into the harbour. As the vessels were moored, the British sailors were surprised by the degree of devastation that had taken place in this area during the siege and the raid:

> Indeed, when our ships came into the harbour, there was hardly any part of it, which had not the appearance of distress and desolation, and presented to our view frequent pieces of wrecks and remnants of destruction — five or six ships sunk in one place with their mastheads peeping out of the water — the stranded hull of *Le Prudent* on the muddy shoal of the other side, burned down to the water's edge, with a great deal of iron and guns staring us in the face — buoys of slipped anchors bobbing very thick upon the surface of the water in the channel towards the town — a number of small craft and boats towards that shore, some entirely under water, others with part of their masts standing out of it; besides the stranded hulls, irons, and guns of the three ships burned on the 21st, upon the mud towards the barrasoy — and in the N.E. harbour little else to be seen but masts, yards and rigging floating up and down, and pieces of burned masts, bowsprits etc, driven to the waters edge and some parts of the shore edged with tobacco leaves out of some ships that had been destroyed — the whole a dismal scene of total destruction![156]

This sombre description of this desolate scene was in fact a testimonial to the efficiency and professionalism of the British gunners and sailors. Boscawen had not forgotten the bravery displayed by his two naval officers, who had conducted this amazing *coup de main*. Captain George Balfour was given command of *Le Bienfaisant* and Captain John LaForey was given command of the captured frigate *L'Écho* (32 guns).[157] Lieutenants Affleck and Bickerton, who boarded *Le Bienfaisant* during the raid, were given command of the fire ship *Aetna* and the sloop *Hunter*, respectively.[158]

This latest major colonial campaign highlighted the depth of new experience gleaned by the British senior army and naval officers. It also demonstrated the aggressiveness and initiative of a seemingly new breed of army officers such as Brigadier James Wolfe, and naval officers such as Captains Balfour and Laforey. Faced with inhospitable terrain, a skilled enemy and a complex operation, these commanders nonetheless honed their skills and successfully conducted a well-organized and synchronized assault beach landing, coordinated an effective ground artillery fire against warships and French entrenchments, and, more importantly, planned and executed a disciplined naval night raid. Clearly, these daring actions emphasized that these commanders and their troops developed skills in combined operations that were specifically honed for the ruggedness of North America's climate, terrains, and waterways.

Notes

1. The squadron consisted of three vessels that arrived from Antigua. Soon after, they were joined by the *Eltham* (44 guns) and the *Bien Aimé* (24 guns) from New England; a captured French warship *Vigilant* (64 guns); and five vessels from England, the *Princess Mary* (60 guns), *Hector* (44 guns), *Chester* (50 guns), *Sunderland* (60 guns), and the *Canterbury* (60 guns). Last to arrive and join up with Warren's squadron was the *Lark* (44 guns), which sailed from her station in Newfoundland. Canadian naval historian Julian Gwyn states that Warren's squadron "was the greatest display of British sea power in North America since 1711, when Rear Admiral Hovendon Walker's expeditionary forces had gathered off Cape Breton to sail up the St. Lawrence and attack Quebec." Julian Gwyn, *The Royal Navy and North America: The Warren Papers: 1736–1752*, (London: Printed for the Navy Records Society, 1973), xxi; and Julian Gwyn, *Dictionary of Canadian Biography Online* s.v. "Sir Peter Warren," (by Julian Gwyn) http://www.biographi. ca/EN/ShowBio.asp?BioId=35832&query=sir%20AND%20peter%20AND%20 warren, [hereafter cited as *DCB Online*] (accessed 15 October 2007).
2. Gwyn, *The Royal Navy*, xviii; *DCB Online*, s.v. "Sir Peter Warren," (by Julian Gwyn) "Sir William Pepperrell" (by Byron Fairchild) http://www.biographi.ca/EN/ShowBio. asp?BioId=35702&query=sir%20AND%20william%20AND%20pepperrell.
3. The French returned all captured territories located in the Netherlands to Britain's allies. In exchange Britain returned Louisbourg to the French. Terry Crowley, *Louisbourg: Atlantic Fortress and Seaport*, (Ottawa: The Canadian Historical Association, Historical Booklet No. 42, 1990), 21.
4. The King authorized that the Second Battalions of the Régiment D'Artois and the Régiment de Bourgogne be stationed in Louisbourg. He ordered that these

troops, totalling 1,050 soldiers, be used to defend the fortress, and also be used by Louis Franquet, the fortress's head engineer, as labourers for his numerous ongoing construction projects and repair works. Order from the King to Drucour, 17 March 1755, folio 22; and Order from the King to Drucour and Prévost, 10 April 1755, folio 30, Library and Archives Canada, [hereafter cited as LAC], MG1, Archives de Colonies, Série B, lettres envoyées, Vol. 101, microfilm C-15660.

5.   Guy Frégault, *La Guerre de la Conquête,* (Montréal: Fides, 1955), 281–294; C.P. Stacey, "The British Forces in North America During the Seven Years' War," in Francess G. Halpenny, ed., *Dictionary of Canadian Biography, Vol. III* (Toronto: University of Toronto Press, 1974), xxiv–xxx; W.J. Eccles, "The French Forces in North America During the Seven Years' War," in *Dictionary of Canadian Biography* [henceforth DCB], *Vol. III, 1741 to 1770* (Toronto: University of Toronto Press, 1974), xv–xxiii.

6.   Letters, Loudoun to Pitt, 30 May 1757, 69–73; and 17 June 1757, 74–80; Letter, Holburne to Pitt, 6 June 1757, 73–74; Letters, Pitt to Holburne, 7 and 18 July 1757, 84–85 and 89–90; Letter, Pitt to Loudoun, 18 July 1757, 88. Gertrude Selwyn Kimball, *Correspondence of William Pitt when Secretary of State with Colonial Governors and Military and Naval Commissioners in America,* (London: MacMillan & Co., 1906), 69–80, 84–85.

7.   Disposition que M. Le Comte Du Bois de Lamotte, et M. Le Chev. De Drucour Governeur de l'Île Royale y ont faites en 1757 pour s'opposer à la descente des Anglais, LAC, MG 2, Archives de la Marine, Série B4, Campagnes, Vol. 76, folios 20r–23v, microfilm F-757.

8.   Admiral's Despatches, Vol. 481, quoted in J.S. McLennan, *Louisbourg From Its Foundation To Its Fall, 1713–1758,* (Halifax: The Book Room Limited, 1979), 204.

9.   The *Windsor, Kingston, Northumberland, Newark, Orford, Terrible,* and *Somerset* sustained minor damages. The *Invincible, Captain, Sunderland, Grafton, Nassau, Devonshire, Eagle, Prince Frederick,* and *Centurion* sustained various levels of damages to their masts, sails, and riggings. The *Bedford* and *Defiance* were not damaged. Only one vessel was lost. It was the ship of the line — the *Tilbury* (60 guns). State of the Squadron, under the command of Vice Admiral Holburne, 28 September 1757. Public Records Office, Admiral's Despatches, Vol. 481; and Admiral's List Book, Vol. 32, quoted in J.S. McLennan, 210.

10. Letter, Pitt to Abercrombie, 30 December 1757, Kimball, 143–150.

11. *Ibid.*

12. *Ibid.*

13. To gain, ensure, and maintain control of the North American waters, the British outfitted two large fleets during the last months of 1757, and January and February 1758. One fleet was commanded by Admiral Edward Boscawen. He was ordered to sail to Halifax and oversee the preparations for the upcoming Louisbourg campaign. Admiral Osborn commanded the other fleet and was ordered to sail to the Mediterranean. Osborn's mission was to intercept the French fleet commanded by Admiral La Clue. Intelligence reports confirmed that this

French fleet was to sail from Toulon to North America. Osborn was successful in confining La Clue's vessels to the Mediterranean. Concurrently, Sir Edward Hawke sailed with seven ships of the line and intercepted a French squadron, which transported much-needed supplies and reinforcements from the port of Rochefort to North America. These successful naval actions enabled Boscawen to operate unhindered during the entire course of the Louisbourg siege. Francis Parkman, *Montcalm and Wolfe*, (Markham, Ont.: Viking, Penguin Books Canada, 1984), 332–333. For information on French naval activities, during the Seven Years' War, along the French Atlantic coast and in the Mediterranean, consult G. Lacour-Gayet, *La marine militaire de la France sous le règne de Louis XV* (Paris: Librairie ancienne Honoré Champion, 1910), 270–341.

14. Letter, Pitt to Abercromby, 20 January 1758, Kimball, 166–167; *DCB Online*, s.v. "Jeffery Amherst," (by C. "James Wolfe," (by C.P. Stacey) "Edward Whitemore," "Charles Lawrence," (by Julian Gwyn).

15. Letter, Pitt to Boscawen, Whitehall, 3 February 1758, Kimball, 180.

16. *Le Prudent*, a 74-gun ship of the line was built in Rochefort, France in 1753. The vessel measured 175 feet in length. E. Willis Stevens, *Louisbourg Submerged Cultural Resource Survey*, (Marine Archeological Section, National Historic Parks and Site Branches, 1994), 42. This restricted report was consulted with the kind permission of the staff of the Fortress of Louisbourg, National Historic Site of Canada.

17. Louis-Joseph Beaussier de Lisle commanded the squadron hailing from Brest. The squadron comprised the following four ships of the line: *L'Entreprenant* (74 guns), *Le Célèbre* (64 guns), *Le Capricieux* (64 guns), *Le Bienfaisant* (64 guns), and one frigate, *La Comète*. Extrait du journal tenu par le Commissaire de la Marine, Querdisien-Tremais, ci devans à la suite de le Marine de vx du Roi *L'Entreprenant, Le Célèbre, Le Capricieux, Le Bienfaisant*, et la frigate *La Comète*, armés au port de Brest sous le commandement de M. Beaussier de L'Ile, capitaine de VX et de Port, destinés pour Louisbourg, LAC, MG 2, Archives de la Marine, Série B4, Campagnes, Vol. 80, folios 186r–194v, microfilm F-757. The squadron from Rochefort was under the command of Count Du Chauffault de Besné. It comprised four warships, *Le Dragon* (64 guns), *Le Belliqueux* (64 guns), *Le Sphinx*, *Le Hardi*, one frigate, *Le Zéphyr*, and one vessel from the Compagnie des Indes, *Le Brillant*. Escadre de Duchauffault de Besné, 29 June 1758, folios 211r–217r, [hereafter cited as Journal of Duchauffault de Besné], LAC, MG 2, Archives de la Marine, Série B4, Campagnes, Vol. 80, folio 207, microfilm F-757.

18. Additionally, the King instructed Desgouttes to patrol the surrounding areas and provide an escort to Louisbourg for all ships of the line arriving from France. These ships were dispatched to augment the commodore's naval squadron for the upcoming defence of Louisbourg. Letter from King to Marquis Desgouttes, Versailles, 29 January 1758, folios 14r–v, LAC, MG 1, Archives des Colonies, Série C11C, Amérique de Nord, Île Royale, Vol. 10, Prise de Louisbourg, microfilm F-518.

19. "A Journal of Proceedings of his Majesty's Squadron under the Command of the

Hon. Edward Boscawen, Admiral of the Blue to North America between the 8th day of February 1758 and the day of November following," [hereafter cited as Admiral Boscawen's Log], LAC, MG 12, Admiralty 50, Admirals' Journals, Vol. 3, folio 59, microfilm C-12891.

20. *Le Raisonable* returned to France for urgent repairs, while *Le Message* was burnt at sea due to damages to her masts. Nevertheless, Desgouttes continued his voyage escorting the frigates, *La Fidèle* (36 guns), *La Mutine*, *La Diane* (22 guns), and *La Chèvre* (16 guns). Letter, Desgouttes to the Minister, aboard *Le Prudent*, Louisbourg harbour, 6 May 1758, LAC, MG 2, Archives de la Marine, Série B4, Campagnes, Vol. 80, folios 64r–68r, microfilm F-757.

21. *Ibid.*, folio 64r. Desgouttes reported that his sailors had contracted an illness that he describes as "le mauvais air de la maladie," from the sailors of Dubois de la Motte's squadron, while outfitting his vessels in the Port of Rochefort. Extrait du "Siège de Louisbourg à commencer du premier Juin, jour ou j'ai apercu la flotte des Anglais, faite par M. Le Marquis Desgouttes," folios 18r-v, [hereafter cited as Journal of Desgouttes], LAC, MG 1, Ministère de la France d'outre-mer, Dépôt des fortifications des colonies, Amérique septentrional, numéro d'ordre 240, microfilm F-557.

22. *La Mutine* left the convoy and sailed for the Îles du Vent for repairs. Once the vessel was seaworthy, it continued its voyage. It then came upon some British vessels, was chased, and never reached Louisbourg. *La Fidèle* had been separated from Desgouttes's squadron due to bad weather conditions off the Grand Banks, however, its captain was able to reach Louisbourg a few days later. Lastly, *La Flûte* was taking on water and, being beyond repair, was burnt at sea. Journal du siège de Louisbourg, 16 avril–27 juillet, 1758, folio 2r, [hereafter cited as Journal anonyme I], LAC, MG1, Archives des Colonies, Série C11C, Amérique du Nord, Vol. 10, Île Royale, Prise de Louisbourg, 1758, microfilm F-507.

23. *DCB Online*, s.v. "Louis-Joseph Beaussier de Lisle," (by Étienne Taillemite), http:// www.biographi.ca/EN/ShowBio.asp?BioId=35329&query=louis-joseph%20 AND%20de%20AND%20lisle (accessed 15 October 2006). The vessels under the command of Beaussier de Lisle were the following ships of the line : *L'Entreprenant* (74 guns), Louis-Joseph Beaussier de Lisle, *Le Célèbre* (64 guns), Chevalier de Marolles; *Le Capricieux* (64 guns), Chevalier de Tourville; *Le Bienfaisant* (64 guns), Chevalier de Courserac; and the frigate, *La Comète*, Chevalier de Lorgeril. These vessels were loaded with great quantities of supplies and men. Thus, most of the guns were removed and stored in order to provide extra storage space. Once the vessels were emptied, all guns were remounted by 10 May. Desgouttes's ships of the line were now ready for operational duty. Their captains received their orders and were assigned to protect the harbour's entrance. Journal anonyme I, folios 2r–2v. *L'Entreprenant* was a 74-gun ship of the line. The identity of the naval yard that built this vessel and date of construction could not be confirmed. The vessel measured 175 feet in length. *Le Célèbre*, a 64-gun ship of the line, was built in naval yards in Brest, France, in 1755. The vessel measured 150 feet in length. *Le*

Capricieux , a 64-gun ship of the line, was built in the naval yards in Rochefort, France. The date of construction could not be confirmed. The vessel measured 150 feet in length. E. Willis Stevens, 5 and 46.

24. Letter, Desgouttes to Drucour, aboard *Le Prudent*, in Louisbourg harbour, 6 May 1758, folio 66r. LAC, MG 2, Archives de la Marine, Campagnes, Série B4, 1758, Vol. 80, microfilm F-757.

25. Relation de la descente des anglais à Louisbourg, 29 juin 1758. LAC, MG 2, Archives de la Marine, Série B4, Campagnes, Vol. 80, folios 21r–v, microfilm F-757.

26. "Registre contenant tous les ordres que M. Le Marquis DesGouttes a donnés pendant le temps qu'il a comandé la division de Rochefort pour Louisbourg et ainsy que ceux qu'il a donnés après son arrivée à cette même division et à celle de Brest," 31 May–8 June 1758, folios 108r–124r, [hereafter cited as Desgouttes's Orders Register], LAC, MG 2, Archives de la Marine, Série B4, Campagnes, Vol. 80, microfilm F-757.

27. Daily entries of 3 May to 6 June 1758, Desgouttes's Order Registry, folios 101r–122v.

28. Journal of Desgouttes, folios 18r–v.

29. Letter, Desgouttes to Drucour, aboard *Le Prudent*, in Louisbourg harbour, 6 May 1758, folio 6v. LAC, MG 2, Archives de la Marine, Campagnes, 1758, Vol. 80, microfilm F-757.

30. Even though Sir Charles Hardy's squadron was patrolling actively off the coast of Louisbourg, a great number of sailors manning these vessels were ill. Boscawen was very concerned by this ongoing situation and feared that the combat efficiency of Hardy's vessels to counter possible sorties attempted by the French ships of the line could be greatly reduced. Letter, Boscawen to Amherst, *Namur*, 10 June 1758, 13. LAC, MG 18, L4, Amherst, Sir Jeffery and family, Vol. 1, Packet 4, Letters from Admiral Boscawen, [hereafter cited as Correspondence Boscawen to Amherst]. On 14 June, a troubled Boscawen further reports that of the 2000 seamen aboard four of Hardy's ships of the line, the crews were now reduced to 300 fit for duty, and this only after eight weeks at sea. This situation came about due to serious problems with alcohol due to the lack of control of daily rum rations. "It [the rum] has been the destruction of the Navy," reported the frustrated admiral. Letter, Boscawen to Amherst, *Namur*, 14 June 1758, 20–21. Correspondence Boscawen to Amherst.

31. To enforce and maintain the blockade, Sir Charles Hardy had under his command the following eight ships of the line. As of 5 April: *Northumberland* (74 guns), *Summerset* (70 guns), *Terrible* (74 guns), *Orford* (70 guns), *Defiance* (60 guns), *Captain* (64 guns), *Kingston* (60 guns), *Southerland* (50 guns), and one frigate. On 2 May, Boscawen dispatched the *Juno* to join up with Hardy's squadron. On 20 May, the *Royal William* (84 guns) and the *Prince Frederick* (64 guns) joined Sir Charles Hardy's squadron for blockade duty. Despite the earlier mentioned problems, the blockade was maintained and had proved efficient. During this

period a total of seven supply ships and the French frigate, *La Diane* (22 guns), were captured and sent to Halifax. Letter, James Cunningham, on Abercromby's staff to Lord Sackville, on board the *Ludlow Castle* at sea, 30 May 1758, quoted in J.S. McLennan, 237–241. Boscawen also dispatched on 16 May the *Squirrel* (20 guns), and the *Scarborough* (20 guns) to further bolster the blockade. Admiral Boscawen's Log, 16 and 19 May 1758, folios 84r, 85r. Hardy's blockade forced the Count Du Chaffault de Besné's Rochefort squadron, which transported supplies, and the Second Battalion of the Régiment de Cambis, to change course and set sail for Port Dauphin (Englishtown) where he dropped on 29 May 1758. Escadre de Du Chauffault de Besné, LAC, MG 2, Archives de la Marine, Série B4, Campagnes, Vol. 80, folio 207, microfilm F-757.

32.   Boscawen's fleet comprised 23 ships of the line, armed with 1,544 guns, 18 frigates armed with 418 guns, and 144 assorted transport vessels. This fleet transported 14 infantry regiments totalling 11,021 rank and file; 550 Rangers, 324 artillery rank and file, and 10 engineers. "Journal Kept by [Robert] Gordon, One of the Officers engaged in the Siege of Louisbourg under Boscawen and Amherst, in 1758," *Collections of The Nova Scotia Historical Society For the Year 1887–1888*, Vol. VI (Halifax: Nova Scotia Printing Company, 1888), 98–99, [hereafter cited as Journal of Gordon]. In his book *Louisbourg From Its Foundation To Its Fall, 1713-1758*, J.S. McLennan also complied a detailed list describing Boscawen's fleet. The author provided the following information for each ship of the line, frigate, sloop, fire vessel, and armed ship: Rates, names, number of guns, number of sailors, names of commanders, names of lieutenants, dates that the vessels sailed from England to Halifax, and their dispositions, 261.

33.   Journal of Desgouttes, 1 June 1758, folio 1r.

34.   Admiral Boscawen's Log, 2 June 1758, folio 90r. Above and beyond his numerous logistical support responsibilities, Boscawen also had to ensure the constant protection of his vast fleet of unarmed transport, hospital, and supply vessels. Luckily, the admiral's protective duties of these defenseless vessels had been greatly facilitated due the concerted efforts of other British squadrons operating off the French coast and in the Mediterranean during 1757 and in the first months of 1758. Correspondence between Boscawen and Amherst, *Namur*, 13 June 1758, 18–19.

35.   Admiral Boscawen's Log, 28 May to 3 June 1758, folios 88r–91r.

36.   Both British naval gunners and French artillery gunners enjoyed limited success in the days preceding the assault landing. A shell fired from a British frigate into one of the French coastal positions hit a small powder magazine and set it on fire. The explosion injured an officer and a few soldiers. However, the marksmanship of a French 6-pdr gun crew forced the enemy frigate to pull away. Journal of Desgouttes, 4 June 1758, folio 2r. The French engineer François-Claude-Victor Grillot de Poilly provides, in his journal, a detailed account as to the number of troops and locations of the French coastal defences. As of May 1758, the following six positions located along the coast on Gabarus Bay and in the vicinity of Louisbourg were occupied by French forces: La Cormornadière, 979 men; Pointe

Platte, 710 men; Pointe Blanche, 200 men; L'Isle de l'Entrée 100; Montage du Diable and surrounding areas in Gabarus Bay, 192 men; Port Dauphin and Port Toulouse, 30 men totalling 2202 soldiers, sailors, militia, and gun crews. Entry of 6 June 1758, 82. Mémoire de evenemens qui interesseront cette colonie pendant l'année 1758 par François-Claude-Victor Grillot de Poilly, [hereafter cited as Journal of Grillot de Poilly], LAC, MG 4, C2, Comité du Génie, Archives de l'inspection générale du génie, Vol. 1, no. 66, 3–137, microfilm F-760. Governor Drucour explained in his post-campaign report that a total of 27 artillery pieces of various calibres, two mortars, and eight *pierriers* had been installed in the various coastal defensive positions. "Artillerie mise et laissée aux retranchements depuis Cap Noir jusqu'au pointes Blanches, pointe Platte et la Cormorandiere, au fanal, et aux anses à Gautier et Laurembec, in Journal ou Relation sur ce qui se passera des mouvemens pour l'attaque et la défense de la place de Louisbourg pendant la présente année 1758," folios 174r–v, [hereafter cited as Journal of Drucour], LAC, MG1, Archives des Colonies, Série C11B, Correspondence générale, Île Royale, microfilm F-167.

37.   Admiral Boscawen's Log, 3 June 1758 folio 90r; Journal of Desgouttes, 6 June 1758, folio 2r.

38.   On 8 June, the surf was so severe, reported Admiral Boscawen, that it took the sailors manning his small embarkation three hours to return to the *Namur*. Correspondence between Boscawen and Amherst, 8 June 1758, 9.

39.   This scorched-earth tactic was carried out over the course of the next few days following the British landing in areas adjoining to the fortress. On 11 June, Governor Drucour ordered Desgouttes to send all his squadron's rowboats, manned by sailors, to transport workers to the abandoned Royal Battery. The men quickly demolished all gun platforms, as well as adjacent civilian buildings. Extrait du "Journal par le commissaire de la marin, ci devans à la suite des vaisseaux du Roi, *L'Entreprenant*, *Le Célèbre*, *Le Capricieux*, *Le Bienfaisant*, et la frégate *La Comète*, armés au Port de Brest sous le commandement de M. Beaussier de l'Isle capitaine de vaisseaux et de Port, et destiné pour Louisbourg, 11 June 1758," folio 190v, [hereafter cited as Journal of Kerdisien-Trémais], LAC, MG 2, Archives de la Marine, Série B4, Campagnes, Vol. 80, microfilm F-757. The Royal Battery was part of a five-battery harbour defense system: Royal Battery (15 large-calibre canons); Island Battery (39 canons); Rochefort Battery (12 guns); Dauphin Circular Battery (8 guns); Lighthouse Battery (3 guns). The batteries were positioned in such a manner as to cover all angles and approaches to the harbour's entrance. Journal de Drucour, folio 108v; Drawing, anonymous artist, La Batteries de L'Isle de L'Entrée. Photograph copy held by Fortress of Louisbourg, National Historic Site of Canada; and Bruce W. Fry, *An Appearance of Strength, The Fortifications of Louisbourg*, Vol. 1 (Ottawa: National Historic Parks and Sites Branch, Environment Canada, 1984), 141–146.

40.   The selected vessels were *La Chèvre* and *L'Apollon*. *La Ville de Saint-Malo*, a merchant ship, was also converted into a hospital ship. Journal of Desgouttes,

8 June 81758, folios 2v–3r; and Desgouttes's Order Register, 8 June 1758, folios 124r–126v; and 20 June 1758, folio 137v.

41.   Journal of Grillot de Poilly, 8 June 1758, 83–85. Louis Franquet, head engineer of the fortress of Louisbourg, was plagued by a series of health issues. "Ma santé dérangée par l'escorbut," explained Franquet, "et une menace d'hydropsie accompagne de fiévre tierce, depuis deux mois." His condition hindered his mobility. Thus, Franquet conferred the majority of the siege-work operations to Grillot de Poilly. Letter, Franquet to the Minister, 22 June 1758, LAC, MG 1, Archives des colonies, Séries C11C, Amérique du Nord, Île Royale, Vol. 10, Prise de Louisbourg, 1758, microfilm F-518.

42.   Journal of Desgouttes, 9 June 1758, folios 3v–4r; and letter, Franquet to the Minister, Louisbourg, 10 June 1758, 5 o'clock in the afternoon, LAC, MG 1, Archives de colonies, Série C11C, Amérique du Nord, Île Royale, Vol. 10, Prise de Louisbourg, 1758, microfilm F-518. The poor state of the fortifications and inclement weather continually plagued the work and repair efforts of the French engineers posted to Louisbourg since 1716. During the British occupation following the 1745 siege, Commodore Charles Knowles provided Thomas Pelham-Holles, Duke of Newcastle, with a very thorough insight as to the fortress's dilapidated state. "The fortifications are badly designed and worse executed I have already informed your grace. It may be said these are things that may be remedied. To which I answer not! For unless the climate could be changed it is impossible to make works durable. The frosts begin to cease towards the middles of May and are succeeded by fogs. These last till the end of July or beginning of August, with the intermission perhaps of one or two days in a fortnight. Towards the close of September or very early October the frosts set in again, and they continue with frequent snow till May or often the beginning June. So that allowing the fortifications to be repaired with the best materials and in the most workmanlike manner, your grace will observe, they have scarce two months in the year for the cement to dry in. This is impossible to do. Therefore it is certain, after the nation has been at the expense of perhaps more that one millions pounds, we should have to go on again with repairing where we had begun at first. As it will take upwards of twenty years to do it in, consequently the works will be rotten and tumbling down before that time, as they are now." Letter #249, Commodore Charles Knowles to Thomas Pelham-Holles, Duke of Newcastle, Louisbourg, 9 July 1746, 290–291. Julian Gwyn, ed., *The Royal Navy and North America: The Warren Papers, 1736–1752*, (London: Printed for The Naval Records Society, 1973).

43.   Drucour's war council included Louis Franquet, Chief Engineer; Jacques Prévost de LaCroix, colonial administrator; Mathieu-Henri Marchant de La Houlière, commander of all the ground troops; Jean Mascle de Saint-Julhien, commanding officer of the Second Battalion of the Régiment d'Artois; Michel Marin de Bourzt, commanding officer of the Second Battalion of the Régiment de Bourgogne; Henri-Valentin-Jacques D'Anthonay, commanding officer of the Second Battalion of the Régiment des Volontaires Étrangers; Claude-Élizabeth Denys De Laronde

de Bonnaventure, the king's lieutenant. They were convened by the governor during the course of the siege to deliberate the implementation of all important operational decisions. Despite entertaining a very cordial, professional relationship with the commodore, the governor, nevertheless, became very disappointed in Desgouttes's repeated requests to leave Louisbourg. "It would be disgraceful," wrote the governor to the minister, "to see this squadron leave a mere 24 hours after the British landing. Such an action, would totally discourage the garrison who up until now worked well." Letter, Drucour to the minister, Louisbourg, 10 June 1758, four o'clock in the afternoon, LAC, MG 1, Archives des Colonies, Série C11B, Correspondance générale, Île Royale, Vol. 38, folio 23v, microfilm, F-518. Desgouttes Orders Registry, 9 June 1758, folios 134r–135v.

44.   Journal of Desgouttes, June 9, 1758, folios 3v–4r.

45.   Correspondence Desgouttes–Drucour 8 June–28 July 1758, 9 June 1758, folio 2v, LAC, MG 1, Archives des Colonies, Série C11C, Correspondance générale, Amérique du nord, Île Royale, Vol. 10, Prise de Louisbourg, microfilm F-518.

46.   Only two of the eight council members, Jacques Prévost de la Croix, the colonial administrator, and Lieutenant-Colonel Mathieu Henri Marchant de la Houlière, commander of all the ground troops, understood Desgouttes's arguments to leave. However, both stipulated that they would allow the vessels to leave only when it became evident to all that the fortress would fall into enemy hands. *Ibid.*

47.   Even though Desgouttes's warships were ordered to remain and defend the harbour, Drucour nevertheless authorized Desgouttes to order Du Chauffault de Besné to immediately set sail with his squadron and proceed in all haste to Quebec. Order of Desgouttes, and Order of Drucour, Louisbourg, 8 June 1758, 9 o'clock in the morning, in Journal of Du Chauffault de Besné, folio 213r. Three other smaller vessels were authorized to leave Louisbourg and carry dispatches informing the French authorities of the successful British landing. Under the cover of darkness on 11 June 1758, *Le Bizare* and *L'Écho* set sail for Quebec, while *La Comète* on the other hand, sailed for France. Journal du Siège, Louisbourg, March–August, 11 June 1758, folios 39v–40r, [hereafter cited as Journal anonyme II.] LAC, MG 1, Archives des Colonies, Série C11C, Amérique du Nord, Vol. 10, Île Royale, Prise de Louisbourg, 1758, microfilm F-507.

48.   Even though Boscawen focused the majority of his efforts to land large quantities of much-needed supplies to Amherst, the admiral nevertheless continued to monitor very closely the French naval activities within the harbour. He hoped that the continual presence of his large fleet would force Desgouttes to favour a defensive strategy rather than consider and attempt bold sorties. The only French naval action during the course of the days following the assault landing was a quick sortie made by a carcass launch, armed with two 18 pounders, manned by 60 sailors under the command of M. de Gosquil. This small vessel attacked one of Hardy's frigates. However, when a ship of the line came to the frigate's rescue, Gosquil quickly retreated into the harbour. Journal of Desgouttes, 9 June 1758, folio 3v.

49.   Information concerning the possible presence of a guerilla force commanded by
      Charles Deschamps de Boishébert et de Raffetot was forwarded by Boscawen to
      Amherst after the interrogation of wounded French prisoners captured in the
      defensive costal positions, on 8 June 1758. Correspondence between Boscawen and
      Amherst, 10 June 1758, 16. Though British personnel were briefed to stand ready
      to counter-raid, Deschamps de Boishébert et de Raffetot's men never constituted
      a serious threat to Amherst's deployed ground forces and artillery positions.
      "Journal de ma campagne de Louisbourg," *Le bulletin des recherches historiques*,
      Vol. XXVII, No. 2 (February 1921, 48–53. *DCB Online*, s.v. "Charles Deschamps
      de Boishébert et de Raffetot," (by Phyllis E. Leblanc), http://www.biographi.ca/
      EN/ShowBio.asp?BioId=35972&query=Charles%20AND%20Deschamps%20
      AND%20de%20AND%20Boish%E9bert%20AND%20et%20AND%20de%20
      AND%20Raffetot (accessed October 15, 2007).

50.   Boscawen interrogations revealed that the French commodore wanted to leave
      Louisbourg. The admiral quickly informed Amherst of possible escape attempts
      and ordered that all ships of the line cruising off the coast with Sir Charles Hardy
      sail directly to Louisbourg and position themselves near the harbour's entrance
      and be ready to intercept fleeing French vessels. Correspondence between
      Boscawen and Amherst, *Namur*, 10 June 1758, 13–14.

51.   For this mission Wolfe had under his command four companies of grenadiers,
      and 1,220 light infantry men. Journal entry of 12 June 1758. Sir Jeffery's Journal,
      No. 8, from 14 January 1758 to 18 June 1758, Packet 19, LAC, MG 18, L4, Vol.
      3, Amherst, Sir Jeffery and Family, 56, [hereafter cited as Jeffery Amherst's
      Journal]. For detailed information regarding the history of Island Battery please
      consult, Eric Krause, *The As-Built History of the Island Battery, 1713–1768*,
      Volumes 1–2, Report 2005-71 (Nova Scotia: Krause, House Info-Research
      Solutions, 2006), and *The Chronology Of Historical Events At The Island Battery,
      1713–1768: Transcribed and Précised Documents*, Report 2005-73 (Nova Scotia:
      Krause, House Info-Research Solutions, 2006), http://fortress.uccb.ns.cs/island
      battery.

52.   Journal of Desgouttes, 12, 14 June, 1758, folio 5r. That same day, the sloop was also
      dispatched to attack a transport vessel in the vicinity of Green Island, located just
      outside the harbour's entrance. The British reacted immediately and dispatched
      a frigate, forcing the sloop to withdraw. Journal of Drucour, June 14, folio 96r.
      During that night, on 14 June, *L'Écho* sailed out of the harbor for Quebec. The
      governor ordered her captain to deliver copies of all his correspondence to the
      officials in Quebec, so as to apprise them of the latest tragic developments. This
      evasion, however, was unsuccessful. *L'Écho* was captured shortly after by the *Juno*.
      Mémoire ou Journal du Siege de Louisbourg avec la capitulation faite le 25 juillet.
      The authorship of this manuscript is unknown. A handwritten note on the cover
      page of the manuscript states that this document was found in the possessions of
      Poisson de Londes, 14 June 1758, 21, LAC, MG 4, Archives de la Guerre, Série
      C1, Comité technique du génie, Place étrangère, Louisbourg, Vol. 7 Article 15,

pièce 4, transcript, [hereafter cited as Journal of the Siege of Louisbourg]. Admiral Boscawen's Log, June 19, 1758, folio 98.

53. Correspondence Boscawen to Amherst, 13, 14, 16 June 1758, 18–29. The increasing pressure placed on Boscawen's shoulders to unload substantial quantities of equipment along different parts of the coastline tested his sailors' navigational abilities, as well as the loading and unloading skills of the crews manning his supply and transport vessels. The admiral was uneasy with the fact that these unarmed vessels were moored over such a large area. "It is very lucky for us," confided Boscawen to Amherst, "the French Fleet were so disabled last year as not to be able to push us by sea, this far at the bottom." Additionally, seven of the admiral's ships of the line, *Dublin* (74 guns), *Terrible* (74 guns), *Northumberland* (70 guns); *Devonshire* (66 guns); *Defiance* (60 guns), *Vanguard* (70), and *Arc-en-Ciel* (50 guns) were experiencing a variety of problems. Depending on the length of this current operation some of the vessels would have to be sent to Halifax for repairs. Correspondence Boscawen to Amherst, aboard the *Namur*, 13 June 1758, 18–19.

54 This information was obtained by Boscawen following the interrogation of the captured crew of *L'Écho*. The vessel was seized on 15 June 1758. Letter from Boscawen to Amherst, *Namur*, 19 June 1758, 36. Correspondence Boscawen to Amherst.

55. Wolf provided Amherst with the following detailed information regarding the composition of his batteries, their locations, and anticipated targets. "The battery at the end of the N.E. Harbour of 1-24 pounder and 1-12 pounder, Hautbiser Battery under the Hill near the Careening Wharf to fire ricochet. Great Bomb Battery, in the bottom, before Goreham's Camp of 4 Mortars and 6 Royals. 2-24 pounders to fire Ricochet at the Masts & rigging from the bottom, between Goreham's Camp and the Light House Hill. 1-24 pounder & 2-12 pounders from the Right of the light house Hill, to fire likewise a ricochet at the Masts & rigging. 2-24 pounder to be placed in Battery, to fire at the Ships Hulls and Lower Masts." Copy of very long orders given at the lighthouse point, 28 June 1758. LAC, MG 18, L4, Amherst, Sir Jeffery and family, Vol. 2, Packet 8, Letters from General Wolfe during the sieges & shortly after the surrender of Louisbourg, 10–12, [hereafter cited as Correspondence Wolfe to Amherst].

56. *Ibid.*, 11.

57. In the 19 June entry of the Gordon Journal, the author provides additional information regarding the guns fired that night against Desgouttes's squadron and the Island battery. "The Bomb Battery consisted of two thirteen Inch, 2 of eight and 6 Royals, some distance from them were two eight inch Howitsers add to these Batteries of 1, 2, and 3 Pieces of Canon each 12 & 24 Pounders, which with those mentioned before made 7 properly desposed of along the Shore of the Light House." Journal of Gordon. Also, map drawn by Capitan-Lieutenant Samuel Holland, acting engineer to Brigadier Wolfe, 60th Regiment, Royal American Regiment, explanations of the works and approaches made by the directions of Brigadier Wolfe.

58. Letter, Wolfe to Amherst, End of the N.E. Harbour, 19 June 1758, 14.

59. Journal of Grillot de Poilly, 19 June 1758, 90–91.

60. Desgouttes reported that his vessels were being bombarded by a battery of 11 mortars and a battery of four canons. To make matters worse, it was a very bright night, and the moonlight reflected off the vessels. During that night, *Le Prudent* was hit several times. Desgouttes reported that his top mast, the large mast, and catwalk had been damaged. Journal of Desgouttes, 19 June 1758, folio 5v.

61. *Ibid.*

62. Letter, Wolfe to Amherst, 20 June 1758, 17. Correspondence Wolfe to Amherst.

63. A frustrated Wolfe reported to Amherst that the Hautbitzer's (Howitzer) carriage broke down after only firing 10 rounds. Furthermore, two 24 pounders, which were being pulled to their positions were stuck in the soft ground and could not be moved. Additionally, two batteries located near Lighthouse Point were still not yet operational and another 24 pounder "was so stuffed in the touch hole, that it could not be employed all night." Letter from Wolfe to Amherst, 20 June 1758, 16. Correspondence Wolfe to Amherst. Using the scale of the map drawn by Captain-Lieutenant Samuel Holland, Royal American Regiment, the distance between the three batteries and the French warships varied between 1,800 to 2,400 yards.

64. Letter, Wolfe to Amherst, 20 June 1758, 16. Correspondence Wolfe to Amherst.

65. Letter, Boscawen to Amherst, *Namur*, 23 June 1758, 41. Correspondence Boscawen to Amherst.

66. Journal of Drucour, 20 June 1758, folio 108r.

67. Journal Anonyme I, Night of 19–20 June 1758, folio 8v.

68. Letter, Wolfe to Amherst, 20 June 1758, 16. Correspondence Wolfe to Amherst. The term "lumbered" used by Wolfe, described construction work carried out on board the French ships of the line. The sailors used planks, netting, and wooden barrels to bomb-proof certain parts of their vessels.

69. Journal of Kerdisien-Trémais, 19 June 1758, folios 191r–v.

70. Journal of Desgouttes, folio 6r. General Amherst noted that the French naval gun crews waited for high tide to engage the main British entrenchments. The additional water under their vessels improved their range and gun elevation. Letter, Amherst to William Pitt, Camp of Louisbourg, 27 July 1758, 8–9. LAC, MG 18, L4, Amherst, Sir Jeffery and family, Vol. 4, Packet 22.

71. Journal of Kérdisien-Trémais, 24 June 1758, folio 192r.

72. Journal of Desgouttes, folios 6v-7r; Drucour's Order Register, folios 108v-109r; and Journal of Drucour, folios 70r-v.

73. Journal Anonyme I, 23–24 June 1758, folio 9v.

74. The deserter stated that when the French defenders would focus their attention on the harbour, the ground forces deployed in front of the landward fortifications would make a push to further consolidate their siege works. Journal Anonyme III, 25 June 1758, 99. The soldier probably got this information, as a rumour or gossip, while talking to sailors during his trip from Halifax to Gabarus Bay. No information regarding such an operation was found in Boscawen's correspondence

to Amherst, or his ship's log. Similar information had been provided to the French governor, earlier, on 19 June, by a sailor who had been captured by Acadians, led by Mr. Villejoint, fils. Villejoint forwarded the following intelligence to Drucour. "Admiral Boscawen who commands this expedition will attempt to force the harbor with six vessels of 90 guns. He has learned from the prisoners taken in the costal positions, that the harbor is only defended by five ships of the line." Additional information regarding the assault of the harbour was obtained during the interrogation of an Irish deserter from the Warburton Regiment. Again, no mention of such an operation was found in Boscawen's correspondence, or ship's log. Journal of Drucour, 19 June 1758, folio 67r; Journal of Desgouttes, 20–23 June 1758, folio 7r.

75. Journal of Drucour, 28 June 1758, folio 75v.

76. Journal of Tourville, 28 June 1758, folio 319v.

77. Jeffery Amherst's Journal, 30 June 1758, Book 9, 6. Boscawen comments that this attempt to cut the masts in order to conceal the exact locations of the scuttled vessels was, in fact, a wasted effort. "The masts of the ships being cutt away will make them easier to weigh, and more difficult for the others to get out in the night, and as they cannot cut them far under water, we shall as easily find them by the stumps, as by any marks we can take." Correspondence Boscawen to Amherst, *Namur* in Gabarus Bay, 30 June 1758, 55.

78. Correspondence Boscawen to Amherst, *Namur*, 29 June 1758, 54. Amherst simply noted this French action in his diary, and reported this in a letter to William Pitt. Jeffery Amherst's Journal, 30 June 1758, Book 9, 6; and Kimball, Letter from General Amherst to Pitt, Camp before Louisbourg, 6 July 1758, 291–293.

79. Correspondence Boscawen to Amherst, *Namur* in Gabarus Bay, 30 June 1758, 55.

80. Gordon reports that five 24 pounders were firing on these two positions. The French gunners returned fire but had little success due to the great distance. Journal of Gordon, 25 June 1758, 126.

81. Nevertheless, Drucour ordered his commodore to engage this battery. Desgouttes carefully maneuvered his ship and fired upon the battery with little success. After having sustained a direct hit to his poop deck and other parts of his vessel, Desgouttes ordered his sailors to pull away and returned to his original position by the town's wharf. Journal of Desgouttes, 27 June 1758, folios 7v–8v.

82. Grillot de Poilly reports that the following ships of the line were hit between 19–30 June 1758: 19 June, *Le Prudent*, and *Le Bienfaisant*; 28 June, *L'Entreprenant*; and 29 June, *Le Capricieux*, 90, 95–96.

83. Journal of Grillot de Poilly, 29 June 1758, 96.

84. Journal of Desgouttes, 1 July 1758, folio 8v. On 3 July 1758, four shells hit *Le Prudent*. When this bombardment took place, Desgouttes was in a meeting with the governor. A naval officer rushed in, and informed the commodore that the enemy was now firing red shots (heated shells that cause fires) against the vessels. Journal of Drucour, 3 July 1758, folios 112r–v.

85. Journal of Desgouttes, 3 July 1758, folio 9.
86. Journal of Tourville, July 5 July folio 324r.
87. Journal of Desgouttes, July 6 July folio 10r.
88. *Ibid.*
89. Journal of Desgouttes, 15 July 1758, folio 12r.
90. Correspondence Boscawen to Amherst, *Namur*, 7 July 1758, 67–68. The vessels manning the blockade were: *The Royal William* (84 guns), *The Dublin* (74 guns), *The Devonshire* (66 guns), *The Bedford* (64 guns), *The Prince Frederick* (64 guns), *The Pembroke* (60 guns), *The Diana* (32 guns), *The Nightingale*, (24 guns), *The Port Mahon* (24 guns), *The Kennington* (20 guns), *The Gramont* (18guns), and *The Hunter* (14 guns).
91. Journal of Jeffery Amherst, 24 June 1758, Book 9, 3.
92. Journal of Gordon, 29 June 1758, 127. An *epaulement* is an elongated breastwork of temporary nature, constructed out of gabions (wicker baskets ca. 1.0 m in diameter, filled with earth to give cover on the parapets, batteries and trenches, precursor of sandbags) or *fascines* (bundles of brushwood, 2–60 cm in diameter and 1.5–2 m long, bound tightly together) and earth to provide shelter for troops' movement. Frequently refers to a work thrown up to defend a flank. Bruce W. Fry, 202.
93. Journal of Kerdisien-Trémais, 4 July 1758, folio 193r.
94. Journal of Jeffery Amherst, 9 July 1758, Book 9, 11.
95. As of 6 July, *Le Prudent* and *L'Entreprenant* would be manned by skeleton crews consisting of two officers and 100 sailors. The other three ships of the line, *Le Capricieux*, *Le Célèbre*, and *Le Bienfaisant* would be manned by two officers and 60 sailors. Journal of Kerdisien-Trémais, 6 July 1758, folio 193r; and Disposition pour le service des vaisseaux, Desgouttes's Orders Register, 6 July 1758, folios 150v–151r.
96. During the night of 6 July 1758, a bomb fell on the hospital. Two surgeons were wounded, and the surgeon of the Second Battalion of the Volontaires Étrangers was killed. Journal of Drucour, 15 July 1758, folio 12r.
97. Copy of Admiral Boscawen's reply, folios 80r–v; Copy of Amherst's reply, folios 80v–81r. Journal of Drucour, 6 July 1758. By 11 July 1758, Wolfe had a total of 18 guns firing upon four targets: six guns aimed at the right flank of the citadel; six guns against the ships of the line; two guns against the right flank of the cavalier and Bastion Dauphin; three guns firing ricochet ordinance against the previously mentioned targets; and one gun to scour the glacis, and ground in front of that Bastion Dauphin. State of Brigadier Wolfe's guns as of 11 July 1758. Letter, Wolfe to Amherst, 20 June 1758, 16. Correspondence Wolfe to Amherst.
98. Journal of Desgouttes, 19 July 1758, folios 12v–13r.
99. *Ibid.*, folio 13v.
100. Journal of Tourville, 21 July 1758, folios 324r–v. Boscawen reports that these shells were fired from the Marine Battery. It was designated as such because the battery had been built and manned by marines from Boscawen's vessel the *Namur*. This battery contained five guns and two howitzers. Admiral Boscawen's Log, 21

June 1758. Map of Samuel Holland, Captain–Lieutenant of the Royal American Regiment published in MacLean's book.

101. Journal of Tourville, 21 July 1758, folios 324r–v.

102. Journal of Desgouttes, 21 July 1758, folio 13v.

103. *Ibid.* These large warships were so close to the wharfs that they now were at risk of going aground.

104. Journal of Gordon, 21 July 1758, 138.

105. Journal Anonyme I, 20–21 July 1758, folio 15v.

106. On 22 July 1758, two additional batteries were unveiled. One gun battery of eight 24 pounders and another of five 24 pounders, and a mortar battery of one 13-inch, two 10-inch, and another of four 2-inch mortars. Now, a total of 37 cannons and 11 mortars, and numerous coehorns and royals were firing upon the French squadron, fortifications, and the town. Journal of Gordon, July 22, 1758, 138–139.

107. In his post siege report, governor Drucour stated that approximately 50 percent of the Island Battery's 37 guns, and two mortars had been damaged by enemy fire and rendered unserviceable. There were other artillery pieces positioned within the Island Battery. However, their emplacements covered other areas within the harbour. Since Sir Hardy's vessels were still operating in the immediate vicinity of Island Battery, the French gunners did not want to move and relocate these guns in case British vessels forced their way into the harbour. État de l'artillerie laissée dans la place de Louisbourg lors de la rédition aux anglais, le 26 juillet 1758. Journal of Drucour, folio 108v.

108. Journal of Gordon, July 23, 1758, 139.

109. Admiral Boscawen's Log, July 24, 1758, folio 111r. No written report or correspondence was uncovered listing Captain Balfour's observations made during the course of this reconnaissance mission. However, it is most likely that Balfour either met with Boscawen or forwarded his recommendations in a short message. Regardless, Boscawen initiated the necessary preparations for the raid, during 25 July 1758.

110. Journal of Desgouttes, July 26, 1758, folio 15r.

111. Letter, Boscawen to Amherst, *Namur*, July 25 1758, 6. Correspondence Amherst to Boscawen.

112. Journal of Grillot de Poilly, 25 July 1758, 113–115.

113. Note from Boscawen to Captain William Parry of the *Kingston, Namur*, 25 July 1758. Boscawen sent notes to all the captains who were to supply small crafts and sailors. The rendezvous timings for this mission were also indicated in his notes. LAC, MG 21, Additional Manuscripts, Add. Mss. 11813, Vol. 8, Captain Parry's Account of the Expedition to Louisbourg, 1758, 38.

114. Letter, Boscawen to Amherst, *Namur*, 25 July 1758, 6. Correspondence Amherst to Boscawen. The embarkations were divided into four groups and sent to Hardy. The first group left at 1200 hours, the second at 1300 hours, the third at 1400 hours, and the last group at 1500 hours.

115. Admiral Boscawen's Log, 25 July 1758, folio 111r. Letter, Boscawen to Amherst, *Namur*, 25 July 1758, 5. Correspondence Amherst to Boscawen.

116. Captain Balfour's Log, [hereafter cited as Captain Balfour's Log]. Public Records Office, ADM 51/111, 26 July 1758. Fortress of Louisbourg, National Historic Site of Canada, microfilm LSBG 487.

117. Letter, Boscawen to Amherst, *Namur*, 25 July 1758, 6. Correspondence Amherst to Boscawen.

118. Journal of Jeffrey Amherst, 25 July 1758, Book 9, 19. Letter, Boscawen to Amherst, *Namur*, 25 July 1758, 6. Correspondence Amherst to Boscawen. Since 12 July, another seven batteries were built and opened fire upon Louisbourg's main landward fortifications and the town. On 13 July, two mortar batteries were unveiled, each comprising two mortars. On 22 July, one eight-gun battery, one six-gun battery, and a seven mortar commenced firing upon enemy positions. A last battery composed of four guns and one howitzer was unveiled on 26 July. Information drawn and complied from the Samuel Holland map and the Journal of Gordon.

119. Journal of William Amherst, 25 July 1758, Book 2, 7, LAC, MG18, L4, Amherst, Sir Jeffery and family, Vol. 4, Packet 20. The scaling ladders were delivered during the day on 25 July 1758. These had been noted by the defenders who now had to post a larger number of troops on the main walls and bastions, fearing an imminent full-out ground assault. *An Authentic Account of the Reduction of Louisbourg, in June and July 1758 by a spectator* (London: Printed for W. Owen, 1758), 46, [hereafter cited as *An Authentic Account*]; "Admiral Sir John Laforey, Bart," in James Rolf, *The Naval Biography of Great Britain* (Boston: Gregg Press, 1972), 45.

120. Captain Balfour's Log.

121. Due to the intense bombardments that took place during the course of that day, the French sailors could not man their quarterdecks or forecastles. This reduced the skeleton crews' abilities to survey and observe the areas around their respective vessels. Journal of Desgouttes, 26 July 1758, folio 15r.

122. Letter from Amherst to Pitt, Camp of Louisbourg, 27 July 1758, 9. Correspondence between Jeffrey Amherst and Boscawen, Pitt and Abercromby, July–September 1758, LAC, MG18, L4, Amherst, Sir Jeffery and family, Vol. 4, Packet 22. In his diary, however, regarding when the raid took place, Amherst reports that he, "... went to the trenches and stayed there until two o'clock and began to despair of the boats coming ..." Journal of Jeffrey Amherst, 25 July 1758, Book 9, 19.

123. This information was provided shortly after the raid by an unidentified French officer who had been on board *Le Prudent*. Journal anonyme II, 26 July 1758, folio 76r.

124. *An Authentic Account*, 46; Rolf, 232; The raiders also liberated a total of 20 English sailors who had been captured by French privateers prior to the siege. Admiral Boscawen's Log, 26 July 1758, folio 111r.

125. Journal of Desgouttes, 26 July 1758, folio 15r. Following the raid, Desgouttes interceded on behalf of his sailors. The commodore explained that the reason

why the majority of the skeleton crews were below deck was to avoid being unnecessarily exposed to shrapnel and wood splinters. However, during the night of 26 July the British gunners did not fire upon the vessels for fear of injuring of killing the raiders.

126. Admiral Boscawen's Log, July 26, 1758, folio 11r.

127. M. de Lionne, ensign, sustained a hand injury, and M. de Mouillebert, ensign, sustained a cutlass injury. Journal anonyme II, folio 76r; and Journal of Desgouttes, July 1758, folio 15r.

128. Journal of Drucour, 26 July 1758, folio 87v.

129. *An Authentic Account*, 46.

130. Journal of William Amherst, 26 July 1758, Book 2, 7. Journal of Captain John Montresor, *Collections of the New York Historical Society for the year 1881* (New York: Printed for the Society, 1882), 172; *An Authentic Account*, 47.

131. Laforey ensured that a large schooner and *Le Prudent's* boats were left by the hull so that the French seamen could safely evacuate the burning vessel. *An Authentic Account*, 47.

132. *Ibid.*, 47.

133. Journal of Captain John Montresor, 172.

134. *An Authentic Account*, 49.

135. Correspondence Amherst to Boscawen, *Namur*, 26 July 1758, 8; The British discovered that these vessels were used as floating prison. General Amherst noted in his diary that among the prisoners were sailors who had been captured by Desgouttes during his trip from France to Louisbourg. Journal of Jeffery Amherst, 25 July 1758, Book 9, 19; Additionally, a British deserter had been held captive aboard the *Prudent*, and was killed during the raid. *An Authentic Account*, 47; Captain Balfour interrogated the liberated English prisoners. All stated that they had never seen army deserters and had been held captive for a 12-month period. Letter, Amherst to Boscawen, *Namur*, 2 August 1758, 14. Correspondence Amherst to Boscawen.

136. Captain George Balfour's Log, 26 July 1758.

137. *An Authentic Account*, 48. To further protect his vessels and provide his crews with additional protection, Desgouttes ordered that barrels containing tobacco leaves be placed on the desk and heavy netting be nailed to various parts of the ships. These measures were carried out to limit the damages to the ships and to reduce the trajectory of deadly wood splinters following an explosion. Journal of Desgouttes, 2–23 June 1758, folio 7r. Another interesting fact was that the raiding parties' officers and sailors were appalled when they realized that the French commodore had not posted aboard these last two vessels naval captains or lieutenants to coordinate and oversee their protection.

138. Despite obtaining excellent intelligence regarding the state of Desgouttes's vessels, and the very poor health of the French crews, Boscawen nevertheless remained cautious, and did not want to force the harbour for fear of losing some of his ships of the line. In the event that he had chosen such a bold course of action and

attacked the harbour, the siege could have ended within 10 days of the landing. See intelligence report of interrogation of French prisoners following the landing. Letter, Boscawen to Amherst, 10 June 1758, 15–16. Correspondence Boscawen to Amherst. Additional information in Boscawen's letter of 15 July 1758 provides valuable insight as to his earlier decisions why he did not want force the harbour. The admiral explained that the French Island Battery and the Rochefort Point Battery were still very active and well defended. Boscawen rationalized that a well-concealed battery "of two guns would sink the Navy of England, unless they can come within Pistol shott and drive the men from their guns, by small arms fire." Letter, Boscawen to Amherst, 15 July 1758, 85. Correspondence Amherst to Boscawen.

139. Letter, Pitt to Admiral Boscawen, Whitehall, 3 February 1758; Kimball, 180.
140. Letter, Brigadier James Wolfe to Major Walter Wolfe, Louisbourg, 27 July 1758. ed. Beckles Willson, *The Life and Letters of James Wolfe* (London: William Heinemann, 1909), 384–385. Despite the problems incurred by the defenders during the siege, and the time-consuming destruction of the French squadron, Desgouttes and his captains did in fact successfully delay Amherst's bid to then head to Quebec. "This sojourn of the vessels did extend the duration of the siege," reflected a pensive Desgouttes, "and during the course of this campaign could easily have launched other operation, giving the size of the 14,000-man army and the 24 ships of the line." Réflexion sur cette campagne, in Journal of Desgouttes, folio 18v.
141. Letter, Brigadier James Wolfe to Lord George Sackville, Louisbourg, 30 July 1758. ed. Beckles Willson, *The Life and Letters of James Wolfe* (London: William Heinemann, 1909), 387.
142. Letter, Brigadier James Wolfe to his father, camp before Louisbourg, 27 July 1758. Willson, 384.
143. Letter, Brigadier James Wolfe to Lord George Sackville, camp before Louisbourg, 30 July 1758. *Ibid.*, 387.
144. Letter, James Wolfe to Captain William Rickson, Salisbury, 1 December 1758. LAC, MG 18, L5, Wolfe, James, Vol. 5, MS 2207, (Antiquaries' Papers), folios 64r–66r, microfilm A-1780.
145. Letter, Brigadier James Wolfe to his mother, camp before Louisbourg, 27 July 1758; Willson, 383.
146. Letter, Admiral Boscawen to William Pitt, *Namur*, Gabarus Bay, 28 July 1758; Kimball, 307–309.
147. *An Authentic Account*, 47–48.
148. Journal of Desgouttes, 26 July 1758, folio 14v.
149. Letter XXIII, [from an unidentified French infantry officer to Thomas Pichon] The siege of Louisbourg continued. Resistance of the garrison, who are at length obliged to capitulate. Treatment of them and the inhabitants, etc. non-dated. Thomas Pichon, *Genuine Letters and Memoirs, Relating to the Natural, Civil and Commercial History of the Islands of Cape Breton, and Saint-John, From the First Settlement There to the Taking of Louisbourg, by the English, in 1758* (London:

Printed for J. Nourse in the Strand, 1760), 372–373.

150.   Journal of Grillot de Poilly, night of 25 July to 26, 1758, 115.

151.   Mémoire ou Journal sur le siège de Louisbourg avec la capitulation faite le 26 juillet, 1758, 62. LAC, MG 4, C1, Comité Technique du Génie, Place étrangère. Louisbourg, Île Royale, Article 14, pièce 53.

152.   Journal anonyme I, folio 16v.

153.   Copie du mémoire de M. Franquet directeur des fortifications, formé a la demande de M. le chevalier de Drucour, sur l'état actuel se trouve la place et Louisbourg, le 24 juillet au soir. Supplément au mémoire ci-dessus du 25 juillet conformement à la visite faitte le 24 au soir des ouvrages de la place. This report and addendum were transcribed in Drucour's journal, following the entry of 26 July 1758. Journal of Drucour, 26 July 1758, folios 88r–91r.

154.   Journal of Jeffery Amherst, 26 July 1758, Book 9, 19.

155.   The six articles are as follows: 1) The garrison shall be prisoners of war and transported to England. 2) All artillery and war provisions located in Louisbourg, Île Royale and the island of St. John must be turned over, without the least waste. 3) The troops on Island of St. John must report to the vessels that will transport them to England. 4) The Porte Dauphin will be opened and made accessible to British forces at eight o'clock 27 July and the garrison will lay down their arms, colours, implements, and ornaments of war: the garrison will be sent to England in a convenient time. 5) The sick and wounded will be attended to and cared for in the same manner as those of his Britannic Majesty. 6) The merchants and their clerks that did not bear arms will be sent to France. Journal of Drucour, 26 July 1758, folios 100v–101r.

156.   *An Authentic Account*, 49–50.

157.   *L'Écho* was captured by Sir Charles Hardy's squadron on 18 June 1758. "An Account of the Ships in the harbor of Louisbourg, when the troops landed," *An Authentic Account*, 58; Boscawen stated that *L'Écho* was captured on the 15 June, by the *Scarborough* and the *June*. Letter, Boscawen to Amherst, *Namur*, 19 June 1758, 36. Correspondence Boscawen to Amherst.

158.   Letter, Boscawen to Pitt, *Namur*, Gabarus Bay, 28 July 1758; Kimball, 307–309.

LAC, C-36181.

Major-General Isaac Brock, the British commander in Upper Canada who believed the province could be defended against American attacks. Despite a lack of campaign experience, he proved a shrewd leader, willing to take great risks. His luck ran out at Queenston Heights, where he was killed in October 1812.

CHAPTER 4

"The determination … to undertake the most hazardous enterprize": The British Attack on Fort Mackinac and Fort Detroit During 1812

JOHN R. GRODZINSKI

Sometime after mid-morning on 16 October 1812, near the northern tip of the Niagara Peninsula in Upper Canada, British artillery pieces at Fort George commenced firing. Under the command of Captain William Holcroft of the Royal Artillery, the two of the seven 9-pounder (pdr) guns[1] fired one round per minute for a period of time and then they all quickly fired three rounds each. Across the river, at Fort Niagara, American gunners responded and fired also, and soon other guns erupted along the frontier until sunset. Although considerable skirmishing had occurred along the Niagara River over the last several weeks and a battle had been fought at Queenston Heights on 13 October, this particular gunfire was not in anger, but served as a salute to the fallen commander of the British forces in Upper Canada and chief administrator of the province, Major-General Isaac Brock.

In the early morning of 13 October 1812, having ridden hastily from his headquarters at Fort George to the sound of the guns at Queenston, Brock fell, mortally wounded from American small-arms fire during an attempt to retake a British gun position on the heights. Now, three days later, he and his aide, Lieutenant-Colonel John Macdonell, were being interred in the northern-most corner of the fort. A large crowd had assembled for the service, including soldiers, militiamen, and Natives and Holcroft's gunners were firing a salute to their commander. Lieutenant-Colonel Winfield Scott, an American artillery officer taken prisoner at Queenston, had arranged for the minute guns at Fort Niagara to fire "out of respect for the very high character of the deceased."[2]

There was great sorrow throughout Upper Canada at the loss of Brock, who, in a matter of weeks, had transformed a near hysteria that any effort to repel an American invasion of Canada was hopeless, to a spirit that Canada would prevail as Brock had "effected the preservation of the Upper Province."[3] For an officer with relatively little campaign experience, Brock proved a shrewd judge of character, able leader of men and builder of alliances, ready to risk all and act boldly against an opponent he considered poorly led and ill-prepared for war. During the summer of 1812, Brock ordered a daring move against the American fort at Mackinac[4] Island on Lake Huron and then led an audacious advance against Fort Detroit. His luck eventually ran out during his second battle in Canada, at Queenston Heights, which resulted in his death.

LAC, C-273.

Artist conception of the death of Brock during the Battle of Queenston Heights, 13 October 1812.

The War of 1812 was fought between the United States and Great Britain and came about from a mix of economic and diplomatic differences that set the two countries increasingly apart between 1807 and 1812. By 1812, these differences had festered, leaving President James Madison convinced that war was necessary to vindicate American sovereignty and national honour. Britain, heavily committed to the struggle in Europe against Napoleon and, hoping to avoid any diversion to that effort, withdrew a key restriction on American trade with French-dominated Europe at the last minute, but that gesture proved too late and the United States declared war on 18 June 1812.

Having never fought a major war, the United States was largely unprepared for what lay ahead. In January 1812 Congress increased the establishment of the regular army from 4,000 to 35,603 (all ranks), but many of the experienced pre-war units were scattered in garrison along the western frontier, while the new recruits did not receive adequate training or equipment. The War Department was not ready for the coming demands of formulating and implementing strategy, providing logistical support for its field forces, or in allocating priorities.[5] The abilities of the secretary of war, William Eustis were distrusted, while his department was insufficiently staffed, forcing him to deal with minutiae, which in wartime became overwhelming.

There was no professional officer present at the War Department to provide advice on strategy. Consequently, planning for the first campaign was left to Major-General Henry Dearborn, a distinguished veteran of the War of Independence and former secretary of war, now 61 years old and in poor health, who was selected over several other serving general officers to command the northern theatre and operations against Canada. His scheme, developed in the months leading up to the war, was to mount four attacks. Three of these were secondary operations and would be conducted by militia forces, seizing several points in Upper Canada: the first the important naval and military posts at Kingston, cutting off Upper Canada from Lower Canada; the second against the Niagara frontier, where the main British garrison in the province was located, and finally, at Fort Malden near Amherstburg in the southwestern end of Upper Canada. The main attack would be conducted from Lake Champlain towards Montreal.[6]

Despite the myriad difficulties faced by the Americans, they did enjoy several advantages. British North America was a vast territory consisting of the colonies of Upper Canada, Lower Canada, New Brunswick, Nova Scotia, Cape Breton, Prince Edward Island, Newfoundland, and Bermuda. With a population of only 600,000 people and limited infrastructure, it was at a serious disadvantage to the United States, which boasted a population of 7 million. Any British military effort would be a secondary one at best, given their commitments in Europe and elsewhere. Although the Canadian militia could augment British regulars, their assistance would be limited as they received little or no training and lacked equipment. The defence would therefore rely on British regulars troops, which in July 1812 numbered less than 10,000 in total — with the possibility of some reinforcements. The one advantage the British held was that the quasi-military inland naval service, known as the Provincial Marine, run by the Quartermaster General's Department, held superiority on Lake Ontario, Lake Erie, and the Upper Great Lakes, including the Detroit River, while the main line of communications, by which all equipment, troops and weaponry would be brought into Upper Canada, the St. Lawrence River, was also controlled by the British.

Given the paucity of personnel and equipment, many held that the best option to defend British North America was to concentrate forces in Lower Canada and await help from London, with the help of the Royal Navy. As navigation on the St. Lawrence limited the reach of the Royal Navy to Montreal, any policy advocating defence farther inland in Upper Canada was deemed unacceptable since the Navy could not support it.[7] The British commander in chief in Upper Canada, Lieutenant-General Sir George Prevost, acknowledged this problem, when he wrote "it would be in vain … with the hopes of making an effectual defence of the open country [i.e. Upper Canada], unless powerfully assisted from Home."[8] The best the British could do would be to reinforce the only major fortification in the colony at Quebec and to withstand a "vigorous and well conducted siege" and await reinforcement from the empire.[9]

Such was the thinking in 1811. Enter Isaac Brock. Born in 1769, the same year as Napoleon and the first Duke of Wellington, Isaac Brock entered the 8th Foot as an ensign in 1785. In 1791, he transferred to the 49th Foot and by 1799 was commanding the battalion. In August 1799, Brock experienced his first taste of battle during the attack on Egmond-aan-Zee, near Amsterdam, where the 49th was eventually heavily engaged. In 1801, Brock's regiment joined the military force accompanying the expedition to destroy the Danish fleet at Copenhagen, during which he met Admiral Horatio Nelson. In 1802, the 49th was ordered to Canada and moved into Upper Canada the following year. After being promoted to colonel in 1805, Brock took leave to England until the apprehension of war with the Americans caused him to cut his leave short and return to Canada. Brock became temporary commander in chief of the forces in Canada and set about improving the defences in Quebec, the training of the militia, and the quality of the marine service. In 1807, Brock was appointed brigadier-general and in command at Montreal until July 1810, when he was sent to take charge in Upper Canada.

During these years, Brock earned a reputation as a stern disciplinarian who also understood the lot of the life of a soldier. He disliked his prolonged service in Canada and sought a more active posting to the Iberian Peninsula, which he then turned down during 1812, as war loomed in North America. In June 1811, Brock was promoted to major-general and later that year he became the political administrator of Upper Canada.[10]

Brock initially agreed with the assessments regarding the defence of Upper Canada,[11] but soon after his appointment there his views underwent a dramatic change. Following a tour of the province, Brock explained his plans to Prevost. He emphasized fortifying key points around the province, naval construction, improvements to the militia, and raising new units locally to augment the 1,200 regulars. Cooperation was sought with the North West and South West [trading] companies, whose assistance was critical for transportation, while the cooperation of the Natives was actively pursued.

On Lake Huron, the American post on Mackinac Island would be taken and offensive operations launched against Detroit. While advocating an overall defensive strategy, the bold attacks were designed to divert American attention from both eastern Upper Canada and Lower Canada. If the British maintained naval superiority on Lake Ontario, and Lake Erie and Detroit and Mackinac were taken, the only other place left for an American attack would be the Niagara region, which would be strongly reinforced, thus confounding the anticipated American offensives against Montreal and Quebec.[12]

To summarize, those in the British and American camps believed that advantages in manpower and seizing the initiative would lead to quick American victories. While the British enjoyed naval superiority on Lakes Ontario, Erie, and the Upper Great Lakes, they might be forced to relinquish Upper Canada. Last-minute attempts to avoid conflict failed and, faced with irreconcilable disputes over trade and impressment, the Americans declared war on 18 June 1812. Pre-war plans were now implemented.

Although operations in the northwest were not intended as the main effort, for President Madison, the situation in the American northwest territories was critical. The Americans had been combating Natives there since the 1790s, and although their victory against the Natives at Tippecanoe in 1811 had settled things down, settlers faced repeated attacks from the Natives and were seeking refuge in the forts scattered throughout the region.[13] Secretary of War Eustis believed that these incidents would rise, particularly if the British achieved victories early in the conflict. Thus, the administration not only viewed this as an internal security threat from the Natives, as well as a problem of frontier security with the British. Simply put, the Detroit frontier required protection, as well as an army positioned there to defend the region, deal with the Natives, and march into Canada.[14]

Cobbling together the force for the upcoming offensive was simpler than the other three planned attacks — which all fizzled out as appropriate forces could not be collected — since there were several regular garrisons scattered throughout the northwest. Fort Detroit, the principal garrison, had 90 men from a company of the 1st Infantry and a company of artillery. Three hundred miles to the north was another garrison at Fort Mackinac, while at Fort Wayne, at the fork of the Maumee River in northern Indiana, was another company of 50 men. At the mouth of the Chicago River were 60 men in Fort Dearborn. Finally, at Vincennes were 300 men of the 4th Infantry.[15]

Lieutenant-Colonel James Miller was ordered to move his 4th Infantry from Vincennes to Dayton, Ohio, while the governor of Ohio was asked to provide 1,200 militiamen. A commander also had to be nominated and both Eustis and President Madison agreed that William Hull, the governor of Michigan, was ideal for the job.

The expansion of the U.S. Army demanded the appointment of additional general officers and 12 were nominated during 1812. Seven were serving regular officers, while the remainder were veterans of the American War of Independence or had more recent experience with state militias. In most cases, their military experience was distant or limited. William Hull fell into the latter category. Hull was born in Derby, Connecticut, on 24 June 1753, and graduated with honours from Yale at 19 before going into the law. He obtained a commission from Congress and eventually rose to the rank of colonel.

Held in high esteem by George Washington, Hull was sent to Quebec

"The determination … to undertake the most hazardous enterprize"

Brigadier-General William Hull, commander of the Army of the Northwest, faced considerable challenges with his campaign and proved himself unsuited to the task. Uninspiring and indecisive, Hull succumbed to his own fears and surrendered without firing a shot.

in 1784 to request the evacuation of the western posts. After the peace of 1783, he held a judicial post in Massachusetts and became a senator. Hull went to Canada again in 1793 to request assistance with negotiating terms of peace with the western Natives. In 1805 he was appointed the first governor of Michigan and commissioned as a brigadier-general on 8 April 1812. When Hull was offered the appointment, he first turned it down, but eventually gave in to the president's request.[16]

Hull received a difficult task. He was to march his Army of the Northwest 200 miles from Ohio to Detroit, building a road through the wilderness. Once at Detroit, Hull would be at the end of a tenuous line of communication, facing the British across the Detroit River at Fort Malden. During his preparations, Hull presented several ideas on how the campaign should be conducted, including the recommendation that efforts be made to secure control of the Great Lakes. He also urged the dispatch of an additional 3,000 reinforcements to Detroit. The government ignored both recommendations.[17]

The only regular unit in Hull's army was the 4th Regiment of Infantry, the sole regular unit of the U.S. Army ready for active service in 1812. With a paper strength of 46 officers and 1,024 men, the 4th, like many of the American regiments, was under strength and had only approximately 400 men.[18] Formed in 1808, the regiment helped defeat the natives at Tippecanoe in 1811 and was currently led by Lieutenant-Colonel James Miller.[19]

Joining the regulars were three regiments of Ohio militia, totalling 900 men. The 1st Regiment was led by Colonel Duncan McArthur, the 2nd by Colonel James Findlay and the 3rd Regiment by Colonel Lewis Cass.

A private soldier of the 4th American Regiment. It was the only regular U.S. infantry regiment in the field on the northern frontier at the outbreak of the war. Reconstitution by Don Troiani.

Courtesy Parks Canada, PD 738.

While the commanding officers were also general officers in the state militia, only McArthur had anything resembling experience gained in earlier campaigns against the Natives.[20] By 1 June, the army was assembled at Dayton and began its trek to Detroit. They advanced slowly and along the way received their final reinforcements, giving Hull a total of 2,075 men. After a difficult journey, Detroit was reached on 5 July 1812.[21]

The town of Detroit[22] was home to about half of the 4,800 inhabitants of the Michigan territory. On the western side of the town was Fort Detroit, a quadrilateral bastioned fortification about 100 yards long on each face, enclosing a parade ground of just under three acres. It had a parapet 11 feet high and 12 feet thick at the top, while a ditch that was 12 feet wide and six feet deep surrounded the walls. It was well armed with 34 guns of various calibres. About three miles to the south of the fort was the small community of Spring Wells and just south of that was the mouth of the River Rouge. Six miles farther south was the small community of Maguaga and seven miles farther south was Brownstown. A riverfront road provided communication between these communities.

At Detroit, Hull had 2,300 men in three regiments of Ohio militia, a 48-man troop of Cincinnati Light Dragoons, totalling 1,592 men, the 300 regulars of the 4th Infantry, augmented by 118 men in a company of the 1st U.S. Infantry and a small artillery detachment at Fort Detroit. There were also some 300 members of the Michigan Territorial Militia. A portion of these men were deployed in a defensive posture in five separate detachments along the line of communications. In addition, Hull maintained a standing garrison at the Fort itself.[23]

Across from Detroit was the western district of Upper Canada. Along the river were two major settlements; the first lay a mile downriver from Detroit and was known as Sandwich (modern Windsor) with 50 houses. From Sandwich, a shoreline road continued south and within two miles crossed Turkey Creek. Five miles farther, a bridge crossed the Canard River. Continuing south, a second, larger, community of Amherstburg was situated on the Detroit River at the head of Lake Erie, 15 miles below Sandwich. It was about half the size of Detroit and had 150 houses. It was also home to the dockyard and marine arsenal for the upper Great Lakes and an assemblage point for the Natives. Just offshore lay Bois Blanc Island and across the river was Brownstown.[24]

Fort Malden lay north of Amherstburg. Built during 1796 as the British prepared to turn Detroit over to the Americans, Fort Malden had a quadrilateral shape with four bastions and a redoubt. The fort was described immediately before the war as "a temporary Field Work in ruinous state ... undergoing a repair to render it tenable."[25] Some improvements were completed during 1812 under the supervision of Captain M.C. Dixon, Royal Engineers (RE), by which time the fort boasted 20 guns.

Lieutenant-Colonel Thomas Bligh St. George commanded the fort. He had been in Canada since 1808 and was currently the senior of several regular officers serving as "inspecting field officers of Canadian militia,"[26] responsible for the efficiency of the militia, and providing Prevost a ready supply of experienced senior officers that could be appointed to various field commands. The garrison included a detachment of artillery, 120 men of the 41st Regiment. Even if 500 local militiamen joined the garrison, Hull's army still outnumbered them.[27]

The one advantage the British enjoyed was in naval strength, which gave them command of the Detroit River, Lake Erie, and the Upper Great Lakes. The Provincial Marine squadron included the brig *Queen Charlotte*, with fourteen 24-pdr carronades and six long guns, the schooner *General Hunter* mounting six 6-pdr guns, and the *Lady Prevost* with ten 12-pdr carronades. Some local merchant vessels could also be pressed into service. In contrast, the Americans had only one vessel, the brig *Adams*, with six 6 pdrs for the entire Upper Great Lakes.[28]

Before the war, Brock had received important intelligence on Detroit, including detailed reports listing the ordnance in the fort, the size of the garrison, a list of vessels and their tonnages, and the general mood of the local Natives.[29] Brock had also worked out a rough plan to defend Fort Malden and eventually attack Fort Detroit. He intended to reinforce the 41st Foot and send 50 more gunners and four to six eight-inch mortars "suited to the Reduction of Detroit." He also hoped the local Canadian militia would contribute 700 men and the Natives would provide 2000–3,000 warriors.[30]

On 9 July, Hull received a letter from Secretary Eustis informing him that war had been declared, while a second letter instructed him to "take possession of Fort Malden," extending operations "as circumstances may justify."[31] Although Hull was concerned with the number of Natives in the area and the strength of the Provincial Marine, his preparations generally went well. A small flotilla of boats was assembled that could transport 400 men across the river at a time. In order to deceive the British, Hull made a visible feint of crossing below Detroit during the evening of the 11th. These troops were then countermarched and met up with the main body at Bloody Bridge, about two miles above Detroit, where 1,200 men crossed the river on 12 July and took Sandwich without any opposition. Hull had left most of the Michigan militia at Detroit while 100 of the Ohio men refused to cross the river.[32]

Hull ordered batteries erected on both shores, to command the crossing point and to prevent the Provincial Marine from moving into the Upper Lakes. He then issued a proclamation to the local residents, promising them freedom from tyranny, guaranteeing their rights, and respect for their property. He welcomed anyone who chose to join the American ranks. It also warned that anyone found fighting alongside Natives would be killed. This seemed to have the desired effect as locals offered their services, many of the local militia returned home, and the Natives even began reconsidering their alliance with the British. Hull sent several parties into the province to spread the proclamation and secure supplies. One group, under Colonel McArthur, advanced 60 miles inland to the valley of the Thames River and secured considerable supplies plus a few settlers willing to join Hull's army.[33]

Another party of 280 men under Colonel Cass was sent out on 16 July to reconnoitre the river road as far as the Canard River Bridge near

Amherstburg. Around mid-morning, Cass neared the Canard River and observed the bridge spanning the 30-yard-wide expanse. Despite orders to the contrary, Cass was determined to take the bridge, guarded by picket of 50 regulars, militia, and Natives under Captain Joseph Tallon of the 41st. Sending a 40-man detachment down the road towards the bridge, Cass then marched his main body inland, hoping to appear on the flank of the defenders. The American approach warned the British of their intentions, allowing them time to prepare, although two men from a forward detachment, under Lieutenant John Clemow, became stranded on the north side of the bridge. Refusing to surrender, one of the men was killed and the other taken prisoner, making them the first British casualties of the war. The battle opened before sunset, and after a spirited and confusing battle, the Americans cleared the bridge. Cass reported his success to Hull, who sent him some of the regular infantry as reinforcements.

A while later, when it appeared that the British were preparing an effort to retake the bridge, a council of war quickly decided to retire, especially since it was evident that Hull had no intention of reinforcing the success of Cass, who was now isolated and threatened with being cut off from Hull. Before leaving, Cass had the bridge destroyed. Although forced to withdraw, and despite his disobedience of Hull's instructions, Cass earned widespread fame for his aggressive stance at the Canard River. The failure to exploit this success or make any attempt on Fort Malden brought "serious grumbling within the army regarding Hull's capacities and leadership."[34]

Hull was indeed inactive at his camp. Surprisingly, this inactivity bore unexpected results as the Canadian militia at Fort Malden deserted in large numbers and many of the Natives simply left. Now facing reduced numbers, Hull then began planning to lay siege to Fort Malden by first reducing it by a bombardment and then assaulting it. Sieges were time-consuming operations that seemed to fit Hull's temperament. On 21 July, Hull left McArthur in charge at Sandwich and moved back to Detroit to check on the preparation of the guns that would be used to bombard Fort Malden. The reports were not good, as it would take an additional two weeks to complete the gun carriages. He also ordered the construction of rafts to move the guns once they were ready.

Hull also sought to drive a wedge between the Native-British alliance. He called a council with the Wyandottes, the Six Nations, and other tribes at Brownstown and convinced them to remain neutral, leaving only two chiefs, Tecumseh and Marplot, supporting the British from Fort Malden. With the Natives quiet, the militia deserting, and the population generally receptive to his proclamation, Hull felt no urge to hasten his preparations.[35]

Then, on the evening of 28 July, two Chippewa warriors arrived at Hull's camp with news that Fort Mackinac, an isolated post 290 miles north of Detroit, had fallen to the British. While seemingly unrelated to events at Detroit, this event would undo much of what Hull achieved thus far and further undermine his confidence.

The British had maintained a post in the Straits of Mackinac since 1761 when Fort Michilimackinac was established on the northern end of the Michigan peninsula. The straits linked Lakes Huron and Michigan and were 50 miles south of Lake Superior. For many years, this site had been an important crossroads, not only for the local Natives, but for the European fur trade as well. A French settlement was located on the north shore of the straits in 1660 and in 1715 a palisaded village was constructed on the south shore. In 1781, during the American War of Independence, the British established a more defendable location at nearby Mackinac Island, which also afforded a deep harbour. It was here that a new fort was built on the 150-feet-high limestone bluffs.[36]

With the end of the war in 1783, several British outposts now in American territory, including Fort Detroit, were to be turned over to the Americans, but the British refused to do so for several reasons. The abandonment of Fort Detroit and Fort Mackinac would have threatened the alliance with the Natives and resulted in a loss of a hub for the fur trade. After some negotiation, the British agreed to turn over all these posts in 1796. As British forces withdrew from their former outposts, they built new ones, such as Fort Malden, on the shore opposite their former fort. Fort Mackinac was transferred to the United States on 17 August 1796[37] and a detachment from the British garrison was sent fifty miles to the northeast to St. Joseph Island where the St. Mary's River flows into Lake Huron, to begin clearing land for a new fort.[38]

Fort St. Joseph became the westerly-most British garrison in the Canadas and one officer described the isolated outpost as "the military Siberia of Upper Canada."[39] In 1812, the commander of a motley group of veteran soldiers stationed there was Captain Charles Roberts. Originally commissioned into the 34th Foot in January 1796, he eventually transferred to the 57th Foot, serving some ten years in the West Indies before repeated attacks of fever forced a move to the 6th Royal Veteran Battalion in October 1806. Early the next year, Roberts was transferred to the 10th Battalion, formed in Britain for service in Canada. Roberts arrived at Quebec in the fall of 1807 and was soon on detached service to Fort St. Johns, known today as Saint-Jean-sur-Richelieu in Lower Canada. In 1811 Roberts was selected for a more rigorous command at Fort St. Joseph.[40]

The garrison included of a company of the 10th Royal Veteran Battalion. Veteran units were recruited from "meritorious Soldiers, who by Wounds, Infirmity or Age, are become unequal to the more active Duties of the Line, but who retain sufficient strength for the less laborious Duties of a Garrison." A further incentive to join was the promise of land grants.[41] These were not particularly young or able men and many were "worn out" as the expression went at the time. They were certainly not the same as line infantry. In 1812 Captain Roberts was aged 40, while his adjutant, Lieutenant Joseph Lambeth was 59, and Ensign John Lambton was 49, while many of the rank and file were even older.[42] While Roberts knew his men were disciplined and would follow his instructions, they were "so debilitated, and worn down by unconquerable drunkenness, that neither the fear of punishment, the love of fame or the honour of their Country can animate them to extraordinary exertions."[43] Consequently, Roberts would need additional help from local voyageurs and the Indian Department.

On 8 July 1812, Roberts received instructions from Brock, written on 25 June, ordering him to make an immediate attack upon Fort Mackinac, or, if he found the Americans moved first, to defend Fort St. Joseph to the utmost.[44] Then, on the heels of Brock's first letter, came another countermanding these instructions. Two days later, these instructions were cancelled and Roberts was instructed to adopt "the most prompt and effectual measures to possess himself of Michilimackinac [Mackinac]," with the aid of fur traders and Natives. Then, to make matters more difficult, Roberts then received a letter from the adjutant general, Colonel Edward Baynes, on behalf of Sir George Prevost, the commander-in-chief of British North America. Roberts was instructed to observe "the greatest vigilance and Caution for the Protection of the Post and for the ultimate security of the Party Committed to your Charge."[45] He was also told that the North West Company had promised cooperation in the prosecution of the war.

While the role played by the Natives during the War of 1812 is rightly acknowledged for its importance to the British cause, the significant part played by the North West Company is largely forgotten. It was evident that each needed the other and the North West Company agreed not only to aid with defence, but also to provide whatever assistance it could to support offensive operations against the Americans.[46] Company representatives assisted in determining which routes could be maintained to ensure the flow of communication and goods between Montreal and the northwest and also recommended moving the garrison at Fort St. Joseph up to the falls of St. Mary's, as the current post was not only exposed but offered no protection to their trade. Four company vessels on the Upper Great Lakes, some of them armed, and a contingent of men were also offered. They would also use their contacts with the Natives to promote the British cause.[47]

On 15 July another letter arrived from Brock, authorizing Roberts to act at his own discretion. Well aware of the shortfalls of Fort St. Joseph's location and the fact that it afforded less protection than Fort Mackinac, Roberts decided the next day to set out with every man available and take the American fort.[48]

The regular troops under Roberts's command included two lieutenants, one ensign, two sergeants, four corporals, and 36 rank and file of the 10th Royal Veteran Battalion, and a sergeant and two gunners from the Royal Artillery. With 48 men, this was not much of an assault force.[49] Roberts soon increased that number to an impressive 630 men. He achieved this by negotiating the creation of a "battalion" of 180 Canadians and Métis voyageurs led by fur trader Lewis Crawford. Through the Indian Department, which had been created in 1755 to manage Native affairs, 400 Natives arrived in two groups. John Askin Jr., the Indian Department storekeeper and interpreter at Fort St. Joseph, collected 280 Ottawa and Chippewa warriors, while 130 Sioux, Menminee, and Winnebago warriors were secured by Robert Dickson and joined Roberts's command.

Dickson was a prominent fur trader who had lived in the region for 25 years and had become increasingly bitter over American encroachment, transforming him into a zealous friend of the British cause, particularly in raising Native forces for the British effort.[50] The Sioux chief Wabasha explained the reason for the Natives' loyalty to the Crown in a speech made to an assembled council in June 1812. "We live by your English traders who have always assisted us," he stated, "and never more so, in the last year, at the risk of their lives, and we are always ready to listen to them on account of the friendship they have always shewn us."[51]

Roberts also engaged in diplomacy on his own to secure help from the allied Natives. On 12 July 1812, he held a council with most of the principal chiefs of the Outawas during which, Roberts was pleased to learn, they had "decided unanimously in our favour."[52]

The North West Company gave important assistance to the expedition by providing supplies and the use of the 70-ton armed schooner owned by the Company, which had conveniently stopped at Fort St. Joseph while en route from Sault Ste. Marie. Roberts acknowledged this help in a letter to Brock and wrote of "their ready and effectual aid and personal exertions voluntarily contributed." In addition, Roberts reported that a company official had "thrown open his Store houses to Supply my [Roberts's] requisitions in the handsomest manner."[53]

Roberts also needed firepower for his expedition. By 1812, Fort St. Joseph was armed with four 6-pdr guns — capable of firing a solid shot weighing six pounds at a distance of 1,200 yards — and six-and-one-half-pound swivel guns, which were not of much use.[54] Roberts took two of the 6 pdrs, the only serviceable ones remaining, and loaded them onto the schooner.[55] Fort Mackinac was 50 miles away, so to get there, the small force was to move by the North West Company vessel *Caledonia*, 10 of the traders' bateaux, and 70 canoes.[56]

These preparations did not go unnoticed by the Americans. The concentration of so many Natives at the British outpost and the failure of others to return to the American fort gave credence to the warning the commander of Fort Mackinac, Lieutenant Porter Hanks, had received from one Native that his post was about to be attacked. Hanks was a native of Massachusetts and commissioned in the U.S. Army in January 1805. At the end of the following year he was promoted to first lieutenant and sent to Fort Mackinac, where he was appointed commander of the station,[57] home to 61 men of the First U.S. Regiment of Artillery under his command.[58] Wanting to learn more, Hanks asked a local resident, Michael Dousman, to pay a visit to Fort St. Joseph and investigate.

Unfortunately for Hanks, Roberts's advancing flotilla captured Dousman before he reached St. Joseph Island.[59] Ironically, it was Dousman who revealed an important piece of intelligence to Roberts. He stated that the commander of Fort Mackinac was unaware that war had been declared.[60] Again, Roberts had benefited from the North West Company as his orders had been included with other papers dispatched for the western agents of the Company, whose directors had chosen to use express post rather than regular mail, which the Americans used.[61]

The expedition departed Fort St. Joseph at 1000 hours on 16 July 1812. To get to Fort Mackinac, the flotilla moved from the southern end of St. Joseph's Island into the St. Mary's River and headed southeast for several miles before they entered Lake Huron and turned westward for the final leg to Mackinac Island. As the fort was on the southern end of the island, the American garrison could not observe Roberts's movements, whose route took them around the northern end of Mackinac Island before turning south and heading for their landing site on the northwestern side of the island. As Roberts's small convoy approached Mackinac Island, he sent Dousman forward to move the civilian inhabitants to the end of the island to avoid any fighting.[62]

Mackinac Island is shaped like an obtuse triangle, with the hypotenuse forming the eastern side. The island is almost four miles square in area and is about two miles wide and three miles long with a distance around the shoreline of about eight miles. On the south end of the island are the harbour and the limestone heights where the fort was built. To the north of the fort, the ground continues to rise and near the south-centre of the island, forms a feature known as the Turtle's Back, which is 150 feet above the fort.[63] Although the British and later the Americans were aware that possession of the feature would dominate the fort, Hanks lacked the resources to fortify it, while the British only placed a fortification on it in 1814, well after they had retaken the island.[64]

The fort sat on a limestone bluff overlooking a natural harbour. Fort Mackinac was constructed of logs and was roughly quadrilateral in shape, with a long wall along the bluffs, a short wall on the west side, a longer one on the east, and another wall along the north end. Blockhouses were built into the walls on the northern and eastern ends.

The interior included a number of buildings, including a barracks, storehouses, magazine, and hospital.

The fort was also well armed, with two 5-and-one-half-inch howitzers, two brass 6 pdrs, one brass 3 pdr and two iron 9 pdrs. The 3 pdr and two 6 pdrs were placed in the blockhouses. Hanks had 61 men under his command, including two lieutenants from the artillery and a surgeon's mate. Half of the men were sick or unfit for service. The fort was in better condition than Fort St. Joseph, but there were also some problems. The masonry walls of the well within the fort had collapsed and had not been repaired, forcing the garrison to obtain their water from outside the walls, in a location that was not commanded by the guns of the fort.[65]

Just after 0300 hours on 17 July 1812, Roberts and his men landed on the northwestern side of the island, at a place now known as British Landing. Roberts and his veteran soldiers landed in the centre, Askin's Natives to their left, and Dickson's to the right.[66] Preparations were then made for the move across the island towards the south shore and the rear of the fort, a distance of about four miles. The group then set off into the darkness of the forest. While several men carried scaling ladders that had been built specifically for an assault, others had the difficult task of dragging the 6-pdr gun to the fort.

There is no description of how the gun was conveyed, other than what Captain Roberts noted in two reports. The first stated that he had taken two guns on the boats and that "by the exertions of the Canadians one of the Guns was brought up to a height commanding the Garrison,"[67] while in a letter to General Brock he revealed the enormity of this task as it was achieved through the "almost unparalleled exertions of the Canadians who manned the boats."[68]

Quite a task indeed. Following a 17-hour trip by boat, the guns, which were between seven or eight feet long and weighed about 2,350 pounds each,[69] were first manhandled onto the shore and then placed on a sled. As these pieces had come from a fort, they were probably not mounted on a wheeled travelling carriage that field guns used. That meant in order for a gun to be of any use it required a garrison carriage, made up of two wooden sides joined together by a transom that was moved by four small wheels, or trucks, which weighed several hundred pounds.[70]

Then there was the powder, the solid shot, the gunner's tools, and other items that also had to be hauled uphill through brush and woods, mostly in the dark to Fort Mackinac. While one might consider it impossible for men to move guns in this manner, one must remember that the voyageurs were used to shifting heavy loads, each man normally carrying 200 pounds or more at portages and working 16 to 18 hours a day. It would appear that only one of the guns was hauled to the fort.[71]

As Roberts's men approached the rear of Fort Mackinac, their single gun was manhandled into position. Saving themselves the effort of hauling the gun up onto Turtle's Back, Roberts's men found a piece of rising ground offering a more advantageous fire position from which they could dominate the walls of the fort at a shorter range, about 200 yards behind the fort.[72] By 1000 hours, everything was in place and the British commander sent Toussaint Pothier with a note addressed to the garrison commander, requesting him to surrender.[73]

Accepting the note, Hanks then surveyed the area around the fort and found the village was deserted. Hanks knew he could withstand neither a lengthy siege nor a major assault and was concerned the Natives might take matters into their own hands and massacre his men. Following a brief parley with his officers,[74] he agreed to capitulate and the colours were struck at noon. The American garrison was granted the full honours of war and Hanks and his men would be allowed to go to Detroit.[75] Aside from the 63 regulars in Fort Mackinac, there were 9 vessels in the harbour having another 47 men on board, for a total of 110 in all.[76] Not a shot had been fired. Roberts's daring did much to "save the effusion of blood, which must of necessity follow the attack of such Troops [Natives] as I [Roberts] have under my Command."[77] Fort Mackinac was again in British hands and would remain so for the remainder of the war.

The capitulation transferred the fort to British control. Private property was not to be seized or destroyed, including the merchant vessels in the harbour, which were to be retained by their owners. Finally, all American citizens in the area had to take an "oath of allegiance to His Britannic Majesty," or depart with within 30 days.[78] The British also secured a large quantity of stores and supplies from the government storehouse. Three British deserters were taken into custody, as were 20 other men who Roberts claimed to be British deserters.[79] Later that month, 18 of these men, many with French-Canadian names, agreed to serve for a limited period in British service, taking an oath of allegiance to King George III.[80]

Despite American fears of Native reprisals, they departed upon learning of the capitulation, but not without first making their presence known. Matthew Irwin, who was with the Indian Trade Office and later became a Chief Justice of the County Court in Michigan, recorded that the Canadians and Natives did depart for their canoes after the fort fell, but "on their way thither, they discharged their pieces in the air & kept up a most hideous yelling, to the Consternation of several American prisoners." Once in their boats and canoes, at the "bow of each were British streamers," they made for the harbour and moved towards the fort, keeping "up a very animated discharge of small arms." Not to be outdone, the British in the fort returned this celebratory fire "very often from the fort, with ordnance."[81]

Those officers, soldiers, and residents of Mackinac Island who chose not to become British subjects left on 26 July 1812 in two American vessels as cartels flying British flags. Fear of Native reprisals by "Canadians & Indians" during the passage let to a request that two interpreters accompany them. The passage was complicated by the recent invasion of British North America by General Hull and the American passengers spent several tense hours uncertain whether their passage would be safe.[82] However, they arrived in Detroit on 2 August.

Brock learned of Roberts's success on 29 July, which was welcome in contrast to the silence from Amherstburg. Earlier, on 20 July, Brock had sent Colonel Henry Procter, also of the 41st, to take command and "ascertain accurately the state of things in that quarter,"[83] while 50 men of the 41st, under Captain Peter Chambers, were sent to Moraviantown, near modern London, Ontario, to rally the militia. As nothing was heard from Procter or St. George, Brock considered going there to examine the situation, but an upcoming session of the legislature made it impossible. Brock faced a difficult situation as he tried to repel an American invasion, deal with disaffection amongst the populace, and recall the militia during harvest. He also faced a shortage of specie to purchase supplies.[84]

When he arrived at York on 27 July, Brock found the situation more desperate, with the legislature "passive," while public officials "appear quite confounded and decline acting." There were also significant difficulties in governing the militia, with the officers failing to exert their authority and legal limitations to his powers over them.[85] This led Brock to tell Colonel Baynes that the residents of Upper Canada were possessed by a belief "that this Province must inevitably succumb," fuelled by a fear that they would pay a hefty price in vengeance if they resisted the Americans.[86]

But reinforcements were on the way. Selecting Long Point on the north shore of Lake Erie as a rendezvous point, Brock sent 90 members of the 1st Flank Company of the 1st York Militia and two flank companies of the 3rd York there on 30 July. From the Niagara, the 1st Flank Company of the 5th Lincoln Regiment and two companies of the York Regiment joined this force. This Herculean effort to raise, equip, dress — some in cast-off British uniforms — and move the militiamen was organized by regular British officers from Brock's staff. Brock only joined them after proroguing the legislature on 5 August. He left that night for Long Point, where 300 militia and 50 regulars with one 6-pdr gun awaited him. On 8 August, they embarked on bateaux and five days later they were in Amherstburg.[87]

By this time, the situation had changed considerably due to the British victory at Mackinac. Hull was in trouble and wrote the Governors of Ohio and Kentucky, requesting reinforcements. He ordered Fort Dearborn, site of modern Chicago, to be abandoned and wrote Eustis to request reinforcements. He also requested operations on the Niagara frontier to commence, hoping it would divert troops. Hull then witnessed the agreement achieved during the council at Brownstown unravel and the Natives now openly supporting the British.

The new British commander at Fort Malden, Colonel Proctor, sent soldiers across the Detroit River to escort the Natives into his lines, leaving Hull with another problem. Hull had counted on the Natives to protect his supply convoys moving through their territory and a large convoy needing protection was now approaching the River Raisin. With this latest defection, Hull was forced to detach troops from his army.[88]

Hull sent a 200-man detachment under Major Thomas Van Horne from Colonel Findlay's regiment to escort them in. The American commander had a difficult task, as he failed to locate the backwoods trail Hull told him to use, forcing him to move by the main road. However, Colonel Proctor dispatched the Shawnee chief Tecumseh and 24 warriors to the American shore to intercept American communications. Tragically, Van Horne dismissed reports that the Natives were setting an ambush.

On 5 August, the Natives hit the Americans while they crossed a bridge near Brownstown. The Americans suffered 17 killed and 12 wounded compared to one Native killed and one wounded for the British. The supplies were lost and, more significantly, the mail had fallen into the Natives' hands, with Tecumseh's warriors capturing more mail heading to Detroit later that same day. The contents of Hull's official dispatches and the letters written by garrison members revealed much of the morale of the Americans and influenced British actions thereafter.[89]

The loss of official correspondence in this manner was not unusual for this period and this was not the first time that Hull's papers had fallen into British hands. During the march to Detroit in July, Hull had his heavy baggage, medical supplies, and an assortment of people taken there by two vessels. By mistake, Captain Abraham Hull, the general's son and aide, also loaded a chest of all the general's military papers on the schooner *Cuyahoga Packet*. Ignorant of the declaration of war, the captain of the schooner chose a route on the Detroit River that brought him under the guns of Fort Malden and, as the vessel moved upriver on 2 July 1812, it was seized by Lieutenant Charles Rolette, master of the Provincial Marine brig *General Hunter* and a veteran of the Nile and Trafalgar. Rolette was accompanied by six soldiers in a bateau. Everything was taken from the captured American schooner, including the papers, which included muster rolls and other records. But most important, the documents revealed the enemy's plans and objectives and left the British knowing "almost more about the army than General Hull himself at this point." Sheepishly, Hull wrote the British commander at Fort Malden, Lieutenant-Colonel St. George, requesting his correspondence back, noting they "will be of no service to the British government." His request was refused.[90]

Hull called a war council on 7 August and the majority of those in attendance agreed to assault Fort Malden, supported by guns mounted on the rafts. Hull then learned that British reinforcements were en route to Amherstburg from the Niagara frontier, leading Hull to believe the American offensive along the Niagara had failed and that he could not expect any relief. Panicking, Hull cancelled his previous orders and directed most of his army in Canada back to Detroit, a move one soldier called a "dastardly evacuation." A detachment of 130 soldiers remained in Canada, instructed by Hull to "hold possession of this part of Upper Canada" and to protect "the well-disposed inhabitants" that had collaborated with the Americans. A report that 5,000 natives were moving south towards Detroit further unnerved the already worn Hull.[91]

Once back on the American shore, Hull regained some of his wits and mounted another attempt to reopen his communications once more. This second effort was trusted to Lieutenant-Colonel Miller, who left Detroit with 600 men, one 6-pdr gun and a howitzer on 8 August. Halting on the River Rouge that night, his march continued the next day and at Maguaga they were met by a force of 200 British regulars and militia under Captain Adam Muir, supported by 200 Natives led by Tecumseh. They had been sent to Brownstown earlier to disrupt the American's line of communications. Warned of Miller's approach by his Native scouts, Muir marched to meet him. The ensuing battle was hard fought and the British were forced to re-cross the river and withdraw to Fort Malden. Miller suffered 18 killed and 64 wounded, but had held his ground. He was soon reinforced and his wounded were evacuated, but Miller made no further moves and was ordered back to Detroit on 11 August. However, he endured the fire from the ships of the Provincial Marine before arriving at the fort the next day.[92]

The action at Maguaga confirmed Hull's defensive mood and he now faced disaffection from the militia officers, who circulated petitions demanding his removal. The situation had changed dramatically due to the aggressive stance by Proctor's regulars and Tecumseh's Natives. Moreover, the fall of Mackinac and the belief that American efforts in the Niagara had failed, left Hull's army isolated. The net

Drawing by Pierre Le Dru, From Benson J. Lossing, *The Pictorial Field-Book of the War of 1812*, New York, 1868

A conjectural portrait of Tecumseh, the Shawnee chief who aspired to establish a Native homeland in the Michigan territory. At Detroit, Tecumseh and his warriors played an important role in cutting the American supply lines and undermining their morale.

effect on the American commander was profound, leading Colonel Cass to write the governor of Ohio that Hull was contemplating surrender. As a result, he asked the governor for help.

On 11 August Hull also ordered the remaining works at Sandwich, known as Fort Gowris, razed and the troops withdrawn across the Detroit River. Thus, after 30 days in Upper Canada, Hull had not made any move against Fort Malden and did little more than secure supplies and to distribute his proclamation. He now surrendered control of the river to the British, leaving Detroit open to their guns.

Colonel Proctor took advantage of their departure and two days later ordered a battery of one 18 pdr, two 12 pdrs, and two five-and-one-half inch howitzers constructed at Sandwich, which would later serve with devastating effect. This work was done under the protection of the guns of the *Queen Charlotte*, which moved upriver to cover the battery and the bridge over the Canard River.[93]

Meanwhile, Brock was moving rapidly towards Amherstburg. Travelling by the Grand River, Brock arrived at Long Point on 8 August, and, after mustering 350 militia and 20 more warriors, continued on, arriving at Amherstburg just before midnight on 13 August. Proctor informed Brock of the collapse of Hull's invasion and his withdrawal to Fort Detroit and of other details. Brock congratulated Proctor for his pressing the enemy and also met Tecumseh for the first time, cementing one of the most famous bonds of Canadian history. He also examined the recently acquired American papers, learning much about the state of his opponent.[94]

Tecumseh was born in Ohio around 1768 and spent much of his early years attempting to limit American colonization in Native lands by building alliances between Native groups aimed at limiting American encroachment, or in fighting against them. Native defeats through the 1790s diminished his prestige somewhat, yet, despite these setbacks, he still believed in his dream of a pan-Native movement that would secure a homeland for his people. Unaware that Britain and the United States were now at war, he decided in the summer of 1812 to move into British territory and by July was at Sandwich in Upper Canada. Although earlier British promises amounted to little, Brock, at least to Tecumseh and a few other Native leaders, was different and seemed willing, and capable enough, to take American territory in support of the Native objectives.[95]

The next day, both Brock and Tecumseh addressed the 1,000

Wyandot, Ottawa, Pottawatomi, Ojibwa, Shawnee, Sac, Winnibego, and Menominee warriors. Afterwards, the two leaders retired with the principal war chiefs to discuss war plans, which received the unqualified support of those present.[96] The captured dispatches also revealed that Hull's position was precarious and that he was awaiting reinforcements. Brock's plan was to cross the river and force the Americans out to an open battle. Guns at Sandwich and from the Provincial Marine vessels would bombard the fort. Another proposal for a direct assault on the fort, which was a much more deliberate and potentially costly affair, was opposed by all, except Lieutenant-Colonel Robert Nichol, the quartermaster general of the Provincial Militia. Brock may have also been driven to conclude matters quickly, so he could attend to matters along the Niagara.[97]

On 14 August, Brock organized the 300 regulars, 400 militiamen, and about 1,000 Natives for the coming attack. The troops of the Western District were formed into a small division of three brigades, as follows:[98]

1st Brigade, commanded by Lieutenant-Colonel Thomas St. George, 63rd Regt
- Royal Newfoundland Regiment, Major Robert Mockler (50 men)
- First Regiment Kent Militia
- First Regiment, Essex Militia
- Second Regiment, Essex Militia

2nd Brigade, commanded by Major Peter Chambers, 41st Regt
- 41st Regiment (50 men)
- First York Regiment and Third Regiments York Militia
- Fifth Lincoln Regiment
- Oxford Militia
- Second Regiment Norfolk Militia

3rd Brigade, commanded by Major Joseph Tallon, 41st Regt
- 41st Regiment (200 men)

Artillery
Detachment, 4 Battalion, Royal Artillery, with three 6 pdrs and two 3 pdrs, with 30 gunners.

Colonel Proctor was appointed commander of the division, while Brock held overall command.

The units in the division were drawn from the British regulars serving in Upper Canada and the provincial militia. The 41st Foot was formed in 1715 and had been stationed in Canada since 1799. It was rotated between Upper and Lower Canada twice before returning to the upper province in 1811. The 41st was to have left Canada during 1812, however, that was cancelled when war seemed likely. The Royal Newfoundland Regiment of Fencible Infantry was formed in 1803 as one of several "fencible" units — serving only within a designated geographic region, in this case British North America — raised between 1802 and 1812 to augment the few regulars in Canada. Their pay, clothing, arms, and discipline put them on par with line regiments, making the fencibles the most capable of the units raised in Canada.

In 1812 the militia of Upper Canada included all men between 16 and 60 organized in sedentary and volunteer units that received almost no training or equipment, which meant they were incapable of fighting with line units in open battle. A revision to the militia act put forward by Brock in February 1812 changed their terms of service and offered better training to a portion of each sedentary unit. These "flank companies," so-called because they took their position on the flanks of the battalion, became the best-trained and most efficient element of the militia, giving Brock a core of dependable troops that could support the regulars. Each company had 35–50 men and could be called up for a maximum of eight months. Most of the militia that were at Detroit were from these flank companies, while others were from sedentary units.[99]

On 15 August, Hull ordered Colonel McArthur to make a third attempt at opening the lines of communications. Assisted by Colonel Lewis Cass, McArthur left with 400 of the best Ohio men to meet a supply column on the upper Huron River. Had Hull known that Brock had arrived at Amherstburg, he may not have detached so many men from Detroit, although Brock received no intelligence that the Americans had dispatched a party from Detroit.[100]

Brock issued instructions for the movement into American territory the next day on 15 August. His force would march north from Amherstburg to a crossing site south of Sandwich, where the troops would be loaded into boats and land between the River Rouge and

Spring Wells, south of Detroit. Colonel Matthew Elliot of the Indian Department was to lead the Natives to the eastern shore of the River Rouge and place the them in a position to take the enemy in the flank and rear. While waiting at the embarkation site, the men would get whatever rest they could in the houses. The commissariat was instructed "to supply the troops employed on the opposite shore with provisions and every article required," including one gill of spirits per day. Brock hoped to cross with 2,000 men. Lieutenant Edward Dewar of the Quartermaster General's Department was given responsibility for organizing the British landing.[101]

On 15 August, Brock's army marched to Sandwich, from where the British general decided to test Hull and sent an aide to deliver an ultimatum demanding his surrender. Brock was playing upon fears he knew the Americans held of Native reprisals, warning as much in his letter: "It is far from my intention to join in a war of extermination," he wrote, "but you must be aware of that the numerous body of Indians who have attached themselves to my troops, will be beyond control the moment the contest commences."[102]

Hull's reply came five hours later: "I have no reply to make, than to inform you that I am prepared to meet any force which may be at your disposal."[103] Brock then ordered Commander George Hall of the Provincial Marine, commanding the Sandwich batteries, to open fire upon Fort Detroit. Guns from the *Queen Charlotte* and *General Hunter* joined in and the bombardment lasted until nightfall. Guns at Detroit returned fire, but neither side inflicted much damage on the other.

That night on Bois Blanc Island, the Native warriors prepared themselves for battle. They painted their tattooed bodies in vermillion, blue, black, and white, and covered their faces in charcoal. Drums beat as they performed a war dance that continued into the morning. This was designed to prepare them psychologically for the upcoming battle, which was described by one European observer as "horrifying beyond expression."[104]

During the night of 15–16 August, Brock assembled 1,460 men for the attack, made up of regulars, militia, provincial marine, the Sandwich gun detachment, commissariat, and garrison of Fort Amherstburg. Before sunrise on 16 August, the Natives commenced crossing from McKee's Point to Spring Wells, and once they secured the area, Brock's 700 regulars and militia crossed the river, covered by the guns from the shore battery at Sandwich and the *Queen Charlotte* and the *General Hunter*. To make the number of regular troops appear larger to the Americans, Brock had the militia decked out in red coats and instructed them to move with double intervals between the men. With 600 warriors, Brock had 2,000 men, a number he had hoped to achieve.[105]

The Natives moved off at once, protecting the flanks, while Brock led the main body towards the fort, about three miles away. Brock's expectation that the bombardment would force the Americans onto the field had not yielded the desired result. An assault of Fort Detroit was out of the question, as none of the troops carried scaling ladders, essential for getting up the walls and into the fort, which was still very well armed. Brock then received intelligence of Colonel McArthur's departure three days earlier with a detachment estimated at 500 men. Other reports indicated that American cavalry was some three miles to the British rear. Thus, without any real plan, a relatively small force, five guns, and no scaling ladders, Brock "decided on an immediate attack," hoping the presence of Tecumseh's Natives would make the jittery Hull avoid bloodshed and surrender. While Brock may have known his enemy, he was taking a huge risk.[106]

Meanwhile, the British artillery continued their bombardment and soon found the correct range. The five pieces rained rounds down upon the fort. Outside, one man was killed, while another round ricocheted inside, killing an ensign and a soldier. An 18-pdr round deflected into the officers' mess, killing Dr. James Reynolds. The round continued to bounce and found yet another target — Lieutenant Porter Hanks, the former commander of Fort Mackinac, who was taking recess from the court marital investigating his surrender. The round killed Hanks instantly. Its energy not yet dissipated, the round continued on, finding one more victim, Dr. Hosea Blood.[107]

As the British approached the fort, they came within range of two 24-pdr guns with fuses burning, ready to fire. These guns could hurl a spherical ball weighing 24 pounds to an effective range of 1,200 yards, bowling down everything in its way. About a mile from the fort, Brock's men moved from column into line, seeking the cover of an orchard behind a low ridge, while the Natives were sent forward to penetrate the American camp. Then, just as it appeared the American guns were going to open up, Captain Samuel Dyson, the senior artillery officer at the fort, rode up with sword drawn swearing "that the first man who would attempt to fire on the enemy, should be cut to pieces." On Hull's orders, Dyson also instructed the river batteries silenced, while another officer was sent under a white flag to Sandwich, authorized to discuss terms of surrender.[108]

This was an astonishing development. During Brock's approach, Hull had mulled over the options and succumbed to his fears. Fort Detroit's defences were intact, with 26 artillery pieces, considerable ammunition with 1,000 men in the immediate area. There was enough food for a week. Although there were a large number of warriors present, they would be of little use in a deliberate assault, thus leaving Hull with the advantage. But things were not well in the fort. At 0900 hours that day, Captain Abraham Hull, the general's son and aide, was involved in an altercation with a group of Ohio miltiamen, where he chased them to their posts at sword-point.

Lieutenant-Colonel Findlay, the commanding officer of the men, demanded that Captain Hull be placed under arrest, at which point the younger Hull challenged Findlay to a duel. Distressed over this news, concerned over how the Natives would treat the non-combatants, General Hull then received more bad news, namely the effect of the British artillery fire, of desertions among the Michigan militiamen, and of the surrender of two companies. A greater man may have tried to rally his men and lead them against the attacker, but William Hull was not that kind of man. One witness observed the general's "lips quivering, the tobacco juice running from both sides of his mouth upon the frills of his shirt." With two of his senior officers away on a sortie and the next most capable officer, Lieutenant-Colonel Miller, bedridden, Hull decided enough was enough. About twenty minutes later, at 1000 hours, on 16 August, Hull ordered the white flag hoisted and sent an aide to seek terms from Brock.[109]

At Sandwich, Hull's envoy discovered that Brock was on the American shore, so he crossed the river and found Lieutenant-Colonel John Macdonnell of the York Militia and Captain John Glegg of the 49th Foot, aides of the British general, who were authorized to negotiate on his behalf. The three men then moved into the fort to discuss the terms of capitulation. The artillery fire had by this time stopped and everyone awaited the results.

An hour later when the terms were presented to Brock, he was pleased to read that they included not only the surrender of Detroit, but the detachments under McArthur and Cass, another at Frenchtown and the garrison of a blockhouse at Maumee Rapids and all of Michigan. Brock struck out a provision allowing the Americans to march out with the honours of war and thus, Fort Detroit came under British control once again. A 40-man guard of honour was quickly assembled, and, accompanied by elements of the 41st and militia, marched into Fort Detroit to the tune of "The British Grenadiers." There was also a scramble to find an ensign to fly over the fort, until a sailor produced one that had been tied to his waist. Legend has it that Brock rode into the fort with Tecumseh riding beside him, wearing a sash given to him by the general. Brock moved inside the fort and was challenged by Abraham Hull, who had awoken from a drunken slumber. Another American officer quickly removed the young captain.[110]

Brock issued a proclamation guaranteeing the inhabitants of Michigan freedom of religion and protection of person and property, while all public property was to be surrendered. Returns showed 1,606 Ohio militia and 582 regulars surrendered, although this figure included those captured at Mackinac and Cayuga.[111]

Hull and the regulars became prisoners of war, while the militia was paroled and allowed to go home. A total of 35 artillery pieces, 2,500 muskets, thousands of rounds, powder, flints, and considerable military stores were seized, most of which was transferred to Fort Erie by ship. Wagons, powder, ordnance stores, and a variety of other equipment were also received, as was the brig *Adams*, and the commercial schooners *Salina* and *Mary* joined the Provincial Marine, the *Adams* being renamed *Detroit*. The colours of the 4th Infantry were also surrendered, becoming the first ones taken by the British in the war.[112] Brock valued the public property at between £30,000 and £40,000. The prize money[113] alone meant that a private soldier would receive £3, the equivalent of a year's pay![114] There was even better news for those who had been at Mackinac, as each private received £10![115]

Brock did not stay to enjoy his victory and the next day, on 17 August, boarded a vessel at Amherstburg for Niagara. Brock's bloodless victory was met with much approbation and he was praised throughout British North America.[116] Aside from written praise from Prevost and others, Brock was soon awarded the Army Large Officer's Medal, an award intended for general officers and the only such award presented for the War of 1812, however, he did not live long enough to receive it.

The medal was suspended by a crimson ribbon with blue edges and on the obverse was a figure of Britannia, while the reverse was engraved with the name of the respective action surrounded by a laurel wreath. Ten other officers received the Army Small Gold Medal, normally for officers of field rank.[117] As for everyone else, no medal acknowledging their efforts was available until 1848, when the Military General Service Medal was instituted. Those surviving veterans, British, Canadian, and Native, could apply for the medal with the bar "Fort Detroit."[118]

Detroit became one of only five engagements that the Horse Guards in London would award a battle honour for, granting it in 1816.[119] It was borne by only one regiment, the 41st Foot, which today is the Royal Regiment of Wales. No Canadian unit has ever had this or any other War of 1812 battle honour on its colours.[120] A banner was made by the women of the provincial capital and presented to the 3rd York Militia by Sir Roger Hale Sheaffe, Brock's successor, at a large ceremony on 23 March 1813.[121]

In contrast to Brock, Hull suffered public disapprobation. Accusations were mounted almost immediately that he had surrendered to an inferior force. Hull responded by pointing out that while he seemed to hold the advantage in numbers, 1,182 of his men were non-effective — including McArthur's detachment, paroled soldiers, convalescents, wagoneers, marines, and artificers — leaving him with only 976 men. Hull estimated he could only bring 600 of these onto the field. Hull appears to have discounted, including 600 Michigan militiamen recently taken under arms into these figures, but his point was probably valid, particularly given the quality of his troops.[122] Hull did have overwhelming advantage in artillery, although he appears to have not laid much hope in successfully defeating a siege. Finally, given their recent experience, Hull's fears about the horrors of Native reprisals were probably valid. Hull was not only a military commander, but also the Governor of the Michigan Territory, which caused him to also consider the safety of its inhabitants and to act upon wider political concerns.

In the spring of 1814, Hull was court-martialled on charges of treason, cowardice, neglect of duty, and bad conduct, and found guilty of the latter two charges. He was sentenced to be shot, which was suspended by President Madison, in acknowledgement of Hull's valiant service during the War of Independence. Hull spent the rest of his life trying to clear his name, while his son Abraham was killed at Lundy's Lane in July 1814.[123]

The defeat of the Northwest Army was more complete than either commander realized. The fall of Mackinac brought the immediate evacuation of other posts, such as Fort Dearborn, and the surrender of Detroit left the Western District of Upper Canada secure. Hull's capitulation detached the Michigan Territory from the United States and it came under British rule, giving hope to some quarters that Michigan and the lands north of the Ohio River, previously surrendered by the Natives to the Americans in 1795, might be regained and form a Native state, serving as a buffer between the United States and British North America. This was never to pass. Unwittingly, while British operations around Detroit sought to end the war, Brock's victory may have had the opposite effect. Determined to regain Michigan and establish a presence on the upper lakes — an idea proposed by General Hull that was rejected — the American president soon earmarked considerable financial and military resources to achieve just that. In fourteen months, the fruits of Brock's victories would be destroyed, the dream of a Native homeland in the northwest gone, while Tecumseh lay dead, killed in battle. Nonetheless, Brock's initiative, boldness and leadership, aided by similarly motivated subordinates, such as Roberts and Proctor, and his strong bond with Tecumseh, rebuilt the Native alliance and achieved an important victory. Brock, his soldiers and the Natives had isolated, worn down, and psychologically defeated their opponents, completely altering the military situation and securing the independence of British North America.

NOTES

1. "Pdr" is a contraction of "pounder," indicating the weight of a solid spherical shot a gun could fire. In this case, a 9-pdr round weighed nine pounds. For specific technical data, see Major-General B.P. Hughes, *British Smooth Bore Artillery* (Harrisburg: Stackpole Books, 1969).
2. Robert Malcomson, *Burying General Brock: A History of Brock's Monuments* (The Friends of Fort George, 1996), 3–8; Lieutenant-General Winfield Scott, *Memoirs of Lieutenant-General Scott, Written by Himself* (New York: Sheldon and Company, Publishers, 1864), 76.
3. Letter, Sir George Prevost to Earl Bathurst, 26 August 1812. E.A. Cruikshank, *Documents Relating to the Invasion of Canada and the Surrender of Detroit, 1812* (Ottawa: Government Printing Bureau, 1912), 184. Cited hereafter as Cruikshank, *Invasion of Canada.*

4.	Although often referred to "Michilimackinac," the modern usage of Mackinac will be used throughout this chapter to differentiate it from the fort at Michilimackinac in northern Michigan.

5.	Robert S. Quimby, *The U.S. Army in the War of 1812: An Operational and Command Study, Volume 1* (East Lansing: Michigan State University Press, 1997), 2–4. Cited hereafter as Quimby, *U.S. Army War of 1812.*

6.	Quimby, *U.S. Army War of 1812,* 18.

7.	Gerald S. Graham, *Sea Power and British North America, 1783–1820* (London: Cambridge-Harvard University Press, 1941), 93.

8.	*Ibid.,* 200

9.	Letter Sir George Prevost to Lord Liverpool, 18 May 1812. Royal Military College of Canada Special Collections CO 42/146, 197–202.

10.	*Dictionary of Canadian Biography, Volume V, 1801–1820,* s.v. "Isaac Brock"; Robert Malcomson, *A Very Brilliant Affair: The Battle of Queenston Heights, 1812* (Toronto: Robin Brass Studio, 2003), 32–36.

11.	J. Mackay Hitsman (Updated by Donald E. Graves). *The Incredible War of 1812* (Toronto: Robin Brass Studio, 1999), 8, 14 (cited hereafter as Hitsman, *Incredible War*).

12.	Memorandum to be Submitted to His Excellency, the Gov.-in-Chief, by Desire of Major-General Brock, December 1811. E.A. Cruikshank, ed., *Documentary History of the Campaign Upon the Niagara Frontier, 1812 to 1814, Vol. III* (Welland, n.p., n.d.), 28–29; Hitsman, *Incredible War*, p. 41.

13.	Quimby, *U.S. Army War of 1812,* 18.

14.	*Ibid.,* 19.

15.	*Ibid.,* 18.

16.	Donald E. Graves and Rene Chartrand, *The United States Army in the War of 1812: A Handbook* (unpublished manuscript in author's possession), 55, 56 (cited hereafter Graves and Chartrand, *Handbook United States Army)*; Quimby, *U.S. Army War of 1812,* 21. Cruickshank, *Invasion of Canada,* 1n1.

17.	Quimby, *U.S. Army War of 1812,* 21.

18.	Graves and Chartrand, *Handbook United States Army,* Chart II-12.

19.	*Ibid.,* 197. Sandy Antal, *A Wampun Denied: Proctor's War of 1812* (Ottawa: Carleton University Press, 1997), 52n5. Cited hereafter as Antal, *Proctor's War.*

20.	Quimby, *U.S. Army War of 1812,* 22.

21.	Antal, *Proctor's War,* 54n5. Quimby, *U.S. Army War of 1812,* 26–28.

22.	The French first visited the site in 1610 and again in 1701 when Detroit was founded. It was ceded to the British in 1763 and given to the Americans by the treaty of 1783, although not surrendered until 1796.

23.	Extract from E.A. Cruikshank, ed., *Documentary History of the Campaign Upon the Niagara Frontier, 1812 to 1814, Vol. III* (Welland, n.p., n.d.), 39; Quimby, *U.S. Army War of 1812,* 30.

24.	Quimby, *U.S. Army War of 1812,* 31.

25.	Letter Sir George Prevost to Lord Liverpool, 18 May 1812 Royal Military College of Canada Special Collections, CO 42/146.

26. Stuart Sutherland, *His Majesty's Gentlemen: A Directory of British Regular Army Officers in the War of 1812* (Toronto: ISER Publications, 2001), 323. Cited hereafter as Sutherland, *His Majesty's Gentlemen.*

27. Letter Sir Prevost to Lord Liverpool, 18 May 1812. Royal Military College of Canada Special Collections CO 42/146.

28. Robert Malcomson, *Warships of the Great Lakes, 1754–1834* (Annapolis: U.S. Naval Institute Press, 2001), 85 (cited hereafter as Malcomson, *Warships of the Great Lakes*); Quimby, *U.S. Army War of 1812,* p. 31.

29. Letter Colonel Matthew Elliot to Major-General Brock, 11 January 1812. Cruikshank, *Invasion of Canada*, 4–6.

30. Memoranda of General Brock on Plans for Defence of Canada, no date, in Cruikshank, *Invasion of Canada*, 12–14.

31. Secretary of War to Brigadier-General Hull, 24 June 1812, Cruikshank, *Invasion of Canada*, 37.

32. Quimby, *U.S. Army War of 1812,* 32.

33. *Ibid.*, 32.

34. Quimby, *U.S. Army War of 1812,* 33–34; D.A.N. Lomax, *A History of the Services of the 41st (the Welch) Regiment (now 1st Battalion The Welch Regiment) from its Formation in 1719 to 1895* (Devonport: Hiorns & Miller, 1899), 90; Antal, *Proctor's War*, 47.

35. *Ibid.*, p. 37.

36. Brian Leigh Dunnigan, *The Eagle at Mackinac: The Establishment of United States Military and Civilian Authority on Mackinac Island, 1796–1802* (Mackinac Island State Parks, 1991), 5.

37. *Ibid.*, 7–8.

38. Brian Leigh Dunnigan, *King's Men at Mackinac: The British Garrisons, 1780–1796* (Mackinac Island State Park Commission, 1984), 13; John Abbott, Graeme S. Mount, Michael J. Mulloy, *The History of Fort St. Joseph* (Toronto: Dundurn, 2000), 45, 47.

39. Elizabeth Vincent, *Fort St. Joseph: A History.* Manuscript Report Series Number 355 (Ottawa: Parks Canada, 1978), 150. Cited hereafter as Vincent, *Fort St. Joseph.*

40. Stuart Sutherland, *His Majesty's Gentlemen* 315; *Dictionary of Canadian Biography, Volume V, 1801–1820,* s.v. "Charles Roberts," (by Glenn A. Steppler).

41. Adjutant General's Office, *Regulations and Orders for the Army, 12th August 1811* (London: Horse Guards, 1816), 223, 307.

42. L. Homfray Irving, *Officers of the British Forces in Canada during the War of 1812–15* (Toronto: Canadian Military Institute, 1908), 235; Brian Leigh Dunnigan, *British Army at Mackinac* (Mackinac City, MI: Mackinac Island State Park Commission, 1992), 10 (cited hereafter as Dunnigan, *British Army at Mackinac);* Sutherland, *His Majesty's Gentlemen,* 221.

43. Letter Captain Charles Roberts to Captain John Glegg, 29 July 1812. National

Library and Archives Canada, RG 8 C 688A.

44. Sir Edward Baynes to Charles Roberts, 25 June 1812. William Wood, *Select British Documents of the War of 1812* (Toronto: The Champlain Society, 1920–1928, Volume 1), 428.

45. Sir Edward Baynes to Charles Roberts, 25 June 1812. Cruikshank, *Invasion of Canada*, 37–38.

46. Charles Gray to Sir George Prevost, 13 January 1812. Cruikshank, *Invasion of Canada*, 9–10.

47. Memoranda on the Defensive Strength and Equipment of the North West Company, 13 January 1812. Cruikshank, *Invasion of Canada*, 11–12.

48. Hitsman, *Incredible* War, 73.

49. Dunnigan, *British Army at Mackinac,* 11.

50. *Ibid.*, 11; *Dictionary of Canadian Biography, Volume VI, 1821–1830*, s.v. "Robert Dickson," (by Robert S. Allen).

51. "Confidential Communication Transmitted by Mr Robert Dickson," 18 June 1812, in William Wood, *Select British Documents of the War of 1812* (Toronto: The Champlain Society, 1920–1928, Volume 1), 425. The correspondence includes similar statements by two of the other chiefs present.

52. *Ibid.*, p. 52.

53. Letter Charles Roberts to Major-General Brock. Cruikshank, *Invasion of Canada*, 53.

54. Major-General B.P. Hughes, *British Smooth Bore Artillery* (Harrisburg: Stackpole Books, 1969), Table 10, 76.

55. Vincent, *Fort St. Joseph,* 97, 101.

56. "Capitulation, Mackinac," 17 July 1812, *Niles Weekly Register*, Vol. II, No. 51, 22 August 1812 (Baltimore: Franklin Press, 1812), 425.

57. Francis B. Heitman, *Historical Register and Dictionary of the United States Army from its Organization, Volume I* (Washington: Government Printing Office, 1903), 497; Robert Malcomson, *Historical Dictionary of the War of 1812* (Lanham, MD: Scarecrow Press, 2006), 234.

58. Some sources say 59 men.

59. Vincent, *Fort St. Joseph,* 180.

60. Keith R. Widder, *Reveille Till Taps: Soldier Life at Fort Mackinac, 1780–1895* (Mackinac Island: Mackinac Island State Parks, 1994), 28–30.

61. Vincent, *Fort St. Joseph,* 177.

62. *Ibid.*, p. 181.

63. Brian Leigh Dunnigan, *Fort Holmes* (Mackinac Island: Mackinac State Island Park Commission, 1984), 5.

64. *Ibid.*, p. 6.

65. Vincent, *Fort St. Joseph,* 182.

66. Dunnigan, *British Army at Mackinac,* 11.

67. Letter Charles Roberts to Sir Edward Baynes, 17 July 1812. Cruikshank, *Invasion of Canada*, 65.

68.   Letter Charles Roberts to Major-General Brock, 17 July 1812. Cruickshank, *Invasion of Canada*, 66.

69.   David McConnell, *British Smooth Bore Artillery: A Technological Study* (Ottawa, Parks Canada, 1988), 88.

70.   *Ibid.*, 165.

71.   Vincent, *Fort St. Joseph*, 181.

72.   Until 1870, it was believed the gun had been placed on the Turtle's Back, which was dispelled by J.A. Van Fleet after interviewing elderly residents of the island who had been present in 1812. See Dunnigan, *British Army at Mackinac*, 12.

73.   Vincent, *Fort St. Joseph*, 180.

74.   Letter Matthew Irwin to John Mason, 16 October 1812, ed. Clarence Edwin Carter, *The Territorial Papers of the United States, Volume X: The Territory of Michigan, 1805–1820* (Washington, DC: U.S. Government Printing Office, 1942), 413.

75.   Quimby, *U.S. Army War of 1812*, 37.

76.   "Capitulation, Mackinac," 17 July 1812, *Niles Weekly Register*, Vol. II, No. 51, 22 August 1812 (Baltimore: Franklin Press, 1812), 425.

77.   Dunnigan, *British Army at Mackinac*, 12.

78.   "Capitulation, Mackinac," 17 July 1812, *Niles Weekly Register*, Vol. II, No. 51, 22 August 1812 (Baltimore: Franklin Press, 1812), 425.

79.   The men were Hugh Kelly, 49th Foot, Alexander Parks of the Royal Artillery, and Redmond Magrath of the 5th Foot. Magrath had deserted the British Army, only to join the U.S. Army, where he served as a fifer. At his court martial he was sentenced to 50 lashes. Kelly was sent to York for trial in September 1812, while Parks and Magrath remanded at Fort Mackinac for most of the war, until they were discharged, old and tired, in 1815. See Dunnigan, *British Army at Mackinac*, 13.

80.   Dunnigan, *British Army at Mackinac*, 13.

81.   Matthew Irwin to John Mason, 16 October 1812, ed. Clarence Edwin Carter, *The Territorial Papers of the United States, Volume X: The Territory of Michigan, 1805–1820* (Washington, DC: U.S. Government Printing Office, 1942), 413.

82.   Matthew Irwin to John Mason, 16 October 1812, ed. Clarence Edwin Carter, *The Territorial Papers of the United States, Volume X: The Territory of Michigan, 1805–1820* (Washington, DC: U.S. Government Printing Office, 1942), 414; Malcomson, *Warships of the Great Lakes*, 86.

83.   Letter Major-General Brock to Sir George Prevost, 20 July 1812. Cruikshank, *Invasion of Canada*, 73.

84.   Letter Major-General Brock to Sir George Prevost, 26 July 1812. Cruikshank, *Invasion of Canada*, 91–92.

85.   Major-General Brock to Sir George Prevost, 28 July 1812. Cruikshank, *Invasion of Canada*, 99–100.

86.   Major-General Brock to Sir Edward Baynes, 29 July 1812. Cruikshank, *Invasion of Canada*, 107.

87.   Hitsman, *Incredible* War, 78.

88.   Quimby, *U.S. Army War of* 1812, 38.

89. *Ibid.*, 38–39.

90. Antal, *Proctor's* War, 35–37; Quimby, *U.S. Army War of 1812*, 28; Letter General Hull to Lieutenant-Colonel St. George, 16 July 1812, Cruikshank, *Invasion of Canada*, 69.

91. Quimby, *U.S. Army War of 1812*, 39; Antal, *Proctor's War*, 79, 80.

92. Hitsman, *Incredible* War, 78.

93. Quimby, *U.S. Army War of 1812*, 43.

94. Antal, *Proctor's War*, 92, 93.

95. *Dictionary of Canadian Biography, Volume V, 1801–1820*, s.v. "Tecumseh," (by Herbert C.W. Goltz).

96. *Ibid.*, 92–93.

97. *Ibid.*, 93.

98. Compiled from "District General Orders, Fort Amherstburg, August 14th, 1812," and General Order, 16 August 1812, in Cruickshank, *Invasion of Canada,* 142, 148.

99. Charles H. Stewart. *The Service of British Regiments in Canada* (Ottawa: Department of National Defence Library, 1964), 199; Colonel G.W.L. Nicholson, *The Fighting Newfoundlander: A History of the Royal Newfoundland Regiment* (Government of Newfoundland, 1963), 60; William Gray, *Soldiers of the King: The Upper Canadian Militia, 1812–1815* (Erin, Ont.: Boston Mills Press, 1995), 85–86; Antal, *Proctor's War*, 92.

100. Antal, *Proctor's War,* 94.

101. District General Orders, 15 August 1812. Cruikshank, *Invasion of Canada,* 145–146; Antal, *Proctor's War*, 94.

102. *Ibid.*, 94.

103. *Ibid.*, 94.

104. *Ibid.*, 94.

105. *Ibid.*, 94.

106. Major-General Brock to Sir George Prevost, 17 August 1812. Cruikshank, *Invasion of Canada*, 158; Antal, *Proctor's War*, 94.

107. Antal, *Proctor's War*, 96.

108. Major-General Brock to Sir George Prevost, 17 August 1812. Cruikshank, *Invasion of Canada*, 158.

109. Antal, *Proctor's War*, 97; Quimby, *U.S. Army War of 1812*, 44–45.

110. Antal, *Proctor's War*, 98.

111. "General Return of Prisoners of War Surrendered by Capitulation at Fort Detroit, Aug 16, 1812," Cruikshank, *Invasion of Canada*, 153.

112. These colours were originally displayed at the Royal Hospital Chelsea and in 1961 were presented to the Welch Regiment (now the Royal Regiment of Wales) and are on display in their museum in Cardiff Castle, Wales. See Robert Malcomson, "War of 1812 Flags at the Royal Hospital Chelsea," *Military Collector and Historian*, Vol. 58, No. 2 (Summer 2006): 58–60.

113. Prize money was awarded by "shares," with a private having one share, a corporal

one and a half, a staff sergeant three, and a general officer 80. For Detroit, Native warriors were rated as privates, whereas a chief received a subaltern's prize of eight shares. See "General Order, Quebec, 30 December 1813," in L. Homfray Irving, *Officers of the British Forces in Canada During the War of 1812* (1908), 257.

114. Antal, *Proctor's War*, 99.

115. L. Homfray Irving, "Officers of the British Forces in Canada During the War of 1812" (1908), 257.

116. D.B. Read, *Life and Times of Sir Isaac Brock* (Toronto: William Briggs, 1894), 187–190.

117. E.C. Joslin, A.R. Litherland, B.T. Simpkin, *British Battles and Medals* (London: Spink, 1988), 67.

118. *Ibid.*, 76.

119. Alexander Rodger, *Battle Honours of the British Empire and Commonwealth Land Forces, 1662–1991* (Ramsbury, UK: The Crowood Press, 2003), 34.

120. The 41st Foot was present at four of the five engagements that resulted in battle honours, including Detroit, Queenston Heights, Miami, and Niagara. The one it did not receive was for Baldensburg in 1814. These were awarded between 1815 and 1826.

121. D.B. Read, *Life and Times of Sir Isaac Brock* (Toronto: William Briggs, 1894), 191–192; Francis J. Dunbar and Joseph H. Harper, *Old Colours Never Die* (Ottawa, 1992), 34.

122. Antal, *Proctor's War*, 99.

123. Graves and Chartrand, *Handbook U.S. Army*, 66–67.

CHAPTER 5

The Lake Erie Expeditions:
Confederate Naval Commandos on the Great Lakes,
1863–1864

JOHN BELL

Despite its relatively small size and limited resources, the Confederate States Navy (CSN) made a significant contribution to the overall Confederate war effort during the American Civil War.[1] Much of the success of the South's naval strategy can be attributed to the farsightedness of Stephen R. Mallory, the Confederate secretary of the navy, who recognized the importance of confronting the formidable Union Navy, which had imposed a blockade on Confederate ports, with "technical surprise."[2] Mallory's commitment to technological innovation encouraged the development of not only ironclads and commerce raiders, but also revolutionary forms of submarine warfare.[3]

The Confederate Navy's willingness to innovate in its struggle against a vastly superior enemy was not restricted to technological developments. It also extended to other tactical and strategic initiatives. Starting in 1862, Mallory, who was, of course, aware of the success of Confederate cavalry raiders and partisans in various theatres of the war, became increasingly supportive of the idea of applying asymmetric guerilla tactics to naval warfare, creating amphibious commando forces that could seriously harass Union shipping and the blockading fleets — and perhaps even seize enemy warships.[4] Not surprisingly, the commanders of these new forces were drawn from among the navy's younger officers, men who were eager to see action and win promotion through meritorious conduct in combat. John Taylor Wood, who went on to become probably the most prominent Confederate naval commando leader (he was sometimes referred to as the "Horse Marine"), spoke for this younger generation when he wrote: "promote for fighting; otherwise the Navy never can be kicked into vitality."[5]

Although there were aggressive young officers chomping at the bit scattered throughout the various CSN squadrons, Wood and many of the other early commando leaders were drawn from the James River Squadron, which was charged with defending the Confederate capital of Richmond, or from the naval headquarters, which was located in the capital.[6] Following the North's Peninsula Campaign during the spring and early summer of 1862 (which saw the South turn back a much larger Union force under Major-General George B. McClellan), service on the upper James became rather routine, prompting many officers in the "Capital Navy" to seek alternative duties.

LIEUTENANT MURDAUGH'S PLAN

Among the restless young men in the James River Squadron during this period was Lieutenant William H. Murdaugh, then serving on the gunboat Confederate States Ship (CSS) *Beaufort*. A converted tugboat that had served earlier in the year as a tender to the ironclad CSS *Virginia* during her historic encounter with the United States Ship (USS) *Monitor* in Hampton Roads, the *Beaufort* was not a particularly desirable assignment for an ambitious young naval officer hungry for action.[7] Rather than simply await a new assignment, Murdaugh took the initiative and tried to create an opportunity for more challenging service.

On 7 February 1863, following consultations with fellow CSN Lieutenants Robert R. Carter and Robert D. Minor, Murdaugh wrote to the secretary of the navy, proposing a bold plan for a commando raid on the Great Lakes to be launched from British North America:

C.S.S. *Beaufort*,
Richmond, February 7, 1863

Sir: I have the honor to submit the following plan of operations proposed to be carried out on the Northern Lakes:

The party to leave the Confederacy at the earliest possible day, to be ready for commencing operations with the opening of navigation, which will be probably about the middle of April.

The commanding officer to be issued with a letter of credit for $100,000, although it is not presumed that more than half this amount will be expended.

After reaching Canada to purchase, through the agency of some reliable merchant, a small steamer, say one of 200 tons, that can pass through the Welland Canal. If practicable, to let the agent equip and victual the vessel and collect a crew of 50 men, ostensibly with a view to mining operations on Lake Superior. If this is not practicable the officers will separate and each collect a party and join the vessel at some point on Lake Erie. The object of the expedition not be made known to the men until the vessel is clear of the Canadian coast, when strong inducements in the way of pay, etc., must be held out to them for making the attempt and still stronger ones for its successful accomplishment. Those not willing to make the attempt to be returned to the Canadian shore; those who are willing to be shipped into the Confederate service. In collecting men much judgment must be exercised in the selections. The crew will be armed with cutlasses and revolvers. The vessel will be provided with a number of small buoys to be used as torpedoes and also the powder, fuses, etc., to charge and fire them. These are to be used in the destruction of canal locks. She must also have on board plenty of spirits of turpentine and incendiary composition for rapid work in starting fires.

The first point to be aimed at is Erie, Pa., the arrival there to be so timed as to make it about 1 a.m. The steamer to be laid alongside the U.S.S. *Michigan* and that vessel to be carried by boarding with as little noise as possible. If there is a reasonable hope that the vessel has been carried without its being known beyond the vessels engaged, both vessels will leave the harbor and proceed towards the Welland Canal, with a view to getting the small steamer through into Lake Ontario before the news of the capture should have reached the Canadians, who might interpose objections to her doing so should the objects of her voyage be apparent. But if the capture is not made secretly, then the work of burning every particle of Federal property afloat will be immediately commenced. Even in this latter contingency the attempt will still be made to get the small steamer into Lake Ontario, when she, under the command of the second officer of the expedition, would have a fine field, but the most important part of her work would be to destroy the aqueduct of the Erie Canal, which crosses the Genesee River at Rochester, 7 miles from the lake, and the locks of a branch of the canal at Oswego. If a passage through the Welland Canal for the small steamer should be refused by the Canadians, both vessels would operate in Lakes Erie, Huron, and Michigan. In Lake Erie, after leaving the town of Erie, Buffalo would be the first point to be visited, the fleet of trading vessels in its harbour and the locks of the great Erie Canal to be destroyed. The next place would be Tonawanda, distant about 30 miles from Buffalo, where there is also an entrance to the Erie Canal, which would be destroyed. Then, coasting along the southern shore of the lake, destroy the locks of the canals leading to the Ohio River, four in number, and burn the vessels fallen in with. Then pass Detroit in the night, and if possible without notice; pass through Lake Huron and into Lake Michigan, and make for the great city of Chicago. At Chicago burn the shipping and destroy the locks of the Illinois and Michigan Canal, connecting Lake Michigan and the Mississippi River. Then turn northward, and, touching at Milwaukee and other places, but working rapidly, pass again into Lake Huron, go to the Sault Ste. Marie, and destroy the lock of the canal of that name. Then the vessel would be run into Georgian Bay, at the bottom of which is a railway connecting with the main Canadian lines, and be run ashore and destroyed.

Four officers will be required for this expedition. I respectfully volunteer my services and ask that Lieutenants Minor, Robert Carter, and Wood may be selected.

Very respectfully, etc.,

Wm. H. Murdaugh,

Lieutenant, C.S. Navy[8]

Secretary Mallory, who, by this time had already authorized successful naval commando operations in the fall of 1862 under the leadership of John Taylor Wood (whom Murdaugh hoped would be free to participate in the Great Lakes operation), was enthusiastic about Murdaugh's plan, strongly recommending it to President Jefferson Davis and the Confederate Cabinet. With Mallory's backing, the operation was eventually approved (although Wood's participation was ruled out, as he was by this time serving as an aide to his uncle, President Davis), and $100,000 was earmarked for the expedition.[9]

However, as Murdaugh, Carter, Minor, and Lieutenant Walter R. Butt (Wood's replacement), prepared for their clandestine operation in Canada, Davis and his cabinet began to have second thoughts. According to Murdaugh, the Confederate leadership grew concerned about the expedition's potential impact on the Confederacy's crucial relations with Great Britain. "When everything was ready for a start," Murdaugh later recounted, "President Davis said that he thought the scheme practicable and almost sure of success, but that it would raise such a storm about the violation of the neutrality laws that England would be forced to stop the building of some ironclads which were on the stocks in England and take rigid action against us everywhere. So the thing fell through and with it my great chance."[10]

Robert Minor shared his friend's disappointment. Reflecting on the aftermath of the plan's collapse, Minor wrote, "With the expedition thus broken up, Murdaugh disheartened, sought other duty, and he, Carter, and Butt were ordered abroad, leaving me here on my regular ordnance duty, as the only representative of a scheme whose prospects were so inviting and so brilliant."[11] However, as it turned out, Minor's involvement with the plan was not over. The summer of 1863 saw such momentous changes in the Confederacy's fortunes (most notably the defeat at Gettysburg and the fall of Vicksburg) that by the autumn of that year a Confederate raid on the Great Lakes took on not only a new viability, but perhaps even an urgency. Lieutenant Murdaugh's plan would be resurrected and revised to reflect new realities.

The chief reason for the survival of the plan was its basic soundness. Anyone contemplating a map of North America in 1863 from the point of view of naval defences could not help but be struck by the fact that the Great Lakes were a region of profound vulnerability for the Northern States. Under the provisions of the Ashburton Treaty, America's inland seas were protected by a single warship of fourteen guns based in Lake Erie: USS *Michigan* (686 tons displacement), the U.S. Navy's first iron-hulled ship.[12] Seize this Union Navy vessel, and the South could wreak havoc in some of the North's most important cities and industrial centres. Moreover, there was a very inviting target sitting three miles offshore in Sandusky Bay, Ohio: the prisoner-of-war camp on Johnson's Island (the southernmost of the Lake Erie islands), which was now swelling with more than 1,500 prisoners (mostly officers), following the defeat at Gettysburg and the collapse of the Confederacy on the Mississippi.[13]

However, for the plan to work, the Confederates would confront serious logistical challenges, launching their operations from British North America, where they ran the risk of precipitating a serious diplomatic incident and where they were obliged to rely on the assistance of sometimes untested Confederate expatriates and agents, as well as local sympathizers, while at the same time confronting a new class of opponents, comprising detectives, secret agents, con artists, and opportunists. Naval personnel, accustomed to service on blue water and brown water, would now have to function in the even murkier waters of cross-border intrigue, counter-intelligence, and dirty tricks.

The First Lake Erie Expedition

In August 1863, Robert Minor, the only member of the original group of officers designated for the Lake Erie commando force still in Richmond, was summoned from the Naval Ordnance Works to a meeting with two members of the Confederate cabinet: Navy Secretary Mallory and Secretary of War James R. Seddon. Seddon read to Minor from a letter proposing a raid on the Great Lakes. This new proposal centred on a goal that had not figured in Murdaugh's original plan, namely, the freeing of the prisoners at the Johnson's Island camp.

Although the letter's author was not identified by Minor, it is likely that it came from a senior Confederate imprisoned on Johnson's Island. One possible candidate would be Brigadier-General John Jay Archer, who had been captured on the first day of battle at Gettysburg. It is known that Seddon received the following unsigned message (by way of a paroled soldier) from Archer late in September:

> We count here 1,600 prisoners, 1,200 officers. We can take the island, guarded by only one battalion, with small loss, but have no way to get off. A naval officer might procure in some way a steamer on the lake and with a few men attack the island and take us to Canada. C.C. Egerton of Baltimore, would, I think, furnish a fitting crew to one of our naval officers who carried your indorsement to him, and would give valuable advice regarding how to get the men armed, in steamer &c. There is no truer man in our service, and he has a large body of men sworn to obey him and help us. Lieut. George Bier or William Parker are suggested.[14]

In order to ensure that he succeeded in communicating with the War Department in Richmond, it is very probable that Archer used several different messengers over the course of the summer of 1863. Of course, it is also possible that other prisoners, perhaps even before Archer's arrival at the camp, were trying to contact Seddon to recommend a similar plan.[15]

Whatever the case, Minor, who had remained a firm believer in the potential of a Great Lakes raid, was asked for his opinion of a new proposed operation that would, in effect, combine Murdaugh's plan with a proposal to free the prisoners on Johnson's Island. Minor did not hesitate to support the operation, remarking, "I need not inform you, gentlemen, how much pleasure it would give me to be engaged upon such duty."[16]

Following this consultation with Seddon and Mallory, Minor anxiously awaited word regarding the new raid's authorization. A month later, he was summoned again to Mallory's office, where he received the welcome news that the operation was, indeed, a go, and was ordered to "organize the expedition, select the officers, make all the necessary preparations." Mallory concluded his instructions by offering Minor command of the operation. Although Minor was keen on the expedition, he declined the offer to lead it, deferring, he later reported, "in favor of my friend, John Wilkinson (who was in a manner somewhat committed to the plan by the letter which I have mentioned as being shown to me by Mr. Seddon, the Secretary of War), with this proviso, however, that on our arrival in Canada, in the event of adopting two lines of operations, I was to have one of them as my command."[17]

Although Minor's friend Lieutenant John Wilkinson was an experienced and well-respected officer, best known, at this point, as the commander of CSS *Robert E. Lee*, a government-owned blockade-runner operating out of Wilmington, North Carolina, he was not an obvious choice for a secret commando operation in British North America. Nonetheless, he accepted the assignment, noting that his orders were deliberately vague: "it was left to the officer in command how the details were to be arranged, his sole explicit instructions being not to violate the neutrality of British territory." The latter requirement was a dubious formality, as Wilkinson well knew. "How this was to be avoided," he remarked, "has ever seemed impossible to me, but having been selected to command the expedition, I resolved to disregard all personal consequences, and leave the responsibility to be borne by the Confederate Government."[18] Clearly, the latter now had a different attitude regarding an attack on the Great Lakes. According to Minor, President Davis, who had previously agonized over the international repercussions of a Lake Erie operation, stated it was "better to fail than not to make the attempt."[19]

One likely reason that Wilkinson was chosen to lead the expedition was the fact that, as an experienced blockade-runner, he could not only be counted upon to deliver the Lake Erie commando contingent to Halifax, Nova Scotia, on the *Robert E. Lee*, but he could also take charge of a sizable cargo of cotton from the War Department and negotiate its sale in order to complement the $35,000 in gold that had been supplied by the Navy Department, thereby providing, in Minor's words, "the sinews of the expedition."[20] Some of the gold would be spent in Halifax in order to outfit the men for their trip across the Maritime provinces to Montreal and

Lieutenant John Wilkinson, CSN. Following the Civil War, Wilkinson lived in exile for several years in Halifax, Nova Scotia.

then on to the Great Lakes; however, the lion's share would be reserved for the outfitting of the liberated prisoners of war (PoWs) on Johnson's Island.[21]

Twenty-two men, mostly officers, were selected for the operation.[22] Among their number were several who had already served — or would later serve — with the renowned commando leader Wood, including Lieutenant B.P. Loyall, Lieutenant G.W. Gift, chief engineer Charles Schroeder, and assistant surgeon William G. Shepardson. (The latter, in addition to serving as a medical officer, was also an experienced journalist and was probably assigned to the expedition so that he could prepare a stirring account of the operation, should it prove successful, for the Confederate newspapers, as he had done for other naval commando operations.[23]) The party also included two gunners, Crawford H. Gormly and John Waters. Only Wilkinson, Minor, and Loyall knew that their destination was Halifax.[24]

On the night of 7 October 1863, the *Robert E. Lee*, under Wilkinson's command, left Smithville, North Carolina (now Southport), below Wilmington.[25] The night was clear, but Wilkinson was confident he could run the gauntlet of the Union blockade. "The fact is," he later explained, "a blockade-runner was almost as invisible at night as Harlequin in the pantomime. Nothing showed above the deck but the two short masts, and the smoke-stack; and the lead colored hull could scarcely be seen at the distance of one hundred yards."[26] Despite her commander's assurance, the *Lee* did not entirely escape the notice of the blockading fleet. After running at full speed for nearly an hour, she came under fire. Following a first shot that was a little long and a second that was just short, the vessel was struck by a shell that hit the starboard bulwarks, setting a cotton bale ablaze, destroying a small hoisting engine, and wounding three men with splinters and shell fragments.[27]

The Confederates promptly threw the burning bale overboard and tended to the men, whose wounds were relatively minor. Although several more shots were fired, the *Lee* soon reached safer waters. As she sailed up the coast, the blockade-runner showed American colours to all vessels that she encountered, including, in very dirty weather off New York, a Union man-of-war.[28]

On 16 October the *Lee* reached Halifax, where Wilkinson consigned his cargo of cotton (worth $76,000) to the wholesale merchant Benjamin Wier, the port's unofficial agent for the Confederacy.[29] Wier, later a Canadian senator, was one of the most prominent and influential members of the large group of Confederate sympathizers found among Halifax's business and social elite.[30] Wilkinson then passed on the command of the ship to John Knox. (Much to Wilkinson's dismay, the *Lee* would be captured on her return voyage, soon thereafter becoming the Union blockader USS *Fort Donelson*.)[31]

Realizing that the "arrival of so large a party of Confederates in Halifax attracted attention," Wilkinson began preparations for the next stage of the operation, namely, the trip to Montreal in Canada East. Assuming that they were now under surveillance, presumably by agents of the vigilant American Consul in Halifax, Judge Mortimer M. Jackson, and/or British authorities, Wilkinson took several measures to safeguard the integrity of his operation.[32] First of all, he dismissed a civilian named Leggett, whom he and other officers suspected of being "a traitor and a spy."[33] Second, he broke the commando group into small parties of three and four, which were to travel to Montreal by one of two different routes: "one via St. John, New Brunswick, and thence up through the province via Fredericton and Grand Falls to Rivière du Loup, on the St. Lawrence, to Quebec and Montreal, and the other via Pictou, through the Northumberland Strait to Bay of Chaleurs, via Gaspé, up the St. Lawrence to Quebec, and thence by railroad to Montreal."[34] Finally, Wilkinson sent ahead his own agent, a "canny Scotchman," who would travel to Montreal via Portland, Maine, and prepare for the commandos' arrival.[35] By this time Montreal was a hotbed of Confederate activity, much of it centred in St. Lawrence Hall.[36]

As they made their way along "their long and devious route through the British Provinces," the Confederates were struck by the brazen activities of "recruiting agents for the United States army ... scarcely affecting to disguise their occupation."[37] (These efforts at foreign enlistment were extremely fruitful for the North, as many Maritimers would serve in New England regiments or the Union Navy.[38])

The various Confederate parties began arriving in Montreal on 21 October. According to Minor, all members of the contingent were ordered to take precautions to avoid detection by Union and Canadian agents: "As it was of vital importance that the utmost secrecy should be observed, the officers were directed to take lodgings in quiet boarding houses, to avoid the hotels, not to recognize each other on the street, and not to be absent from their rooms for more than half an hour at a time. Finding Marshal Kane and some of our friends in Montreal, we set to work to prepare and perfect our arrangements, the first object of the plan being to communicate with the prisoners on Johnson's Island."[39]

Accordingly, with the assistance of a cross-border network of Confederate sympathizers, Wilkinson utilized the personal columns of the *New York Herald* to contact Brigadier-General Archer and confirm that an attempt would be made to free the Confederate prisoners. Wilkinson's message stated "that a few nights after the 4th of November a carriage would be at the door, when all seeming obstacles would be removed, and to be ready." The obstacles alluded to, Minor later clarified, "were the U.S.S. *Michigan* and the prison guard."[40] (In response to rumours regarding Confederate attempts to free the prisoners on Johnson's Island, the *Michigan* was ordered to take up station in Sandusky Bay in late October.[41])

Once he had established contact with the Confederate prisoners, Wilkinson was determined to act quickly in the hope that he and his men could avoid detection. Over the course of the last week of October and the first week of November, he finalized the key elements of his operation, adjusting for changing circumstances and contingencies, including regular intelligence reports received from Ohio; all the while trying to weigh the reliability of the various sympathizers and agents who offered assistance and advice.[42]

With logistical support from the Confederate exile George P. Kane, a trusted Southern operative and a former Baltimore Chief of Police, Wilkinson focused on three key issues: ordnance, the composition of his commando force, and the final details of his assault plan.[43]

Robert Minor described the creative approach that was adopted for weaponry: "Two small 9-pounders were quietly purchased; Colt furnished us with 100 navy revolvers, with an ample supply of pistol ammunition, of course through several indirect channels. Dumb-bells were substituted for cannon-balls, as it would have excited suspicion to have asked for such an article in Montreal; powder, bullets, slugs, butcher knives in lieu of cutlasses, and grapnels were obtained, and all preparations made to arm the escaped Confederate officers and soldiers."[44]

As for the final assault force, Wilkinson initially resisted the temptation to recruit a large number of men from among either the members of Montreal's sizeable Confederate colony or several British North America volunteers; although, he did make an exception for a few former prisoners who had escaped from Johnson's Island. Because they knew the lay of the land, these men might be able to provide crucial information. During the actual attack, Wilkinson's commando force would also be assisted by a number of prisoners who had volunteered to rise against their captors.[45]

However, as the Confederates' plans progressed, the enormity of the task of seizing the *Michigan* prompted a reconsideration of the size of the assault force. As one of the participants later recalled, the expedition leaders came to the realization that "more men were necessary, and some Confederates, who had recently escaped from camps Chase and Douglas were taken as volunteers."[46] With this augmentation, the final commando party numbered 54.[47]

Although no British North Americans figured among the members of the assault team, two did play important roles in the operation. The first, an unidentified retired British Army officer, traveled to Sandusky, where, under the pretext of duck-hunting, he observed the movements of the USS *Michigan* and relayed information about the vessel and other activities in the vicinity of the Johnson's Island camp to Wilkinson on a daily basis, using a "pre-arranged vocabulary," presumably in cables or newspaper advertisements.[48] The second Canadian, James Simeon McCuaig, the manager of the Bay of Quinte and Saint Lawrence

Steamboat Co. and later a federal member of Parliament, ultimately had an even more critical impact on the operation; however, his initial role was to convince Wilkinson to alter his assault plan.[49]

Wilkinson's original plan, probably developed in consultation with Minor and Loyall, was to travel to Windsor and take passage on a steamer to Detroit. Once out on Lake Huron, Wilkinson's commandos would seize the vessel and then make their way to Lake Erie and Johnson's Island, where they would find a way to board the *Michigan*. However, based on information received from McCuaig, who had been introduced to the commando leaders by Kane, the plan was revised, with the Welland Canal chosen as the departure point.[50] Minor summarized the new plan as follows:

> From Ogdensburg, in New York, there is a line of screw steamers plying to Chicago in the grain and provision trade, and as they return nearly empty to Chicago, and sometimes carry the Adams Express Company's safe, we decided to take deck-passage on board one of them as mechanics and laborers bound to Chicago to work on the city waterworks there, and with this view one of our clever privates, named Connelly, was sent over to Ogdensburg, who paid the passage money for 25 of us in advance, to be taken on board at some point on the Welland Canal, and while doing so he made an agreement to take as many more laborers as he could obtain, their passage being fixed at the same price, to which the New Yorker consented, and gave him the ticket to show to the captain of the boat. We were then to assemble at St. Catharines, on the canal, go on board the steamer (one of our men, apparently entirely unconnected with us, having charge of the guns, powder, pistols, etc., boxed up in casks, boxes, etc., and marked 'Machinery, Chicago,' going on board the same steamer with us), and when fairly out in Lake Erie, and well clear of British jurisdiction, we were to rise on the officers and crew, overpower them, seize the steamer, mount our two 9-pounders, arm the men, secure the prisoners,

and push on for Sandusky, timing our arrival so as to reach the *Michigan* about daylight, collide with her as if by accident, board and carry her by the cutlass and pistol, and then with her guns, loaded with grape and canister, trained on the prison headquarters, send a boat on shore to demand an unconditional surrender of the island, with its prisoners, garrison, material of war, etc., upon penalty of being fired into and the prisoners being released without restraint upon their actions.[51]

Once the *Michigan* and the PoW camp were captured, the Confederates would seize several small steamers known to be at the wharf at Sandusky and then transport the bulk of the prisoners to Canada West. Then the *Michigan*, with a crew drawn from Wilkinson's commando force and about 50 freed PoWs (some of whom would likely serve as marines), would set out to attack Northern shipping. As Minor observed, the Confederates would have "the lake shore from Sandusky to Buffalo at our mercy, with all the vast commerce of Lake Erie as our just and lawful prey."[52]

Having completed all his preparations, Wilkinson placed a final notice in the *Herald*, notifying Archer that "'the carriage will be at the door on or about the tenth.'"[53] The commandos then embarked — presumably once again in small parties — for St. Catharines, where they would meet

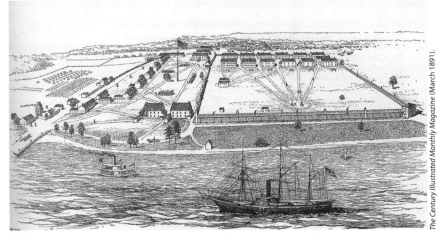

The Century Illustrated Monthly Magazine (March 1891).

View of the Johnson's Island prison and the USS *Michigan*.

The Lake Erie Expeditions

and await the arrival of the steamer on which they had booked passage. About a month after the *Robert E. Lee*'s departure from Wilmington, Murdaugh's plan was about to be realized — or so it seemed.[54]

On or about 12 November, with his commando force assembled on the canal at St. Catharines, awaiting the imminent arrival of the steamer that would carry them to Lake Erie, Wilkinson's party received devastating news, which, in his words, "fell among us like a thunderbolt."[55] The news came in the form of a proclamation, issued by the governor general, Lord Monck, warning of Confederate plans to launch a naval attack from British North America and threatening serious repercussions for anyone violating British neutrality. In addition, there were further reports indicating that Monck had ordered that the Welland Canal be carefully watched and that any suspicious parties travelling through its waters be arrested. As well, the governor general notified the U.S. authorities of Confederate designs, prompting the American secretary of war, Edwin M. Stanton, to send warning telegrams, on the evening of 11 November, to the governors, mayors, and military commanders of the Great Lakes region and to order the defences at Sandusky to be significantly bolstered.[56]

Although Wilkinson was loath to abandon his operation, he promptly withdrew his force from the canal and endeavoured to obtain more intelligence. Meanwhile, his Canadian contact at Sandusky wisely ended his duck-hunting excursion and quickly returned to Canada, where he reported on the increased garrison at Johnson's Island and, in Wilkinson's words, "such other measures adopted as to render our success impossible."[57]

Following a war council with his senior officers, Wilkinson concluded that the operation had been seriously compromised. "There was a possibility of a successful issue to this enterprise," he later wrote, "but not a probability."[58] Robert Minor summarized the final decision of the commando leaders: "With our plan thus foiled, and with the lake cities in a fever of fear and excitement, and with the rapid advance of reinforcements, both naval and military, to reinforce the garrison at Johnson's Island against our compact little band of 52 Confederates, we had, as a matter of course, to abandon the design, and leave Canada as soon as possible, but to do so in a dignified and proper manner."[59]

As they prepared for the journey back to Halifax, the Confederates received intelligence suggesting that they had been betrayed at the last moment by the Canadian McCuaig, who, apparently, had come to regret his connection with the operation and had revealed the details of the plot to Luther Holton, a noted steamship and railroad entrepreneur and the Canadian finance minister.[60] (Holton also apparently served as the unofficial liaison between Monck and the U.S. Consul General Joshua Giddings.[61]) Wilkinson was not entirely certain about the reliability of this intelligence. In fact, he later speculated that the operation had been doomed from the start: "It is quite probable, indeed, that we were closely watched through the whole route."[62]

Whatever the case, the disappointed Confederates recognized that Monck was under enormous pressure to curry favour with the increasingly belligerent and hostile North by publicly thwarting the Confederate plan. Fortunately for the Confederates, the Canadian authorities were prepared, in the interests of maintaining neutrality, to let the commando force return to the South unmolested.[63]

For their trip back through British North America, the Confederates broke up into at least two groups.[64] As winter began to set in, the disconsolate commandos returned to Nova Scotia, travelling by various means and routes. After visiting briefly with Halifax's Confederate sympathizers, Wilkinson's men took passage for Bermuda on the Royal Mail steamer *Alpha*, arriving on 17 December. At St. George's, the commando force began to disperse. Wilkinson was soon offered command of a small blockade-runner, *Whisper*, which, after a rather harrowing voyage, arrived in Wilmington on 7 January. Among his passengers were Minor and about one-third of the original commando force.[65]

While Wilkinson remained in Wilmington for a time, Robert Minor returned to Richmond, where he resumed command of the Naval Ordnance Works. Over the course of the next few weeks, as time permitted, he drafted a lengthy report on the Lake Erie expedition for Confederate States Navy Admiral Franklin Buchanan. Completed on 2 February 1864, about a year after he and Murdaugh had first planned an attack on the USS *Michigan*, the report reflected its author's bitter disappointment. "So, but for treachery," Minor wrote, "which no one can guard against, our enterprise would have been the feature of the war, and our little Navy another laurel wreath of glorious renown."[66] Although Robert Minor would have no further involvement in efforts to capture the *Michigan*, the CSN would soon have another opportunity to win renown on Lake Erie.

THE SECOND LAKE ERIE EXPEDITION

As the South's military situation deteriorated throughout 1864 (one of the most devastating setbacks being General William Tecumseh Sherman's inexorable advance on Atlanta, starting in May), the Confederate leadership grew increasingly open to desperate measures that might serve to undermine Northern support for the war and perhaps even contribute to the electoral defeat of President Abraham Lincoln in the fall. One of the key figures given responsibility for implementing this new strategy was Jacob Thompson, a former United States congressman and secretary of the interior, who was dispatched to British North America as a confederate commissioner in May 1864. Based at the Queen's Hotel in Toronto, in Canada West, Thompson was provided with large amounts of money to finance various irregular operations against the North.

Thompson's mandate was broad and deliberately vague:

> Richmond, Va., April 27, 1864
> Hon. Jacob Thompson:
>
> Sir: Confiding special trust in your zeal, discretion, and patriotism. I hereby direct you to proceed at once to Canada; there to carry out the instructions you have received from me verbally, in such manner as shall seem most likely to conduce to the furtherance of the interests of the Confederate States of America which have been entrusted to you.
>
> Very respectfully and truly yours, Jeff'n Davis[67]

Although President Davis did not mention the fact in writing, Thompson had the authority to sanction a wide variety of actions against the North, including sabotage and some plots that were probably best characterized as terrorism.[68]

Thompson's biggest challenge was to conduct his covert operations (which together came to be known as the "Northwest Conspiracy") under constant scrutiny by American and Canadian authorities. "The bane and curse of carrying out anything in this country," he later complained, "is the surveillance under which we act. Detectives, or those ready to give information, stand at every street corner. Two or three cannot interchange ideas without a reporter."[69] In this Canadian netherworld of Civil War intrigue, populated by detectives, double agents, fraud artists, criminals, and a large but motley pool of Confederate exiles (including paroled soldiers and numerous escapees from Union PoW camps) and sympathizers, Thompson was also confronted with the problem of distinguishing between realistic and authentic plans and proposals that were unrealizable and/or fraudulent.

One plan that seemed particularly promising to Commissioner Thompson was the seizure of the USS *Michigan*. As a result, he was keen to authorize another commando operation against the vessel. He did not have long to wait. In July, Thompson was approached by Charles H. Cole, who presented himself as an escaped army captain who had served with Nathan Bedford Forrest's celebrated cavalry force. Cole also indicated that he held the rank of lieutenant in the CSN.[70] (In reality, Captain Cole had no naval commission. He had been paroled in April 1864 and allowed to return to his family home in Pennsylvania after taking an oath of allegiance to the Union. He was, thus, taking a considerable risk by resuming hostile activities against the North.[71])

In any event, Cole seemed to have the right stuff and was promptly sent by Thompson on a reconnaissance mission: "I sent him around the Lakes with instructions to go as a lower-deck passenger, to familiarize himself with all the channels and different approaches to the several harbors, the strength of each place, the depositories of coal, and especially to learn all that he could about the war steamer *Michigan*, and devise some plan for her capture or destruction. This duty he performed very satisfactorily."[72]

Cole ended his journey in Sandusky, where, with generous financing from Thompson, he presented himself as a free-spending oil-company executive, registered at the West House with a woman companion, and began a deliberate campaign to win the confidence of the *Michigan*'s officers, especially the vessel's commander, Captain John C. "Jack" Carter.[73] He also recruited a few conspirators from among Ohio's numerous Confederate sympathizers (known as Copperheads).[74] Reporting back to Thompson, Cole observed that "Lake Erie furnishes a splendid field for operations."[75] He also asked Thompson to formally authorize his activities:

Hon. Jacob Thompson

Sir: I have the honor to ask to be placed in secret detached service, in undertaking the capture of the gunboat *Michigan* at Johnson's Island. Combination can be made without infringing the neutrality laws of Canada. I send this by special messenger. An immediate answer requested.

Charles H. Cole,
Captain, C.S.A.[76]

While Cole was engaged in his tour of the Great Lakes, Thompson had begun to seek other personnel for the Lake Erie operation. Fortuitously, he was soon contacted by John Yates Beall (pronounced "Bell") and asked to authorize a privateering expedition on Lake Huron. Beall, a recently exchanged acting master in the CSN, who had been involved in several daring commando operations in Chesapeake Bay in the fall of 1863, was the ideal person to serve as Cole's second in command and to lead the naval side of the operation. Accordingly, Thompson persuaded Beall to abandon his Lake Huron plans and to join the second Lake Erie expedition. This was probably an easy decision for Beall, as his primary goal was to strike against the Yankees on the Great Lakes, something he had been pressing for before his meeting with Thompson.[77]

In fact, in late May or early June of 1864, Beall had apparently received consent for an operation against Johnson's Island from Secretary Seddon of the War Department. Beall's

John W. Headley, *Confederate Operations in Canada and New York* (Neale Publishing Company, 1906).

Acting Master John Yates Beall, CSN.

original plan was to assemble some of the commandos who had served with him on the Chesapeake for "special service" in British North America.[78] However, before he could finalize arrangements, he abruptly left the Confederacy. According to William Washington Baker, who had been chosen to serve with Beall, the latter "learned … of an easy way to get through the lines of the enemy to Canada, and left several of us in Richmond because we could not be assembled in time to leave with him."[79] Beall was clearly very eager for action.

With Beall on board, Thompson did not hesitate to send authorization to Cole, albeit with the usual pro forma admonition regarding British and Canadian neutrality:

> Charles H. Cole, Captain C.S.A. and Lieutenant C.S. Navy
>
> Sir: By the authority in me vested, specially trusting in your knowledge and skill, you are assigned to the secret detached service for the purpose mentioned in your letter. To aid you in this undertaking, John Y. Beall, Master in the Confederate States Navy, has been directed to report to you for duty. In all you may do in the premises, you will carefully abstain from violating any laws or regulations of Canada or British authorities in relation to neutrality. The combinations necessary to effect your purposes must be made by Confederate soldiers, with such assistance as you may draw from the enemy's country.
>
> Your obedient servant,
> Jacob Thompson[80]

Thompson then sent Beall to Sandusky to confer with Cole and finalize an assault plan. In many respects, the resulting plan resembled that of Wilkinson and Minor; however, it deliberately avoided the bottleneck of the Welland Canal, where the first expedition had come to such a disappointing end.

Essentially, the plan called for Cole to stay in Sandusky and continue to cultivate his relationship with Carter and the other officers of the

Michigan, with a view to arranging for a party on board the vessel on the evening of 19 September, at which Cole would ply the ship's officers with drugged wine. Meanwhile, Beall would return to Canada and recruit a commando force. Beall's raiders would seize the small side-wheel steamer *Philo Parsons* (222 tons) on the morning of 19 September, during its regular run from Detroit to Sandusky.[81] At Kelleys Island they would rendezvous with a messenger from Cole who would confirm that all was ready for an attack on the *Michigan*.[82] Beall's commandos would then steam to Sandusky, about 12 miles away, and await a final signal from Cole to commence their nighttime assault. Ordnance would consist primarily of Navy Colts and small axes, which, together with grappling hooks, would be taken on board the *Philo Parsons* in a trunk. As was the case with the first Lake Erie expedition, contact was also made with senior officers on Johnson's Island and an uprising was planned to coincide with the attack on the *Michigan*.[83] According to Thompson, "Their plan was well conceived and held out the promise of success."[84]

With the plan completed, John Yates Beall returned to Windsor to assemble his commando force. Here again, fortune seemed to be smiling on the Confederate operation as Beall was soon joined by another CSN officer who had served with him during his depredations against Union shipping in Chesapeake Bay, fellow Acting Master Bennett G. Burley, a Scottish soldier of fortune.[85] Beall also recruited an additional 17 raiders, including an army surgeon, J.S. Riley.[86] Beall was assisted in his efforts by Thompson, who, in order to supervise preparations and provide logistical support, had taken up temporary residence at the home of Colonel Steele, a Confederate exile living outside of Windsor.[87]

On 18 September, Burley was sent to Detroit with orders to contact the part-owner and clerk of the *Philo Parsons*, William O. Ashley, and arrange for the vessel's captain, Sylvester F. Atwood, to make an unscheduled stop at Sandwich, Canada West, in order to pick up a few men who would be joining Burley for an excursion to Kelleys Island. Burley explained that the stop would be a favour to one of the men, who was extremely lame. The next morning, Burley took passage at Detroit. As requested, the vessel stopped briefly at Sandwich, where John Yates Beall and two other commandos boarded. The *Parsons* then put in at Malden (now Amherstburg) on the Canadian side of the Detroit River, where a large group of passengers came on board.[88] Among them were

187

16 Confederate raiders, who brought with them a large trunk. Ashley mistakenly assumed that they were "skedaddlers" (Union draft-evaders), a relatively common sight in the border communities during the war.[89]

The *Parsons* then continued on to the Lake Erie Islands. At Middle Bass Island, the captain disembarked to spend the night with his family. The vessel, now under the command of the mate, De Witt C. Nichols, proceeded to Kelleys Island, the presumed destination for Burley and the men who had come on board at Sandwich. However, once at Kelleys Island, they informed the ship's clerk that they had decided to go on to Sandusky. Some new passengers got on at Kelleys Island,

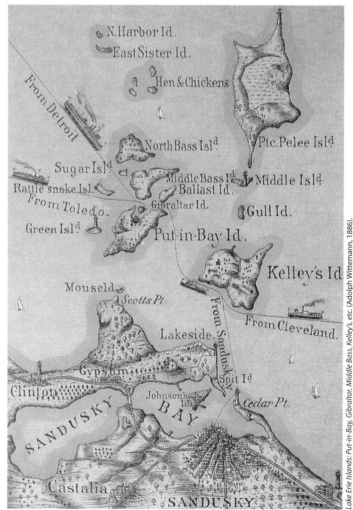

The Lake Erie Islands chain. Middle Bass Island, the small island below Pelee Island, is the southern-most point in Canada.

Lake Erie Islands: Put-in-Bay, Gibraltar, Middle Bass, Kelley's, etc. (Adolph Wittemann, 1886).

possibly including an associate of Cole's, but apparently not the promised messenger with news from Sandusky. Although Beall realized that this might point to a problem, it did not deter him from his mission.[90]

Shortly after the vessel left Kelleys Island for Sandusky, at about 1600 hours, the commandos struck. Beall began the seizure of the vessel on the hurricane deck, where he confronted the mate. According to Nichols, Beall declared, "I am a Confederate officer. There are thirty of us, well armed. I seize this boat, and take you prisoner. You must pilot the boat as I direct you." Beall then pulled a revolver from his pocket and continued his instructions: "And here are the tools to make you. Run down and lie off the harbor."[91] An unarmed Nichols wisely complied.

Meanwhile, Burley and the other commandos promptly armed themselves and set out to take control of the vessel. About ten Confederates were assigned to the subduing of the clerk, the wheelman, the engineer, the fireman, and the deckhands. Two crew members tried to evade their captors, prompting the firing of several warning shots, which seemed to have the desired effect, as the outnumbered crewmen soon realized that resistance was ill advised. The remaining commandos rounded up the passengers and made sure that they were unarmed before herding them into the fire hold. Much of the crew was also sent below. Any crew members not in the hold were accompanied by guards. Most commandos were armed with two Navy Colts. Some also brandished small axes.[92]

As the vessel steamed towards Sandusky, the Confederates brought the wheelman up from the hold, as well as several deckhands. The latter were ordered to clear the decks by throwing a cargo of pig iron overboard. Once the *Parsons* arrived outside of Sandusky harbour, at a point that offered an unobstructed view of the USS *Michigan*, Beall took stock of the situation. He also had one of the commandos press the mate, Nichols, for information about the warship and her current position in the harbour. Then Beall himself interrogated Nichols about the *Parsons*'s fuel supply, determining that it was low. Following a brief war council, Beall ordered the wheelman to turn back for the wooding station at Middle Bass Island.[93]

The *Parsons* arrived back at Middle Bass Island about sundown and tied up at the wharf alongside the fuelling station. Here, the Confederates were obliged to fire several warning shots at the owner of the wood supply and two other men on the wharf. They then released several deckhands from the hold to assist with the loading of the wood. They also apparently transferred the remaining prisoners from the hold to the cabin.[94]

As the loading continued, the commotion on the wharf soon came to the attention of the *Parsons*'s captain, Atwood, who rushed from his home to the dock to find out "what in hell was up."[95] Within minutes, he found himself a prisoner on his own vessel. Dr. Riley, the surgeon assigned to the commando force, was then one of the guards in the steamer's cabin and tried to offer some comfort to Atwood. "He said," the *Parsons*'s captain later recalled, "he thought I'd get my boat again."[96]

As Riley and Atwood conversed, the latter heard the familiar whistle of the *Island Queen* (173 tons), a small steamer that also plied the waters of Lake Erie. As the *Queen* came alongside, Beall prepared to seize the boat, pulling guards from the cabin to assist in the assault.[97]

It was essential that Beall quickly gain control of the *Queen*. Although the crew and passengers (which included about 25 unarmed soldiers on their way to being mustered out at Toledo) were promptly subdued, this seizure met with some resistance. As a result, one person was cut in the head by a hatchet, several others were knocked down, and a number were struck with the butt ends of pistols or hatchets.[98] As well, the vessel's engineer, Henry Haines, suffered a minor gunshot wound. Perhaps because he could not hear very well above the noise of the engine, Haines had not responded to orders to stop it. He later recalled what happened next: "I heard someone exclaim, 'Shoot the son of a bitch,' and was immediately shot, the ball passing my nose and through my left cheek. The bell rang, and I stopped the engine, and came out on deck."[99]

Once the *Island Queen* was in Confederate hands, Beall had to address two urgent problems, namely, what to do with his surfeit of prisoners and what to do with the *Queen*.

His first step was to transfer the new prisoners from the *Queen* to the *Parsons*'s cabin. Then, under the direction of Burley, most of the men were escorted, three at a time, to the hold. Beall then met with the *Parsons*'s captain, Atwood, and asked him to give his word that he would not try to contact the mainland for 24 hours. Once Atwood agreed to these terms, Beall told him that he was releasing most of the prisoners into Atwood's care, starting with the women, children, and other prisoners held in the cabin. The released prisoners were also obliged to take an oath similar to Atwood's.[100] Once Atwood was ashore and had begun to escort the prisoners to his house, Beall released most of the men from the hold. The only remaining prisoners were some crew members from the two steamers.[101]

The *Parsons* then finally left Middle Bass Island and steamed towards Sandusky Bay with the *Island Queen* in tow. Before departure, one of the commandos had consulted with the *Queen*'s engineer and verified the location of the boat's valves. The engineer later described what happened next: "I showed him the pony pipe in the hold, and he thereupon chopped it off. He then took a big sledge hammer and broke the big cock off the side of the boat and let the water in."[102]

After towing the smaller steamer for about five miles, the Confederates cut her loose and let her go adrift. They then imprisoned her crew members in the hold.[103] Beall's commandos next prepared for an attack on the *Michigan*. In addition to the equipment and ordnance that they had originally brought on board, they now had a supply of fireballs made from hemp, which they had ordered the *Parsons*'s porter to fashion under their supervision.[104]

At about 2200 hours, the *Parsons* arrived opposite Marblehead Lighthouse, which marked the entrance to Sandusky Bay.[105] It was a clear night, and, as they proceeded into the Bay's entrance, the commando's target was visible in the bright moonlight. The Confederates now awaited Cole's signal to attack. It did not come, which was a serious problem. Two more would promptly follow.[106]

First of all, the *Parsons*'s wheelman, Michael Campbell, told Beall that "it was too dangerous to run into Sandusky Bay by night ... the channel was too narrow."[107] This warning probably gave Beall pause, but apparently it did not deter him from his plans. However, the second problem proved to be fatal to the operation. "I then started back to attack the *Michigan*," Beall later recounted, "when seventeen of my twenty men mutinied and refused to go forward ... a most cowardly and dishonorable affair."[108] Beall's raiders had split along predictable lines. The experienced naval commandos, Beall and Burley, together with two other men, were determined to proceed. (Captain George W. Orr of the *Island Queen* later recounted that he had overheard a hurried war council that ended with Beall stating: "I have a notion to make the attempt, anyhow."[109]) The other Confederates, consisting mostly, if not entirely, of ex-soldiers, viewed an attack on the gunboat under the current circumstances as suicidal and doomed to failure.

An angry Beall did not want his own record besmirched by what he viewed as a failure of courage on the part of his volunteers and thus insisted that they sign a declaration:

> On Board the *Philo Parsons*
> September 20, 1864
>
> We, the undersigned, crew of the boat aforesaid, take pleasure in expressing our admiration of gentlemanly bearing, skill, and courage of Captain John Y. Beall as a commanding officer and gentleman, but believing and being well-convinced that the enemy is already apprised of our approach, and is so well prepared that we cannot by any possibility make it a success, and having already captured two boats, we respectfully decline to prosecute it any further.

J.S. Riley, M.D.	Wm. Byland
H.B. Barkley	Robert G. Harris
R.F. Smith	W.C. Colt
David H. Ross	Tom S. Major
R.B. Drake	N.S. Johnston
James Brotherton	John Bristol
M.H. Duncan	F.H. Thomas
W.B. King	J.G. Odoer
Joseph Y. Clark[110]	

As it turned out, the mutineers were right about the prospects for success — as Beall surely must have realized, despite his protests. Cole was not signaling the *Parsons* because he had been arrested that afternoon, before his party was scheduled to start. An attack on the vessel therefore have resulted in either certain capture or death.

Unfortunately for Beall and Cole, on 17 September, the military commander of the District of Michigan, Bennett H. Hill, had received intelligence from a Confederate double agent indicating that an attack on the *Michigan* was imminent.[111] He had promptly conveyed this warning to Carter. Two days later, on the day of the planned attack, Hill supplied Carter with far more explicit information:

> Detroit, September 19, 1864
> C. J.C. Carter, U.S. Navy
> U.S. Steamer *Michigan*, Sandusky, Ohio:
>
> It is said the parties will embark to-day at Malden on board the *Philo Parsons*, and will seize that steamer or another running from Kelly's Island. Since my last dispatch am again assured that officers and men have been bought by a man named Cole; a few men to be introduced on board under guise of friends of officers; an officer named Eddy to be drugged. Both Commodore Gardner and myself look upon the matter as serious.
>
> B.H. Hill,
Lieut. Col., U.S. Army,
Acting Assistant Provost-Marshal-General[112]

Later that day, Carter assured Hill that he had acted on the intelligence:

> Sandusky, September 19, 1864
> Col. B.H. Hill:
>
> Your dispatch of 19th received. I have Cole and a fair prospect of bagging the party.
>
> J.C. Carter,
Commander, U.S. Navy[113]

With Cole and several of his associates in custody, Carter prepared his vessel for an encounter with Beall's commandos. He was determined to capture the *Philo Parsons* and spent most of the night of 19 September awaiting her approach.

As the *Michigan* lay in wait, her quarry slipped away and made for the Canadian shore of the Detroit River. The ever-aggressive Beall intended to destroy all American shipping that he encountered on the way. However, according to Campbell, the *Parsons*'s wheelman, Beall decided to forego his only possible capture: "We saw but one vessel near to us as we went up; they told me to go alongside of her, and then asked what waters she was in. When I told him she was in British waters, they said they would not touch her."[114]

Just above Malden, Beall sent two commandos ashore in one of the *Queen*'s lifeboats with a cargo of seized property (and probably some Confederate materiel). Farther along, at Fighting Island, most of the prisoners were released. The *Parsons* then proceeded to Sandwich, where, shortly after 0800 hours, the vessel docked and the remaining prisoners and commandos disembarked. Before leaving the vessel, the Confederates removed a sizable amount of property, including such improbable plunder as a piano and an easy chair. They also forced the engineer to cut the *Parsons*'s injection pipes. The Confederates then made their way to Windsor, accompanied much of the way by the wheelman, engineer, and mate of the *Parsons*. At Windsor, the commandos scattered.[115]

Upon his arrival at Windsor, Beall reported to Commissioner Thompson. The naval officer was soon sent north into the Canadian woods on a hunting trip in the vicinity of Balsam Lake in the Kawartha Lakes region. Here, in hiding, he would be beyond the reach of American and Canadian authorities, thus ensuring that he would be available for another operation; for neither Thompson nor Beall were prepared to abandon their designs on the *Michigan* and Johnson's Island.[116] Beall's firm resolve was evident in a letter to a friend on 11 October: "You know that I am not the giving up kind. We are going to try again on my plan."[117]

The Third Lake Erie Expedition

Although Jacob Thompson was eager to initiate another naval operation on Lake Erie, despite the increasingly formidable obstacles — logistical and otherwise — his first priority was to come to the defense of Charles Cole, who was now a prisoner on Johnson's Island and facing the prospect of a trial before a military tribunal. On 22 September, Thompson, together with fellow commissioner, Clement Clay, wrote to Jefferson Davis asking for official support for Cole.[118] That same day, they also wrote to Colonel Charles W. Hill, the commandant at Johnson's Island, insisting that Cole be treated as an escaped prisoner, and not — as had been reported — as a spy. In addition to pleading Cole's case, the commissioners included a blunt warning: "If you proceed to extremities with Captain Cole we should feel it our duty to call on the authorities of the Confederate States to adopt proper measures of retaliation."[119] Such admonitions usually had the desired effect.

During the month of October, Thompson's colleague Clay was largely preoccupied with the final planning, execution, and aftermath of the St. Albans Raid of 19 October, which saw a Confederate cavalry force of about 20 men launch an attack on a sleepy Vermont town located about 15 miles from the Canadian border. The raid caused great panic and much outrage in the North and also became a major source of tension between British North America and the United States.[120]

In late October, undeterred by the diplomatic furor caused by the Vermont raid, Thompson, Beall, and Burley stepped up their preparations for a third Lake Erie expedition. The new plan differed from the previous commando operations in one key respect. Rather than seize a Great Lakes steamer, the Confederates would purchase a suitable vessel in Canada, outfit her for war, assemble a crew under Beall, and then commence attacks against Union shipping and cities on the eastern end of Lake Erie, beginning with Buffalo. As the Confederates raids continued, three additional steamers would be captured and armed. Crews would be drawn from among Confederate volunteers at various lakeshore communities. Once assembled, the small Confederate fleet would be divided. Assuming that their attacks would lure the *Michigan* from Sandusky Bay, one group would continue diversionary raids in the eastern part of Lake Erie; the other, comprising two steamers under Beall's command, would steam west and take advantage of the *Michigan*'s absence, attacking Johnson's Island and freeing the prisoners. The four steamers would then rendezvous and confront the *Michigan*.[121]

In its broad outline, the plan was daring to the point of audaciousness. It was also extremely complicated and far-fetched, probably too much so. However, the crucial part of the operation — the acquisition and arming of a steamer — was potentially a feasible goal.[122] The key question was: could the Confederates outmanoeuvre their most daunting enemies, namely, the informers in their own ranks and the American and Canadian agents who were determined to monitor their every move?

Confident that he could obtain a ship, Thompson's first step was to send Burley, probably at the end of September or early in October, to Guelph, where, at the foundry of a fellow Scotsman, Adam Robertson, a Confederate naval officer who apparently had some previous experience as a mechanic, began work on the production of a gun carriage, torpedoes, solid shot, shells, grapeshot, and other ordnance.[123] He also arranged for the purchase of an old 14-pounder gun from a Guelph resident and paid for it to be rebored.[124] On 17 October, Burley reported on his progress: "Everything is going on finely and I anticipate having the things finished early, perhaps this week, anyway in the fore part of next."[125]

Thompson then focused on the acquisition of a vessel, which he wanted to accomplish without alerting Union and Canadian authorities. In this effort he relied on a proxy, Dr. James T. Bates, a Kentucky expatriate and former steamboat captain. Late in October, at Toronto, Bates purchased the steamer *Georgian* (350 tons) from A.M. Smith and Co. and George H. Wyatt, for approximately $16,500.[126] Ostensibly acquired for use in the timber trade, the *Georgian* was an impressive ship. Launched in Georgian Bay early in 1863, she was powered by a screw propeller and would serve as an excellent Lakes raider.[127]

Now that they had a suitable ship, it was imperative that the Confederates move quickly and simultaneously on three operational fronts: preparing the vessel for warfare, completing the manufacture of the necessary naval ordnance, and assembling a crew and commando force. Probably in an effort to elude surveillance, Thompson undertook these activities under different leadership at several different locations.

Bates was given responsibility for overseeing the conversion of the ship, which was delivered to him at Port Colborne on Lake Erie, at the southern end of the Welland Canal, on or near 1 November. Under the guise of strengthening her beams for the towing of lumber rafts, he sought to have her hull reinforced and a ram attached which could be used against the *Michigan*. Bates also hired a crew, including an experienced Great Lakes captain, Milne, who was known as a Confederate sympathizer.[128]

Meanwhile, as Burley continued his ordnance work at Guelph, Thompson established a second ordnance operation in Toronto, at the home of a Confederate agent named William Lawrence "Larry"

MacDonald. As ordnance was completed, the Confederates began shipping it (much of it in boxes and barrels labeled "potatoes"), to various lakeshore towns, including Sarnia and Spanish River. This would allow the *Georgian* to acquire its armament and munitions in stages during its inaugural cruise as a warship. Among the weaponry being assembled was "Greek Fire," which was apparently being manufactured at Windsor for use in various Confederate operations.[129]

In Toronto, Thompson and MacDonald also worked on recruitment.[130] As was the case with the second Lake Erie expedition, naval veterans were in short supply, so the Confederates would have to rely mostly on army personnel to serve as naval commandos. However, they were able to recruit a number of experienced cavalry raiders, including Colonel Robert M. Martin, Lieutenant John W. Headley, and George S. Anderson, all of whom had served with the celebrated Kentucky cavalry commander General John Hunt Morgan. In an effort to avoid detection, it was decided that commandos would join the Confederate State Ship (CSS) *Georgian* in small groups at various points on the Great Lakes.[131]

Despite the seeming promise of the operation, the third Lake Erie expedition soon began to unravel. At Port Colborne, Bates discovered that the *Georgian*'s propeller required repairs. Consequently, ensuring that the ship was seaworthy quickly took precedence over the installation of a ram. Following repairs, the vessel began her westward cruise on 6 November, heading for Sarnia on Lake Huron. It soon became clear, however, that the ship was being watched by both American and Canadian authorities. Not only was she boarded along her route, but she was carefully inspected by custom officials at every port where she stopped. Furthermore, the propeller malfunctioned again, and Bates had to go to Toronto and make arrangements for a new one to be shipped to Collingwood.[132]

To make matters worse, on 19 November, J.J. Kingsmill, the county Crown attorney for Guelph, acting on instructions received from John A. Macdonald, the attorney general of Canada West, arranged for the arrest of Bennett Burley at Guelph, where he was residing at Ferndell, the home of Adam Robertson.[133] Interestingly, it is evident from Kingsmill's initial report that the authorities first assumed they were arresting Beall: "The person was arrested here this morning as Captain Bell, who on 20 September last on Lake Erie seized the steamer *Island Queen*."[134] In addition to arresting Burley, Canadian authorities intercepted several Confederate ordnance shipments.[135] Clearly, Monck, MacDonald, and other Canadian officials were no longer willing to tolerate Confederate acts of aggression against the North launched from British North America.

Difficulties also plagued the Confederates when it came to manning the vessel. For instance, the three veterans of Morgan's Raiders, Martin, Headley, and Anderson, were all sent to Port Colborne by Thompson and told to await Beall's arrival. Headley later recounted what transpired: "We waited for him two days and nights. His failure to come (he being twenty-four hours overdue) became a mystery and we returned to Toronto."[136]

Upon his arrival in Toronto, Headley met with Commissioner Thompson, who informed him that the third Lake Erie expedition was being aborted. Thompson cited two main reasons:

> ... Canadian authorities had instituted such surveillance of the vessel that it had been impossible to get arms or other supplies on board ... And besides the United States authorities ... had alarmed all points on the lakes and tugs were being fitted up at Buffalo and other cities, with artillery for her destruction. The panic could not have been greater if we had captured a city.[137]

Thompson could have added a third factor: winter would soon be setting in and the navigation season on Lake Erie would be coming to an end.

Once he had decided to terminate the operation, Thompson's first concern was to dispose of the *Georgian*. Probably with a view to taking heat off the vessel and thereby ensuring her availability for future use, he ordered Bates to transfer ownership to a Toronto lawyer, George T. Denison.[138] A noted militia officer and scion of a prominent United Empire Loyalist family, Denison was also one of the most rabid pro-Confederates in British North America.[139] In assuming ownership of the vessel, he, like Bates, was serving as a proxy. Although Denison insisted that he had purchased the vessel for $13,000 and intended to use her for commercial purposes, American and Canadian authorities were not convinced. The *Georgian*, now at Collingwood, thus, remained under careful surveillance.[140] Of course, Denison, as he later recounted, was under no illusions about the attention he had invited from the detested Yankees as a result of his association with Thompson: "Any persons seen communicating with him about the hotel ... were shadowed by the United States secret service men."[141]

With no possibility for any further actions against Johnson's Island until the following spring, on 13 December, Thompson sent Martin, Beall, Headley, Anderson, and six other commandos to Buffalo, where their mission was to stop a train and rescue seven Confederate generals (reportedly including Brigadier-General Archer) who were allegedly being transferred to Fort Lafayette in New York from Johnson's Island on 15 December. Apparently based on faulty intelligence, this operation proved to be exceedingly perilous and ill conceived; so much so that it was abandoned a day later. However, not all the Confederates made it safely back to Canada. Beall and Anderson were arrested at the New York Central Railroad depot at Suspension Bridge.[142]

The arrest of the two commandos would soon be followed by a succession of calamities that would preclude any possibility that the Confederates would ever resume their efforts to capture Johnson's Island. On 5 February, Bennett Burley was extradited to the United States to

Bennet Burleigh, *The Natal Campaign* (George Bell, 1900).

stand trial for robbery.[143] On 24 February, Beall, after having earlier been found guilty of acting as a spy and "guerrillero" by a military tribunal, was executed at Governor's Island, New York.[144] There have been suggestions — probably apocryphal — that Beall's execution contributed to John Wilkes Booth's deci-

Bennet Burleigh, the renowned Victorian war correspondent, who, during the Civil War, made his mark as Bennett Burley, Acting Master, CSN.

sion to assassinate Abraham Lincoln on 14 April. Whatever the case, Booth is known to have spent two weeks among Confederate operatives in Montreal during October 1864.[145]

On 2 April, Richmond fell and the Confederate government, in disarray, fled southward. Five days later, the *Georgian* was seized by Canadian authorities in preparation for her transfer to the American government (Denison would mount a legal fight against this action for months, but to no avail).[146] On 9 April, Robert E. Lee surrendered the Army of North Virginia at Appomattox. Other surrenders by key Confederate military commanders still in the field soon followed. Within weeks the Confederacy collapsed and the war was over.[147]

As many senior Confederates escaped to Canada to avoid what they assumed would be certain prosecution, Jacob Thompson, who was, for a time, suspected of involvement in the conspiracy to kill Lincoln, resolved to flee from British North America to Europe. On 14 April, he left Montreal and made his way to Halifax, where he took passage for England. Uncertain of his possible legal jeopardy, he would live in exile for several years.[148] Confederate operations in British North America had come to an end.

Conclusion

Although the three naval commando operations launched on the Great Lakes by the Confederacy during the 1863–1864 period were ultimately unsuccessful, they did not fail for lack of will. The Confederates committed serious resources to these operations, both in terms of finances and personnel (this is particularly true of the first Lake Erie expedition). Furthermore, all three operations were led by experienced Confederate naval officers who had demonstrated an appetite for fighting. If the *Michigan* had been seized or destroyed by any one of the commando parties that were dispatched against her, the blow against the Union in the Great Lakes region would likely have been considerable; as would the impact on Northern morale and confidence.

The 1863 Lake Erie expedition, involving more than 20 naval officers, was probably the most promising, but even it was compromised virtually from the start by an extremely efficient and pervasive surveillance network maintained by the American and Canadian authorities. It was also undermined by the effective and timely use of disinformation. Clearly, well-placed informers and other agents allowed the Union to constantly remain one step ahead of their Confederate adversaries on the Lakes. Both George P. Kane in Montreal and Jacob Thompson in Toronto, who were responsible for logistical support and security for their respective commando operations, seemed incapable of undertaking effective counter-intelligence measures. From a security point of view, their organizations were sieves, which meant that the Confederates were always at a serious disadvantage when it came to the critical war in the shadows.

Furthermore, as the prospect of a Confederate defeat became more and more probable, British and Canadian authorities were increasingly determined to avoid provoking the North. In fact, from the Confederate perspective, British neutrality slowly evolved into tacit support for the Union.

Nor were American and Canadian surveillance and governmental cooperation the only obstacles to Confederate success. With each successive raid, Union defences and military preparedness on the Great Lakes were bolstered. In fact, as the war ended, the Union was preparing to increase its naval presence on the Lakes.[149] Nonetheless, the allure of Murdaugh's original plan for a commando raid on the Great Lakes persisted, probably until the end of the Southern Rebellion (otherwise, Jacob Thompson would have sold the *Georgian* outright, rather than continue in his efforts to disguise the vessel's Confederate ownership).

Although Confederate naval commandos on the Great Lakes did not win the glory that William Murdaugh and Robert Minor had hoped for in 1863, they did conduct themselves with daring against formidable odds. Far from home, in enemy waters, they attempted the impossible. Certainly there was no dishonour for them in their failures — only bitter disappointment (even the *Parsons* "mutineers" acted in an honourable fashion). Contemplating the collapse of the first Lake Erie expedition, a philosophical Minor pointed to the reality that ultimately faced all the Southern commandos on the North's inland seas: "The fortunes of war were against us."[150]

Notes

1.   The two best works on the history of the Confederate States Navy are Raimondo Luraghi's *A History of the Confederate Navy* (Annapolis, MD: Naval Institute Press, 1996) and J. Thomas Scharf's *History of the Confederate Navy From Its Organization to the Surrender of Its Last Vessel* (New York: Rogers and Sherwood, 1887).

2.   Luraghi, *A History of the Confederate Navy*, 67–69.

3.   Mallory's career is examined in detail in Joseph T. Durkin's *Stephen R. Mallory: Confederate Navy Chief* (Chapel Hill, NC: University of North Carolina Press, 1954).

4.   For a useful overview of the Confederate States Navy's main commando operations, see Luraghi, *A History of the Confederate Navy*, 300–314. For more on the Confederacy's approach to the authorization of irregular naval operations, see United States War Department, *The War of the Rebellion: A Compilation of the Official Records of the Union and Confederate Armies in The War of the Rebellion* (Washington, DC: Government Printing Office, 1880–1901) [hereafter cited as *OR*], ser. 1, Vol. 22, 1001–1003, Stephen Mallory to E.C. Cabell, 10 September 1863.

5.   United States Department of the Navy, *Official Records of the Union and Confederate Navies in the War of the Rebellion* (Washington, DC: Government Printing Office, 1894–1927), [hereafter cited as *ORN*], ser. 2, Vol. 2, 256–257; J. Taylor Wood to Catesby, R. Jones, 30 August 1862. For more on Wood's career, see Royce Gordon Shingleton, *John Taylor Wood: Sea Ghost of the Confederacy* (Athens, GA: University of Georgia Press, 1979); John Bell, *Confederate Seadog: John Taylor Wood in War and Exile* (Jefferson, NC: McFarland & Company, 2002).

6.   For a history of the James River Squadron, see John M. Coski, *Capital Navy: The Men, Ships and Operations of the James River Squadron* (Campbell, CA: Savas Publishing Company, 1996). For the basic service records of most of the Confederate States Navy personnel mentioned in this article, see Thomas Truxton Moebs, *Confederate States Navy Research Guide* (Williamsburg, VA: Moebs Publishing Co., 1991), 183–298.

7.   See the *Beaufort*'s entry in the online *Dictionary of American Naval Fighting Ships*: http://www.history.navy.mil/danfs/cfa1/beaufort.htm.

8.   *ORN*, ser. 1, Vol. 2, 828–829, William Murdaugh to Stephen Mallory, 7 February 1863.

9.   *Ibid.*, 829; *ORN*, ser. 1, Vol. 2, 823, Robert Minor to Franklin Buchanan, 2 February 1864. Minor's letter also appeared n the *Richmond Dispatch* (15 December 1895) and *The Southern Historical Society Papers*. See *Southern Historical Society Papers*, Vol. XXIII (Richmond, VA: Southern Historical Society, 1895), 283–290.

10.   *ORN*, ser. 1, Vol. 2, 829–830, Murdaugh to Mallory.

11.   *ORN*, ser. 1, Vol. 2, 823, Minor to Buchanan.

12.   *Ibid.*; Bradley A. Rodgers's *Guardian of the Great Lakes: The U.S. Paddle Frigate Michigan* (Ann Arbor: University of Michigan Press, 1996) provides a scholarly account of the career of the USS *Michigan* (renamed USS *Wolverine* in 1905).

Launched in 1843, she was not decommissioned until 1912. The prow of the vessel has been preserved and is now on display at the Erie Maritime Museum in Erie, Pennsylvania.

13.   It is estimated that 10,000 Confederates passed through the military prison camp on Johnson's Island from April 1862 to September 1865. Of these, about 300 died while in custody. Charles E. Frohman's *Rebels on Lake Erie: The Piracy, The Conspiracy, Prison Life* (Columbus, OH: Ohio Historical Society, 1965) remains the most thorough account of the camp's history. For information on current preservation activities and ongoing archaeological investigations relating to the camp, see http://www.heidelberg.edu/johnsonsisland/.

14.   *ORN*, ser. 1, Vol. 2, 823, Minor to Buchanan; *OR*, ser. 2, Vol. 6, 311, Y.H. Blackwell to James A. Seddon (with unsigned enclosure from John Jay Archer), 21 September 1863. The C.C. Egerton mentioned in Archer's letter was probably the Baltimore businessman and senior militia officer Charles C. Egerton, Jr. By the time that Archer's message arrived in Richmond, neither of the two naval officers recommended by him were available for the operation. Bier had resigned his naval commission in 1862, and transferred to the army, where he served as a staff officer (ordnance) with Lieutenant-General T.J. "Stonewall" Jackson. As for Parker, he was about to take charge of the Confederate Naval Academy, a pet project of Secretary Mallory.

15.   Minor indicates that the naval officer John Wilkinson was specifically recommended in the letter that Seddon shared with him, which might suggest an author other than Archer. See *ORN*, ser. 1, Vol. 2, 823, Minor to Buchanan. It is also possible that Seddon — and not the letter writer — recommended Wilkinson, as the two were close friends. See John Wilkinson, *The Narrative of a Blockade-Runner* (New York: Sheldon & Co., 1877), 174.

16.   *ORN*, ser. 1, Vol. 2, 823, Minor to Buchanan.

17.   *Ibid.*

18.   Wilkinson, *The Narrative of a Blockade-Runner*, 169.

19.   *ORN*, ser. 1, Vol. 2, 823, Minor to Buchanan.

20.   *Ibid.*, 824.

21.   Wilkinson, *The Narrative of a Blockade-Runner*, 169.

22.   *ORN*, ser. 1, Vol. 2, 824, Minor to Buchanan.

23.   Shepardson often wrote under the pseudonym "Bohemian." For more on his wartime journalistic career, see J. Cutler Andrews, *The South Reports the Civil War* (Princeton: Princeton University Press, 1970), 448–551.

24.   *ORN*, ser. 1, Vol. 2, 824, Minor to Buchanan.

25.   *Ibid.* In his memoirs, Wilkinson gives the date of departure as 10 October (see Wilkinson, *The Narrative of a Blockade-Runner*, 169). It may be that the *Lee* left Wilmington on October 7 and Smithville on October 10; however, I have assumed that Minor's nearly contemporaneous account is more reliable in this regard than Wilkinson's memoir, written more than a decade after the events.

26.   Wilkinson, *The Narrative of a Blockade-Runner*, 171.

27. *ORN*, ser. 1, Vol. 2, 824, Minor to Buchanan; Wilkinson, *The Narrative of a Blockade-Runner*, 170.

28. *Ibid.*, 173.

29. *Ibid.*, 174; *ORN*, ser. 1, Vol. 2, 824, Minor to Buchanan.

30. For more on the activities of Wier and the other leading Confederate sympathizers in Halifax during the American Civil War, see Greg Marquis, *In Armageddon's Shadow: The Civil War and Canada's Maritime Provinces* (Montreal and Kingston: McGill-Queen's University Press, 1998).

31. Wilkinson, *The Narrative of a Blockade-Runner*, 174–176; Stephen R. Wise, *Lifeline of the Confederacy: Blockade Running During the Civil War* (Columbia, SC: University of South Carolina Press, 1988), 139, 318.

32. Wilkinson, *The Narrative of a Blockade-Runner*, 176, 187. For more on Judge Jackson's efforts to counteract Confederate operations in the Maritimes, see Marquis, *In Armageddon's Shadow*, 103–104.

33. Wilkinson, *The Narrative of a Blockade-Runner*, 176; *ORN*, ser. 1, Vol. 2, 824, Minor to Buchanan.

34. *Ibid.*, 173.

35. Wilkinson, *The Narrative of a Blockade-Runner*, 180.

36. For more on Confederate operatives in British North America, see John W. Headley, *Confederate Operations in Canada and New York* (New York, and Washington, DC: Neale Publishing Company, 1906); Robin W. Winks, *Canada and the United States: The Civil War Years* (Baltimore: Johns Hopkins Press, 1960); Oscar A. Kinchen, *Confederate Operations in Canada and the North* (North Quincy, MA: Christopher Publishing House, 1970).

37. Wilkinson, *The Narrative of a Blockade-Runner*, 181.

38. Marquis, *In Armageddon's Shadow*, 105–133.

39. *ORN*, ser. 1, Vol. 2, 824, Minor to Buchanan.

40. *Ibid.*

41. The first request to have the *Michigan* stationed at Sandusky Bay came in the late spring of 1862, not long after the establishment of the Johnson's Island PoW camp. However, she apparently did not take up her new station until more than a year later. See *OR*, ser. 2, Vol. 4, 42, William S. Pierson to William Hoffman, 19 June 1862; *Ibid.*, *OR*, ser. 2, Vol. 6, 435, William S. Pierson to William Hoffman, 28 October 1863.

42. Wilkinson, *The Narrative of a Blockade-Runner*, 181–185.

43. Kane, who had been imprisoned in 1861 for his secessionist activities, was often referred to as Marshal Kane. The *Maryland Online Encyclopedia* offers a useful biographical entry on him (http://www.mdoe.org/kanegeorge.html), although it should be noted that the article overlooks his exile in Canada.

44. *ORN*, ser. 1, Vol. 2, 825, Minor to Buchanan.

45. Wilkinson, *The Narrative of a Blockade-Runner*, 182; *ORN*, ser. 1, Vol. 2, 825, Minor to Buchanan.

46. Canada Parliament, *Sessional Papers of the Dominion of Canada; Volume VI; No.*

75; *Second Session of the First Parliament of the Dominion of Canada, Session 1869* (Ottawa: Hunter, Rose, 1869) [hereafter cited as *1869 Sessional Papers No. 75*], 79. The Camp Chase military prison was located at Columbus, Ohio. The Camp Douglas prison was in Chicago.

47. *ORN*, ser. 1, Vol. 2, 825, Minor to Buchanan.

48. Wilkinson, *The Narrative of a Blockade-Runner*, 184–185.

49. *Ibid.*, 185; *ORN*, ser. 1, Vol. 2, 825, Minor to Buchanan. For a brief biography, of McCuaig, see J.K. Johnson, ed., *The Canadian Directory of Parliament, 1867–1967* (Ottawa: Public Archives of Canada, 1968), 391.

50. *ORN*, ser. 1, Vol. 2, 825, Minor to Buchanan.

51. *Ibid.*, 825–826.

52. *Ibid.*, 826.

53. Wilkinson, *The Narrative of a Blockade-Runner*, 185–186.

54. *Ibid.*; *ORN*, ser. 1, Vol. 2, 826, Minor to Buchanan.

55. Wilkinson, *The Narrative of a Blockade-Runner*, 186.

56. *Ibid.*; *ORN*, ser. 1, Vol. 2, 826, Minor to Buchanan; *OR*, ser. 3, Vol. 3, 1013–1015; *1869 Sessional Papers No. 75*, 75–78. The behind-the-scenes story of the gathering and analyzing of intelligence relating to the first Lake Erie expedition is beyond the purview of this article, as is the diplomatic response to the attempted raid and its aftermath. The best summary of these aspects of the expedition is found in Winks, *Canada and the United States*, 145–154.

57. Wilkinson, *The Narrative of a Blockade-Runner*, 186.

58. *Ibid.*, 187.

59. *ORN*, ser. 1, Vol. 2, 826, Minor to Buchanan. Minor indicates here that the force comprised 52 men, whereas he had previously indicated that there were 54. In this instance, he is probably referring to the number of men who were under his and Wilkinson's command.

60. *Ibid.*

61. Winks, *Canada and the United States*, 148. Unfortunately, Henry C. Klassen's recent biography of Holton, *Luther H. Holton: A Founding Canadian Entrepreneur* (Calgary: University of Calgary Press, 2001) sheds very little light on Holton's role during the Civil War. Although the Confederates were convinced that McCuaig had gotten cold feet, it is possible that he had been asked to deliberately plant disinformation that would undermine the Confederate operation.

62. Wilkinson, *The Narrative of a Blockade-Runner*, 186–187.

63. *Ibid.*, 188; *ORN*, ser. 1, Vol. 2, 826, Minor to Buchanan.

64. Another party of returning Confederates, including George P. Kane and about 16 other men, mostly former PoWs, left Montreal for Halifax in late January or early February. It is possible that some of the former prisoners who had volunteered to serve in the commando force were among this group. See Halifax *Citizen* (4 February 1864).

65. *Ibid.*, 826-827; Wilkinson, *The Narrative of a Blockade-Runner*, 188–193.

66. *ORN*, ser. 1, Vol. 2, 826, Minor to Buchanan.

67. ORN, ser. 2, Vol. 3, 174, Jefferson Davis to Jacob Thompson, 27 April 1864.

68. For more on Thompson's activities in Canada, see Headley, *Confederate Operations in Canada and New York*; Winks, *Canada and the United States*; Kinchen, *Confederate Operations in Canada and the North*.

69. OR, ser. 1, Vol. 43, pt. 2, 934, Jacob Thompson to Judah P. Benjamin, 3 December 1864.

70. *Ibid.*, 932.

71. OR, ser. 2, Vol. 8, 708, A.A. Hosmer to W. Hoffman, 18 July 1865; Headley, *Confederate Operations in Canada and New York*, 310. Headley's book includes transcriptions of some archival documents that are not found in the OR or the ORN.

72. OR, ser. 1, Vol. 43, pt. 2, 934, Thompson to Benjamin.

73. *Ibid.*; Headley, *Confederate Operations in Canada and New York*, 231–235; Frohman, *Rebels on Lake Erie*, 73, 78p. For more on Carter's career, see David W. Francis, "The United States Navy and the Johnson's Island Conspiracy: The Case of John C. Carter," *Northwest Ohio Quarterly* LII, 3 (Summer 1980): 229–243. Interestingly, Carter was born in Virginia and was descended from a distinguished Southern family. His strong connections to the South may have raised some doubts regarding his commitment to the Union and probably contributed to the decision to relieve him of his command of the *Michigan* in October 1864. See Francis, "The United States Navy and the Johnson's Island Conspiracy," 232.

74. The infamous leader of the Copperheads (also known as Peace Democrats), Clement Vallandigham, was exiled in Canada from 1863 to 1864, during which time he ran for the governorship of Ohio. See Winks, *Canada and the United States*, 143.

75. Headley, *Confederate Operations in Canada and New York*, 233.

76. *Ibid.*

77. *Ibid.*, 241–248, 252; Luraghi, *A History of the Confederate Navy*, 303–304, 312.

78. William Washington Baker, *Memoirs of Service with John Yates Beall* (Richmond, VA: The Richmond Press, 1910), 47–49. It has been suggested that Beall was actually the first person to propose a Lake Erie raid. See Daniel Bedinger Lucas, *Memoir of John Yates Beall: His Life; Trial; Correspondence; Diary; and Private Manuscript Found Among His Papers, Including His Own Account of the Raid on Lake Erie* (Montreal: John Lovell, 1865), 19–20; Headley, *Confederate Operations in Canada and New York*, 242–243.

79. Baker, *Memoirs of Service with John Yates Beall*, 49.

80. Headley, *Confederate Operations in Canada and New York*, 233.

81. OR, ser. 1, Vol. 43, pt. 2, 226, John A. Dix to E.M. Stanton, 30 September 1864.

82. Kelleys Island is also known as Kelley's Island.

83. *Ibid.*, 234–235, 252.

84. OR, ser. 1, Vol. 43, pt. 2, 932, Thompson to Benjamin.

85. Headley, *Confederate Operations in Canada and New York*, 248. After the American Civil War, Bennett Burley changed his name to "Bennet Burleigh"

(possibly reverting to the original spelling). After several years of travel and campaigning as a soldier of fortune, he embarked on a career as a journalist, first in the United States and then in Britain, where he emerged as one of the leading war correspondents of the late Victorian era. For more on his remarkable career, see Lucas, *Memoir of John Yates Beall*, 20–22, 42–45; Headley, *Confederate Operations in Canada and New York*, 243–244, 462; Roger T. Stearn, "Bennet Burleigh: Victorian War Correspondent," *Soldiers of the Queen: The Journal of the Victorian Military Society* 65 (June 1991), 5–10. Apparently Burleigh never did write about his experiences as a Confederate naval commando. In fact, according to an obituary, he was reticent about this period of his life: "it has never been possible to get a very clear and consistent story of the young fire-eater's adventures during these stirring times." See *The Times* (18 June 1914).

86. Headley, *Confederate Operations in Canada and New York*, 251; *OR*, ser. 1, Vol. 43, pt. 2, 239, affidavit of S.F. Atwood, 25 September 1864.

87. *Ibid.*, 229, Dix to Stanton.

88. The Confederate's seizure of the *Philo Parsons* is now commemorated by an Ontario provincial heritage plaque at Amherstburg. See the web page http://www.ontarioplaques.com/Plaques_DEF/Plaque_Essex05.html.

89. *Ibid.*, 242–243, affidavit of W.O. Ashley, 25 September 1864.

90. *Ibid.*, 243–244; 240, affidavit of De Witt C. Nichols, 25 September 1864; Headley, *Confederate Operations in Canada and New York*, 250.

91. *OR*, ser. 1, Vol. 43, pt. 2, 240, affidavit of Nichols.

92. *Ibid.*, 235–237, 240, 243, affidavits of James Denison, Michael Campbell, Nichols, Ashley.

93. *Ibid.*, 236–237, 240–241, 243, affidavits of Denison, Campbell, Nichols, Ashley.

94. *Ibid.*, 236–239, 241, 243, affidavits of Denison, Campbell, Atwood, Nichols, Ashley.

95. *Ibid.*, 239, affidavit of Atwood.

96. *Ibid.*, 240.

97. *Ibid.*, 228, Dix to Stanton; 239, affidavit of Atwood. Interestingly, the *Island Queen* was the first vessel to transport prisoners from Sandusky to Johnson's Island, in April 1862. See Frohman, *Rebels on Lake Erie*, 8.

98. *Ibid.*, 227, Dix to Stanton; 236, 239, 243, affidavits of Denison, Atwood, Ashley.

99. *Ibid.*, 244–245 affidavit of Henry Haines.

100. After the Confederates' departure, one of the released prisoners, George Magle, the mate of the *Island Queen*, apparently crossed from Middle Bass Island to Put-in-Bay, on South Bass Island, where he alerted the residents to the Confederate plot. John Brown, Jr., a son of the fiery abolitionist, was then living on the island and quickly organized an armed force and prepared for a possible Confederate attack. Early the following morning, Brown, together with three other men, crossed to the mainland in very rough seas and then made their way to Johnson's Island. See Theresa Thorndale, *Sketches and Stories of the Lake Erie Islands* (Sandusky, OH: I.F. Mack & Brother, 1898), 71–74. Thorndale was a pseudonym of the journalist

Lydia J. Ryall. Her book, a second edition of which was issued under her own name in 1913, includes a first-person account of the Confederate raid by George W. Orr, the *Island Queen*'s captain. For more on Brown's role, also see *OR*, ser, 2, Vol. 7, 903, Charles W. Hill to E.A. Hitchcock, 1 October 1864.

101.   *OR*, ser. 1, Vol. 43, pt. 2, 236, 239, 241, affidavits of Denison, Atwood, Nichols.

102.   *Ibid.*, 245, affidavit of Haines.

103.   *Ibid.*

104.   *Ibid.*, 244, affidavit of Ashley.

105.   Thorndale, *Sketches and Stories of the Lake Erie Islands*, 78.

106.   *OR*, ser. 1, Vol. 43, pt. 2, 236–237, 241, 245, affidavits of Denison, Campbell, Nichols, Haines; Headley, *Confederate Operations in Canada and New York*, 250.

107.   *OR*, ser. 1, Vol. 43, pt. 2, 237, affidavit of Campbell.

108.   Lucas, *Memoir of John Yates Beall*, 296.

109.   Thorndale, *Sketches and Stories of the Lake Erie Islands*, 78.

110.   Headley, *Confederate Operations in Canada and New York*, 250–251.

111.   *OR*, ser. 1, Vol. 43, pt. 2, 233, B.H. Hill to C.H. Potter, 21 September 1864. Although Hill does not identify his informant, it probably was Godfrey Joseph Hyams, who was active in Jacob Thompson's Canadian network of Southern operatives and later openly betrayed the Confederates. See Headley, *Confederate Operations in Canada and New York*, 215, 281, 308, 381; *1869 Sessional Papers No. 75*, 112, James Cockburn to Denis Godley, 1 June 1865; Canada Parliament, *Journals of the House of Commons of the Dominion of Canada from November 6, 1867, to May 22, 1868, Both Days Inclusive; In the Thirty-First Year of the Reign of Our Sovereign, Lady Queen Victoria; Being the 1st session of the 1st Parliament of the Dominion of Canada; Session 1867–8* (Ottawa: Hunter, Rose, [1868]) [hereafter cited as *Journals of the House of Commons of the Dominion of Canada from November 6, 1867, to May 22, 1868*], Appendix No. 7, [1–3]. See also *OR*, ser. 1, Vol. 3, 496, extract from D. Hunter's consular dispatch No. 21, 7 April 1865. Hyam's name in this latter document is misspelled as "Hyarns." It is interesting to note that John Wilson Murray, the most famous Canadian detective of the Victorian era, claims to have been a gunner on the USS *Michigan* during the Civil War and insists that he was ordered by Captain Carter to uncover and foil the Confederate plot to seize the gunboat. While his account of the incident, which was co-authored, if not entirely ghosted, by Victor Speers, is colourful and entertaining, it is so riddled with gross errors and improbabilities that it must be regarded as fiction. See John Wilson Murray, *Memoirs of a Great Detective: Incidents in the Life of John Wilson Murray* (London: William Heinemann, 1904), 10–19. For a scholarly critical assessment of the reliability of Murray's memoirs as a source, see Jim Phillips and Joel Fortune, "Murray, John Wilson," *Dictionary of Canadian Biography Online,* http://www.biographi.ca/EN/ShowBio.asp?BioId=41073&query=. See also Frohman, *Rebels on Lake Erie*, 99–100.

112.   *Ibid.*, 235, B.H. Hill to J.C. Carter, 19 September 1864.

113.   *Ibid.*, J.C. Carter to B.H. Hill, 19 September 1864.

114. *OR*, ser. 1, Vol. 43, pt. 2, 237–238, affidavit of Campbell.

115. *Ibid.*, 236, 238, 241, 242, 245, affidavits of Denison, Campbell, Nichols, Haines.

116. Headley, *Confederate Operations in Canada and New York*, 251–252; Lucas, *Memoir of John Yates Beall*, 45.

117. *Ibid.*

118. *OR*, ser. 2I, Vol. 7, 864–865, Jacob Thompson and Clement C. Clay, Jr. to Jefferson Davis, 22 September 1864.

119. *Ibid.*, 864, Jacob Thompson and Clement C. Clay, Jr. to B.H. Hill, 22 September 1864.

120. For more on the St. Alban's Raid, see *inter alia* Winks, *Canada and the United States*, 295–336; Kinchen, *Confederate Operations in Canada and the North*, 127–147; Oscar A. Kinchen, *Daredevils of the Confederate Army: The Story of the St. Albans Raiders* (North Quincy, MA: Christopher Publishing House, 1959); Dennis K. Wilson, *Justice Under Pressure: The St. Albans Raid and Its Aftermath* (Lanham, MD: University Press of America, 1992).

121. Headley, *Confederate Operations in Canada and New York*, 254.

122. In some respects this third Lake Erie plan resembled an earlier proposal, probably by James D. Bulloch, the Confederacy's chief agent in England, to purchase a steamer in the United Kingdom that could be converted into a warship and used to strike against the Union on the Great Lakes. One drawback to this plan was that the vessel would have to pass through the Welland Canal without her true ownership and purpose being detected by British, Canadian, and Union authorities — an increasingly unlikely scenario as the war progressed. See Wilkinson, *The Narrative of a Blockade-Runner*, 188.

123. United Kingdom Parliament, *North America No. 1 (1865); Correspondence Respecting the Attack on St. Albans, Vermont and Naval Force on the North American Lakes; With Appendices* (London: s.n., 1865), [hereafter cited as *North America No. 1 (1865)*], 37–39, 41; *OR*, ser. 1, Vol. 3, 495–496; Headley, *Confederate Operations in Canada and New York*, 244. It has been suggested that the Scotsmen Burley and Robertson were actually cousins. See Claire Hoy, *Canadians in the Civil War* (Toronto: McArthur & Company, 2004), 246.

124. *North America No. 1 (1865)*, 39, J.J. Kingsmill to John A. Macdonald, 19 November 1864.

125. *OR*, ser 1, Vol. 3, 496, Bennett Burley to Dr. S.B. [James T.] Bates, 17 October 1864. This letter was intercepted by the double agent Godfrey Hyams and supplied to Union authorities.

126. See the *Georgian's* entry in the online *Dictionary of American Naval Fighting Ships*: http://www.history.navy.mil/danfs/cfa4/georgian.htm.

127. *OR*, ser. 1, Vol. 43, pt. 2, 934, Thompson to Benjamin; *1869 Sessional Papers No. 75*, 88-90.

128. *Ibid.*, 89–91. Among the documents cited here is a report from "Fides," a Toronto-based undercover detective who was supplying information on Confederate activities to William G. Fargo, the mayor of Buffalo.

129. *North America No. 1 (1865)*, 37–39, 41–42, 53–55; Toronto *Globe* (17 April 1865); *OR*, ser 1, Vol. 3, 496, Burley to Bates; *1869 Sessional Papers No. 75*, 84–87. The Greek Fire of the Civil War era was an incendiary liquid that apparently consisted of a mixture of phosphorous and carbon bisulphide. The concoction was designed to burst into flames when exposed to the air, but was not an entirely reliable weapon. See Headley, *Confederate Operations in Canada and New York*, 272–273; Kinchen, *Confederate Operations in Canada and the North*, 60–61.

130. Toronto *Globe* (17 April 1865).

131. Headley, *Confederate Operations in Canada and New York*, 254–255.

132. *1869 Sessional Papers No. 75*, 90, 93–95; *ORN*, Vol. 1, No. 3, F.A. Roe to Gideon Welles, 6 December 1864.

133. *North America No. 1 (1865)*, 39, Kingsmill to Macdonald. Now designated as a provincial heritage property, Ferndell is operated as a bed and breakfast. See the website www.ferndell.ca.

134. *North America No. 1 (1865)*, 39, Kingsmill to Macdonald.

135. *North America No. 1 (1865)*, 36–42.

136. Headley, *Confederate Operations in Canada and New York*, 255.

137. *Ibid.*

138. *1869 Sessional Papers No. 75*, 92–94.

139. For more on Denison's early career and his relationships with many leading Confederates, see Lieutenant-Colonel George T. Denison, *Soldiering in Canada: Recollections and Experiences* (Toronto: George N. Morang and Company, 1900), 29–82. In 1877 Denison won an international contest, sponsored by the Czar of Russia, for the most authoritative text on the history of cavalry. Denison's study includes an interesting chapter on the role of cavalry in the American Civil War. See Lieutenant-Colonel George T. Denison, *History of Cavalry from the Earliest Times, with Lessons for the Future* (London: Macmillan and Co., 1877), 436–484.

140. *1869 Sessional Papers No. 75*, 93–94.

141. Denison, *Soldiering in Canada*, 59.

142. Headley, *Confederate Operations in Canada and New York*, 301–307.

143. *1869 Sessional Papers No. 75*, 83. See also Charles S. Blue, "Famous Canadian Trials VIII: The Case of Bennett Burley, the Lake Erie 'Pirate,'" *The Canadian Magazine* XLV, 3 (July 1915): 190–196.

144. *OR*, ser 2, Vol. 8, 398–400. Beall's trial is documented in Lucas, *Memoir of John Yates Beall*, 91–216; see also *Trial of John Y. Beall: as a Spy and a Guerrillero, by Military Commission* (New York: D. Appleton and Company, 1865).

145. For more on the Booth–Beall connection and Booth's time in Canada, see *inter alia* Isaac Markens, *President Lincoln and the Case of John Y. Beall* (New York: Isaac Markens, 1911); Clayton Gray, *Conspiracy in Canada* (Montreal: L'Atelier Press, 1957); William A. Tidwell, *April '65: Confederate Covert Actions in the American Civil War* (Kent, OH: Kent State University Press, 1995).

146.   *1869 Sessional Papers No. 75*, 96–97; *Journals of the House of Commons of the Dominion of Canada from November 6, 1867, to May 22, 1868*, 291, 412; Appendix No. 7, [1–3].

147.   See Jay Winik, *April 1865: The Month That Saved America* (New York: HarperCollins, 2001) for an authoritative account of the war's end, which was less abrupt — and far less inevitable — than many historians have implied.

148.   Kinchen, *Confederate Operations in Canada and the North*, 210–216; Winks, *Canada and the United States*, 361–362. Winks states that Thompson travelled to Halifax by way of Portland, Maine, an extremely unlikely route, given the circumstances. Kinchen's arguments for an all-Canadian escape route are far more persuasive.

149.   *North America No. 1 (1865)*, 101–106.

150.   *ORN*, ser. 1, Vol. 2, 822, Minor to Buchanan.

CHAPTER 6

Accidental Heroes:
The "Royal Canadians" Redeem British Honour
at Paardeberg

BERND HORN

Shots continued to ring out from the Boer entrenchments as the early morning dawn began to leak light onto the cold, forbidding South African landscape. Nervous Boer sentries, still recovering from the night attack scant hours ago, bolstered their courage by maintaining a steady stream of lead at the British lines. However, their anxiety was quickly replaced by shock as daylight revealed Canadian soldiers in newly dug trenches not even 100 yards away! British forces now outflanked the besieged Boer position. Within minutes white flags began to appear.

The British had finally won their first victory of the war. Even though it was the colonials, namely largely inexperienced volunteers from The Royal Canadian Regiment, who were responsible, the victory was celebrated as an Imperial accomplishment. Undeniably, it was a seminal triumph. The victory changed how British regulars, and the English people, viewed colonials (at least for a short while). It also bestowed on a recently independent Canada international recognition, which is often only earned through military prowess and sacrifice. And finally, the battle was the turning point in the war. In its aftermath, the momentum dramatically shifted and British victory became only a question of time. However, when the battle of Paardeberg is closely examined, the question arises of whether it was a daring feat of arms or whether the Canadians were accidental heroes.

On 11 October 1899, Britain officially went to war with the republics of Transvaal and the Orange Free State. Conflict in South Africa was long in brewing and by the summer of 1899, the relationship between the British and the Boers had deteriorated dramatically, ostensibly over the denial of civic and social rights of the Uitlanders (non-residents) in the

Boer republics. This affront to the fair treatment and democratic freedom of British subjects was too much for some to bear. The fact that large deposits of precious minerals were recently discovered in the breakaway territories did not help ease the tension.[1]

The British, however, were largely unconcerned. Their political and military leadership were confident that the conflict would be quickly concluded. The Boers, after all, were little more than "the levies of two insignificant Republics whose forces were but loose gatherings of armed farmers."[2] Lord Dundonald so doubted the capability of his opponents that he actually queried an officer of the locally raised scouts, on the eve of battle, if "the Boers would [actually] fight when they saw Her Majesty's troops."[3]

Despite the British optimism, they still aggressively sought support from their colonies. The British government wanted colonial contingents for political reasons — a show of Imperial unity — not for their military application or worth. "We do not want the men," wrote Chamberlain to the Canadian Governor-General, "the whole point of the offer would be lost unless it was endorsed by the Government of the Colony."[4] Colonial contingents, as far as the British were concerned, would be absorbed into British units and formations. Moreover, they would be used largely for garrison, picket, and rear area security tasks, since British regulars had little faith in the martial prowess of militiamen, and even less of colonials.

However, British arrogance quickly disappeared. The conflict did not go as they expected. As the war progressed in the autumn of 1899, British soldiers and politicians alike were shocked at the fighting prowess of the Boers, who, on one occasion after another, inflicted humiliating and costly defeats on the British field force. These unexpected "drubbings" pointed out that the Imperial Army was woefully inadequate to meet the challenges of modern warfare. The humiliating climax came during the week of 10–15 December 1899 when three separate British formations were decisively beaten at Stormberg, Magersfontein, and Colenso. These fateful seven days were appropriately labelled "Black Week."[5]

The impact in South Africa was enormous. During "Black Week" the high commissioner in Capetown, Alfred, Lord Milner despondently cabled Joseph Chamberlain, the colonial secretary in London, "This is the worst blow we have sustained yet during the war." He added, "The impression it has created here is simply deplorable, and this is sure to be the case throughout the Colony." Milner's alarming entry in his diary the next day had more than a hint of panic:

> December 12th [1899] — The news to-day is again extremely bad. There can be no doubt that General Gatacre's defeat on Sunday was a very severe one, and the effect of a large number of British prisoners being taken through a rebel district of the Colony into the Orange Free State cannot but be most injurious. One consequence is that, as reported by various magistrates, armed men are leaving their homes in various parts of the eastern districts, and going to join the enemy.[6]

Two days later, he acknowledged that there existed a "deep depression in loyal circles in consequence of the three disasters of the past week." He lamented, "General Buller's defeat on the Tugela [River], coming on the top of Stormberg and Magersfontein, has been rather too much for the bravest." By Christmas, he informed Chamberlain "The effects of the reverses at Stormberg, Magersfontein, and Colenso is cumulative." He warned, "Even in the remotest country districts it is now known that the enemy have had great successes." He ominously added, "the spirit of rebellion has received an enormous impetus — even in districts hitherto comparatively quiet."[7]

The effect elsewhere in the Empire was similarly dramatic. "The military situation is without doubt at this moment most grave and critical," reported Winston Churchill, the future prime minister of Britain, who was a correspondent at the onset of the conflict. "We have been at war three weeks," he explained, "[and] the army that was to have defended Natal, and was indeed expected to repulse the invaders with terrible loss, is blockaded and bombarded in its fortified camp." He added, "At nearly every point along the circle of the frontiers the Boers have advanced and the British retreated. Wherever we have stood we have been surrounded … All this is mainly the result of being unready … It is also due to an extraordinary under-estimation of the strength of the Boers."[8] England now turned to their former colonies in a desperate plea for troops, no longer for political impact, but rather for fighting men.

And so, the 1,039 largely inexperienced Canadian volunteers forming the 2nd Special Service Battalion of The Royal Canadian Regiment entered what appeared to be a desperate struggle against a wily and very capable enemy. Nonetheless, the "green" Canadian soldiers were eager to get to the fight. Despite their inexperience — the raw material was there. "Of the physique and high intelligence of all ranks of the Battalion," wrote Lieutenant-Colonel William Otter, their commanding officer, "I could not but form the very highest opinion, and it was in a great measure due to these qualities that ultimate success accrued."[9] Hence the disappointment of the men when their expectations of battle were not immediately met.

The Battalion disembarked at Cape Town on 30 November, but it was not allowed to linger long. The desperate situation in the field necessitated their presence at the front. Therefore, they entrained the next day for Belmont. However, contrary to their expectations and desires, they were not deployed to battle. Rather, they spent the next two hot and monotonous months securing the lines of communication. Their battles were more with boredom, hunger, and the harsh environment. These conditions, exacerbated by a rigid, uncompromising, and dispassionate commanding officer (CO), created morale problems.

Outpost duty was both demanding and particularly tedious. "Our present duties has I think," penned Otter in the Battalion report, "a depressing effect upon the men — these duties consist of outpost fatigues and working parties and are very heavy."[10] Private Ramsay explained, "We sleep in our tents with most of our clothes on and our accoutre-

Lieutenant-Colonel W.D. Otter, Commander First Canadian Contingent, the 2nd (Special Service) Battalion, The RCR.

LAC, C-14234.

216

ments at our side." He added, "I haven't had my boots off for nearly two weeks and have forgotten what a bath is like."[11]

The harsh environment also tested the troops. Their indoctrination came immediately. The first day introduced the "Royal Canadians" to conditions they would soon come only too familiar with. "Little or nothing to eat, stinking slushy water to drink, no tents for shelter on a hot summer day in Africa and a terrible rain storm," reported one participant.[12] And when it was not raining, there was the other constant irritant. "There is nothing but sand, sand, sand and a few little tufts of sage brush here and there and then there are sand storms," complained Private Jesse Briggs, "They are dense, choking, blinding and penetrate every crevice."[13]

The shortage of food was another major dissatisfier. "Things are going from bad to worse here in the way of grub," complained Private Bennett, "we are on poor rations and we are even on water rations."[14] On a number of occasions, Bennett, like others, passed on advice to those who may have been considering volunteering for the Second Contingent. "Well if the boys took my advice they would stay at home," he counselled, "for there is nothing here but a burning sun and desert storm." He added, "This is the most forsaken country I have ever seen."[15]

Lieutenant-Colonel Otter was another major aggravation. "How the boys dislike that man," revealed Private Perkins.[16] Although an experienced and skilled soldier, he was dour and uninspiring, and the men found him rigid and uncompromising. They chaffed at his discipline and endless drills. Moreover, they resented his refusal to allow a dry canteen, such as existed in all other regimental bivouacs. More odious yet, he would not even allow the YMCA to provide such a service. In addition, they felt he did not push his British superiors for better, more active, employment. "I don't think much of Colonel Otter ... The boys call him the Old Woman and many other pretty stiff names," confided one soldier in a letter home. "He is too fond I think of giving the men too much marching, and that at a time when it interferes with a fellow's grub time."[17]

The fact that Otter was the interim commandant of Belmont station did not help matters. His seeming preoccupation with garrison duties and mundane training created resentment. The eventual arrival of the British-appointed commandant, Lieutenant-Colonel Thomas Pilcher, just enflamed the problem. Within his first week, he organized a flying column that included "C" Company, The RCR, and launched a highly successful strike against a group of Boers who were conducting operations near the town of Douglas.

On 1 January 1900, his flying column surprised the Boers at Sunnyside Kopje. As the artillery shelled the unprepared enemy, the Royal Canadians seized a small *kopje* 1200 metres from the enemy position and opened fire on the Boers. As the other British forces closed the noose on the Boers, the Canadians advanced on the enemy position closing to approximately 200 metres and now awaited the order to charge. However, after four hours of fighting and almost totally surrounded, the Boers fled towards Douglas. The fight had been a great success. The small British force had killed six enemy, wounded 12, and captured 34.[18]

This engagement represented the first experience under fire for the Canadians, yet it seemed they conducted themselves well. "Although the fire of the Boers was apparently very hot for a time," reported Otter, "LCol Pilcher who commanded the flying column ... speaks very highly of the steadiness under fire and general good conduct of the Royal Canadians during this special service."[19]

The attack at Sunnyside simply increased the grousing. It was not lost on the RCR soldiers that Pilcher, even though newly arrived as Commandant of Belmont Station, spent his time planning and conducting offensive operations instead of miring himself in administration. Not surprisingly, the criticisms of Otter continued and grew.

But the expectations of the soldiers were somewhat misguided as well. Their inexperience could be fatal. Otter's memories of the fight at Ridgeway in 1866 against the Fenians and later combat in the North-West Rebellion in 1885, taught him the importance of drill, discipline, and fitness. His emphasis on marching and battle drill, specifically the new "rushing tactics" that stemmed from the lessons of the defeats of "Black Week," were instrumental in preparing the Royal Canadians for their upcoming campaign. So too were the occasional forays into the outlying areas on reconnaissance. In all, these activities improved the physical endurance of the troops and gave them experience in operating in the harsh environment, as well as a better knowledge of the country and terrain. As late as 11 February, Otter noted, "I confess to being somewhat disappointed in the condition of many of the men ... I find that there are many who it is unsafe to put upon any extra strain for the reason that they are constitutionally unable to meet it."[20] Therefore, this initial period, as monotonous as it may have seemed, was instrumental in preparing the men for what lay ahead.

The adage *be careful of what you ask for* never rang more true. The Battalion clamoured for action and they would soon realize their wish. On 12 February the Battalion moved to Gras-Pan and joined 19 Brigade under Major-General Horrace Smith-Dorrien.[21] The Battalion was now to begin an epic campaign. Lord Roberts's army of 35,000 men was set to march to Bloemfontein, which would effectively relieve the siege of Kimberley and Ladysmith since it would force the withdrawal of the besieging Boer armies from their positions of vantage in Natal and Cape Colony or risk themselves being cut off and surrounded. The march, however, would be done without railway support. This necessitated the bare minimum of supplies. Tents, extra equipment, and all other super-fluous materials were left behind.[22]

The march for The RCR, who now numbered 31 officers and 865 other ranks, commenced on 13 February 1900. The first three days were exceedingly difficult. Although only marching an average of 19 kilome-tres a day, the hot climate, difficult terrain, and supplemental fatigue duties, such as assisting heavy naval guns cross rivers, took its toll. The capture of a convoy of 200 British supply wagons by the Boers on the morning of 15 February also had a significant impact. It meant that all, despite the arduous conditions, would be on short rations for the fore-seeable future.

The next day the Battalion moved into Jacobsdal and remained there during the day. Due to the excessive heat, the advance was resumed at night. That evening at 2100 hours, the Battalion departed for Klip Drift on the Modder River. Seven hours later, they arrived at their objective and rested until 1800 hours, when they set off once again for Paardeberg Drift. At 0600 hours, on 18 February, the Royal Canadians arrived at their destination, extremely fatigued and famished. Immediately, arrangements were made for a much-anticipated breakfast, despite the meagre rations available.

The meal was barely started when shots rang out in the distance. The British field force had caught General Piet Cronje's army of 5,000 on the Modder River. The hunter had become the hunted. The Boer army

Photographer Reinhold Thiele, LAC, C-014923.

RCR soldiers crossing the swift flowing Modder River at Paardeberg Drift, 18 February 1900.

that had just recently besieged Kimberley was now itself trapped. The RCR were ordered to dislodge or capture them. By 0720 hours, the Royal Canadians, most without a meal, deployed from their lines.

The troops were not impressed. "The state of many of the men was now pitiable," reported one embedded journalist. "The short rations, want of water, lack of sleep, and long, tedious and irregular marches had told on them," he wrote. "Others were chafed and bleeding with the sand," he added, "we threw ourselves down half-dead and were just in the act of getting breakfast, when the order came that we were to form for the attack."[23]

The perspective of the soldiers was not much different. "We were pretty well fatigued as we had not slept or ate or even had a drink of water since yesterday," scribbled Lance-Corporal John Kennedy Hill in his diary.[24] Another account reinforced the state of exhaustion. "On the night of the 17th we made a forced march (about 23 miles) arriving on the scene at daybreak," recorded Private F. Dunham in his diary. "We thought that before we went into action we should receive some food to fill our shrunken stomachs but no, we had hardly halted when we were ordered to wade the Modder [river] & attack the N[orth] side," he wrote acidly.[25]

The river proved to be a formidable obstacle. It was five deep and the current ran at approximately 25 kilometres an hour. Ropes were

Royal Canadian Regiment Archives and Museum.

5.A.M. AFTER 22. MILES MARCH. 39.

Exhausted "Royals" snatch some rest after a gruelling 35-kilometre march over the harsh African veldt.

strung from bank to bank to assist with the crossing, but, to speed up the process, groups of four men linked arms and struck for the opposite side. "We did wade across that swiftly flowing river right up to our necks, four abreast," explained Dunham, "If one slipped he was supported by his comrades. Thus we gained the opposite bank."[26] Lance-Corporal John Kennedy Hill, with a timeless understatement, recounted, "We had quite a time crossing as water was up to our chins and current very strong."[27]

Once on the other side, the men were immediately deployed into extended order in the direction of the Boer positions. By 0930 hours, the Battalion was firm on the other bank and began what would be nine days of fighting for Paardeberg Drift.[28] Their baptism of fire was a true test of their mettle. "This was the first time [18 February] our Regiment as a whole were engaged," wrote Dunham. "Within 1800 yards of their position the bullets began to hum around … But nothing daunted us as we kept steadily marching forward." He explained further:

> A sort of wild excitement to be at them came upon us so we hastened forward.… Within 800 yards we supported the front or firing line. Things began to be rather hot so we adopted the rushing tactics, that is running fifty yards then lying down for a few minutes for breath and again pushing on. This we kept up to within 450 yards for the fire was too hot and their aim too sure. Here we lay for several hours keeping up a hot fire all the time. The sun showed no mercy on us. Instead it seemed to shine with greater fierceness so that the sweat rolled from us as it never rolled before.[29]

The Battalion had advanced with "A," "B," and "C" Companies in the forward firing line under Lieutenant-Colonel Lawrence Buchan, the Battalion second-in-command (2IC). "D" and "E" Companies were in support and the remainder in reserve. They were flanked by the Duke of Cornwall's Light Infantry (Cornwalls) on the right (but on the other side of the river), and the King's Own Shropshire Light Infantry (Shropshires), and Gordon Highlanders on the left.

Not surprisingly, the confusion on the battlefield was great. "The bullets were whizzing past us, and throwing little sprays of sand in all directions as they struck the ground," recalled Sergeant W. Hart-McHarg, "in a very few minutes we were well in the fire zone, and were ordered to lie down."[30] He quickly observed that all around them were men of the other British regiments. The advance continued until the Royal Canadians reached the forward firing line where they intermingled with the British regulars. Often men could not fire at the Boers for fear of hitting their comrades who were in the line of fire.

Nonetheless, once the Canadians reached the firing line the advance came to a grinding halt. The Boer fire was simply too overwhelming. Their accurate and smooth firing bolt-action Mauser rifles cracked ceaselessly at any target that showed itself. "We lay in the burning sun, under the cover of small bushes or anthills, or lying flat on the open, jamming ourselves into the very ground to escape the peppering hail of bullets which ripped, whirred, and whinged a continual chorus of malignant warning," recounted one participant.[31]

The Royal Canadians were now strung out in front of the Boer positions from approximately 400 metres on the right to 700 metres on the left, the difference owing to the terrain that allowed the troops on the right more cover. Many, overcome with fatigue and feeling the effects of the relentless burning sun, fell asleep clinging to the ground or behind whatever scanty cover they could find. Some died this way — the target of Boer marksmen who continued to shoot at any target they could locate. The official Battalion report noted that "The enemy's fire was … delivered when the least exposure was made by our men … on our part the fire discipline was excellent, the men being cool and collected, but they laboured under the difficulty of fighting an invisible enemy."[32]

At 1530 hours a brief thunderstorm drenched the pinned-down soldiers, providing some relief. But the storm seemed almost an omen for the tempest that would shortly engulf the Royal Canadians. Approximately 30 minutes later the commanding officer of the Cornwalls, Lieutenant-Colonel William Aldworth, who had been ordered by Lord Kitchener to "finish this thing," arrived on the battlefield.[33] After a very brief and unpleasant discussion with Otter, he "proposed going in with bayonet." He then ordered three of his companies across the river and moved them forward to the firing line. Then, at approximately 1715 hours, after "offering five pounds to the first man in the enemy's trenches," Aldworth ordered his men to charge and "invited" all others from the wide array of gathered regiments to join them.[34] The effect was electric. Along the whole line, the intermingled soldiers of the various regiments who had been paralyzed by inactivity were seized by the sudden excitement. The Canadians were no different and immediately rose and joined the charge.

"It was about 4:30 in the afternoon that the order passed along the line like a thunderbolt to 'fix bayonets,'" recalled Private Dunham. "Never for a moment did we flinch, so when the order came to prepare to charge we jumped to our feet with a stifled cheer & charged."[35] Excitement and enthusiasm, however, were not enough. "And, oh! That wild, mad charge against an invisible enemy," explained Reverend O'Leary. "Hell let loose would give but a faint idea of it."[36] Had those on the ground been questioned, they would have answered that a charge was a very foolish idea.

"When we started to move," recalled Lieutenant J.C. Mason, "the bullets fell like a perfect hailstorm."[37] One journalist present wrote, "The men tumbled like skittles on every side."[38] Private Dunham explained, "It was too hot for us; we were compelled to stop."[39] Another participant observed that the enemy "opened a fearful fire on us which compelled us to lie down again and take cover as to advance ... would have been mere madness and could have done no good."[40] Both Mason and Dunham agreed it was a needless act. Mason felt that "it was a hopeless undertaking to cover 600 yards of open ground when the enemy had the exact range," and Dunham wrote resignedly that "the order to charge was another of those blunderings which cost our army so dear."[41] The brigade commander, Major-General Smith-Dorrien, later told his troops he had not ordered the charge — which was the truth.[42]

The charge occurred nonetheless. Lieutenant-Colonel Aldworth was one of the first to fall in the ill-fated assault. In the end, the charge netted only another 200 yards.[43] At that point the soldiers once again were forced to fling themselves to the ground and desperately attempt to melt into any available crack and crevice to avoid the deadly reach of the Mauser bullets. Darkness now became their only hope and salvation. At about 1900 hours, once the battlefield was cloaked in obscurity, Otter gave the order to withdraw. "Within a few hundred yards of the enemy we lay till night closed around us, then quietly retired," scribbled Dunham in his diary. "It was a sad moment for us, to leave the ground we had so dearly won."[44] The day's action cost the Battalion 21 killed and 60 wounded.

Although darkness provided a reprieve, it was clear to all — the Battalion had been blooded. Moreover, its young adventurers who sought "action" now realized war's grim side. "We all agree," wrote one young soldier, "that we have had all the fighting we want, and will be glad to get back to the line of communication as soon as possible."[45]

Despite the unsuccessful assault, the British had achieved some success. At nightfall the Boers, too, withdrew, albeit to better a defensive position. Regardless, Cronje's large army was now completely surrounded by an overwhelming British force. Moreover, the trap was sufficiently strong that he could not break out, nor could Boer reinforcements relieve the pressure or save him. As such, the siege progressed with antagonists manning entrenchments and continuing a constant harassing fire by both artillery and small arms.

The Royal Canadians took their turn manning both outposts and the main entrenchment facing the Boers. On the 19th, the Battalion buried its dead and manned a series of outposts five kilometres up river and approximately 3,500 metres from the Boer *laager*. Two days later the Battalion was sent to Artillery Hill to support the naval guns that were shelling the Boers with lyddite, as well as man a series of outposts at night. On the 22nd they were relieved, but the arrival of a large Boer force that intended to break the siege meant that they were reassigned with the remainder of 19 Brigade to man a line of *kopjes* to the West as a blocking force. On the 24th, after three days — during which time there was an incessant heavy rain — the Battalion was sent back to Paardeberg Drift for a rest. This proved to be of little value as the torrential rains continued throughout the night turning their bivouac into a quagmire.

The mud, however, was the least of their concerns. The heavy rains caused the river, which ran through their bivouac and which was the only source of drinking water, to flood. The swift current that also ran through the Boer laager now carried the debris of the besieged camp — specifically its dead and its waste. Otter reported that the greater part of their "rest day" was spent polling off dead men and animals from

LAC, C-3477.

Temporary bivouac in Bloemfontein. The primitive living conditions and inability of the British Army to provide adequate logistical support to colonial troops fuelled Canada's future position on national command for its contingents overseas.

the banks of their bivouac to prevent them creating a dam. In the brief 24-hour period spent in the camp, Otter estimated that a minimum of 720 bodies and carcasses drifted down from the Boer *laager*. This fouling of the drinking supply would later create grave problems in the form of enteric and typhoid fever that eventually affected 350 men in the Battalion, 10 percent of which would actually die from disease. [46]

On the morning of 26 February, the Battalion was ordered into the trenches to relieve the Cornwalls. The entrenchments were gradually being pushed towards the enemy position. When the Royal Canadians arrived they found themselves approximately 600 metres from the Boer lines. For the remainder of the day the Canadians engaged the Boers with small arms fire. All hoped for an end to the siege and most felt that the end was near. "At present we are surrounding Cronje and his force, and now have them cooped up like rats in a hole, though it has been at a great cost," wrote one participant. "We are shelling them continually with shrapnel and lyddite [high explosive], and they are readily famished, as we have learned from prisoners and almost ready to surrender."[47]

With such a turn of events the British commanders decided to put additional pressure on the Boers. In the afternoon, the Battalion received word that a night attack would be conducted at 0200 hours. Preparations were undertaken and the Battalion braced for its second major engagement of the war. However, the soldiers were not all overly enthusiastic. "Nothing is so trying on the nerves as a night attack," confided Private Dunham to his diary, "and we had lots of time to ponder on it."[48]

The plan of attack was for six RCR companies in the main trench (i.e. "C," "D," "E," "F," "G," and "H" companies) to advance on the Boer trenches at the assigned hour. In support, in the main trench to the right of the RCRs were 200 Gordon Highlanders. To the left at approximately 1,500 metres was the Shropshire Light Infantry. These battalions were to provide covering fire if required. For the assaulting Royal Canadians, the front rank of each company was to move with fixed bayonets and they were not to fire until fired upon by the enemy. The rear rank, with engineer support, was to sling their rifles and carry shovels and picks with which to entrench. Once the advance ground to a halt and could go no farther, the rear rank, supported by the fire of the front rank and adjacent units, was to dig in.[49]

At 0215 hours, in the inky Transvaal darkness, the Royal Canadians crept out of their entrenchments and moved forward. They maintained an interval of one pace between men and a distance of 15 paces between ranks. Initially, the advance seemed too good to be true. The front rank moved forward without interruption for about 400 metres. Then, suddenly, a few stray shots rang out and a terrific fire engulfed the darkness. Luckily, the initial shots served as a warning and many of the soldiers threw themselves down to the ground before the fire erupted. "Silently we advanced for several hundred yards, then the order came to ease off to the left," explained Private Dunham. "We hardly had moved two steps when a wall of fire opened up in front of us, not fifty yards away and a hail of bullets whizzed past us, sending death with it. We all dropped as flat as pancakes and lay there while the fusillade lasted."[50]

But not all were so lucky. "Now we are in for it and no mistake," reflected Gerald Carogan. "Crossfire everywhere the Boers are only 100 yards from us now but, there is a solid wall of lead between us and them — the hail of lead is pouring in on us from every side … in our ranks men are dropping on every side — hundred be dead or dying in our wake, and hundreds more must die before those trenches are reached — but no its impossible — no human being can move against that hail of lead."[51]

Another participant recalled: "The first news we had of the enemy was a sheet of flame not twenty yards away."[52] The noise of the battle impressed Private William Jeffery. "The explosive bullets," he wrote, "sounded like flying devils hissing and smacking through the air."[53] One journalist witnessing the event described it as "a brief fight, but a long half hour of deadly combat … ten minutes of triple hell and twenty minutes of an ordinary inferno."[54] The Boer volley had a disastrous effect on the "F" and "G" companies, which were caught in the open within 60 metres of the enemy's advanced trench. Combined, they suffered six killed and 21 wounded in mere minutes.[55] Private Perkins wondered, "How we got back is a wonder to us all. It was like being in a swarm of bees."[56]

The assaulting Canadians in the front rank now hugged the ground and returned fire. They were supported by the Shropshires, who unleashed volleys of fire from their distant entrenchments in a vain effort to provide covering fire and distract the Boers. The rear rank of the Royal Canadians began to entrench, but progress was mixed. The trench

This contemporary drawing, *Dashing Advance of the Canadians at Paardeberg* is utterly inaccurate, but it does capture the excitement and boost to public morale the victory bestowed.

on the right, being constructed by Royal Engineers (RE) who "worked liked demons" and supported by "G" and "H" companies, made rapid progress and was approximately 100 metres from the enemy position. The trenches on the left were not faring as well.

Then, suddenly, the fog of war took hold of the battlefield — the friction that the great theoretician Carl von Clausewitz warned of, and the same that is the bane of existence of all commanders. In the murky darkness, amidst the carnage, death, and fear of battle, an authoritative voice ordered all "to retire and bring back your wounded."[57] The apparent directive was enough for most — the entire left side of the line, four companies in total, collapsed in a rush to the rear, back to the main trench. "I think all records for the 100 yards," penned Private Dunham, "were broken that night."[58]

The precipitous withdrawal angered Otter. The hasty retreat put the reputation of the Canadians at risk. Conscious of the disdain that the British regulars held for the colonials, Otter was concerned this would

228

simply reinforce their perceptions. However, fate smiled on the RCR that night. Daylight found "G" and "H" Companies well entrenched, with the Royal Engineers still pushing on with their work. It has never become clear whether the tenacious troops simply were oblivious to the supposed order and general withdrawal that took place in the dark, or whether strong decisive local leadership prevailed. Regardless, at 0400 hours, as the light of dawn slowly seeped onto the battlefield, the Boers rose from their trenches to investigate their night's work. Suddenly, the tables were turned as they came under fire from the newly constructed trench less than 100 metres from their position. The firefight continued for over an hour, at which time, unexpectedly, a white flag fluttered over the advanced enemy trench. The Boers had had enough. However, the Canadians were very leery since this tactic had been used before as a ruse. As a result, they kept up a well-disciplined fire until 0600 hours, when an individual carrying a white flag emerged from the enemy trenches. The firing stopped immediately. Soon, groups of Boers began to flow from their entrenchments.

The battle for Paardeberg was over. By 0615 hours, the division commander, General Sir Henry Colville, arrived and dispatched an officer into the Boer *laager* to discuss the terms of surrender — which were unconditional. Despite the questionable night attack, the daring tenacity of "G" and "H" Companies had not only saved the reputation of the Battalion, but had in fact created the conditions for the first major British victory of the war. It has also been widely recognized as the turning point of the conflict. Moreover, the date of the victory was very significant. Nineteen years earlier to the day, in 1881, the Boers had inflicted a humiliating defeat on the British, and thus secured their independence. That embarrassment was now avenged.

The victory was a distinctly Canadian one. "The supporting companies of the Gordon Highlanders were not engaged, although the trench which protected them was subjected to a fairly heavy fire from the enemy," reported Otter. He added that, "The battalion of the Shropshire Light Infantry on our left, fired volleys at long ranges for some time after our attack developed and materially assisted us." However, he was clear in his appraisal. "That the duty entailed on the Royal Canadian Regiment was most difficult and dangerous no one will deny," he wrote, "and though the advance was not so successful at all points as was hoped for, yet the final result was a complete success, and credit can fairly be claimed by the battalion for such, as it was practically acting alone."[59]

The Battalion had made Canada proud. The effects of the battle were quite profound. After Paardeberg, Field Marshal Lord Roberts, the British commander-in-chief in South Africa, told survivors that they "had done noble work, and were as good a lot of men as were in the British Army." Roberts went on to say that "Canadian now stands for bravery, dash and courage."[60] Another British general stated, "Those men [Canadians] can go into battle without a leader — they have intelligence and resourceful-ness enough to lead themselves."[61] Praise poured in from throughout the Empire, congratulating the Royal Canadians for their "brilliant achieve-ment," "gallant conduct," and "distinguished gallantry."[62]

The success of the Canadian troops and the seemingly international respect they garnered soon triggered a nationalist outpouring of pride in Canadian military prowess. Even Canadian Prime Minister Wilfrid Laurier, who was initially hesitant to send troops to South Africa, was not immune from exploiting the success in the field. "Is there a man whose bosom did not swell with pride, the pride of pure patriotism, the pride of consciousness," thundered Laurier in the House of Commons, "that day [Paardeberg] the fact had been revealed to the world that a new power had arisen in the West?"[63]

In light of the eventual success, Otter's anger waned over the actual conduct of the troops during the attack, specifically their unauthorized retreat. For the soldiers, however, the adulation was of little immediate value. What mattered to them was the fact that Cronje's surrender meant a brief rest. However, on 7 March the drive towards Pretoria, the Boer capital, commenced. The British forces entered the capital city approximately three months later on 5 June 1900. Unfortunately it was not the end of the war that all had hoped for. The Boers now reverted to guerilla warfare and the bitter conflict dragged on for an additional two years.

In all, the Royal Canadians had done Canada proud. They served with distinction and demonstrated a martial spirit, endurance, and tenacity that rivaled the vaunted British regulars. "There are no finer troops or more gallant troops in all the world," wrote Major-General Dorrien Smith of the Royal Canadians.[64] He was not alone in his praise. "The men of the RCR," commented the Battalion medical officer, "were a jolly lot and saw the humor in any difficulty."[65] Even the journalists were impressed. "We have seen the First Contingent," wrote one reporter, "side by side with the bravest and the best of the Imperial regiments, taking with them the hardships met with on campaign."[66] In the end, it was the 2nd Battalion, The RCR, which delivered the first British victory in the war at Paardeberg and became the turning point of the conflict. It also awakened a sense of patriotism and national identity at home. The martial victory in a foreign land also earned Canada, through its blood, recognition in the international community. Nonetheless, the seminal victory that redeemed British military honour on the battlefield of South Africa and raised the stock of colonial military prowess was a questionable triumph. In many ways, the Canadians were accidental heroes. But, in the end, it is hard to criticize success.

NOTES

1.   See Thomas Pakenham, *The Boer War* (New York: Random House, 1979), chapters 5 to 9. The most comprehensive, and arguably best work on the Canadian participation in the conflict is Carman Miller, *Painting the Map Red: Canada and the South African War 1899–1902* (Ottawa: The Canadian War Museum, 1993).

2.   "The British Army and Modern Conceptions of War," *Royal United Services Institute (RUSI)*, Vol. 60, No. 40 (September 1911): 1181. See also Sanford Evans, *The Canadian Contingents* (Toronto: The Publishers' Syndicate Ltd., 1901), 36.

3.   Gordon McKenzie, *Delayed Action: Being Something of the Life and Times of the Late Brigadier General, Sir Duncan McKenzie, K.C.M.G, C.B., D.S.O., V.D., Legion d'Honneur* (Private Printing, no date), 163.

4.   Joseph Schull, *Laurier: The First Canadian* (Toronto: MacMillan of Canada, 1965), 381.

5.   For a detailed account of the British military failure see Bernd Horn, "Lost Opportunity: The Boer War Experience and its Influence on British and Canadian Military Thought," in Bernd Horn, ed., *Forging a Nation: Perspectives on the Canadian Military Experience* (St. Catharines, Ont.: Vanwell, 2002), 81–106.

6.   David Throup, ed., *British Documents on Foreign Affairs: Reports and Papers from the Foreign Office Confidential Print*. Part I, Series G, Africa, 1885–1914. *Vol. 8 Anglo-Boer War I: From Eve of War to Capture of Johannesburg, 1899–1900* (Bethesda, MD: University of Publications of America, 1995), 235.

7.   *Ibid.*, 239

8.   Winston S. Churchill, *The Boer War: London to Ladysmith via Pretoria, Ian Hamilton's March* (London: Leo Cooper, 1989), 31–32.

9.   Report A, Otter to Adjutant General, 26 January 1901, in Department of Militia and Defence, *Supplementary Report … 1901*, 11.

10. "South Africa War Records Reports, RCRI, January–June 1900" [hereafter RCR South Africa War Reports], 25 January 1900. Library and Archives of Canada (LAC), RG 9, II-A3, Vol. 32, Microfilm T-10404.

11. Letter, Ramsay to sister, 22 November 1899. LAC, MG 30, Series E-231, File Ramsay fonds, typescript of letters and biographical sketch.

12. Stanley McKeown Brown, *With the Royal Canadians* (Toronto: The Publishers' Syndicate Ltd., 1900), 104. Brown was a war correspondent.

13. Letter, Jesse Biggs to Aunt, 29 December 1899. LAC, MG-29, E-76, Jesse C. Biggs fonds, RCR.

14. Letter, Bennett to his Mother, 13 December 1899. LAC, MG 29, Acession E-59, File 1 – Bennett, S.A. Correspondence 1899.

15. Letter, Bennett to his Mother, 30 December 1899. LAC, MG 29, Acession E-59, File 1 – Bennett, S.A. Correspondence 1899.

16. Letter, J.A. Perkins to mother, 2 January 1900. LAC, MG 29, E-93, J.A. Perkins fonds, RCR.

17. "An Echo of the South African War," *Recollections of J.W. Jeffery*. RCR Archives, Series 3 Boer War 1899–1900, Vol. 2, File 17.

18. Miller, 79–80.

19. "RCR South Africa War Reports," 6 February 1900.

20. "RCR South Africa War Reports," 11 February 1900.

21. 19th Brigade was composed of the 1st Bn, Duke of Cornwall's Light Infantry; 2nd Bn King's Own Shropshire Light Infantry; 1st Bn Gordon Highlanders; and the 2nd Bn RCR.

22. Lord Roberts's army also included 5,000 Native drivers and 25,000 animals.

23. "South African Letter from Our Own Correspondent," near Paardeberg Drift, 25 February 1900, The *Canadian Military Gazette*, Vol. XV, No. 7 (3 April 1900): 7.

24. Lance-Corporal J. Kennedy Hill Diary, South Africa, 1899–1900 [hereafter Kennedy Hill Diary], LAC, John Kennedy Hill fonds, microfilm M-300.

25. "Diary of Private F.H. Dunham, South African Campaign," [hereafter Dunham's Diary] Part III, Paardeberg. RCR Archives, Series 3 Boer War 1899–1900, Vol. 2, File 15. Also available from LAC, "Diaries of Pte. F.H. Dunham South African Campaign, 1899–1900," MG 29, Accession E-89, File 4, typescript of original diary.

26. Dunham's Diary.

27. Kennedy Hill Diary. See also Letter, J. Cooper Mason to Father, 21 February 1900 and Letter, Mason to Mother 27 February 1900. LAC, MG 30, Series E 397, File correspondence.

28. See "RCR South Africa War Reports," 23 February 1900.

29. Dunham's Diary.

30. W. Hart-McHarg, *From Quebec to Pretoria With the Royal Canadian Regiment* (Toronto: William Briggs, 1902), 108.

31. "South African Letter," 7.

32. "RCR South Africa War Reports," 23 February 1900.

33. "RCR South Africa War Reports," 23 February 1900.
34. See "RCR South Africa War Reports," 26 February 1900; "South African Diary, 2nd Bn (SS) Royal Canadian Regiment, Otter's Diary [henceforth Otter's Diary]," 19 February 1900. LAC, RG 9, 11-A-3, Vol. 34, Microfilm T-10405; and Miller, 92–97.
35. Dunham Diary.
36. Letter, reproduced in a contemporary clipping, by Reverend O'Leary, RC Chaplain to The RCR, at Paardeberg. LAC, MG 30, E-372, file — Robert Gordon Stewart fonds.
37. Letter, J. Cooper Mason to Father, 21 February 1900 and Letter, Mason to Mother 27 February 1900. LAC, MG 30, Series E 397, File correspondence.
38. "South African Letter," 7.
39. Dunham Diary.
40. Kennedy Hill Diary. See also "RCR South Africa War Reports," 23 February 1900.
41. Letter, J. Cooper Mason to Father, 21 February 1900; and Dunham Diary.
42. See Kennedy Hill Diary and Miller, 98–101.
43. See Report A, Appendix A1, Otter to Adjutant General, 26 January 1901, in Department of Militia and Defence, *Supplementary Report … 1901*, 42–44 for Otter's account of the day's events.
44. Dunham Diary.
45. Letter, Bennett to his Mother, 23 February 1900. LAC, MG 29, Acession E-59, File 2 — Bennett, S.A. Correspondence 1900.
46. Report A, Otter to Adjutant General, 26 January 1901, in Department of Militia and Defence, *Supplementary Report…1901*, 18.
47. "Wrote on a Rock," 27 March 1900, clipping from an unknown newspaper. The Royal Canadian Regiment Museum Archives [henceforth RCR Archives], Series 3 Boer War 1899–1900, Vol. 1, File 56.
48. Dunham Diary.
49. See Otter's Diary, 26–28 February 1900; and Report A, Appendix A3, Otter to Adjutant General, 26 January 1901, in Department of Militia and Defence, *Supplementary Report … 1901*, 46–47 for Otter's account of the attack. See also "RCR South Africa War Reports," 2 March 1900.
50. Dunham Diary, Letter sent from Paardeberg Drift, 3 March 1900.
51. Gerald Carogan, "Recollections of the Boer War by June 1902." RCR Archives, Series 3 Boer War 1899–1900, Vol. 2, File 16.
52. Letter, J.A. Perkins to mother, "Modder's Drift," no date. LAC, MG 29, E-93, J.A. Perkins fonds, RCR.
53. Letter, J. William Jeffery to friends, 18 March 1900. LAC, MG 29, E-101, Jos. Wm. Jeffery fonds, RCR.
54. Brown, 217.
55. Report A, Appendix A3, Otter to Adjutant General, 26 January 1901, in Department of Militia and Defence, *Supplementary Report … 1901*, 46.

56. Letter, J.A. Perkins to mother, "Modder's Drift," no date. LAC, MG 29, E-93, J.A. Perkins fonds, RCR.

57. *Ibid.*

58. Dunham Diary.

59. Report A, Appendix A3, Otter to Adjutant General, 26 January 1901, in Department of Militia and Defence, *Supplementary Report...1901*, 47.

60. John Marteinson, *We Stand On Guard* (Toronto: Ovale, 1992), 63; and Miller, 109.

61. Brown, 138.

62. "Gen. Cronje's Surrender," *Globe and Mail*, 27 February 2000, 1; and Report A, Otter to Adjutant General, 26 January 1901, in Department of Militia and Defence, *Supplementary Report ... 1901*, 33–35.

63. Quoted in Robert Page, *The Boer War and Canadian Imperialism* (Ottawa: Canadian Historical Association, 1987), 14; and C.P. Stacey, "Canada and the South African War, Part IV," *The Canadian Army Journal*, Vol. 4, No. 5 (October 1950): 10.

64. Quoted in "Considerations Leading Up to Decision to Provide a Contingent," 275.

65. McCormick, 8.

66. Brown, 291.

CHAPTER 7

Daring Innovation:
The Canadian Corps and Trench Raiding
on the Western Front

ANDREW GODEFROY

I hope that the Canadians are not in trenches opposite you, for they on the darkest night jump suddenly into our trenches, causing great consternation and before cries for help can be answered disappear again into the darkness ...

— From a letter found on a
captured German soldier, 1917[1]

Decisive battles that led to operational victories or strategic outcomes on the western front eluded both sides for much of the war. After a spurt of offensive and defensive engagements between late 1914 and early 1915, the two very evenly matched enemies prepared to dig in for what was sure to be a long, gruelling, and deadly contest. For the German Army, adopting a defensive stance on the Western Front was a matter of pragmatism. Prussia and her allies were heavily engaged in the east against Russia and other foes and had no desire to wage an aggressive two-front war if it could be avoided. Therefore, while the Germans prepared largely for the defence of their initial gains on the Western front, the British, French, and their Commonwealth allies prepared for daring actions to unhinge them.

As battlefields of the period went, the Western Front was nothing if not unique. One could not simply advance in closed ranks against the German front lines or form squares to beat off attacks as was done during the late Victorian age. Taking an objective was no longer just a matter of marching towards it. Modern artillery and machine guns made short

Photographer W.I. Castle, LAC, PA-1326.

The miserable existence in the trenches, France 1917.

work of cavalry and foot soldiers who were bunched closely together, so much so that a single machine gun with a well-trained crew could put a complete stop to an entire squadron or battalion advancing against them. Combined with an extensive series of fixing and delaying obstacles such as barbed wire, trenches, pillboxes, and artillery, the Western Front soon settled into a series of largely static front lines that required not only new technologies but also new ideas in order to break through them.

When not engaged in major operations to break their enemy, the British and Commonwealth forces routinely harassed German defensive positions with a program of bombardment and raiding. The Canadian Expeditionary Force (CEF) became particularly adept at these activities, gaining both experience and a reputation that eventually led to the Canadian Corps becoming one of the most operationally successful corps in all of the British armies on the Western Front. At the heart of the Canadian success was daring innovation and a desire to employ the

Photographer W.I. Castle, LAC, PA-568.

On sentry duty in a front-line trench. From these positions, Canadian soldiers would mount their intrepid forays into enemy lines.

art of trench raiding as a means to perfect fire and maneuver tactics for larger set-piece battles that could break the enemy lines.

The Canadian initiative was a success — after nearly three years of slugging it out on the Western Front, the Canadian Corps, led by General Sir Arthur Currie, delivered a series of operational victories that historians later described as the "spearhead to victory." But before the set-piece battles of the last hundred days could be carried out, many smaller groups of Canadian soldiers had to learn the lessons the hard way — through repeated and often daring raiding of the enemy lines.

THE SCHOOL OF HARD KNOCKS

The trench raid, noted historian Bill Rawling, was the laboratory by which the Canadians developed a successful battlefield doctrine for cracking German defences.[2] Tactics for not only surviving the routine of trench warfare, but also for overcoming the barren wasteland in between that was so often an obstacle in the attack, were tested and retested in hundreds of trench raids before being adopted by the whole Canadian Corps for larger battles. It was a trying process and not always victorious. Some trench raids were daring successes, others spectacular failures.[3] In all cases, however, there were casualties. At such close quarters and often fighting with pistol and grenade or hand to hand with clubs, the chances of being wounded and killed were always high.

To properly understand how trench raids differed from many other operations on the Western Front, a few definitions of terminology are helpful. Trench raiding was essentially any raid or minor operation whose purpose it was not to take ground from the enemy and hold it, but rather to complete smaller objectives against the enemy such as inflicting casualties, destroying enemy equipment, collecting intelligence, creating deceptions, lowering morale, and, in general, cause havoc within the enemy lines. For example, an operation order from the 21st (Central Ontario) Infantry Battalion in early 1917 described an upcoming raid as follows: "The 21st Battalion attacking party will enter the enemy trench from M.15.b.6.½. to M.15.b.9.8½. at ZERO HOUR plus 4 minutes for the purpose of inflicting casualties, making prisoners, securing booty and wrecking dugouts in the system of trenches in the area attacked."[4]

Trench raiding was an effective way of testing the enemy defences and measuring (and therefore also lowering) the morale of the enemy. When prisoners were taken, enemy units could be identified and enemy strengths estimated. The capture of documents and equipment were also important for intelligence purposes. Enemy installations were destroyed, especially dugouts, saps, and mines leading towards friendly lines, and havoc and disruption were generally caused in that particular part of the enemy line. Raiding also often induced the enemy to mobilize and send forward reserves to counterattack, which enabled friendly artillery to shell them and thus cause further casualties. Raiding also gave the artillery regular opportunities to practise and improve its own techniques in registering enemy targets and conducting counter-battery fire. In the latter function especially, Canadian gunners became noted for their expertise.

In addition to causing temporary grief to the enemy, the raid acted as a "mini-version" test of potential larger-scale operations. At the outbreak of the First World War, infantry tactics were not designed to operate in such an environment, as was witnessed on the Western Front, and modern technology had put an end to the doctrines of the Victorian age. Small arms had developed to such an extent that some branches of the military, such as the Cavalry, were facing a crisis over their future utility on the battlefield. For example, the machine gun, explained Canadian military historian John Swettenham, was, "cheap, light, requiring few soldiers to man it and firing 450 rounds per minute of relatively lightweight ammunition which posed no very difficult supply problem."[5] It was an inexpensive investment that could put a quick end to even the most determined assault. By conducting trench raids, British and Canadian troops gained experience, honed their tactics, technique, and procedures, and tested new ideas without fear of substantial troop losses. It was a means to the end of developing the recipe required to break the German lines and force a decision to end the war.

Though the trench raid was by no means a purely Canadian invention, historian Daniel G. Dancocks wrote, "If [Canadians] had not initiated this form of warfare, they certainly elevated it to an art form."[6] Trench raiding had originated as part of the British Expeditionary Force (BEF) policy to maintain the offensive on the Western Front, keeping soldiers from becoming complacent and falling into the monotony of trench warfare, while constantly harassing and demoralizing the enemy. One of the first recorded trench raids was carried out by British Indian troops, the Gerwhal Rifles of the Lahore Division, of which two battalions raided the German lines on the night of the 9–10 November 1914.[7] In February 1915, the Princess Patricia's Canadian Light Infantry (PPCLI) raided the German lines opposite them and, thus, undertook the first operation of what would later become a trademark of the Canadian Corps. The Canadian staff soon realized the advantages of trench raiding, and after the Second Battle of Ypres (April 1915) they implemented a vigorous raiding policy for the division and later, the entire corps.

The most important factor that influenced raiding was the geography of the Western Front. Geography had a direct influence on survivability, being such that the nature of the terrain provided little in the way of natural obstacles for either side to take advantage of. Much of the areas of Belgium and Flanders where the Canadian Corps fought its battles consists of no more than low ridges, rolling hills, or wide expanses of flat open terrain. The many wooded areas had been reduced to nothing more than a collection of burned stumps by tremendous artillery barrages. With little or no natural cover, soldiers were forced to dig themselves down into the ground to survive. Thus within a short while the whole Western Front consisted of a series of interconnected trenches, protected by row upon row of barbed wire entanglements and machine guns. Artillery, machine guns, or snipers meticulously covered every field of fire. In between the German and Allied armies was a narrow strip of cratered and desolate terrain that was commonly referred to as "no man's land" due to the perception that it was impossible for anyone to survive outside beyond his own trench lines for very long. The ability to safely cross no man's land and "put the Boche to the bayonet" was therefore a primary objective of Canadian raiding.

Trenches developed as a result of the need for creating defensive positions from which to repel enemy attacks and counterattacks. As mentioned above, both sides created an extensive series of works, well supplied with small arms, machine guns, and supported by artillery, which led to the inability of either the British or the Germans to continue to operationally manoeuvre without tremendous casualties.

LAC, 2165.

The desolate, hostile terrain that troops were required to traverse in order to mount their raids.

Manoeuvrability was vital to the maintenance of the offensive, and without it, the best either side could hope for was to consolidate their present gains.

All trenches on the Western Front were based on a similar concept or pattern. Trenches were constructed four to six feet in width and approximately six to eight feet deep. Every trench was supposed to have a fire step and parapet so that the infantry could fire at the enemy and be able to take cover if necessary. Trenches were also dug in a zigzag pattern so that if the trench was overrun the infiltrators could not fire their weapons down the length of the trench and hit everyone at once. Trenches were normally connected to other parts of the line and to the rear by smaller communication trenches, normally anywhere from three to five feet wide. Most trench systems had some form of revetting and cover, as well as traverses and sandbagged tops and sidings.

Out beyond the trench lay wire entanglements of every shape. Barbed wire was strewn across the entire Western Front, often without any tactical considerations beyond local needs. Wire was placed on top of wire where it had been damaged, cut, or destroyed. Soon, a sea of entanglement had been created on both sides of no man's land. Wire was normally situated only a few metres beyond the firing step, but was gradually moved out from the trenches so as to deny bombers their range for throwing. Often laid in successive belts and constantly checked by working parties, it was hoped to try and counter infiltration of any kind.

German trench systems were often much more solid and complex than Allied lines. Unlike the Allies, who saw trench lines as a temporary cover in the wake of a continuing advance, the Germans knew that their defensive lines might become home for some time. German trenches contained several interesting features, such as solid concrete bunkers, sniping posts, and protected forward ammunition dumps. These often became the priority targets of Canadian raiders, as more conventional attempts to destroy them completely (i.e. by artillery) often met with mixed results.

THE FIRST TRENCH RAIDS

Trench raiding was first conceived as a temporary solution to British

General Headquarters' (GHQ) fear of idleness in the trenches and a lack of fighting spirit, which had developed between British and German forces during the winter of 1914. GHQ was especially concerned to avoid a repetition of the well-known 1914 Christmas Day truce where British and German troops openly fraternized with each other, exchanging chocolates, brandy, and even playing a game of soccer together. Therefore, as historian Colonel G.W.L. Nicholson wrote, "In contrast to the French, who when not engaged in a major offensive tended to observe an unofficial truce, British GHQ emphasized the necessity for continual aggressiveness in defence."[8]

The first recorded Canadian raid of the war was in fact more of a limited attack, which was carried out by the PPCLI on 28 February 1915, in and around Shelly Farm and the Mound.[10] This was not a raid strictly in the sense that raids were to become known as, for the aim of the PPCLI commander's attack was to stop the Germans from developing their own line to gain the upper hand in the immediate area. After failing to occupy and hold trenches to the left of the Mound and farm, Bavarian troops had been sapping fire-trenches parallel to British ones running in front of Shelly Farm and 300 metres beyond to a point east of St. Eloi. Lieutenant-Colonel F.D. Farquhar, the commander of the PPCLI, sought permission to deliver a local attack against the Bavarian position "partly to break up this work, partly to meet aggression with aggression, partly to put new heart into men who were living in filthy ditches overlooked by an enemy campaigning in far greater comfort."[10]

While the PPCLI unit history does argue that all the essentials of subsequent raids were present in this "first" raid, this is in fact untrue. The reason for deciding to use a small number of troops in the engagement was predefined by the size of the target that the PPCLI had set out to destroy, not because they were attempting a raid by stealth. Agreed, surprise was an important factor, but this was true of any operation and not just raids. The same can be said for the idea of withdrawing before the enemy could counterattack. As one will see this was often not the case with Canadian raiding parties, who had a tendency to take on counterattacks with enthusiasm, and were well capable of repelling the best the Germans had to offer.

Furthermore, it later became part of the aim of the raid to induce the enemy to counterattack so that he could be shelled by the Canadian field batteries and therefore cause further casualties. One of the objectives of the PPCLI attack was supposedly to secure prisoners for identification.[11] This was not necessary either, for the British 80th and 82nd Brigades, which held this part of line prior to their relief by the PPCLI, had already identified the enemy units opposite them.

This engagement also differs from later raids in its lack of preparation prior to execution. The ground that the PPCLI was to cover had not been previously studied, nor had any of the troops involved in the action received any special training prior to the attack. The first reconnaissance of the ground was conducted on the night of 27 February, just prior to the attack itself. Lieutenant Colquhoun, the battalion sniping officer, was sent forward to examine the ground over which he would lead his troops and to verify all possible routes from which the enemy might be able to counterattack. He was further instructed to report on the feasibility of "holding the trench in front of the existing line if the attack succeeded."[12]

This idea was definitely not typical of raiding policy. Colquhoun made two reconnaissance sorties that evening, going out a second time before midnight with the battalion second-in-command, Major Hamilton Gault. During their expedition the two separated at one point, and, while exploring in one of the German communication trenches, Lieutenant Colquhoun was captured.[13]

Men were drawn from No. 4 Company, and officers chosen to lead the raid were briefed on their orders sometime after midnight. The commander had no information about his right front due to Colquhoun's capture, but had obtained enough from Major Gault's report to plan his attack on the main objective — the sap. The party consisted of roughly 75 men divided equally into three groups. Each had been assigned specific tasks but was allowed a great amount of flexibility.

Unfortunately, the composition of the force denied the PPCLI to put that flexibility to its greatest use. The assaulting party consisted of 30 riflemen, supported by a small section of bombers commanded by Lieutenant T.M. Papineau. The second and third parties were identical except that they had no bombers, only shovels with which to break down the parapet. The attack commenced at 0515 hours and soon became, the unit history noted, a race against daylight. The attacking party returned to its own trenches by 0540 hours, after wrecking about 80 yards of trench at the cost of five killed and eleven wounded.[14]

In the final analysis, the attack at Shelly Farm was not a raid by any means. The aim was never clearly and concisely established. There was no prior preparation for the attack. There was no time for preparation of equipment or stores. Indeed, the only item brought over by the PPCLI with which they planned to destroy 80 yards of high-quality trenches was shovels. Colonel Farquhar was very distressed at having to abandon the German trench line at all, which he considered, quite correctly, to be of a much more superior quality than their own. There were no set timings for the attack. At 0530 hours Colonel Farquhar sent a message to Lieutenant Crabbe, commander of the attack, to begin withdrawing his troops in five minutes. Had the message not come through it is unknown as to when the troops would have left, if at all.

Despite these misgivings, some good came of the effort. The attack had been a major morale booster after spending over two months in stale trench routine. Eight decorations were bestowed upon the PPCLI for their actions, amongst them awards to Major Gault and Lieutenant Papineau.[15] In addition, the unit received many congratulatory messages from other British units and commanders, and one from their own 1st Canadian Division. The action also says something of the ability and the initiative of the officers, who had less than three hours from the time they received their orders to be on the German parapets wrecking havoc. This they did successfully, and in doing so caught the attention of GHQ, who would soon hook into the idea of constant aggression towards the enemy, even if it could only be achieved on a small scale.

Raiding, though not considered large-scale engagements, provided the first clues to the Canadians in their search for successful fire and movement on the battlefield. Even more important, however, raiding and other minor operations quickly became the only avenue for learning anything about fighting at all on the Western Front. There is an overriding misconception in the writing of the history of the First World War that the British Expeditionary Force, and hence the Canadian troops within its organization, were constantly flailing themselves against the German wire between 1914 and 1917 in vain attempts that force of mass would eventually break through. In fact, in the period between Christmas 1914 and 9 April 1917, the Canadians were involved in only 35 days of actual battle, and never had more than two divisions committed to the fray. The other 800 days were spent continually rotating in and out of the front line, with the raids serving as the only chance to exercise one's combat skills.

A raid or other minor operation provided the opportunity to train soldiers while on the job. By sending out smaller parties of men with limited yet more attainable objectives, tactics could be practised with a minimal loss of life compared to large-scale attacks. Raiding familiarized the soldier with the terrain in which he would operate for weeks at a time. It exposed him to the realities of trench warfare while still giving the soldier a fighting chance to learn. An old axiom was that if a soldier could survive the first month then he could potentially survive the war. Raiding also familiarized the soldier with the enemy, his style of operations and fighting skills, defences, and tactics. It allowed the soldier to make use of newly acquired skills, such as bomb throwing, and also to test out new equipment, like the employment of the Lewis machine gun in the infantry role.

Towards the end of October 1915, Second Army Headquarters, under which the Canadians were serving, issued further directives to whenever possible harass and exhaust the enemy's troops while training all branches for future operations. Specifically, GHQ wanted trench raiding continued throughout the winter. The first trench raid carried out by the Canadian Corps (then consisting of two divisions) was at the Douve River on the night of 16–17 November 1915. Raiding parties were formed from the 5th (Saskatchewan) Battalion and the 7th (British Columbia) Battalion of the 2nd Canadian Infantry Brigade. At this stage platoons were still organized into four rifle sections, but the organization evolved as lessons were learned on the battlefield. Heavy rains that swelled the Douve River to almost three times its width had postponed the raid from the previous night. The raid itself had three objectives. First, the raiders were to secure prisoners, from which enemy units could be identified and information about their movements gained. Second, the Canadians wanted to coax the Germans into bringing forward their reserves so that they could be shelled by the Canadian Field Artillery (CFA). Third, the raiders were hoping to lower the enemy's morale.

Raiding parties consisted of five officers and 85 volunteers with 23 men in reserve from each battalion. Volunteers always carried out raids unless too few came forward. This, however, was seldom the case in the Canadian experience. Raiders were excused from all other duties while training for the raid, and were usually taken out of the front line to do so. Many preferred to "get it over with" rather than wait around to be killed by a random shell. Others saw raids as an opportunity for souvenirs and a possible "blighty" (a wound that was small yet bad enough to get one a few weeks out of the trenches and back to England). Others simply volunteered, as it was a break from the monotony of trench life. The raiders rehearsed night and day over ground that was similar to the enemy terrain (later Canadian Engineers [CE] would build extensive "dummy" trenches for the infantry to practise in) and produced the same approaches to the objectives.[16]

Immediately north of the Douve River, the German line curved outward across the Messines-Ploegsteert road to form a salient 500 yards long that included a farmstead called La Petite Douve.[17] The angle of the trenches between the river and the farm was 7th Battalion's objective. Meanwhile, the 5th Battalion would stage a diversionary attack to the southeast. During the day of 16 November, the 1st Canadian and 118th British Field Artillery Brigade and the Royal Canadian Horse Artillery (RCHA) began pounding the German wire while a trench mortar battery continually struck La Petite Douve. That evening, parties went out and placed two 60-pound portable bridges over the Douve River while other work parties finished cutting by hand any German wire that the artillery had missed. Meanwhile, the raiders prepared themselves by removing all of their own identifying insignia (even the distinguishable Canadian Ross rifle was traded in for the British-issue Lee-Enfield rifle — a treat to say the least). Flashlights, tied to the rifle stocks, were to be turned on inside the enemy trenches in order to blind the occupants. White armbands were worn by the raiders to distinguish friend from foe in the confusion that would exist inside the enemy line.

At 0230 hours on 17 November the two raiding parties crept up out of their trenches, following previously set white stakes that marked their route of advance into no man's land. In the southeast, leading elements of the 5th Battalion got caught up in wire entanglements that had been placed in a water-filled moat along the base of the German parapet. While trying to free themselves, they were spotted by the Germans and fired upon. Soldiers responded in kind with bombs until everyone had freed himself and withdrawn. Surprisingly, the Canadians suffered no casualties.

Meanwhile, the 7th Battalion had taken their objective completely by surprise, the German sentries having gone under cover from the rain that had begun to fall.[18] The efforts of 7th Battalion's Captain Charles Costigan and his raiding party were later related in the *Calgary Daily Herald*:

> The little force quietly cut the wires strand by strand, folded them back, fastening the ends, leaving a wide path. So silently did they accomplish this work that not a single Germany sentry realized that the Canadians were so near. Seeing a large white platform in front of them which looked solid, Capt. Costigan and his brother officer sprang upon it, when, to their horror, it gave way and they were precipitated headforemost into the trench onto the heads of three German sentries. The latter were more surprised than the Canadian officers, and before they could recover themselves, Captain Costigan and his pal had shot two sentries dead, and the third, wounded in the leg, ran down the trench screaming for help.
>
> The Germans began to pour out of their dugouts into the trenches, but by this time the rest of the squad had sprung into the trench loaded with bombs. Each of the two ends of the sector of the trench were blocked by Canadians armed with bombs. The artillery kept a circle of fire back of the trench, so that the Germans in this section could get no assistance from any others. As the Germans came out of the dugouts they were met by the bayonets ...[19]

There was no resistance, and the Germans made no attempts to counterattack. After about twenty minutes, the Canadians withdrew, having killed or wounded an estimated 30 Germans and having obtained the information they sought. The 7th Battalion only suffered one killed and another wounded, while they brought back with them 12 prisoners. The Germans counterattacked some 40 minutes later, but this was easily broken up by sharp artillery.

The raid had been a complete success, and much of it was credited to the preparations made prior to the attack. The enemy's position had been properly and thoroughly scouted in advance, allowing the Canadians to recognize potential difficulties and prepare for them (i.e. the bridges). Sufficient training and rehearsals had been undertaken prior to the raid so that each man was aware of exactly what his mission was. This allowed the soldier to carry on even if all of his superiors were to become casualties. The orders were clear and concise, and cooperation between the artillery and infantry had been excellent. Information about enemy troop location and strengths was gained, but, above all, the captured prisoners had also brought an additional bonus to the Canadians. They had all been sporting the new German-issue rubber gas masks that were, "a prize to Canadian Intelligence officers."[20]

One British historian saw Douve River as a model raid, but in its simplicity it failed to give the Canadian some much-needed lessons.[21] The ease with which the Canadians reached and occupied the enemy positions gave them no appreciation for the need of a mixed-arms platoon. Later on, Lewis gunners and bombers would play a much more important role in the raid and also in general fire and movement tactics on the battlefield. Blocking of the trench was done with the most basic tools and given no cover. The Canadians blocked the two ends of the trench they occupied with wire, but no bombing parties were placed or Lewis guns set up to cover important arcs of fire. It is uncertain as to whether or not the raiders would have been able to fend off any serious counterattack long enough for them to extricate themselves from the enemy lines. There was no mention of a covering force to protect the raiders while they withdrew, either. It seems that the raiders had been lucky in that the Germans themselves were so confused and therefore failed to make a more concerted attempt to dislodge the Canadians from their lines. In fact, the Canadian withdrawal had been so easy that the raiders were able to reclaim one of the two portable bridges they had laid across the Douve.

Early Canadian intelligence operations lacked any sort of formal instruction from the British. When the Canadian 1st Division landed in England the British Army was hotly entangled in the First Battle of Ypres and had little time to pass on their experience. The Canadians "therefore followed their own initiative" and made intelligence part of operations on the divisional staff.[22] Officers and interpreters were appointed to each brigade and each infantry battalion designated one of its officers as the intelligence officer (IO) for the unit. When the 1st Canadian Division crossed over to France in February 1915, it had the opportunity to receive some training from its British counterparts in Second Army.

By mid-March the Canadians issued their first divisional intelligence summary. British intelligence had correctly identified the threat of attack in the Ypres salient and had even received a report from the French that "a poison gas weapon" may be used. Despite these early warnings it was difficult to convince both the French and British high commands that an attack was imminent due to discrepancies in the supposed date of the German offensive. As a result the British Fifth Army reeled under the weight of the attack while the French and Algerian troops were routed completely. However, despite early misgivings, intelligence within the Canadian Corps steadily improved, fed by a plentiful amount of captured information supplied by raiders. Though not always successful, this infant branch of the military (formed in 1903) did much to convert the "raw" resources of raiding into the doctrine that would be later used to train Canadian troops.

NIGHT RAIDS: LESSONS STILL TO BE LEARNED

As static warfare and limited gains became more of a reality on the Western Front, beginning in 1916, it was more important than ever to develop the traits necessary to survive in such an environment. Despite all the skills, tactics, and equipment, which were designed to help the soldier live, move, and fight, one characteristic — morale — could only be maintained by success.

The newly formed Canadian Corps, now two divisions strong and soon expecting a third and fourth, found itself trying to cope with

LAC, PA-2439.

Ever vigilant — Canadian troops were also the target of German raids and as such were required to maintain a constant watch on "no man's land."

the day-to-day routine of trench life. Battalions continued to rotate through the front lines, spending from four to six days at each of the front, support, and reserve lines of their sector. When in the front line a de facto live-and-let-live policy tended to prevail, occasionally interrupted by indirect shelling and the exchange of small ordnance. This was exactly what GHQ was trying to avoid, and while in many sectors the Germans seemed content with simply defending their line, the Canadian Corps sought to retain the initiative and "own" no man's land.

Not all raids met with the textbook success that the 5th and 7th Battalions experienced at the Douve River. As the Western Front became increasingly hazardous to live in, so too did it become more dangerous to move in. Shelling was a constant feature. Casualties occurred daily on both sides, becoming known as "trench wastage." In essence, this referred to those who became injured or killed simply by chance. Between January and March 1916, the Canadian Corps (three divisions) was not engaged in any offensive operations other than trench raids, and yet still lost hundreds of men (see Table 1.1).

Table 1.1
Casualties suffered by the Canadian Corps —
November 1915 to March 1916

Date	Strength	Losses	Operations
Nov. 1915	52,000	937	Trench raids by 5th and 7th Battalions
Dec. 1915	52,000	753	Trench raids by 5th Battalion
Date	**Strength**	**Losses**	**Operations**
Jan. 1916	53,241	658	Trench raids
Feb. 1916	54,733	553	Trench raids
March 1916	60,087	764	Situation normal

Source: Rawling, B. Surviving Trench Warfare: Technology and the Canadian Corps 1914–1918. Appendix B.

The increased amount of impersonal killing resulted from developments in technology. By December 1915 both German and Canadian troops had developed decent artillery, mortars, hand bombs, and rifle grenades. For example, with a range of about a 100 yards, and the enemy trenches often less than 50 yards distant, rifle grenades made it easy to set up a bombardment.[23] One only required inserting the rod of the grenade into his rifle and firing it off using a blank round. Another tactic was to simply lob large amounts of bombs into enemy trenches that were within range. Captain James Mathewson of the 42nd (Black Watch) Battalion noted in a letter home to his father how effective such an activity could be. A section would lob over a couple dozen bombs, but sometimes somebody would forget to light the fuse of a bomb before throwing it. This was disasterous because the Germans would simply pick up the bomb, light the fuse, and throw it back.

The Highlanders got wise and came up with a trick. They would disassemble some of the bombs and shorten the fuse (normally about four or five seconds long) to one second. Then, along with other lit bombs, they would toss these into the enemy trenches. A German, seeing an unlit bomb arrive in his trench and thinking it to still be good, would attempt to light the fuse and throw it back. The bomb would then explode in his hand and kill him instantly. It was a guaranteed way to produce casualties until the Germans got too paranoid and left intact bombs alone.[24]

Conducting raids at night always invited complications, but darkness was still considered essential to surprise and success. Sometimes, however, even the cover of night offered no respite. A case in point was the 10th (Calgary Highlanders) Battalion raid on the German trenches opposite its position on the night of 4–5 February 1916. The raid was doomed to failure from the start by one disaster after another, but despite the seemingly impossible odds, the raiders still managed to successfully engage the enemy and return with most of its members and many new lessons learned.

The raid was to be commanded by Lieutenant Stanley Kent, who, according to his commanding officer Lieutenant-Colonel Rattray, "[took] a keen interest in the doings and actions of the Huns."[25] Kent, a 23-year-old banker in civilian life, found himself confronting one of the most difficult and daring operations he would face during the entire war. On the evening of 3 February, Lieutenant Kent set out with a wire-cutting party towards the German line to clear the path for the raiders who would follow. Nothing was heard from him for over six hours, and the battalion became concerned. When he finally returned it was with bad news. Not only was the main wire perfectly intact, but the Germans had put in an additional row in front of it and were sending out patrols to check it every few hours. Lieutenant Kent felt that he could not cut sufficient gaps in the wire before daylight and therefore decided to postpone the raid until the next evening.[26]

The following evening the weather conditions remained favourable and Captain Allan Conners of "D" Company ordered Lieutenant Kent to proceed with the operation. Kent and his sergeant, Edward Milne, along with the wire-cutting party and a two-man signal section, crept out towards the German lines covered by a 10-man section under Sergeant James Pringle. Things went wrong right from the beginning. After Kent had brought his cutting party to the nearest German wire he went back to deploy his covering party. It was nowhere to be found. Kent sent Sergeant Milne to search for Pringle and his men and after an hour the party turned up. Sergeant Pringle reported that he had been delayed by a pair of enemy patrols, but had now posted his covering party amongst the shallow willow trees in a ditch that ran through no man's land. Kent detected that something was wrong, but before sending Pringle back to the covering party he reminded Sergeant Pringle, "Don't fail us Sergeant, we are absolutely dependent upon you."[27]

The situation worsened. One of Pringle's covering party, Private Samuel Rider, was discovered and killed by a German sniper. Two more of the covering party crawled back to their own trenches to report Rider's death and that Sergeant Pringle seemed "somewhat excited."[28] Worried about the situation, the regimental sergeant major, Duncan Stuart, set out to stabilize the situation. He ran into Sergeant Pringle in no man's land, where Pringle informed him that the whole raiding party had been surrounded and captured, and that Lieutenant Kent had been taken prisoner. "Are you sure of what you are saying?" Stuart asked Pringle. When he confirmed, Stuart became suspicious. The RSM knew that Lieutenant Kent and the men would not have given themselves up without a fight, so he placed Pringle under arrest on the spot and had him dragged back to the 10th Battalion lines.[29] Stuart then reported to Captain Conners, who sent Lieutenant Lewis Younger, Sergeant Arnold Budd, and half a dozen other ranks to reinforce the covering party at the willow grove. At one point they were almost discovered by a German patrol, but fortunately no one was hit when the Germans lobbed a few bombs blindly in Younger's direction.

The wire cutting took forever, but finally at 0337 hours on the 5 February, they were through it. Word was sent back to the 10th Battalion lines to prepare to send forward the 50-man raiding party. Once it reached the covering party at the grove, Lieutenants Kent and Younger, followed by Sergeant Milne, led the raiders through the German wire. Suddenly, Kent signalled everyone to halt. On the German parapet was a working party. Kent waited 10 minutes, hoping that they would leave, but when the party continued on with its work, the decision was made to rush the party and take as many prisoners as possible, then retire. The raiders were strung out between the two rows of enemy wire and very vulnerable. Kent had to complete the operation before a disaster occurred. He was too late, however. While he was making arrangements for the assault, a German patrol, "consisting of between 20 and 30 men" literally walked right into the Canadians.[30]

The night suddenly erupted, and the two groups clashed in a hand-to-hand battle with rifles, knives, bayonets, knob-kerries, and even fists.

The noise alerted the German working party, which quickly scrambled into their own trench and sent up flares. German sentries then started pouring fire into the group, not caring to distinguish between friend and foe. "Caught in a cross-fire," noted historian Daniel Dancocks, "the German covering party was virtually annihilated."[31] Only one man appeared to have gotten away. The raiders took eight prisoners but none survived. Not wanting to move back with the Canadians they attempted escape, and were shot or bayoneted. With the German working party and garrison crammed into the trench, the raider's bombs found plentiful targets. The Canadians could not get into the German trenches now, however, and with it becoming increasingly dangerous to remain, Lieutenant Kent ordered his raiding party to retire.

Captain Connors, seeing the fight developing from his parapet and noticing Kent's men beginning to return, quickly called the two field batteries standing by to begin shelling the Germans. Twenty seconds after he contacted the battery commanders, the first 18-pounder shells slammed into the German positions. The effect of the high-explosive shrapnel rounds was immediate, and enemy fire decreased significantly. Kent finally returned to his own lines and was the last to enter the trenches, but upon learning that wounded still lay out in no man's land he immediately set back out to get them. When everyone was finally recovered, the total casualties to the raiders were four killed and 17 wounded.

The raid had been a partial success, but there was no doubt that the Canadians had achieved two things. First, despite the endless difficulties the raiders had identified those units opposite to them and had inflicted several German casualties in the process (with a little help from the Germans themselves). Once again the cooperation between the artillery and infantry had been excellent, and both Currie and Brigadier-General Andrew McNaughton would continually attest to the importance of this on the battlefield.

Second, they had established a reputation for the entire Canadian Corps as the masters in this art of warfare. The French sent a liaison officer, Lieutenant S. Dallennes of the 26th Battalion Chasseurs à Pied, to study the methods adopted by the Canadians with regards to patrols at night. The raiders themselves had been visited and questioned by the brigade commander, L.J. Lipsett, 1st Division's General Currie, and even the corps commander, General Alderson. A total of ten decorations

The ever-welcome "Rum Ration" issued in the front lines.

were given out, a rather large amount considering the number of people involved in the raid.[32]

Valuable lessons were learned, such as the need for quicker and better ways to clear enemy wire. It had taken Lieutenant Kent and his cutting party almost six hours to complete their job. This forced a long period of waiting on other troops and when idle the private soldiers were prone to become tired and fall asleep. Staying still for several hours in cold, damp weather caused the body to cramp up and made it difficult for the soldiers to get themselves back up to speed.

The value of the bomb as a raiding weapon was obvious. In future operations raiders would carry an ever-increasing number of bombs with them. Lightweight and effective, bombs could cause several casualties and did not require a line-of-sight target to be lethal. One thing that was missing from Kent's raiding party was a Lewis gunner. In future operations gunners would be employed in all raids for covering purposes. Private Nicholas Purmal recalled engaging the enemy during the 5 February raid at close range. "I opened rapid fire at them and shot two in the breast."[33] Had he been armed with a Lewis gun surely he could have fallen twice as many.

Operations carried throughout 1916 witnessed a series of changes to Canadian troops. First was the issuing of steel helmets on 4 April to replace the soft, peaked cap that the Canadians had worn throughout their first year on the Western Front.[34] After Mont Sorrel (2–13 June 1916) the much-disliked Ross rifle was discarded and the entire Canadian Corps was reissued the more rugged Lee-Enfield short magazine rifle. The rifle platoon was also reorganized, and now consisted of two rifle sections (each with two rifle grenadiers), a bomber section, and a Lewis gun section.[35] This organization was more effective to meet the evolving tactics of the day. The Germans were beginning to abandon line defences for a more secure series of strong points and defences in depth. The increased firepower in the rifle platoon allowed the Canadians to meet the German defences with a good chance of defeating them. Flanking manoeuvres had become an increasingly popular tactic and the Canadians' ability in fire and movement made them naturals at this type of fighting.

TRENCH RAIDING AT ITS PEAK: PREPARATIONS FOR VIMY RIDGE

The Allies spent the first months of 1917 in extensive planning and preparation for the spring offensive. At the end of the previous year the French high command had decided on making a strong thrust across the Aisne rather than continuing the battles of attrition on the Somme. In addition, General Nivelle, commanding the French, asked Field Marshal Alexander Haig that the British continue with their planned attack south of Arras, starting a few days in advance of his own main attack. Haig agreed, but insisted that his attack extend north to include the Vimy sector. Haig was convinced that only strong pressure could force the Germans off the ridge. In January 1917 this area fell within the British First Army sector and was held by the Canadian Corps.[36]

Extensive raiding preceded the attack on Vimy Ridge. Almost every battalion was required to engage in aggressive patrolling and raiding, for the purposes of gaining as much information about the enemy while familiarizing its own troops with the ground that the battalions would eventually have to fight across. Played out like miniature versions of the actual assault, raids were now being mounted in daylight as opposed to under the cover of darkness like the year before. As Allied troops were fighting from west to east, they enjoyed a few hours more twilight behind them while the rising sun silhouetted the German positions.

Raiding parties also increased dramatically in size compared to the handfuls of men who undertook earlier raids. Raiding and patrolling also achieved the aim of keeping the Germans paranoid and nervous, forced them to abandon their own forward posts and patrolling, and limited their ability to detect an attack was being prepared against them. A series of raids were carried out right up until 9 April, constantly testing the German defences and lowering their morale.

Raids carried out between November 1916 and Early January 1917 were given the objectives of obtaining as much information as possible about the enemy and the terrain that lay between the opposing lines. Just prior to the new year the 42nd (Royal Highlanders of Canada) Battalion carried out such a raid with perfection. A party of nine organized under the command of Lieutenant John McNaughton slipped out through their own wire to make a raid on a German post that had been positioned on the lip of a crater not too far from their lines. After placing a covering party of five bombers just outside the enemy obstacles, they then proceeded into the German trenches. After about 20 minutes the party returned with two captured sentries who were quickly hustled back to the Canadian lines. Without firing a single round the 42nd Battalion had confirmed that the unit standing opposite them was the 23rd Prussian Reserve Infantry Regiment.

Another example was the 4th Field Company, Canadian Engineers, who had been located at Bully Grenay in the Calonne sector since 16 October 1916. This location had become the reserve and training area for 4th Brigade, and the engineers under Major H. St. A. Smith had been tasked to begin work there on a full-scale model of a German trench system.[37] 4th Brigade had planned to conduct a large-scale raid on the German trenches just north of Calonne for the middle of January, requiring men from the 20th and 21st Battalions, as well as engineers from the 4th Field Company, and other support troops. The 20th Battalion had arrived there on 28 December, relieving the 18th Battalion.[38] The 21st Battalion arrived a few days later, after which training began almost immediately.

The raid was to employ some 860 specially trained troops in total, formed into four operational companies.[39] Heading the two companies from the 20th Battalion were Major C.C. Wansbrough with No. 1 Company on the right and Major H.W.A. Foster in command of No. 2 Company on the left. Each company consisted of four platoons, and each platoon was accompanied by two sappers from the 4th Field Company.[40]

Major George S. Bowerbank and Major F.D. Raymond led men from the 21st Battalion. An accountant from the Sarnia branch of the Canadian Bank of Commerce, Bowerbank had been with the battalion for almost three years, and would go on to win the Distinguished Service Order and the Military Cross with the unit.[41] He had already been mentioned in dispatches for displaying gallantry and devotion to duty on more than one occasion. Likewise, Major Frederick Raymond would be cited twice for the award of the Military Cross for his gallantry while serving with the 21st Battalion. It was under this type of leadership that the soldiers were able to maximize their aggressiveness against the Germans.[42]

Men chosen for the raid spent a period of time out on aggressive patrols into "no man's land" to familiarize themselves with the terrain. This had become standard practice now, so those soldiers had less chance of becoming lost while on the actual mission. It was also a way of "climatizing" the raiding troops with the environment in which they were going to conduct the operation. This helped to build up the confidence of the individual soldier, in that he was more likely to be able to carry on should his superiors become casualties because he knew where he was going and what he was supposed to do.

Patrolling was complimented by training sessions on the models constructed by the engineers. On the morning of 5 January 1917, the sappers, along with the infantry, went through the dummy German trenches on a practice run under the supervision of the corps commander.[43] Lieutenant-General Julian Byng was satisfied that the men were being properly trained and looked towards the operation with confidence in its success.

On 27 December 1916, the enemy wire was completely scouted and the procedure of systematically destroying it began, using medium trench mortars and stokes guns. The Left Group, 2nd Canadian Divisional Artillery, undertook this task. Enemy entanglements had consisted of five or six rows of angle iron knife rests closely laced together, and it was hoped that the artillery would satisfactorily destroy the wire prior to the raid.[44] If not, members of the first wave in the storming platoons had been outfitted with wire-cutting attachments for their rifles just in case.

Lessons learned from the Douve River raid the previous November indicated the importance of conducting reconnaissance prior to an attack. Too often, assaulting troops discovered rows of barbed wire that were to have supposedly been destroyed prior to an attack directly in their path. The ensuing fiasco always proved to be murderous to the attackers. Therefore, on the night prior to the raid, reconnaissance patrols and scouts were dispatched to confirm the damage done to German wire, as well as to report on the effect of the artillery. The job having been accomplished, the raid was now on.

Each platoon was organized as a separate storming party with riflemen, bombers, carriers, wire-cutters, stretcher-bearers, and, in the case of the second wave, Lewis gunners. In addition to this, two sappers from the 4th Field Company, Canadian Engineers, accompanied each platoon, carrying mobile charges and gun cotton for wrecking dugouts and emplacements.

One section of battalion bombers was attached to the two platoons on the extreme left flank for the purpose of holding the important block on this flank in the enemy front line. Another section was given No. 1 Operation Company as a protection force. Six men in each of these companies carried ten No. 23 rifle grenades per man. Every operation company also had four rolls of wire and canvas slats to throw over the enemy wire if it was necessary.

Only the bare essentials on a soldier were to be carried on an attack, but the sappers equipping themselves for the raid found their loads to still be quite cumbersome.[45] In addition to a rifle, bayonet, 100 rounds of ammunition, and 10 bombs, the sappers were also carrying with them 10 light ladders, each eight feet long, to be used for bridging trenches and, when necessary, to be used as stretchers. Also on the kit list was Stokes mortar adapted for bombing dugouts and a number of "P" bombs (smoke).[46] All the raiders stripped down their webbing, carrying only their bayonets, water bottles, and haversacks. Men wore the P.H. gas helmet instead of carrying the more cumbersome box respirator.

In the pre-dawn hours of 17 January the raiders moved into their positions. A hot meal was issued to all ranks at 0400 hours and a half hour later the troops left Bully Grenay to take up their positions in the front line. The second wave of troops moved into the bays of the communications trench leading into the front line, and those in the third wave occupied the close support trench. At about 0715 hours all troops reported they were in position.[47]

Conditions were quiet and the enemy had just called their "stand down." It was a routine for both the British and the Germans to be at the ready during the dawn of each day, as so many attacks took place during this time. Seeing no immediate threat, the Germans began to go about their daily rituals when suddenly, at 0745 hours, the sky opened up and shells mercilessly poured into the German position.[48] Parties of the 18th and 19th Battalions carried out diversions on the left flank as the assault went in.

The confused Germans were slow to react and could not locate the real attack. A barrage of smoke was laid in front of the assaulting troops and favourable wind conditions gave great assistance in covering their advance. At zero hour plus fifteen minutes the 173rd Tunneling Company, Royal Engineers, exploded a mine near Double Crassier, an important tactical feature to the west of the attack. This effectively drew attention from the real assault as the Germans, thinking that the attack was to be against this point, concentrated their artillery fire there instead.[49]

Troops of the first wave, covered in snow, poured out of their front-line trench with great speed and went forward through 10 lanes that had been cut in their own wire. Surging across no man's land with great accuracy, they reached the German wire in less than five minutes, while the artillery was still pounding the German front line with smoke and shrapnel.[50] Some recently laid concertina wire did little to slow up the infantry, who quickly cut through the obstacle with their rifle wire cutters.

Little resistance was encountered as the infantry and engineers jumped down into the German front-line trenches. The trench itself was very wide at the top but had caved in many places. The bottom was covered in water and almost all the dugouts had been abandoned. The engineers noticed that there were few fire steps and very little sign that any work that had been recently done on them. In all, five sentry groups were quickly killed or captured, with a few more prisoners being taken in two of the dugouts. By 0758 hours, less than 15 minutes after the raid began, Major Raymond was sending back verbal reports by land-line signals phone from the German front-line trenches. Shell fire was still landing in the front lines at this point, and a Lewis gun crew from the 21st battalion was badly mauled by a direct shell burst. The dead and wounded were immediately evacuated back to friendly lines using the newly taken German prisoners to accomplish the task.[51]

The first wave secured the front-line trenches while the second and third waves passed over them. As the infantry worked their way up the communication trenches, the sappers followed close behind, destroying dugouts, emplacements, and bomb stores. Sapper H. Arnold personally took out several emplacements on his own, and also succeeded in destroying a huge bomb store. Other sappers were busy destroying every dugout they came across as the infantry made their way towards the German support line, successfully entering it at Z hour plus 24 minutes.

In the German support line the dugouts were more numerous, but the sappers of 4th Field Company busily engaged themselves with destroying every one. The infantry were hoping to take more prisoners, but the occupants of the dugouts were extremely unwilling to leave their place of hiding and time did not allow for much persuasion. If the Germans did not give up their dugouts immediately they were bypassed and left for the engineers, who threw in mobile charges and annihilated the men and dugouts all together. When a member of the 20th Battalion asked one sapper how he was faring, the reply came as, "Fine!" He then added, "You come to a dugout — light the fuse — drop the charge in and run like hell — look over your shoulder and see the dugout come out the door!"[52] In all, the sappers demolished 35 deep dugouts and two bomb stores.

At Z plus 45 minutes the raiders commenced breaking off their attack. Under the cover of Lewis gun teams set up to cover the withdrawal, soldiers began moving back towards their own lines. Lieutenant W.M. Goodwin of the engineers had exploded an underground tube from a sap running about 85 feet into no man's land, and it formed a decent flanking communication trench that the raiders used during their retirement. German artillery also began to increase in severity, but due to their confusion as to the exact location of the attack, German shells were evenly distributed between the Calonne area, the neighbouring trenches, and the Double Crassier.

Sections returned independently to friendly trenches and completed their withdrawal by 0840 hours. Sapper Arnold had blown the chains of a German machine gun using mobile charges and assisted in bringing it back as booty. In addition, the raiders returned with another machine gun and two trench mortars, as well as 100 prisoners of the German 11th Reserve Division. Thirty-two more had been counted dead, plus an unknown number that were killed in their dugouts. Canadian casualties totalled 40 dead and 135 wounded. Not a single Canadian was left behind.[53] Sapper H. Arnold later received the Military Medal for his bravery and determination during the raid, having been responsible for a majority of the damage caused by the sappers against the German defences.

LESSONS LEARNED

Doctrine and tactics evolved considerably due to the knowledge and experience gained from daring raiding of the German lines. Trench raids had taken on a new purpose. At first designed to simply harass the enemy and cause some damage, by 1917 raids were being used as "on the job training" for new troops while honing the skills of the more veteran soldiers. Raids had also grown in size, from a few dozen men of a single infantry battalion to almost 1000 troops from all arms.

Combined arms warfare solidified itself in Canadian doctrine through these raids, and had become the example for all other armies to follow. Later the implementation of successful unit-level tactics enabled the Canadian Corps to take Vimy Ridge, the muddy heights of Passchendaele in 1917, and to break the German lines of defence in 1918. All of this reflected well on the Canadian Corps commander, Sir Arthur Currie, who had always encouraged his officers to think and use their initiative. He was not of the traditional British stock, having started as an officer in the Canadian militia, and had no qualms about challenging the status quo doctrine of the British Expeditionary Force (BEF).

Although there is no doubt that the BEF made every effort to improve its own tactics on the western front, their depleted ranks, exhausted staffs, and constant changes to their orders of battle had limited success in getting the lessons learned back to the soldiers. Just the size of the British force and its lack of homogeneity right down to the division level were enough to retard the BEF's quick success in applying fire and manoeuvre. These difficulties allowed the Canadian commanders to enter into the spotlight of the western front command, and General Currie himself had few equals as a combat leader.

As previously stated, raiding was not a Canadian invention. The art was, however, mastered by Canadian troops and rightly so. An army of volunteers for much of the war, Canadian soldiers seldom, if ever, were risk-averse in their operations and took naturally to the idea of constantly harassing their adversary. They were pragmatic, resourceful, and aggressive soldiers, respected by their allies and hated by their enemy. Raiding required innovative minds and a good degree of daring initiative. The Canadian soldier had plenty of both.

> *See you that stretch of shell torn mud spotted with pools of mire,*
> *Crossed by a burst abandoned trench and tortured strands of wire,*
> *Where splintered pickets reel and sag and leprous trench-rats play,*
> *That scour the Devil's hunting-ground to seek their carrion prey?*
>
> — James H. Knight-Adkin

Notes

1. Various authors, *Canada and the Great World War: An Authentic Account of the Military History of Canada from the Earliest Days to the Close of the War of the Nations*, Vol. II (Toronto: United Publishers, 1917–21, 6 vols.), 1188–89.

2. Bill Rawling, *Surviving Trench Warfare: Technology and the Canadian Corps, 1914–1918* (Toronto: University of Toronto Press, 1992), 47.

3. For an example of failure see Tim Cook, "A Proper Slaughter: The March 1917 Gas Raid at Vimy Ridge," *Canadian Military History*, 8:2 (1999): 7–23. For an example of success see Andrew B. Godefroy, "A Lesson in Success: The Calonne Trench Raid, 17 January 1917," *ibid.*, 25–34.

4. Library and Archives Canada [LAC], Record Group [RG] 9, Series III D3 Vol. 4930. 21st Battalion Operation Order dated 16 January 1917.

5. John Swettenham, *To Seize the Victory: The Canadian Corps in World War I* (Toronto: Ryerson Press, 1965), 92.

6. Daniel Dancocks, *Spearhead to Victory* (Edmonton: Hurtig, 1987), 21.

7. Rawling, 47.

8. Colonel G.W.L. Nicholson, *Official History of the Canadian Expeditionary Force*

1914–1919 (Ottawa: Minister of Supply and Services, 1962), 122.

9. The official history of the CEF and the official history of the PPCLI both classify this event as a raid.

10. R.H. Williams, R.H. *The Princess Patricia's Canadian Light Infantry.* Vol.1 (Toronto: Hodder and Stoughton Ltd., 1923), 29.

11. *Ibid.,* 30.

12. *Ibid.,* 31.

13. *Ibid.,* 31–32. Lieutenant Colquhoun was awarded the Military Cross for his daring, and survived his long imprisonment in Germany to receive his award in 1919. He remained with the permanent force militia after the war ended.

14. *Ibid.,* 88.

15. Others to receive awards included Corporal Hacking, Piper Robertson, Lieutenant Crabbe, Sergeant Patterson, and Lance-Corporal Nourse.

16. Rawling, 123.

17. *Ibid.,* 123.

18. *Ibid.,* 124.

19. *Calgary Daily Herald*, 22 April 1919. Captain Charles Costigan was recommended for the Victoria Cross for his actions in this raid but was awarded the Distinguished Service Order.

20. Rawling, 124.

21. *Ibid.,* 125.

22. Major S.R. Elliot, *Scarlet to Green: A History of Intelligence in the Canadian Army 1903–1963* (Toronto: Canadian Intelligence and Security Association, 1981), 25.

23. Rawling, 50–51.

24. McCord Museum (Montreal) Military Papers, "Capt. James Arthur Mathewson letters, 42nd Battalion (Black Watch) CEF."

25. LAC, RG9 III C3, Vol. 4070, Book 17, Rattray to L.J. Lipsett, 10/12/15.

26. Daniel G. Dancocks, *Gallant Canadians: The Story of the Tenth Canadian Infantry Battalion 1914–1919* (Calgary: Calgary Highlanders Regimental Funds Foundation, 1990), 70.

27. LAC, RG9 III C3, Vol. 4070, Book 23, summary of evidence, 11/2/16.

28. *Ibid.,* Battalion report.

29. *Ibid.,* Battalion report.

30. *Ibid.,* Volume 4919, folder 372(2)/16-2, S.H. Kent report, 5/2/16.

31. Dancocks, *Gallant Canadians,* 71.

32. The Military Cross was awarded to Captain Connors, Lieutenants Kent, Younger, and Trimmer, and Regimental Sergeant Major Stuart. Sergeants Milne and Budd, and Privates Cox, Sixby, and Zuidema were all awarded the Distinguished Conduct Medal. In addition these members received a week's leave in London to receive their medals personally from the King.

33. LAC, RG9 III C3, Vol. 4919, Folder 372(2)/16-2, Statement by 20187 Pte. N. Purmal.

34. Nicholson, 140.

35. Rawling, 84–85.

36. Colonel A.J. Kerry and Major W.A. McDill, *The History of the Corps of Royal Canadian Engineers Vol.1 1749–1939* (Ottawa: Minister of Supply and Services, 1962), 127.

37. 4th Field Company War Diary, RG9 III D 3, Vol. 4995. *16 Oct 1916.*

38. Major D.J. Corrigall, *The History of the Twentieth Battalion (Central Ontario Regiment) CEF* (Toronto: Stone & Cox, for the Trustees of the Twentieth Canadian Battalion, 1935), 99.

39. Nicholson, 233.

40. Corrigall, 99.

41. *Letters from the Front.* Vol. I (Toronto: 1920), 47–48.

42. Both Raymond and Bowerbank were awarded the Military Cross for their role in the Calonne Raid. See *Letters From the Front.* Vol. I, 47–48.

43. Corrigall, 100.

44. *Ibid.*, 100.

45. Normally sappers went in with the support waves carrying as much as 120 pounds of gear and stores. It is assumed that for raids they would have travelled more lightly, but this was not to be the case.

46. *Ibid.*, 100.

47. *Ibid.*, 102.

48. Nicholson, 233.

49. LAC, RG9 III D3, Vol. 4930. War Diary 20th Battalion, CEF. 17 January 1917.

50. LAC, RG9 III D3, Vol. 4930, 21st Battalion, CEF, Reference memoranda to accompany operation order No.73, dated 16 January 1917. This report contains an appendix attachment of all telephone communications reports that were received during the raid on 17 January.

51. LAC, RG9 III D3, Vol. 4930. DHS File 4-30. 21st Battalion, CEF, *Documents belonging to the late Lieutenant Colonel Elmer Jones, Officer Commanding 21st Battalion.* Each company commander submitted a narrative of their respective area of operations to the Lieutenant-Colonel following the raid. Their notes were donated to the Historical Section of the Canadian Army in June 1928 by Mr. A.S. Fraser who was in possession of the notes at the time.

52. Corrigall, 103.

53. Nicholson, 234; and Corrigall, 103–104.

CHAPTER 8

Soldier's Honour — Commander's Shame: Daring Actions at Dieppe

TONY BALASEVICIUS

In the early morning hours of 19 August 1942, an Allied assault force, comprised primarily of Canadian soldiers, sailed from England in what was to be one of the largest and most daring military raids in history. The objective of the operation was to take the port of Dieppe, located on the French coast, and secure the surrounding area for a short period before returning to England. In the end, the operation was a complete failure and, over the years, there has been considerable debate regarding the choice of the target, the plan for the attack, and the considerations that ultimately resulted in the raid being revitalized after it had been cancelled. Although these issues are extremely important in understanding the mission's failure, they often overshadow the study of Dieppe within the operational context of Britain's raiding policy at the beginning of the Second World War. Regardless, Dieppe proved to be a bold concept and certainly daring in its execution, however flawed in its planning.

In terms of Britain's raiding policy the Dieppe Raid was one of its most daring actions and had it been successful there is little question that the psychological impact on the Germans would have been enormous. Unfortunately, it did not succeed and the price was costly, particularly for the Canadians.[1] In analyzing the tragedy of Dieppe it becomes quickly evident that the soldiers who fought the battle were defeated by a bad plan and not by the superiority of the enemy's soldiers. As Private Haggard of 13 Platoon, "C" Company, the South Saskatchewan Regiment, points out, "In this action the Canadian troops showed themselves far better soldiers than the Germans whom they encountered. Their [Canadian] morale was excellent and they were anxious to fight, whereas the enemy infantry gave in easily when it came to close quarter fighting."[2]

If one accepts that on that particular day the Canadians soldiers were as good as, or better than, their German counterparts, then the question that must be asked is how was it that they found themselves in a position so unfavourable that, despite their best efforts, they never had a chance. To understand this perplexing issue it is important to first comprehend the genesis and development of the Dieppe Raid within the context of Allied strategy. To do this, one must first comprehend the notion of raiding and how it fits into military operations.

The Raiding Concept

Military raids can be described as operations carried out by a small force that have a very specific but usually high value objective. They are characterized by a swift incursion into hostile territory and their purpose is to secure information, confuse the enemy, or destroy his installations.[3] Although this type of operation forms a principal tactic for guerrilla or asymmetric forces, it is also used, under certain circumstances, by conventional forces.[4] Within these constructs, raids can either be carried out on a specific enemy asset, or they can be grouped together as a series of actions that are spread over time and designed to continually harass and thus slowly wear down an opponent. Although raids can be very effective, they do have their limitations.

The biggest drawback to carrying out such operations is the high level of expertise needed by the participants. For example, planning requires a certain level of sophistication so that operations focus on the enemy's centre of gravity, achieve the element of surprise, and are carried out with speed. Consequently, planners need access to detailed, accurate and up-to-date intelligence. Finally, because raiding frequently means travelling and operating behind enemy lines, forces used to carry out these operations must be well trained and highly motivated.[5] If any of these conditions are not met, the chances for success diminish substantially. Conversely, when these components are properly brought together, raiding can play an important part in military success.

Such was the case in the North American colonies where, by the late 17th century, raiding had become a fundamental part of operations to all sides. In fact, both the British and French integrated the Native model of raiding into a viable tactical doctrine that was used within the context of a conventional military structure based on the European model.[6] This innovation gave both sides the means to carry out war within the confines of the North American wilderness, where conventional forces had difficulty operating.[7]

Although not always appropriate to the specific demands of European continental warfare, the raid and its organizational construct was often able to find a niche in more specialized campaigns where low-intensity operations predominated. For example, the concept of integrating conventional operations with irregular raiding units was exported to Spain where Spanish partisans, linked to British regulars, fought a successful campaign against Napoleon in the Peninsular War of 1808–1814.[8] This adaptation also occurred during the later stages of the Second Boer War (1899–1902), where Commonwealth forces often struggled to deal with an enemy that had evolved from conventional operations into a guerrilla campaign that was based on "hit and run" raiding tactics.

In an effort to contain the Boers' mobility, the British developed a system of blockhouses that divided up vast areas into smaller zones that could be better controlled. Directly linked to these static positions were mobile British raiding columns that continually hunted down the Boers.[9] In the end, the combination gave the British an effective operational concept that slowly reduced the Boers' fighting strength by limiting their freedom of manoeuvre.[10] This rich historical experience would not be forgotten by the British when they became engulfed in their own struggle for survival during the early stages of the Second World War.

BRITAIN'S RAIDING POLICY

The startling success of the German invasion of France and the Low Countries in the spring of 1940 caught the Allies by complete surprise.[11] In fact, the efficiency of the German assault was so overwhelming that the British Expeditionary Force found itself forced to either evacuate the continent or face total annihilation. The process of retreat was so rapid that the British were obliged to leave behind nearly all of their equipment, weapons, and transport.[12]

Defeated, virtually alone, and with little to defend itself, England needed time to re-equip, rebuild, and retrain its armed forces. In the meantime, the British prime minister, Sir Winston Churchill, was not prepared to stand idly by as the Germans prepared for a possible invasion of England. He wanted to take the fight back to the enemy any way he could. As Rear-Admiral L.E.H. Maund, a staff officer at Combined Operations Headquarters (COHQ) explained, "The Prime minister had already gone over to the attack. He wanted to start worrying the enemy over the length of the gigantic coastline they now controlled; to attack first here then there and so tie down considerable numbers of troops and material for the defence of the newly won coasts."[13] One of the options proposed to Churchill was the highly mobile Boer commandos who fought the British using raiding tactics in South Africa.[14] It was suggested that Britain could develop a force of highly trained and motivated soldiers that would be capable of executing an aggressive raiding policy against German coastal defences. Churchill, an offensive-minded and innovative thinker, immediately jumped on the idea.[15]

The commandos would be trained to infiltrate behind enemy lines and conduct night assaults against headquarters, tank harbours, and other key installations. They would also ambush enemy forces moving forward to the battle area and infiltrate airfield perimeters to destroy aircraft, as well obtain information about the enemy. Other, more general, tasks included simply creating tension, disruption, and anxiety amongst the enemy defences or carrying out large-scale diversionary raids to induce the enemy to commit his reserves. In preparation for these operations the commandos would also receive special training that would allow them to carry out amphibious landings along the European coastline.[16]

Although it was envisioned that the commandos would play a major role in initially taking the fight to the enemy, they were also expected to become an important element in preparing the Allies for large-scale amphibious assault operations. This second mission was based on the strategic reality of late 1940, which acknowledged the fact that in order to defeat the Germans, a major assault on "Fortress Europe" would be necessary. The difficulty was that in 1940 England had very little recent experience in mounting opposed amphibious landings, or what the British commonly referred to as "combined operations."[17]

In fact, the combined-operations concept was not even part of Britain's strategy during the interwar period. As late as 1938, the naval member of the chiefs of staff indicated he "could not visualize any particular combined operation taking place in the next war." The army member was even more uncompromising. "Plans for a combined operations landing in the face of strong opposition," he asserted, "was not contemplated."[18] With the fall of France, this attitude changed very quickly, and by the end of 1940, not only was the need for a capability well understood, it was also clear that these operations would now have to be carried out on a much larger scale than previously imagined.[19]

However, before large-scale amphibious assaults could be carried out, every aspect of the operation would have to be reviewed, validated, and then incorporated into the Allies' force doctrine and structure.[20] This learning curve would be steep and had to include everything from deciding on what type of landing craft would be needed, to overcoming the difficulties of sustaining large forces once they had landed.[21] To look at these issues and coordinate the various activities that would need to be developed, the British created a special organization appropriately named Combined Operations Headquarters.[22]

Initially headed by Sir Roger Keyes, the combined-operations concept entailed COHQ launching the commandos on a series of raids that would keep the enemy off balance, while gaining the necessary experience for much larger operations.[23] In order to meet this mandate, raids would have to become progressively bigger and more complex as time went on.[24]

During the 18 months that Keyes was director of COHQ, there was significant development of the necessary infrastructure. Unfortunately, there was little motivation to commit this new organization to operations and the failure to do so was becoming extremely frustrating.[25] Quite simply, the conventional military felt the commandos were a waste of resources.

By the early spring of 1941, Keyes was becoming progressively more disenchanted with the chiefs of staff over their lack of support for raiding operations, and with how the commando units should be organized and employed. Finally, Keyes demanded more authority to carry out his job, and when it became clear that this was not forthcoming, he resigned. In the meantime, Churchill, too, was becoming increasingly impatient with the lack of progress in taking the fight to the enemy. In an effort to jump-start the process he decided on a more controversial choice to replace Keyes and appointed the young and energetic Captain (Navy) Louis Mountbatten.[26]

On taking over the appointment, Churchill immediately pushed Mountbatten for progress. "My task," Mountbatten explained, "was twofold: I was to continue the Commando raids in order to keep up the offensive spirit, gain essential experience, and to harass the enemy."[27] However, Mountbatten went on to stress, "But above all, I was to prepare in every possible way for the great counter-invasion of Europe."[28]

If Churchill wanted a man who would get things done then Mountbatten was a good choice. Shortly after his appointment, the scope of COHQ duties increased significantly and there was also a noticeable shift in Britain's raiding policy. As Christopher Buckley, a noted military historian, points out, "… in the raids that followed Mountbatten's appointment — Vaagso, Bruneval, St. Nazaire, and finally Dieppe — there was an increasing tendency to integrate the functions of all three services into a more closely knit and therefore more efficient unity."[29] Although, not evident at the time, the assault on the dry-docks at St. Nazaire in March of 1942 would have particular significance to the Dieppe Raid.

WRONG LESSONS ON THE ROAD TO DIEPPE

By late January 1942 the German battleship *Tirpitz* was starting to cause the British concern. It had sailed into the area of Trondheim on the Norwegian coast, and this move gave the Germans the option of deploying the ship into the North Atlantic, where it could strike Allied convoys. In an effort to prevent this from happening, the British attempted to bomb the *Tirpitz*, but were unsuccessful.[30]

Believing that the Germans would need secure dry-dock facilities on the coast before deploying a battleship into the Atlantic, the British focused on the possibility of destroying the supporting infrastructure. Fortunately, the only port capable of handling the larger German ships was at the French port of St. Nazaire. The British believed that if they could destroy the dry docks located in the port they could eliminate the German surface threat in the Atlantic.[31]

The British plan for the assault was simple and daring. On 28 March 1942, the HMS *Campbeltown*, a converted surplus ship that was modified to look like a German vessel, was packed with explosives and sailed up the St. Nazaire estuary, where it rammed the locks. Commandos carried on the ship and on some of the escorting craft disembarked after the ramming and destroyed much of the dockyard's infrastructure.[32]

Although the attack resulted in the gates being taken out of commission for the remainder of the war, the cost was high. Of the 241 commandos who took part, 59 were killed or missing and 109 were captured. In addition, 85 navy personnel were killed or missing and approximately 20 were captured. Taking into account the high casualties, the overall value of the operation is difficult to measure.[33]

With respect to the Dieppe raid, the specific advantages derived from St. Nazaire are less important than the lessons that were taken from the operation. For example, an air raid had been planned at St. Nazaire as part of an effort to keep the Germans occupied during the initial phases of the operation; however, it did not work because the fear of causing civilian casualties forced tight restrictions on the use of aircraft and aircrew. As a result, the bombing hindered rather than helped the conduct of the operation.[34]

More important to the eventual raid at Dieppe, similar to the assault on the Norwegian port of Vaagso, St. Nazaire was successful despite that fact that the port had been very heavily defended. In fact, "St. Nazaire was proof for Captain Hughes-Hallett, Naval Adviser at Combined Operations Headquarters that raids in strength could succeed, even against heavily defended ports, given darkness and the element of full surprise."[35] These lessons would have an influence on the planning of future raids — particularly Dieppe.

Up to this point, British raiding policy had progressed in a logical and generally progressive manner. As Robin Neilland, historian and member of the British Commission for Military History, notes, "It can therefore be argued that the Dieppe Raid, which took place five months after the St. Nazaire Raid and eight months after Vaagso, was simply a continuation of this process."[36] Although each raid had become better integrated and more sophisticated then the previous, the overall size of the forces involved remained relatively small.

For example, 51 officers and 525 other ranks carried out Operation Archery, the raid on Vaagso and Maaloy, while "C" Company of the 2nd Battalion of the 1st Parachute Brigade only used 120 men at Bruneval to capture the radar station. Operation Chariot, the attack on St. Nazaire, required about 241 commandos.[37] In reality, these low numbers provided planners dealing with the staging, movement, and control of much larger invasion forces with little if any useful information.[38] This issue started to take on greater importance in early 1942 as the Allies began to seriously consider the requirements for an invasion of the continent. They quickly realized they needed additional information.

THE CONCEPT BEHIND OPERATION RUTTER

Planning for what eventually became Operation RUTTER, the original raid on Dieppe, appeared to have started in January 1942, shortly after the Vaagso Raid. The COHQ staff drew up a list of potential targets that included many of the cross-Channel ferry ports from Calais to Le Havre. Dieppe was one of the ports on the list.[39] According to Hughes-Hallett, when the initial list was drawn up, Dieppe held no particular significance as it was simply one of many possibilities then under consideration.[40] However, a number of events occurred during the first half of 1942 that would move Dieppe into the operational framework of Allied strategic thinking.

In early 1942, the Combined Commanders were beginning to look at contingency operations for the invasion of the continent, and one possibility included landings at various points between Calais and the Cherbourg Peninsula. Under this option it was envisioned that at least six ports would be attacked simultaneously and that reserves would be exploited through the most successful of these bridgeheads.[41] It was felt that once these bridgeheads could be linked together the Allies would have a secure foothold on the continent.[42]

However, before detailed planning could be undertaken, a number of questions needed to be answered. These included: the size of the force needed to take a port, the best methods for carrying troops, the various types of support that would be needed, and, most importantly, how the enemy would react? In order to answer these questions the Combined

Commanders sent their outline plan, including the list of ports to COHQ with the request: "Please raid one of these ports in sufficient strength to persuade the enemy to react as if he were faced with actual invasion."[43]

Important to understanding the evolution of the Dieppe plan is the fact that the basic concept for assaulting ports had also already been developed. In this respect, it had been decided that a divisional-size force would carry out brigade-flanking attacks on either side of the objective while the third brigade was held in reserve. A question that was still under consideration was whether the reserve brigade should be used to reinforce the flank attacks or be launched into a frontal assault at the same time that the flank assaults went in.[44] Captain Hughes-Hallett was asked if it would be possible to plan what was to become the Dieppe raid so that it could test one of these tactical concepts. After getting the necessary approvals, the COHQ staff produced an outline plan based on the flanking option. But when the idea was presented to the army it was rejected in favour of a frontal assault.[45]

As a result, two options for Dieppe were developed. The first envisioned a frontal assault with tanks that would follow flank attacks at Puys and Pourville-sur-Mer. While these flank attacks were going in, parachute and glider-borne troops would capture two coastal batteries located at Berneval and Varengeville-sur-Mer.[46] The second option dropped the frontal assault and moved the focus of the attacks to Puys and Pourville-sur-Mer, while increasing the size of the reserve and landing tanks at Quiberville. After much discussion on the issue, the Chiefs of Staff agreed to go with the frontal assault.[47]

Evidence suggests that the army's option was accepted because it focused on the problem of capturing the port's facilities intact. According to Colonel C.P. Stacey, an historian at Canadian Military Headquarters in London, "an attempt to 'pinch out' a port by landings on its flanks might lead to delays which would give the enemy time to demolish the harbour, whereas if the place could be seized by a blow into the centre the problem would be solved."[48] Based on the direction they had received, COHQ approved the plan and tentatively scheduled the raid for sometime in late June or early July 1942, under the code name Operation RUTTER.

At this point the plan should have been passed to the commander heading the operation for more detailed planning and a second sober look. However, this was not the case as the chain of command was somewhat convoluted.[49] So, although the general concept for RUTTER had been produced, there is no evidence to suggest that a detailed evaluation of the specific issues regarding the attack had been undertaken. As Neilland concludes, "... at no point had the proposed operation been subjected to a detailed analysis of its aims and the likelihood of achieving them, a process referred to in the jargon of 1942, and for many years afterwards, as 'making an appreciation of the situation.' This process is ... fundamental to the next step, devising a viable plan." [50]

In general, "making an appreciation of the situation" involves understanding the mission and then analyzing the ground and how the enemy has positioned himself on it for defence. This process allows the planner to then determine the resources necessary to accomplish the task. In examining the possible seizure of Dieppe, it can be easily argued that a frontal assault on the town itself was not the most ideal choice for an amphibious assault option.

The difficulty in attacking Dieppe is the simple fact that the area around the town, like much of northeastern France, is made up of high unscalable chalk cliffs. These cliffs are broken in only a few places by narrow gaps that have been formed as a result of rivers that flow into the sea. In fact, one of these rivers is the Arques, where the port town sits.[51] In front of Dieppe there is a 1.5-kilometre beach, which is about 300 metres deep and forms a natural field of fire from the line of buildings facing the sea. On both sides of the town the beaches are dominated by headlands, making the area of the beach an ideal killing zone where an attacker can get hit with plunging and grazing fire from three sides.[52]

Moreover, during their two years of occupation, the Germans significantly enhanced the natural strength of this region. As Stacey points out, "The Dieppe area was organized as an independent strong point (*Stutzpunkt*) capable of all round defence and girded on the landside with continuous barbed wire obstacles. Defences for this strongpoint had been extended to incorporate Puys to the west and the high ground immediately east of Pourville."[53]

Within this defensive zone the Germans had placed a number of French 75 mm artillery pieces and anti-aircraft guns both on top and inside the headlands. These strong defensive positions were augmented by numerous machine gun and sniper emplacements as well as coastal batteries, which were located farther inland.[54] "In many respects, the

German defences appear to have been at least as strong as those which the Anglo-Canadian-American forces assaulted two summers later."[55]

The state of German defences around Dieppe and Allied knowledge of its detail would be a major controversy after the raid. The focus of this controversy centres on the lack of knowledge regarding the caves and weapons that were located inside the headlands, as well as the number and quality of the units that occupied the area. Fuelling the debate is the first paragraph of the "Outline Plan" submitted with the Dieppe proposal, which reinforces the contention that Allied planners were out of touch with the reality on the ground. It states, "Intelligence reports indicate that Dieppe is not heavily defended and that the beaches in the vicinity are suitable for landing Infantry and Armoured Fighting Vehicles at some points."[56] Based on the evidence of the subsequent battle, this information was clearly wrong.

In terms of raiding operations, the Allies had broken a key requirement for success, which holds that planners need access to detailed, accurate and up-to-date intelligence. The lack of intelligence or the inability to properly interpret what was available would have a significant impact on the tactical plan as assumptions were made based on this best case scenario. The fact that the Allied planners did not understand the full extent of the defences at Dieppe led them to grossly underestimate the resources and time they would need to capture the two headlands. As control of the headlands was a necessary prerequisite to securing the surrounding area, including the taking of Dieppe, this became a critical error and the assaulting units would pay dearly for this mistake on the beaches.[57]

The units that would carry out the attack would come primarily from the 2nd Canadian Division, commanded by Major-General John Hamilton Roberts.[58] The assault plan called for landings at Puys (Blue Beach), which would be carried out by the Royal Regiment of Canada. They had the mission of securing the village of Puys and taking the headlands that dominated the eastern side of the main beach. West of Dieppe, the South Saskatchewan Regiment would land at Pourville (Green Beach), seize the village, and secure the area between it and Dieppe, which included the western headlands.[59]

Half an hour after the South Saskatchewan Regiment had landed at Green Beach, the Queen's Own Cameron Highlanders of Canada would come ashore and advance along the eastern side of the Scie River to the airfield at St. Aubin, and with tanks from the Calgary Regiment, they would assault the German divisional headquarters, believed to be located at Arques. At about the same time as the flank assaults were going in, parachute and glider-borne troops would land and destroy the two coastal batteries located farther inland. The main assault, directly in front of Dieppe, would be carried out by the Essex Scottish Regiment (Red Beach) and the Royal Hamilton Light Infantry (White Beach). With them would be tanks from the 14th Canadian Army Tank Regiment and engineers who were responsible for clearing obstacles on the beaches and in the town.[60] In addition to this, Roberts would have the Fusiliers Mont-Royal Regiment and the Royal Marine "A" Commando as a floating reserve to exploit any success. According to the plan the initial flank assaults were to be made at 0450 hours, while landings on the main beaches would take place 30 minutes after that, but would be preceded by a bombing run on the headlands and the town of Dieppe itself.

The 30 minutes difference in timing between the flanking assaults and the main attack would also become a point of contention regarding the flaws in the tactical plan.[61] The sequencing of the landings was the result of the number of assaults that needed to take place in the Dieppe area, which would be five, based on the initial plan. Planners felt that the area, in the channel around the cleared lanes of the minefield, would become congested and as the success of the frontal assault depended on taking the batteries and the headlands on the flanks; it was decided to sequence the flank attacks before the main assault.[62]

Although there is much logic to the argument, the problem with this approach is that any surprise initially achieved would be lost before the main assault was launched. This meant that even with the headlands secure the only way the frontal assault could succeed was with a massive amount of fire support. Initially, this was not an issue as it was built into the plan. The second problem deals with the belief that the 30 minutes allocated for the capture of the headlands was adequate.

The Army had initially requested the frontal option because they felt the landing on the flanks would take far too long to develop and likely give the Germans significant time to blow the harbour's infrastructure. Logic would suggest that the timings allocated for the plan had to assume that no opposition would be encountered by the flanking forces as they moved onto their objectives. In this respect, there is a clear disconnect between the rational behind the concept and the development of the plan. This oversight reinforces the idea that no real analysis was done for the assault. Rather, tactical planning was based simply on meeting the needs of the general concept.

TRAINING FOR THE OPERATION

As the plan was being refined the assault forces were sent to the Isle of Wight, where they began training.[63] For the infantry, the program was specifically designed to harden and train the soldiers for the challenges of the mission. It involved such things as the clearing of strong points, bayonet drills, and street-fighting. There was a heavy emphasis on marches and assault courses.[64] According to Denis Whitaker, an officer with the Royal Hamilton Light Infantry at Dieppe, the "normal infantry pace was two-and-one-half miles per hour. After four weeks of accelerated training on the Isle of Wight, all ranks were required to march (no running) 11 miles in two hours carrying full kit and weapons. They were expected to cover the first five miles in 45 minutes; with equipment that weighed 50 pounds."[65]

An important part of the training program focused on landing and the re-embarkation from enemy-held beaches under live fire. During this phase, all members of the assaulting force practised deploying from the crafts and getting their weapons into action as quickly as possible.[66] In the later stages of this training, landing craft came under heavy simulated bombardment as they got close to the shore. To get the soldiers into the habit of keeping their heads down, live bursts of fire were sent over the top of the incoming boats.[67]

The infantry were not the only ones carrying out intensive preparations for the operation. Based on the intelligence that was being provided to the assault force it was clear that there was a series of obstacles on the beaches, particularly in front of Dieppe. The task of dealing with them was given to the engineers. From analysis, it appeared that the defences on the beach included tubular scaffolding, barbed wire as well as antitank and antipersonnel mines. Also, there was a six-foot-high seawall, which was supplemented by another six-foot by six-foot reinforced concrete antitank wall covered by a concrete strongpoint.[68] As a result, the engineers

Canadians train with landing craft prior to the Dieppe Raid.

LAC, PA-113245.

spent much of their time on the island searching for innovative methods of overcoming these obstacles and this included carrying out a series of tests that examined the best methods to destroy masonry and breach the sea wall.[69]

Breaching the sea wall quickly would be important as the tanks had to get through the city and meet up with the Cameron Highlanders. To this end, the tanks worked closely with the sappers responsible for blowing gaps in sea walls so that the breaches would be large enough for the tanks to get through. As the raid would be the first amphibious operation where tanks would accompany the assaulting forces, this meant that a number of challenges needed to be worked out before the operation could be undertaken.[70] For example, everything from preparing the tanks for water, getting them on ships, and having them disembark had to be looked at and somehow solved before the mission.[71]

After weeks of intensive training and preparation, most of these issues had been addressed and the soldiers involved were extremely confident with the skills and knowledge they had acquired on the island. As Jack Poolton, a soldier in "D" Company of the Royal Regiment of Canada, at Dieppe, points out with some satisfaction, "The U.S. Rangers that trained with us were amazed at the type of training we were doing. They would tell us that their troops had an awful lot of catching up to do."[72]

By early June, it was time to put all this training to the test and on the night of 11 June 1942, the soldiers boarded ships for Exercise Yukon. Not only was the exercise the first real test of the joint training that had occurred up to that point, it was also intended to be a dress rehearsal for the operation. The exercise called for the assault force to attack the coast on either side of the towns of Bridport and Dorset at first light on 12 June, after which designated units were to advance inland to secure other objectives.[73] By all accounts the exercise was a complete disaster.

For a start, the sea was rough, and many of the men became seasick. More disconcerting was the fact that landing craft landed the soldiers late or landed them at the wrong place. As a result, once the initial landings were completed an atmosphere of general chaos ensued on the beaches. The poor results forced planners to conclude that additional training and another practice would be needed before the actual operation could be carried out. A second exercise was duly scheduled for 21 June 1942; however, this meant that the raid would have to be delayed until early July.[74]

When Exercise Yukon II was finally run on 23 June 1942, it was only slightly better then the first but sufficient to get the go-ahead.[75] A major problem was the Navy's inability to consistently get the soldiers to the right place at the right time. The Royal Regiment reported that landing was affected at the proper beach, and all went smoothly. But the War Diary of the Essex Scottish reveals that "the Assault Landing Craft lost direction and we are late landing."[75] Overall, "while Roberts was resolutely satisfied with the division's performance, he was still disgusted with the way the Navy handled its role. Nor was he at this stage convinced that Combined Operations were fully aware of the naval failings."[77]

Despite this less then stellar performance, RUTTER was now set for the first good weather day between 2 and 8 July 1942. The men of the raiding force boarded their transports while the assault fleet of some 253 vessels assembled in Yarmouth Roads to wait for favourable weather conditions.[78] Unfortunately, the weather did not improve during the designated period. More importantly, as the force sat in Yarmouth, they were hit by German aircraft on the morning of 7 July 1942.

Although the bombing did little damage, the Germans had seen the invasion fleet and would likely conclude that there was an operation ready to be undertaken. This incident, combined with the fact that better weather over the next two days was unlikely, resulted in the cancellation of Operation RUTTER late in the day on 7 July. Shortly after the cancellation was issued, the men and ships were ordered back to their home stations.[79]

Although that appeared to be the end of the operation, less than two weeks later RUTTER, now code-named Operation JUBILEE, was back on the table. The rationale for remounting the raid is still very much a subject of debate, but the evidence suggests that a number of factors were in play.[80] According to Stacey, "First and foremost it had been an important element in preparing the Allies for the eventual invasion of the continent; and its cancellation was viewed as a clear setback to that programme. Also there was the disappointment to the Canadian troops, who had been looking forward to the operation after two years of home guard duty, to consider."[81] In addition, there were a number of strategic reasons that likely influenced the remounting. Foremost was the significant pressure being put on the British to do more in helping the Allied effort — specifically the hard-pressed Soviets, who were desperately fighting for their survival on the Eastern Front.

This "pressure to do something" was rooted in the fact that during the summer of 1942 Axis forces were at the pinnacle of their success. The Germans controlled much of Europe and its navy held the advantage in the Battle of the Atlantic. German forces had also occupied much of North Africa including parts of Egypt, while further to the east, the German Army was on the offensive pushing towards Stalingrad.[82]

Great Britain, the United States, and the Soviet Union were clearly on the defensive and no nation was feeling the pressure like the Soviets. In an effort to relieve the stress of the German onslaught towards Stalingrad, the Russians were pushing for a second front in Western Europe as quickly as possible. However, the British and United States had a number of issues of their own.

In June 1942, German forces had captured Tobruk and the resulting political crises in England threatened Churchill's position as Prime Minister. To deflect some of the criticism, Churchill was looking for success but he needed to undertake some type of offensive action in order to get it.[83] In this respect, Dieppe offered an off-the-shelf solution and a force already trained and practised for the mission. However, the major issue in remounting the raid was security.

When RUTTER was cancelled, thousands of soldiers, sailors, and airmen had been taken out of quarantine and sent back to home bases throughout England. Therefore, it had to be assumed that the enemy was now aware of the operation. Decision-makers realized that the mission could only be revived if it was clear that information about the remounting would not reach the Germans. To overcome this problem,

Hughes-Hallett suggested that the various units move directly from their bases to the ports of embarkation and embark on the same evening they were designated to sail.[84]

This is exactly what happened, according to Jack Poolton: "Shortly after lunch [on the 18 August], we received an order to be out on the street with all arms and equipment in fifteen minutes. We were hustled into waiting trucks. The tarps were tied down across the back, something we had never had done before. Immediately the trucks moved off, carrying the Royals [Royal Regiment of Canada] to Portsmouth, where we were driven into the dock yards. The troops then embarked on two troop carriers.... Once aboard the ship, I was told by one of the sailors that we were headed for Dieppe. Apparently, the raid had been resurrected and it was now called Operation Jubilee."[85]

OPERATION JUBILEE

The plan for Operation JUBILEE was essentially the one that was to be used for RUTTER. However, while the units were training on the Isle of Wight, RUTTER had been significantly altered. In particular, the heavy bombing attack had been taken out of the operation.[86] This change more than any other would remain an enduring controversy as conventional wisdom dictated that the frontal assault to capture Dieppe's port facilities would require a significant amount of fire support to make it work. So what happened to the fire support?

As the Navy was not prepared to risk battleships in the English Channel, it had been decided to use bombing raids to provide the necessary support. However, when asked to support the Dieppe operation, Air Marshal Sir Authur Harris, chief of bomber command, retorted, "I have neither planes nor crews to spare for useless sideshows."[87] This fact was then made known to the three force commanders at a 5 June 1942 conference and, for some unexplained reason, the mission was still allowed to continue.[88] Moreover, Major-General Roberts convinced himself that the bombers would not be accurate and the resulting damage would only hinder the occupation of the town.[89] Even if this assumption was correct, questions regarding why the plan was not altered to adjust for this change are perplexing. In effect, the change meant that the infantry, engineers, and tanks on the main beaches would be carrying out a frontal attack on a heavily defended position in daylight with little support.

Other modifications were also introduced into the plan. In particular, since the use of airborne forces needed almost ideal weather conditions in order to operate, it was decided to substitute this force with commandos, which would take over the task of neutralizing the coastal batteries on either side of Dieppe. As will be seen, this particular change would also have a significant impact on the mission.

Nonetheless, during the afternoon and evening of 18 August 1942, transport vessels were positioned and readied at the staging ports while the Air Force conducted final preparations for what they hoped would be a major battle with the German Luftwaffe.[90] Concurrently, the assault forces under the command of Major-General Roberts were beginning their assembling and loading onto the various naval vessels that would transport them across the channel.[91]

As these final preparations were being carried out, two lanes were being cleared and marked through the German minefield located in the English Channel. At approximately 2125 hours on 18 August 1942, a flotilla of 254 ships began moving to the link-up point located just in front of the minefield. Once at the link-up point they continued moving through the minefield and into position. At the designated position the landing craft were dropped off and started moving to their assigned beaches. It was now approximately 0330 hours on 19 August.[92]

Allied convoy of landing craft en route to Dieppe.

Daring Action on the Beaches

No. 3 Commando, which was commanded by Lieutenant-Colonel R.G. Durnford-Slater, was on the far left side of the assault force and had the mission of taking out the battery near Berneval. As they moved towards their landing point they encountered an enemy convoy at 0347 hours. The Germans were quick to open fire and in the ensuing fight No. 3 Commandos' landing craft scattered into the darkness. As a result, only one of the commandos' landing craft, which contained 18 men, was able to make it to the beach and they did so on time at 0445 hours.[93] Undaunted by this setback, the small party, now under the command of Major Peter Young, continued on with the mission. They quickly succeeded in scaling the cliffs and reached the battery position a short time later.

Although, this force was insufficient to attack and destroy the enemy battery, they were able to effectively harass the gunners, which prevented the Germans from engaging the flotilla for over two and a half hours. Sometime around 0700 hours the Germans were starting to reinforce the area in sufficient numbers that Young decided it was time to leave and began his withdrawal to the beaches.[94] As the after action report for the operation states: "The bold action and extraordinary good fortune of this single craft and the Commando troops who were its passengers is a very bright spot in the general gloom of events on the eastern flank beaches. That 20 soldiers should land completely unsupported, should succeed in interfering effectively with the action of an enemy battery, and should subsequently be withdrawn without loss by the same craft which put them ashore, constituted a truly remarkable episode."[95] For his daring action in taking on the battery, Major Young received a well-deserved Distinguished Service Order.[96]

Despite the fact that No. 3 Commando was having its share of bad luck and a difficult time at Berneval, things were going much better for No. 4 Commando on the far right flank. No. 4 Commando, commanded by Lord Lovat, had the task of destroying a six-gun coastal battery located near Vaengeville. For the operation the Commando was broken up into two groups and landed on two different beaches. The first group, which had landed at Vasterival (Orange Beach I) north of the enemy position, was responsible for setting up a fire base, while the assault element, which

Photo by B. Horn.

View from German pillbox on the high ground overlooking the main beach at Dieppe.

had landed near Quiberville (Orange Beach II), moved around the flank of the gun position to carry out the assault.

The fire base opened up at 0615 hours and included in the supporting fire plan was an air attack that came in on the objective 12 minutes later. This preparatory fire was followed by the assault that went in at 0630 hours. The operation was a complete success and despite significant resistance on the objective, was over in a relativity short period of time. The German guns were quickly destroyed and the commandos then withdrew according to plan and returned to England.

During the fight, Captain Pat Porteous distinguished himself. The platoon commanders leading the assault force were both killed before they were able to get to the gun position. Without hesitation, Captain Porteous, who was already wounded in the hand, took over command and, under his leadership, the attack continued. In fact, he was one of the first to reach the guns and started clearing enemy positions. In the process, he was wounded in the leg and fell to the ground. Incredibly, he got up and continued fighting until he was again wounded and eventually dropped to the ground, unconscious, but not before killing the enemy around him. He was subsequently awarded the Victoria Cross for his daring actions on that day.[97] Unfortunately, the success of No.4 Commando was in marked contrast to what was happening on the other beaches, and particularly with the landing being made by the Royal Regiment of Canada at Puys.

The beach at Puys is fairly broad and dominated by cliffs on either flank with a 10-foot sea wall at the base of the cliffs. The Royal Regiment of Canada was expected to take Puys and then clear the Germans off the eastern side of the headland. Although the plan was relatively simple, the success of the "Royals" depended on achieving surprise and getting to the top of the cliffs before the Germans could gain their balance. A delay in getting the boats to shore meant the "Royals" were late and were forced to land in daylight in front of an enemy that was on the alert. As a result, surprise was not achieved and the unit was exposed to crossfire from the cliffs even before getting out of the landing craft. The result was a complete disaster.[98]

Photo by B. Horn.

The killing ground at Puys.

The ferocity and devastation on Blue beach that day is revealed by Captain G.A. Browne of the RCA, who was a Forward Observation Officer (FOO) attached to the unit. "We were met by intense, accurate Light Machine Gun fire," he described, "sustaining heavy casualties. 'A' and 'B' Coys, who were landed immediately in front of the Blue Beach sea-wall, met intense and unexpectedly heavy MG [machine gun] fire from a number of posts on the wall, sustaining very heavy casualties as they left the [landing craft]."[99] Browne adds, "The survivors, who attained the comparative cover of the wall itself, were pinned to its face by enfilade fire from well-concealed positions on the flanks. Some of the wall MG posts were put out of action however, at further heavy cost…"[100] Despite the carnage that was taking place on the beach, an intrepid group of soldiers was able to make their way past the seawall and up onto the cliffs.

Although much of his unit had been decimated, the commanding officer, Lieutenant-Colonel Douglas Catto, refused to admit defeat. He gathered as many soldiers as he could and was able to lead a small party of about 20 "Royals" off the beach by cutting their way through the wire at the western end of the seawall and climbing up the cliffs. They reached the top and proceeded to clear some houses in the area. Unfortunately, as soon as they made it through the gap the Germans brought machine-gun fire down on the opening, isolating the group. The small group of "Royals" eventually ended up in a nearby wood where they remained until it became obvious that the raiding force had withdrawn. At 1600 hours they surrendered.[101] Interestingly, Lieutenant-Colonel Catto and his intrepid group were not the only "Royals" to make it to the top of the cliffs that day.

Corporal L.G. Ellis leapt out of the landing craft as it hit the beach and quickly ran for the cover of the seawall. Once there he anxiously waited for the others to arrive. However, when he looked back, all he could see was men being cut down by machine-gun fire that was sweeping the beach.[102] More urgently, the wall which he had assumed would provide him with a safe haven had now turned out to be a death trap as machine-gun positions, sited on the eastern side of the cliff, were bringing down enfilade fire onto the area, causing heavy casualties.

Throughout his ordeal, Corporal Ellis remained undaunted and, keeping a cool head, was somehow able to find his way through the barbed wire that was obstructing the steps near where he was positioned. Quickly moving out of the line of fire, he headed up the cliff and came upon a gun emplacement, but found it empty. He then continued onward but was again confronted by a wire obstacle, which "was so thick that he could not shoot through."[103] Fortunately, he was also able to find a way through this obstacle and, a short time later, reached a house at the top of the cliff. Finding the door open, he started to clear the building, but was quickly forced to evacuate the it when it was targeted by Allied ships. Ellis then continued down a path until he came to another gun position.[104] Again, looking inside, he found nothing. However, he did notice a bunker on the opposite side of the valley and "saw dust flying about this pill-box, which he felt indicated that our troops were firing at it."[105] Although he was unable to see fire coming from the bunker, he did see tracers originating from a position close by which appeared to be falling on the beach. More important, Corporal Ellis thought he could see what he assumed to be a face of a person, so he fired at this target and immediately saw the stream of tracer bullets change direction, moving up into the air.[106]

Not seeing any more firing from the position, Corporal Ellis crawled back to the point where he had crested the slope and looked down at the beach. He saw what he assumed was a landing craft embarking so he decided to head back down.[107] Once back near the water, he saw no movement and the landing craft was already pulling out. However, it did not get very far, as it capsized. A short time later he decided to swim for it. Taking off his boots and equipment he plunged into the water and started heading out to sea.

While Corporal Ellis was swimming, a sniper's bullet came within a few inches of his head so he pretended he had been hit and the shooting stopped. After a while he started swimming again and continued to do so for about 1–2 hours until he was just about exhausted. In fact, he started losing consciousness just as he was rescued by a passing vessel.[108]

Despite the actions of leaders like Lieutenant-Colonel Catto, and soldiers such as Corporal Ellis, the "Royals" never really stood a chance on the beaches of Puys. The assault depended on complete surprise and adherence to exact timings. When these two prerequisites had been compromised there was no flexibility built into the plan to alter or stop the operation. As a result, the "Royals" landed in a killing zone with little chance of survival, much less success. By the end of the battle the regiment had lost 88 percent of its strength. Of the 546 that hit the beach, 209 were killed, 262 became prisoners (103 of which were wounded), and only 63 escaped the beaches and returned to England.[109] More importantly, the consequence of this failure would have a direct effect on the success of the landings on the main beaches.

Meanwhile, at Pourville, a much greater degree of surprise was initially achieved by the South Saskatchewan Regiment, which was under the command of Lieutenant-Colonel C.C.I. Merritt. Although the unit landed on time at 0452 hours against very little opposition, they had been put down on the wrong side of the Scie River. Heavy fighting erupted as they were forced to fight their way through the village and then across a narrow bridge before they could start clearing their objective, which was the western headlands overlooking Dieppe.[110]

Among the first to land at Pourville was Private Haggard of 13 Platoon, "C" Company, the South Saskatchewan Regiment. As his platoon started moving off the beach they quickly came under fire from a nearby building. They were able to rapidly overcome the resistance and secure the objective. As they consolidated around the position, civilians in the area told them that the Germans were in position on the hill behind the building. Sergeant H.E. Long, who was in command of the platoon, ordered his men up the hill to clear the enemy. A short time later they came under fire and Sergeant Long was wounded, while a soldier who was standing near him was killed. Leaderless, the men of No. 13 Platoon stopped in confusion.[111]

Haggard, who had been at the rear of the column, came forward to see what was happening and in the absence of leadership he and Private Berthelot took charge of the situation. They quickly discovered that the Germans were firing from slit trenches near a house and close to the edge

Photo by B. Horn.

The German fields of fire covering the exposed beach at Pourville.

of a wooded area, so they organized an attack. As two sections of the platoon were already pinned down by fire, Haggard moved the third section into position where he could attack the Germans from the rear. Although the Germans opened fire when they saw the soldiers advancing, they quickly realized they were about to be encircled and resistance stopped. In all, about twelve enemy prisoners were taken while the rest were killed.[112]

Back near the river, the South Saskatchewans had made it to the bridge, but it was covered by heavy fire from the Germans occupying the headlands. Despite a number of gallant attempts, the soldiers were having difficulty getting across and the bodies of brave soldiers that had tried were starting to pile up, so further movement across the bridge stopped. Hearing that the unit was being held up, Lieutenant-Colonel Merritt moved forward and took charge.

Ignoring the heavy fire, he walked onto the bridge, waving his helmet and yelling to his men, "Come on over, there's nothing to it!"[113] Inspired by this act of heroism, men followed their commanding officer as he moved forward and charged one of the German positions, taking it out with a grenade. Although, the South Saskatchewans were now in a much better position to fight the battle, the Germans were by now on fully alerted and ready for the attack. Lacking communications and almost out of mortar ammunition, the Canadian advance was held in check.[114]

As the South Saskatchewan Regiment was struggling to get a foothold on the headland, the Queen's Own Cameron Highlanders of Canada, commanded by Lieutenant-Colonel A.G. Gostling, came ashore at 0550 hours. They were 20 minutes late, and attempted to quickly pass through the bridgehead established by the South Saskatchewan Regiment. However, by this time the Germans had targeted the landing beach and Lieutenant-Colonel Gostling was killed almost immediately after landing. The fire scattered the unit, which now came under the command of Major A.T. Law.[115] According to Law, the initial plan was for the Camerons to advance towards their objectives at St. Aubin Arques-La-Bataille by the east bank of the Scie River. Along the way they were to make contact with the tanks that had landed on the main beaches to put in the attack.[116]

However, the unit had also developed an alternative plan to move up the west bank of the Scie if circumstances made that option a more desirable choice. Since the South Saskatchewan Regiment had made little

Canadian prisoners of war being led through the streets of Dieppe en route to their internment camps.

progress towards the east side of the river and the Camerons had also been placed on the wrong (west) side of the river, Major Law decided to adopt the alternative plan and quickly issued the necessary orders.[117]

The battalion, less one company that remained in Pourville, began to move inland along the main road towards Bas De Hautot. They immediately came under machine-gun and mortar fire and, as they attempted to evade the fire, the battalion moved into a wooded area and up a "draw" in the direction of Benouville. Although this gave them some cover from the fire, their progress was hampered by German snipers.[118]

When the Camerons finally came of the wooded area they found they were in front of a defensive position, which they quickly attacked and captured. However, the unit was hit by machine-gun fire located in depth and were forced to withdraw. As progress was slow and enemy troops were now concentrating in the area, Major Law concluded that there was little hope of advancing farther and at around 0930 hours he issued orders for a withdrawal back to the beach.[119]

From this point onward, the Camerons carried out a fighting

withdrawal as they moved back to Pourville and caused a significant amount of damage to the Germans. In fact, Major Law believed, "that in all the Camerons may have inflicted 200–300 casualties."[120] By the time the Camerons returned to Pourville it was about 0956 hours and although the Canadians held the village, all of the high ground was still in German hands. This situation made the embarkation extremely difficult and both units would pay a heavy price going over the exposed beaches.[121]

In fact, by the time the embarkation began, Merritt had been wounded twice and his battalion had been reduced to about 300 men. Incredibly, he was still able to supervise an orderly withdrawal. As his soldiers were getting ready to leave, he decided that he would remain behind and cover the re-embarkation, which he did until about 1600 hours that day. Short of ammunition and realizing little could be gain from further action he, along with a small party, surrendered.

Merritt was awarded the Victoria Cross for his heroism.[122] His citation reads:

> Although twice wounded, Lieutenant-Colonel Merritt continued to direct his unit's operations with great vigour and determination and while organizing the withdrawal he stalked a sniper with a Bren gun and silenced him. He then coolly gave orders for the departure and announced his intention to hold off and "get even" with the enemy. When last seen he was collecting Bren and Tommy guns and preparing a defensive position which successfully covered the withdrawal from the beach.[123]

In the end, countless soldiers were evacuated safely because of Lieutenant-Colonel Merritt's courage under fire.

Although there were a number of heroic actions carried out at Green Beach, in the end the operations achieved very little towards the accomplishment of the mission. This was due to the fact that there were insufficient forces to capture the designated objectives and the forces that were allocated lacked the necessary fire support to do the job effectively. Most importantly, the western headland overlooking Dieppe, which was vital to the overall success of the assault on the main beaches, was not captured.[124]

The failure of the flanking attacks would have a knock-on effect on the main assault. In preparation for this attack there was a five-minute bombardment that started at 0510 hours. The ships in the flotilla targeted the buildings along the seafront and after that the fire shifted to the flanks. At that point cannon-firing aircraft swept into attack shortly before the first landing craft touched down on time at 0520 hours. On the right, the attack was made by the Royal Hamilton Light Infantry, commanded by Lieutenant-Colonel R.R. Labatt, while the Essex Scottish, commanded by Lieutenant-Colonel. F.K. Jasperson, was on the left. These units were followed closely by the first wave of tanks from the 14th Canadian Army Tank Battalion (Calgary Regiment), commanded by Lieutenant-Colonel J.G. Andrews.[125]

As the troops landed, they came under devastating fire from concealed positions located inside the cliffs and from guns that were positioned behind the first line of buildings facing the beach. Many of the tanks in the first wave also came under heavy fire as soon as they moved out of the landing craft. Although some of the tanks were able to get over the seawall and make it to the Promenade, none of them were able to get beyond this point. This was due to the fact that the exits had been blocked by anti-tank obstacles and the engineers, who could have cleared these obstacles, were having a number of problems of their own.

During the initial assault many engineers became casualties as they struggled to carry out their tasks. Of the 169 sappers who went ashore on 19 August, 152 were killed or captured and of the 17 that managed to escape the beaches and return to England, 10 were wounded.[126] Lance-Sergeant G.A. Hickson, of the 7th Field Company, Royal Canadian Engineers, provides an example of the outstanding effort put forth by the engineers on that trying day. Sergeant Hickson landed with the Royal Hamilton Light Infantry on White Beach. As the fire on the beach was too heavy to get to his objective, he decided to join an infantry platoon. When the platoon commander and his senior non-commissioned officer (NCO) became casualties, Hickson took command leading the men to the casino. There, he breached the defensive position using explosives and was able to reach a large concrete gun emplacement where he killed the crew and then destroyed the gun.[127] An official military report noted:

He [Hickson] quickly re-organized the remaining men of the platoon and, in the face of heavy enemy opposition, led them into the town as far as the Church of St. Remy. Only when he found that his party was alone and unsupported did he decide to withdraw back to the casino. Later, during the evacuation, he was among the last men to leave the beach. Incredibly, during the course of these actions, two bullets passed through Sergeant Hickson's left sleeve, and one through the leg of his pant trousers; but he received no injury, with the exception of a scratch from some barbed wire.[128]

Another incredible action that took place amidst the turmoil of the killing grounds in front of Dieppe was the courage displayed by honorary Captain John Foote, the regimental chaplain for the Royal Hamilton Light Infantry. Throughout much of the morning he exposed himself continuously to enemy fire as he attempted to carry wounded personnel to safety. During the evacuation, he helped move the wounded from the Regimental Aid Post onto landing craft often under heavy fire. On several occasions he had the opportunity to embark but returned to the beach to care for and evacuate the wounded. In the end, he refused a final opportunity to leave, choosing instead to stay with the men that were going into captivity.[129] For his actions on that day, Captain Foote was awarded the Victoria Cross.

Although, the Royal Hamilton Light Infantry had succeeded in capturing the casino, which was in front of the town, obstacles covered by heavy fire blocked the streets, preventing further progress. In fact, many soldiers were unable to advance beyond the wire obstacles that were positioned on the beach and continually swept by heavy fire. In this respect, the Essex Scottish was particularly hard hit and suffered numerous casualties.

The Essex Scottish Regiment landed on the exposed eastern side of the beach and was unable to make further progress as the enemy covered this area from the buildings along the seafront, as well as from the eastern headland. Attacks made over the seawall were quickly stopped by a deep obstacle belt and any movement towards the obstacle came at a heavy cost. As a result, movement forward for the Essex Scottish was impossible.

Investigations carried out by Stacey revealed that there was only one small group of about 12 men under the command of Company Sergeant Major Cornelius Stapleton that made it as far as the Promenade.[130]

CALLING IN THE RESERVES

Although the situation on the beaches had become desperate, back on the command ship HMS *Calpe* poor communications resulted in Major-General Roberts receiving conflicting information about what was actually happening. Unfortunately, Roberts had completely misinterpreted the situation on the ground as he not only believed that the main attack in front of Dieppe was achieving some success but that operations at Pourville were going well. As a result, he decided to commit his reserve into the carnage of the main beaches.[131]

The Fusiliers Mont-Royal, commanded by Lieutenant-Colonel D. Menard, and the Royal Marine "A" Commando, commanded by Lieutenant-Colonel J. Picton-Phillips, were ordered to land on the beach to reinforce the Royal Hamilton Light Infantry and the Essex Scottish. The Fusiliers Mont-Royal went in at about 0700 hours and were engaged by heavy fire even before their ramp hit the water. Menard was cut down almost as soon as he landed.[132] Within minutes of hitting the beach the once-proud unit was reduced to small groups looking for any shelter from the withering fire that they could find.

The situation faced by the Fusiliers Mont-Royal was vividly recalled by Sergeant Dubuc, who was attached to the battalion headquarters of the regiment. Dubuc was landed from a Landing Craft Personnel (LCP) near the west end of the casino at about 0700 hours. On landing, he ran forward about 150 yards with a Bren gun and took cover in a depression in the beach. He ended up staying there for about an hour as heavy fire was coming in from what appeared to be every direction.[133]

However, Dubuc had no intention of sitting around waiting for something to happen. As soon as an opportunity appeared, he seized it and made his way off the beach. As he did he was followed by approximately 11 other men from the Fusiliers. The small party arrived at the corner of the Rue de Sygogne, where they encountered a machine-gun position that started firing in their direction. In the ensuing fight one of the

Fusiliers threw a grenade at the Germans and the firing stopped. The small group quickly advanced on the position and found three enemy soldiers lying on the ground. They continued fighting their way through the city, under fire the entire time. Eventually they were able to reach the southwest corner of the Bassin. There, approximately 15 Germans suddenly appeared from different directions. Low on ammunition and with few options, Sergeant Dubuc and his group surrendered.[134]

However, surrender did not sit well with these intrepid warriors. The Germans took the captured fusiliers into a backyard and lined them up facing the wall of a building. They then departed, leaving only one German soldier to guard them. It did not take long for Sergeant Dubuc to see an opportunity for escape, which he did by throwing himself upon the guard.[135]

Free from captivity, Sergeant Dubuc was eventually able to find his way to the beach. Coming back just northeast of the casino, he found a group of three tanks on the shingle and also discovered his commanding officer (CO), Lieutenant-Colonel Menard, who was lying on the ground, wounded. As the withdrawal had begun, he helped get the CO safely onto a LCA (landing craft armour) and then returned to the beach, picking up Corporal Cloutier of No. 3 Platoon before embarking himself.[136]

By 0930 hours, the enemy had brought a number of mobile batteries, mortars, and additional infantry into action against the Canadians, and many of the Allied ships were starting to come under increasing threat. At 0940 hours, higher headquarters sent out the message to withdraw all assault forces at 1100 hours. Concurrently, craft-carrying tanks and troops who had not yet been landed were ordered to return to England.[137] As the Allies struggled to withdraw, the Germans, who still controlled all of the high ground, continued to pour a withering fire onto the beach.

As Stacey records, "The Germans on the cliff tops continued to pour down shells and bullets, taking toll of boats and men alike."[138] The South Saskatchewan Regiment and the Queen's Own Cameron Highlanders of Canada at Pourville took most of their casualties during this phase of the operation. Moreover, there was a general state of confusion as too many soldiers were trying to get onto too few craft. Although not pretty, by 1240 hours the evacuation of what was left to take away had been completed. The battle losses from the raid were staggering. Personnel casualties included 3,623 ground troops, 153 air force casualties, and 550 naval casualties. Equipment losses included 27 of the 30 tanks, 106 of 650 aircraft, 33 of 179 landing craft, and 1 of 8 destroyers.[139] The raid had been a debacle.

Shortly after the raid Sir Winston Churchill stood up in the house of Parliament and said about the operation:

> The raid must be considered as a reconnaissance in force. It was a hard, savage clash such as will very likely become increasingly frequent as the war deepens. We had to get all the information necessary before launching operations on a much larger scale ... I, personally, regarded the Dieppe assault, to which I gave my sanction, as an indispensable preliminary to full-scale operations.[140]

German officers survey the aftermath of the battle on Dieppe Beach among the Canadian dead and wounded.

Churchill's contention about getting "all the information necessary before launching operations on a much larger scale" became the major theme for senior officers attempting to justify the raid and its cost.

An article written by Stacey on the first anniversary of the raid observed, "... but some commentators have overlooked the fact that many of the advantages which we gained cannot yet be described in public. A basic object of the Dieppe raid was to gain information essential to the preparation of major assault operations in the future. Important lessons were learned, and our knowledge of both the enemy's defensive system and the means of breaking it — the means too of saving the lives of many thousands of Canadian and other Allied soldiers in the future — were very greatly increased."[141] Although this may in fact be correct it does not address the real issue, which is that the tactical plan was flawed. Had that not been the case the cost of these lessons could have been gained at a much cheaper price.

WHAT WENT WRONG

When looking at the planning and conduct of the raid, it must be put into the context of the times. In this respect, the operational premise for the operation, which was to test the concept of attacking ports, was sound given Allied views in 1942. The raid fell apart at the tactical level where the application of the basic principles for success was not followed.

The cornerstone to any successful raid is intelligence. For intelligence tells the planners what resources are needed and how forces must be employ to achieve the necessary effect. In this respect, intelligence failures at Dieppe led to an underestimation of the defences in the area. This underestimation led to inadequate resources being given to the operation and likely had some impact on the key decision to reduce fire support.

Although planning for the operation was extremely detailed; it was not sophisticated. First, there is no evidence that an analysis on the situation was completed for the attack. This resulted in a plan that had structural flaws and lacked any flexibility to compensate for its weaknesses. In fact, had there been more flexibility built into the plan it is unlikely it would have changed the outcome for the Allies, but it could have saved lives by stopping the main assault if the capture of the headlands did not occur.

Finally a key element in the conduct of a successful raid is the ability to achieve surprise. The unfortunate discovery of No. 3 Commando by the German convoy entering Dieppe should have stopped the operation at that point. Once surprise was lost, the assaulting troops needed firepower to compensate for the now-alerted defences. Loss of surprise and the lack of firepower prevented the raid from developing as quickly as required. This allowed the Germans time to recover from the initial shock. As a result, the assaulting elements became bogged down in front of strong defensive positions and the ability to take key objectives was no longer possible.

The Dieppe Raid was the first time the British had attempted a major amphibious assault since the landing in Gallipoli in 1915. Although they had carried out a number of successful smaller raids, Dieppe showed the Allies they still had much to learn.[142] There is little question that the Allies were able to learn many of those lessons by the D-Day landings on 6 June 1944. However, there was no necessity to learn those lessons by sacrificing soldiers to conduct an operation that was based fundamentally on a flawed plan. This is why Dieppe will forever remain a controversial event in Canadian military history and this is why it should always remain so.

Nonetheless, the actions of Canada's soldiers on the bloody beaches of Dieppe in many ways epitomized the courageous and daring persona of this nation's warriors. Eager to join the fray, the Canadians, representing all regions of the country, fought a tenacious battle against overwhelming odds and wrote with their blood another chapter of Canada's proud military heritage. For that reason, Dieppe will also be forever remembered.

NOTES

1. Colonel C.P. Stacey, *The Canadian Army 1939–1945: An Official Historical Summery* (Ottawa: Kings Printer, 1948), 80. Allied losses during the raid were staggering. Stacy states: "Of the 4963 all ranks that embarked for the raid only 2211 returned to England. 589 were wounded but survived while 28 died from their wounds. No less then 1944 Canadian officers and men became prisoners; at least 558 of those were wounded." To put this loss into perspective, "At Dieppe, from a force of fewer than 5000 men engaged for only nine hours, the Canadian Army lost more prisoners then the whole eleven months of the later campaign in Northwest Europe, or the twenty months during which Canadians fought in Italy." *Ibid.*

2. Memorandum of Interview with L-13282 Private W.A. Haggard, DCM South Saskatchewan Regiment, carried out at Canadian Military Headquarters, 12 Nov 1942. Subject: The Operation at DIEPPE — 19 Aug 1942. Annex E. Accessed through the Directorate of History and Heritage. Canadian Military Headquarters (CMHQ) Reports 1940-1948 (electronic version), http://www.forces.gc.ca/hr/dhh/history_archives/engraph/cmhq_e.asp?cat=1 (accessed 1 May 2007).

3. Department of the Navy. *Fleet Marine Force Manual (FMFM) 7-32, Raid Operations* (Washington, DC: United States Marine Corps, 3 December 1993), 1-1.

4. Guerrilla warfare (the word *guerrilla* comes from the Spanish meaning "little war") is often the means used by weaker nations or military organizations against a larger, stronger foe. Fought largely by independent, irregular bands, sometimes linked to regular forces, it is warfare of harassment through surprise. It features the use of ambushes, hit-and-run raids, sabotage, and, on occasion, terrorism to wear down the enemy, http://www.answers.com/topic/guerrilla-1 (accessed 15 April 2007).

5. Department of National Defence. *Land Force Tactical Doctrine, B-GL-300-002/ FP-000, Volume 2* (Kingston: Director of Army Doctrine, 1997), 3–4. Depending on the mission they may also require access to a significant amount of fire support that must be available in order to reduce the enemy's ability to react should something go wrong. *Raid Operations*, 1–1.

6. Bernd Horn, *Forging a Nation: Perspectives on the Canadian Military Experience* (St. Catharines, Ontario, 2002), 46–47.

7. In fact, the British went so far as to raise specialized units for the purpose of carrying out raiding operations deep into the enemy's territory. Ironically, today's American Army Rangers owe much of their legacy to one such British unit, Rogers's Rangers. The unit had the official title of His Majesty's Independent Company of American Rangers. The original genesis of this unit was organized and trained by Major Robert Rogers in 1756; they had the mission of carrying the war deep into enemy territory by using the raid as the basic operational tactic. His doctrine was published as *Rogers' Rules for Ranging* (1757), and is considered a classic. A modernized version is still issued to all U.S. Army Rangers, http://www.answers.com/topic/guerrilla-1 (accessed 1 June 2007).

8. Jan Read, *War in the Peninsula* (London: Faber and Faber Limited, 1977), 13–15.

9. John Selby, *The Boer War* (London: Authur Barker Limited, 1969), 216–217. However, it should be noted that the success of these columns relied heavily on intelligence provided by native Africans, who were becoming increasingly disenchanted with the Boers in the region.

10. *Ibid.*, 217.

11. Walter Goerlitz, *History of the German General Staff: 1657–1945* (New York: Frederick A. Praeger, Publishers, 1965), 374–377. Although the Germany military conquest of France took just 46 days, the outcome had been decided in ten.

12. Bernd Horn, "Strength Born From Weakness: The Establishment of the Raiding Concept and the British Commandos," *Canadian Military Journal*, Vol. 6, No. 3, (Autumn 2005): 59–68.

13. Rear-Admiral Maund, *Assault from the Sea* (London: Methuen & Co. Limited, 1949), 61.

14. Christopher, Buckley, *The Second World War, 1939–1945: Norway, The Commandos, Dieppe* (London: His Majesty's Stationery Office, 1951), 162. The idea was based on British experience in South Africa "when small mobile armed

bands had successfully harassed hostile forces of many times their own number, and considering above all the activities of the Boer Commandos in the later phases of the South African War, [General Sir John Dill] began to feel that the same type of result might be achieved by means of amphibious Commandos which, taking advantage of our continued command of the sea, might operate successfully in mobile hit-and-run raids across the Channel."

15. Cecil Aspinall-Oglander, *Roger Keyes: Being the Biography of Admiral of the Fleet Lord Keyes of Zeebrugge and Dover* (London: Hogarth Press, 1951), 380. In fact, the British military establishment was less than keen on the idea of the commandos and Churchill had to become directly involved in moving the idea along.

16. "Notes on Commando Training," 1 November 1942, para 1–18; British Ministry of Information. *Combined Operations; 1940–1942* (London: His Majesty's Stationery Office, 1943), 6–8.

17. *Combined Operations*, 15.

18. Kenneth Clifford, *Amphibious Warfare Development in Britain and America from 1920–1940*, (New York: Edgewood, Inc., 1983), 2.

19. Despite the urgency "The concept of Combined Operations developed slowly. On June 14 1940, Lieutenant-General Alan Bourne was appointed Commander of Raiding Operations and Advisor to the Chiefs of Staff on Combined Operations. Over time a clearer vision of the role of the Commandos was formed and on the 17th of July 1940 Roger Keyes was appointed Director of Combined Operations. This was to be followed by the appointment to the post of Lord Louis Mountbatten in October 1941." See *Combined Operations: The Official Story of the Commandos* (New York: The Macmillan Company, 1943), 16.

20. Philip Ziegler, *Mountbatten* (New York: Alfred A. Knopf, Inc., 1985), 153. Ziegler provides an outstanding synopsis of the British weakness in Combined Operations. He states, "Keyes had a chance to put into practice some of the lessons he had learned so painfully at Gallipoli, and did so with striking success. The science of Combined Operations had been born. It did not thrive between the wars. The first specialist flat-bottomed landing-craft were developed, but with limited enthusiasm; only nine were in existence by 1938. A sub-committee of the Chiefs of Staff was set up in 1937 to consider the various problems but, though its conclusions were sensible enough, little was done to implement them. By the outbreak of war Great Britain was as ill-equipped to put an army ashore in the face of opposition and to maintain it once landed as it had been in 1918. Meanwhile, the rapid development of air power had made the traditional techniques of amphibious warfare still more irrelevant. This deficiency did not seem significant to those in charge of British strategy; at a meeting of the Chiefs of Staff on 15 December 1939 the then Colonel Macleod, one of the original apostles of Combined Operations, argued the case for greatly increased numbers of landing-craft. Churchill, who was present as First Lord of the Admiralty, remarked that he could see no need for such facilities except possibly in support of Finland against Russia." *Ibid.*, 153.

21. Robin Neillands, *The Dieppe Raid: The Story of the Disastrous 1924 Expedition*

(London: Aurum Press Limited, 2005), 54.

22. Ziegler, 166. Ziegler makes a good point in that "There were some who argued that raiding Europe was a futile diversion of effort, but the generally accepted judgment was that, pinpricks though such enterprises might be, they raised public morale, maintained an offensive spirit among the troops, compelled the enemy to deploy large forces in defence of the coastline and occasionally achieved useful results in the destruction or capture of key facilities. Since anyway the principle of raiding was insisted on by Churchill and eagerly supported by Mountbatten, the merits or demerits of the policy were not much debated." Interestingly he goes on to say, "In theory the first was complementary to the second; in practice it sometimes seemed that the demands which the raids entailed on limited resources made the two almost irreconcilable."

23. Rear-Admiral Hughes-Hallett, "The Mounting of Raids," *Royal United Services Institute* (RUSI), Vol. 65, No. 80 (November 1950): 580.

24. Neillands, 54.

25. Buckley, 187. Between 1940 and 1942 the number of raids being conducted by COHQ increased each year. For example, in 1940 only three raids were conducted, however, in 1942, 22 were carried out.

26. Brian Loring Villa, *Unauthorized Action: Mountbatten and the Dieppe Raid* (Toronto: Oxford University Press, 1990), 119–120. A few months later, Mountbatten was promoted to the rank of Acting Vice-Admiral (his title being changed to that of Chief of Combined Operations) and he was also granted the honorary rank of Lieutenant-General in the Army and Air Marshal in the Royal Air Force.

27. John Terraine, *The Right of the Line: The Royal Air Force in the European War 1939–1945* (London: Hodder and Stoughton, 1986), 559.

28. Quoted in John Terraine, *The Life and Times of Lord Mountbatten* (London: Arrow Books, 1980), 83. As part of the invasion preparations, Churchill also wanted Combined Operations to undertake a plethora of other tasks, including the selection of bases from which the invasion could be launched, "creating the Training Centers for the assault troops, and bringing in other Services to create a proper inter-Service organization to produce and refine the techniques of modern assault."

29. Buckley, 186–187. The first of the raids to be carried out under Louis Mountbatten's tenure was Operation Archery. Archery was the assault on the Norwegian port of Vagsøy and involved elements from 2, 3, 4, and 6 Commando, a flotilla from the Royal Navy, and air support. Although relativity small, the raid would have a significant impact on the Germans, who diverted 30,000 additional troops to Norway in an effort to upgrade coastal and inland defenses. More importantly, from the British perspective, it established some important precedents. The operation also showed the validity of a number of independent commando operations being carried out simultaneously within the concept of an overall plan.

30. Headquarters received the missive, " We have made desperate attacks on the

Tirpitz in Trondheim but alas although near the target have not achieved any damage (stop)." R.E.D. Commander Ryder, *The Attack on St. Nazaire: 28th March 1942* (London: John Murray, Albemarle Street, 1947), 4.

31. Maund, 124.

32. Jacques Mordal, *Dieppe: The Dawn of Decision* (London: Souvenir Press, 1962), 58–60.

33. Robert Barr Smith, "Raid on St. Nazaire: Operation Chariot During World War II," http://www.historynet.com/magazines/world_war_2/3031626.html (accessed 29 April 2007).

34. Neillands, 53.

35. Terence Robertson, *The Shame and the Glory* (Toronto: McClelland and Stewart Limited, 1962), 31.

36. Neillands, 53.

37. Maund, 124–125.

38. These numbers are small when compared to the 130,000 men that landed on French beaches during D-Day, 6 June 1944. See http://www.junobeach.org/e/2/can-eve-rod-nor-e.htm (accessed 2 April 2007).

39. Robertson, 46.

40. Neillands, 90. According to Neillands, Hughes-Hallett wrote later "that Dieppe was a small seaport and it would be interesting to capture it for a time and then withdraw. It had no particular military significance but was about the right size for a divisional attack."

41. Robertson, 48.

42. John P. Campbell, *Dieppe Revisited: A Documentary Investigation* (London, Frank Cass & Co. Ltd., 1993), 213. Zieglar, points out that: "It was official doctrine in the middle of 1942 that the invasion could not succeed unless the allies secured two or three major ports." *Ibid.*, 187.

43. Quoted in Robertson, 49. Other reasons for the selection of Dieppe included the fact that it was a resort town with a good harbour and was only 67 miles from Newhaven in Sussex, which was within the range of the fighter aircraft of 1942. Equally important was the fact that it was not going to be the sight for the actual invasion.

44. Campbell, 213.

45. *Ibid.*, 213. When Montgomery was briefed on the outline plan for the flanking attack he apparently "asked the naval planners one question: 'is it intended to stay ashore for forty-eight hours or longer?'" "No," was the answer. As a result, he rejected the flanks' only option because he believed there would be insufficient time to get the tanks and infantry to the port facilities before the Germans could get sufficient strength to block the advance. See Robertson, 51. See also Department of National Defence, *The Raid on DIEPPE, 19 Aug 42 Part I: The Preliminaries of the Operation,* (Canadian Military Headquarters, London, 16 July 1943), 13. Accessed through the DHH Canadian Military Headquarters (CMHQ) Reports 1940–1948 (electronic version), http://www.forces.gc.ca/hr/dhh/history_

archives/engraph/cmhq_e.asp?cat=1 (accessed 3 May 2007).

46.   Stacey, 56.

47.   Ziegler, 188.

48.   Department of National Defence, *The Raid on DIEPPE, 19 Aug 42 Part I: The Preliminaries of the Operation,* (Canadian Military Headquarters, London, 16 July 1943), 13–14. Accessed through the DHH Canadian Military Headquarters (CMHQ) Reports 1940–1948 (electronic version), http://www.forces.gc.ca/hr/ dhh/history_archives/engraph/cmhq_e.asp?cat=1 (accessed 3 May 2007). In fact, this was the option proposed by Montgomery. See note 45.

49.   Interestingly, the command structure of the assault force was somewhat disjointed with no one person in command. This too would become a major point of controversy in the future and result in changes shortly after the operation. Captain (Navy) Hughes-Hallett was co-located with Major-General Roberts on the destroyer *Calpe.* Air Vice-Marshal Leigh-Mallory, the Air Force component commander, stayed at Headquarters 11 Fighter Group, at Uxbridge, Middlesex.

50.   Neillands, 90–91. In fact, an appreciation of the situation was completed by the Canadians for the operation. The GSO 1, 2 Canadian Division made an appreciation of the Outline Plan for the military force commander. Lieutenant-Colonel Mann's "Observations upon the Outline Plan" looked at the question of tanks for the operation. See *The Raid on DIEPPE,* 27.

51.   R.W. Thompson, *Dieppe at Dawn: The Story of the Dieppe Raid* (London: Hutchinson & Co. Ltd., 1956), 17.

52.   Buckley, 231.

53.   Stacey, 67.

54.   Eric Maguire, *Dieppe: August 19* (London: Billing & Sons Limited, 1963), 97–98.

55.   Buckley, 231. At Berneval, to the east, was a coastal battery that included three 17-cm and four 105-mm guns, while another over to the west, near Varengeville, had six 15-cm guns, and a third, consisting of four 15-cm Howitzers, was deployed near Arques-la-Bataille. Interestingly, the artillery battalion of the 302nd Division, which had 16 10-cm field howitzers was deployed in four battery positions: two east and two west of Dieppe.

56.   *The Raid on Dieppe,* 15.

57.   Thompson, 156–160. In fact, the Air Force wanted to use Dieppe as a way to bait the German air force to draw them out for a fight. The overhead cover for the operation comprised five squadrons of fighters, one squadron of fighter/bomber aircraft, and bombers.

58.   Stacey, 64–65.

59.   *Combined Operations; 1940–1942,* 110.

60.   Buckley, 237. The concern, and to some extent, debate, was that as soon as the Canadians stepped ashore at Puys and Pourville, German forces throughout Dieppe would be on the alert and would have a half-hour to prepare before the frontal assault came in at Dieppe in full daylight.

61.   *The Raid on Dieppe,* 16.

62. Villa, 11.
63. "On 18 May 42 HQ 2 Cdn Div arrived in the ISLE OF WIGHT. On the same day 4 Cdn Inf Bde arrived on the island, and the following day 6 Cdn Inf Bde. 14 Cdn Army Bn (Calgary Regiment) arrived on 20 May, as did the RCE detachments designated to participate." See *The Raid on Dieppe*, 33.
64. Jack Poolton, *Destined to Survive* (Toronto: Dundurn Press, 1998), 31; Stacey, 59. In fact, the program produced by 2nd Division set out the training priorities. In addition to physical fitness other skills were given to the soldiers. These included fighting in villages, assaulting pillboxes and other strong points, map reading by day and night, techniques in cliff-scaling, grenade-throwing, the use of Bangalore torpedoes and other demolitions, mortar firing, bayonet-fighting, and the firing of Bren guns. See Robertson, 78.
65. Denis and Shelagh Whitaker, *Dieppe: Tragedy to Triumph*, (Whitby, Ont.: McGraw-Hill Ryerson Limited, 1992), 130.
66. *Ibid.*, 131. The Landing Craft Armour (LCA)s were lightly armoured and were able to provide some protection from small-arms fire; however, the wooden "R" boats were viewed as flimsy craft and offered no protection whatsoever.
67. Robertson, 78. However, that was not the end of the live-fire training for when the landing craft hit the beaches, mortars and sniper bullets kicked up sand about their feet.
68. *Ibid.*, 133. According to Whitaker "Here, much reliance had to be placed on intelligence summaries detailing the Dieppe topography and defences, and defining any problems that might be encountered. These reports were disseminated regularly from Combined Headquarters to Second Division Intelligence who, in turn, with the objectives disguised, passed them on to the units."
69. Robertson, 78.
70. More importantly, the tank that would be used was the Churchill, which was brand new and suffered from a number of teething problems.
71. Whitaker, 126. According to Whitaker, a typical day of training looked like this: 0600 hours — Embarking, craft afloat; 0630 hours to 0830 hours – Cruise; 0830 hours to 0900 hours — Disembarking exercise. Craft afloat and withdraw when unloaded; 1000 hours to 1300 hours — Gunnery and S.A.T. (Small Arms Training); 1430 hours to 1800 hours — Troop Training exercise. Whitaker states that during the "[e]venings, the men would often go through the whole thing again in night conditions, usually in closed tanks. Or they would perform the inevitable maintenance duties."
72. Poolton, 30.
73. Mordal, 118–119.
74. See *The Raid on Dieppe*, 37. According to the report, "While planning and execution were on the whole considered to have been satisfactory, certain serious faults appeared during the exercise. The worst of these were that 'the two flanking bns [battalions] were landed at the wrong beaches' and 'the TLCs [Troop Landing Craft] were lost and arrived 1 1/2 hrs late' (undated memorandum (14 Jun) by

Lieutenant-Colonel Henderson, file 8-3-4/Ops, War Diary, 'G,' HQ First Cdn Army, September 1942, Appx 22), LAC. In the case of the Royal Regiment of Canada, 'the assault craft landed some two miles to the west of their proposed landing beach,' and the South Saskatchewan Regiment was put ashore three-quarters of a mile from the proper place (War Diaries of these units, 12 Jun 42)" quoted from paragraph 37.

75.   Whitaker, 135. On his return from the United States, Mountbatten was briefed on the exercise and demanded that the entire exercise be redone.

76.   Quoted in Robertson, 107.

77.   *Ibid.*, 107.

78.   Neillands, 106. According to Jack Poolton, "On July 2, after completing several landing rehearsals on the coast of Devon, the regiment embarked on HMS *Princess Josephine Charlotte* and HMS *Princess Astrid*. When the regiment was aboard, Lieutenant-Colonel Basher announced that this was not an exercise, but an actual operation against the enemy. The troops let out a great cheer."

79.   James Leasor, *Green Beach* (London: William Heinemann, limited, 1975), 63. See also Neillands, 106. At about 0615 hours on the morning of 7 July, four enemy aircraft delivered an attack against landing ships of the force lying in Yarmouth Roads near the west end of the Solent. Four 500-kilo bombs were dropped and the attack achieved considerable success. Both HMS *Princess Astrid* and HMS *Princess Josephine Charlotte* were hit and badly damaged. The troops on board both ships were mainly from the Royal Regiment of Canada. "Fortunately, in both cases, the bombs passed completely through the ships before exploding, and only four minor casualties were suffered in the Battalion" (Royal Regiment of Canada War Diary). See *The Raid on Dieppe*, 51.

80.   Neillands points out that "the finger therefore points inexorably at Mountbatten, who, at a COS meeting in December 1942, stated that he had taken the responsibility to relaunch the raid — and this December response is indeed minuted. However … it is necessary to state, yet again, that there is no documentation, even in the Cabinet papers, to support the claim that the relaunch of the raid had COS approval." Neillands, 117.

81.   Stacey, 61.

82.   Villa, 233–235.

83.   Colonel Matthew L. Murphy, Commander John P. Coray, Lieutenant-Colonel Scott C. Van Blarcum, and Lieutenant-Colonel Jon K. Gray, USAF. Joint Forces Staff College, *Beaches, Bunkers, Barbed Wire, And Blood: The Disastrous Raid On Dieppe*. (Joint and Combined Warfighting School, Senior Class 04-1S, 1 March 2004), 5.

84.   Stacey, 61.

85.   Poolton, 30.

86.   Stacey, 64–65.

87.   Robertson, 93.

88.   *Ibid.*, 93.

89.   Villa, 12.

90.   Maguire, 55.

91.   It should be noted that the operation's chain of command was also different. For Operation RUTTER the responsible military authority had been the General Officer Commanding (GOC) South-Eastern Command. The GOC First Canadian Army held only an undefined "watching" role. For JUBILEE, however, the Commander-in-Chief Home Forces, on General McNaughton's recommendation, made the Canadian Army Commander the responsible military authority. General McNaughton delegated this responsibility to Major-General Crerar.

92.   Murphy et. al, 5–9.

93.   *Combined Operations; 1940–1942*, 112.

94.   Department of National Defence. *Report No. 83 A-6 Report No. 83* (Historical Officer Canadian Military Headquarters, 19 Sep 1942). Accessed through the DHH CMHQ Reports 1940–1948 (electronic version), http://www.forces.gc.ca/hr/dhh/history_archives/engraph/cmhq_e.asp?cat=1 (accessed 3 May 2007).

95.   Department of National Defence, "Operation JUBILEE: The Raid on Dieppe, 19 Aug 42 Part I: The Preliminaries of the Operation," Canadian Military Headquarters, Report 101, 31 Dec 1942, 17. Accessed through the DHH CMHQ Reports 1940–1948 (electronic version), http://www.forces.gc.ca/hr/dhh/history_archives/engraph/cmhq_e.asp?cat=1 (accessed 1 May 2007).

96.   Peter Young, *Storm from the Sea* (London: Wrens Park, 1958), 71.

97.   Will Fowler, *The Commandos at Dieppe: Rehearsal for D-Day* (London: HarperCollins, 2002), 17. See also Stacey, 71. The German casualties numbered approximately 30 killed and 30 wounded, with 4 prisoners taken. No. 4 Commando suffered 45 casualties, including two officers and 10 other ranks killed, its success, however, was complete. As Stacey so eloquently states, "No. 4 Commando was the only unit engaged in this operation to capture all its objectives. Its proceedings are a model of boldness and effective synchronization." See also *Combined Operations; 1940–1942*, 116.

98.   *Report No. 83 A-6.*

99.   Department of National Defence, "Report No. 89 The Operation at DIEPPE, 19 Aug 42: Personal Stories of Participants," Appendix A, by Capt G.A. Browne, RCA FOO attached to Royal Regiment of Canada, A1, Canadian Military Headquarters, 31 Dec 1942. Accessed through the DHH CMHQ Reports 1940-1948 (electronic version), http://www.forces.gc.ca/hr/dhh/history_archives/engraph/cmhq_e.asp?cat=1 (accessed 1 May 2007).

100. *Ibid*. It should be noted that Browne was impressed with the outstanding efforts of the soldiers. During his after-action interview in London he stated, "It may be permitted to mention the conduct of the troops in general on the beach. "In spite of the steady approach to the beach under fire, the ROYALS [Royal Regiment of Canada] in my ALC [Armoured Landing Craft] appeared cool and steady. It was their first experience under fire, and although I watched them closely, they gave no sign of alarm."

101. Leasor, 131.

102. Department of National Defence, "Memorandum of Interview with B-66984, Corporal. L.G. Ellis, D.C.M., Royal Regiment of Canada, Subject: The Operation at DIEPPE, 19 Aug 42," Canadian Military Headquarters, London, 20 Oct 1942, Annex D. Accessed through the DHH CMHQ Reports 1940–1948 (electronic version), http://www.forces.gc.ca/hr/dhh/history_archives/engraph/cmhq_e. asp?cat=1 (accessed 1 May 2007).

103. *Ibid.*

104. *Ibid.*

105. *Ibid.*

106. *Ibid.*

107. Ellis now went downhill towards the beach, and in doing so came across a soldier lying paralyzed. He half dragged, half carried this man downhill as far as the wire obstacle, and, finding another gap in the concertina wire, began to work him through it. He came to what appeared to be another signal wire, and having lost his wire cutters, and believing it to be a continuation of the wires he had previously cut, pulled it. It was, however, connected with a buried booby trap which exploded, killing the paralyzed man and wounding Corporal Ellis slightly in the face, the right hand, and the left foot. He also suffered a punctured eardrum from either this explosion or that of the Bangalore torpedo.

108. *Memorandum of Interview with B-66984, Corporal. L.G. Ellis.* As the report points out, "It is a rather remarkable fact that although Corporal Ellis was probably over an hour on shore (he landed about 0515 or 0520 hours, and his watch stopped when he entered the water at 0630 hours) he did not see a single German, except for the face, if it was a face, in the bush at which he fired, and one man whom he saw on the skyline some 2,000 yards away who may have been an enemy soldier. None of the enemy positions which he inspected were occupied at the time. Near the house he looked into a weapon pit which might possibly have covered the mouth of a tunnel, but he did not investigate further. All this time the enemy was maintaining a most destructive fire on the beach."

109. Neillands, 184–185.

110. Stacey, 73.

111. Department of National Defence. Memorandum of Interview with L-13282 Private W.A. Haggard, DCM South Saskatchewan Regiment, Subject: The Operation at DIEPPE — 19 Aug 1942, (Canadian Military Headquarters, London, 12 Nov 1942), Annex E. Accessed through the DHH CMHQ Reports 1940-1948 (electronic version), http://www.forces.gc.ca/hr/dhh/history_archives/engraph/ cmhq_e.asp?cat=1 (accessed 12 April 2007).

112. *Ibid.*

113. Canada, "Dieppe: Victory Cross Winners : Matchless Gallantry and Inspiring Leadership," *Maple Leaf,* Vol. 5, No. 29 (24 July 2002): 9.

114. Whitaker, 248.

115. Stacey, 74.

116. Department of National Defence, "Memorandum of Interview with Major A.T.

Law, DSO, Camerons, Subject: The Operation at DIEPPE — 19 Aug 42," (Canadian Military Headquarters, London, 3 Dec 1942), Annex G. Accessed through the DHH CMHQ Reports 1940–1948 (electronic version), http://www.forces.gc.ca/hr/dhh/history_archives/engraph/cmhq_e.asp?cat=1 (accessed 9 April 2007).

117. *Ibid.*

118. *Ibid.*

119. Stacey, 74. "Shortly afterwards he received word that a message from Brigade to the South Saskatchewan Regiment had been intercepted. This message said, 'Vanquish from Green Beach at 1000 hours, get in touch with the Camerons.'"

120. Department of National Defence. "Memorandum of Interview with Major A.T. Law, DSO." One of the unit's snipers, Private Huppe, was awarded the Military Medal for taking out about a dozen of the enemy, while another, Private Hebert was mentioned in dispatches for carry out a similar feat.

121. *Ibid.* The Camerons were able to complete their re-embarkation by about 1200 hours; unfortunately, they had suffered more casualities during this phase than at any other time.

122. Canada, "Dieppe: Victory Cross Winners: Matchless Gallantry and Inspiring Leadership," *Maple Leaf,* Vol. 5 , No. 29 (24 July 2002).

123. *Ibid.*

124. Neillands, 205. Incredibly, in the plan, only one company had been allocated to this important task.

125. Stacey, 76.

126. Neillands, 218.

127. Department of National Defence. "Report No. 89 The Operation at DIEPPE, 19 Aug 42: Personal Stories of Participants. Memorandum of Interview with A-19407 L/Sergeant. G.A. Hickson, DCM, 7 Fd Coy, Rce," (Canadian Military Headquarters, 13 Oct 1942), Annex f F1-F12. Accessed through the DHH CMHQ Reports 1940–1948 (electronic version), http://www.forces.gc.ca/hr/dhh/history_archives/engraph/cmhq_e.asp?cat=1 (accessed 1 May 2007).

128. *Ibid.*

129. *The London Gazette*, 14 February 1946. Taken from the Royal Hamilton Light Infantry Heritage Museum page, http://www.rhli.ca/veterans/foote_story.html (accessed 1 June 2007).

130. Stacey, 76.

131. Mordal, 207.

132. Murphy et. al, 9–12

133. Department of National Defence, "Memorandum of Interview with D-62050, Sergeant P. Dubuc, M.M., FUS. M.R., Subject: The Operation at DIEPPE — 19 Aug 42," (Canadian Military Headquarters, London, 7 November 1942), Annex B.

134. *Ibid.*

135. *Ibid.*

136. *Ibid.* In the course of this operation, Sergeant Dubuc was struck in the back by a

piece of shrapnel. He did not know this until three weeks later, when symptoms appeared and he was sent to hospital.

137. Buckley, 252.

138. Stacey, 79.

139. Murphy et. al, 9–12.

140. James, Robert Rhodes, *Winston S. Churchill: His Complete Speeches 1897–1963, Vol. VI 1935–1942* (London: Chelsea House Publishers, 1974), 6667.

141. Department of National Defence, "Report No.98: Article Dealing with the Operation at DIEPPE, 19 Aug 42," (Canadian Military Headquarters, London, 15 Jul 1943), Appendix A, A-21.

142. Whitaker, 302.

CHAPTER 9

Jump into Chaos:
Canadian Paratroopers on D-Day,
5–7 June 1944

BERND HORN AND MICHAEL WYCZYNSKI

Under the cover of darkness, in the late hours of 5 June 1944, 36 C-47 Dakota aircraft transporting the main group of the 1st Canadian Parachute Battalion (1 Cdn Para Bn) and part of the headquarters staff of the 3rd Parachute Brigade (3 Para Bde) took off from Down Ampney Airport in England.[1] The aircraft closed up in tight formation and headed towards the French coast. The steady drone of this armada filled the fuselages and drowned out all other noise. The heavily laden Canadian paratroopers, crammed in the restrictive dark confines of their airplanes, shifted uneasily as the planes bucked and lurched in the wake of the preceding aircraft. The atmosphere was subdued. Some paratroopers slept or prayed, while others nervously went over their assignments. Corporal Harry Reid gazed out a window and observed the ghostly silhouettes of the other Dakotas. "Then it hit home," exclaimed Reid. "We were finally on our way!"[2] To many this flight seemed to take forever. However, in the distant horizon, the French coast was already within sight.

"Stand up!" bellowed the jumpmaster. Despite this much-anticipated order, the paratroopers awkwardly struggled with their heavy loads and leg kit bags to assume their jumping positions within each stick. Each man strained to hook up his static line to the overhead cable. The Dakotas now jerked and rocked violently as the pilots tried to avoid the deadly flak barrage that filled the sky as they crossed the coastline. Due to the heavy fire, many pilots veered off their assigned flight trajectories and dropped to altitudes ranging between four and seven hundred feet in an effort to escape the lethal hailstorm.

As the pilots desperately tried to get back on course, the navigators scrutinized the rapidly unfolding French terrain, hoping to recognize landmarks that confirmed the direction of their final approach to Drop Zone (DZ) "V." Meanwhile, the paratroopers were thrown violently within the aircraft. Static lines became tangled and equipment began to snag on the plane's interior. Individuals cursed as they scrambled to stand up long enough to execute their pre-exiting drills as the jumpmasters barked out orders.

"The pilots took such evasive action because of the flak," recalled one veteran, "that it resulted in some paratroopers not being able to get out of their aircraft."[3] Nineteen-year-old paratroop Private Bill Lovatt explained, "As we approached the DZ the aircraft took violent evasive moves and as I approached the door I was flung back violently to the opposite side of the aircraft in a tangle of arms and legs."[4] Major Dick Hilborn stated: "As we crossed the coast of France the red light went on for preparing to drop. We were in the process of hooking up when the plane took violent evasive action … five of us ended up at the back of the plane."[5] One airborne officer conceded that on D-Day "we lost a number of people over the sea from evasive action who fell out."[6] Sergeant John Feduck was slightly more fortunate. "Before the light changed the plane suddenly lurched," he remembered, "I couldn't hang on because there was nothing to hang on to so out I went — there was no getting back in."[7] Luckily, he was already over France.

Throughout the ordeal, the jumpmasters urgently tried to restore order despite the hot jagged shrapnel that ripped through the thin skin of the Dakota aircraft. Many of the occupants were surprised at "how much the aircraft bounced because of the flak."[8] This extraordinary night jump would forever be etched into the very souls of the young paratroopers. "When I left the aircraft it was pitching," stated Company Sergeant-Major (CSM) John Kemp. "I was standing in the door. There were 20 of us in the aircraft. I had 19 men behind me pushing. They wanted to get the hell out. The flak was hitting the wings." Private Anthony Skalicky's plane was one of those that were actually hit. One of the engines burst into flames, spewing thick black smoke. The plane was losing altitude and even though they were nowhere near the drop zone, "the entire stick just ran out the door," recalled the frightened paratrooper. He conceded that, "I couldn't get out of the plane fast enough."[9]

For the others, the red light came on — the drop zone was now only minutes away. Fear was now forgotten as the paratroopers desperately strained to steel themselves for the coming jump that would allow them to escape this airborne hell. Mercifully, the green light flashed on. "Go!" hollered the jumpmaster as he literally pushed the first jumper out the door. He was followed by the remainder of the stick who were not already wounded. The paratroopers' heavy loads hampered the exiting cadence, causing the stick to be dropped over a much longer distance. "With 60 pounds of equipment strapped to our legs we couldn't run out the door," reminisced Private William Talbot, a member of the anti-tank platoon. "We shuffled to the door and just dropped out."[10]

Some pilots did not reduce their speed, which further complicated the already stressful night jump. "The plane was going much too fast," recollected Captain John Simpson of the Battalion's signal platoon. "When I went out the prop blast tore all my equipment off. The guy must have been going at a hell of a speed. All I had was my clothes and my .45 revolver with some ammo."[11]

The majority of the paratroopers exited on the initial run. Others were not so lucky and had to relive this hellish experience and endure a second pass over the DZ. "I was number 19 in the stick of 20 in my plane," explained Corporal Ernie Jeans, a medic from Headquarters Company. "As I made my way to the door, I heard the engine rev up and the jumpmaster pushed me back." He added, dejected, "I thought to myself that we had come all this way to go back to England." However, the aircraft race-tracked and headed back to the DZ to drop the two remaining paratroopers. A few days later, Jeans learned that the remainder of his stick had been dropped off course on the initial run and were all either captured or killed.[12]

As Private Jan de Vries exited the aircraft he was met by an abrupt rush of wind, which physically yanked him out into the slipstream of the aircraft. Suddenly, the noise and the pandemonium of just a few moments ago disappeared. An eerie silence now surrounded the paratroopers who drifted to earth seemingly alone. "Going down I was surprised at the quietness and the darkness," recollected Corporal Boyd Anderson. "I had expected to hear sounds of shooting or at least some activity."[13] Engulfed in the inky darkness, the paratroopers were given a moment of respite. However, that relief abruptly ended. The solitude and peacefulness of the parachute descent were replaced by the reality of airborne warfare.

The lucky ones hit solid ground, albeit rather heavily. "When I landed flat on my back," reminisced one veteran, "I was in such agony that I cared very little whether I lived or died." But, "then the training took over," he explained, "I immediately pulled out my rifle and at the same time hit the release on my parachute. I placed my pack on my back and with the rifle in my arms I started to crawl toward a clump of trees which I could see very dimly. At this time I heard nothing, not an aircraft, not a bomb, not a shot."[14] Like many that night, he was lost and alone.

While many endured tumultuous exits, others experienced difficult landings. Several paratroopers crashed into trees or slammed onto buildings, resulting in serious injuries and deaths.[15] Among the first casualties was the Battalion's medical officer, Captain Colin Brebner, who had landed in a tree. Due to the darkness, Brebner misjudged his height. The anxious officer proceeded to cut his suspension lines and fell 40 feet down to the ground. His evasive action resulted in a broken left wrist and pelvis.[16] In certain cases the exits from the aircraft were too quick. Corporal Tom O'Connell's chute got tangled up with that of another jumper. "As we plunged towards the earth I heard the other fellow yell from below, 'Take it easy old man!'" Both men crashed to the earth. Around noon, a severely injured O'Connell had finally regained consciousness. Beside him was the body of Padre Captain George Harris. A distraught O'Connell explained that the "two chutes were twisted together like a thick rope."[17]

O'Connell was not alone. Many paratroopers had sustained various injuries upon their landings, however, these landings paled in comparison to those who descended into the dreaded flooded and marshy areas. "Looking out of the plane it looked like pasture below us, but when I jumped I landed in water," recalled Private Doug Morrison. "The Germans," he explained, "had flooded the area a while back and there was a green algae on the water so it actually looked like pasture at night from the air."[18] Many Canadian paratroopers drowned because they were so heavily laden with equipment and ammunition.[19] Sergeant W.R. Kelly was one of the lucky paratroopers who cheated this watery grave. One man found Sergeant Kelly hanging upside down from a huge tree with his head in the water. Kelly's parachute suspension lines were knotted around his legs and feet. The canopy had caught on a limb and suspended Kelly so he was submerged from the top of his head to his neck. The eighty pounds of equipment that he carried was now bundled up around his chest. To stop from drowning, Kelly was required to keep lifting his

Pencil sketch by Ted Zuber.

Many of the Canadian paratroopers found themselves immersed in the flooded fields of Normandy, an attempt by the Germans to restrict the Allied ability to use its airborne capability.

face above the water for mouthfuls of air. He was nearly exhausted when a fellow Canadian found him, cut him loose, and assisted him to dry land.[20] Others, however, were not so fortunate. Many drowned in the fields that the Germans flooded to deter the airborne landings.

But the real problems for the Canadian paratroopers had just begun. The parachute drop had been a disaster. The drops were widely dispersed and scattered. The evasive action of the pilots had created some of the problems. However, the lingering smoke and dust created by heavy *ongoing* bombing made navigation difficult. This situation was exacerbated by the failure of the "Eureka" homing beacons to function properly. As a result, during the next few hours following the airborne insertion, those who had been dropped off course experienced difficulties in identifying their location. Additionally, the dark night and the fields partitioned by high hedgerows, further impeded the paratroopers' abilities to confirm their positions.

"Airplanes dropped us all over hell's half acre," chided Lance-Corporal H.R. Holloway.[21] "On landing," commented Private De Vries, "I wondered where I was and where the others were. I got out of my chute and quietly moved to the hedgerow at the edge of the field. I was lost. I could not recognize anything."[22] Corporal Dan Hartigan acknowledged that "the scattering had an operating influence on the whole battle. We lost more than 50 percent of our officers on D-Day, 15 of 27." He added, "The fighting in the weeks that followed turned from an officer's war to a Senior NCO's war."[23]

Some paratroopers were lucky and would eventually rejoin their units. Others did not. "I tried to find out where I was, but could not," recalled Sergeant Feduck. "I wandered for an hour or so with no success. I laid down in a bomb crater and tried to get my bearings. Finally, I spotted two English Chaps, we moved out to find our respective units."[24] Nevertheless, the paratroopers had been briefed on how to orient themselves after their landings. "If you are in doubt of the location of the RV," stated Lance Corporal D.S. Parlee, "we were instructed to face the line of incoming aircraft and then move off to the left of their flight path. That was all well and good until I discovered that every aircraft I could see was going in a different direction."[25]

Sergeant Denis Flynn felt that the dispersal "changed the whole attitude — once on the ground we all wondered, 'where are we?' Because of the dispersal of the drop I was separated from my group. Things were a little strange. I wondered, 'Where am I? How do I meet up with the others?'" He confessed that "there were a lot of anxious moments."[26] As dawn pierced through the heavy smoke and clouds, the increasing natural light helped numerous paratroopers find their way to the objectives. However, the early morning sunlight proved more of a hindrance to the airborne soldiers who found themselves in the midst of German positions and troops.

The net result of the aerial difficulties now manifested themselves on the ground. Many of the paratroopers who were not drowned or killed on landing were haplessly lost and 82 became prisoners of war.[27] Some, like Private Anthony Skalicky, were captured shortly after their landing. "Another paratrooper and I decided to move out," recollected the unlucky paratrooper. "We walked on a road and were suddenly surrounded by German bicycle troops. We were searched, tied up and marched off."[28] Others were more fortunate and successfully eluded many enemy patrols. "I came face to face with a German patrol," reminisced Private Morris Zakaluk of the heavy machine gun section. "I counted six men in single file about three paces apart. They are in full battle gear, rifles, submachine guns, grenades, one man packing a radio … As I was taking a bead on the lead man, but holding my fire, they turned to the left [and] proceeded along this hedge until they found an opening and disappeared." The bedevilled paratrooper lay silently and held his fire. "A minute or so later three other men showed up," continued Zakaluk. "These men had MG 42s at ready hip position and had I opened fire on the first six-man group I surely would have been a dead duck."[29] In the end, a mere one-third of the Canadian paratroop force was actually able to assemble at their designated rendezvous points and carry on with their missions.

Although this wide dispersal greatly complicated the initial missions allocated to the paratroopers, it also confused the German forces. Unable to confirm the exact area of the drop zones, German commanders delayed, for many hours, the deployment of their reserve units. Landing in the town of Varaville, the deputy commanding officer, Major Jeff Nicklin, witnessed this confusion firsthand. "The Germans were really windy in Varaville," he observed. "They ran around that town like crazy men and shot at anything that moved. Even a moving cow would get a blast of machine-gun fire. They were so jumpy [that] they ran around in twos and threes to give themselves moral support."[30]

However, the dispersal of Battalion headquarters personnel severely limited Lieutenant-Colonel G.F.P. Bradbrooke's command and control capabilities, as well as his communications with brigade and divisional headquarters during the first 24 hours.[31] "I personally was dropped a couple of miles away from the drop zone," related Bradbrooke, the 1 Cdn Para Bn commanding officer (CO), "in a marsh near the River Dives and arrived at the rendezvous about one and a half hours late and completely soaked."[32] "The problems of getting organized," he explained, "into effective fighting units are immense, there is considerable confusion in getting order out of chaos."[33] However, on the bright side, he added, "We [Bradbrooke's stick] were not troubled by the enemy at this time [during and immediately after the drop], I suppose he [the enemy] was just as confused as we were."[34] In the end, concluded the CO, "The hardest part of the job wasn't the fighting, although that was hard enough at times, but getting ourselves organized after we hit the DZ."[35]

As if the dispersion had not created enough problems, most of the paratroopers' heavy equipment was lost due to exits made from aircraft that were travelling too fast, resulting in equipment being ripped away by the heavy wash of the plane or by the hard opening shock of the parachute canopy. In addition, much of the equipment was also lost when the leg kit bags were released by the paratroopers. The shock caused by the sudden full extension of the 20-foot rope was such that the bottom of these canvas bags ripped open. Paratroopers watched helplessly as their heavy weapons, equipment, and much-needed extra ammunition and explosives fell, scattered, and disappeared into the darkness below. A frustrated Major Richard Hilborn, who commanded the heavy machine-gun platoon, reported that he had only two Vickers machine guns, one tripod, and a limited quantity of ammunition.[36] Corporal Ernie Jeans, one of the few surviving medics, was also very concerned. The battle had not even started and, "I hardly had any medical equipment or supplies."[37] In sum, more than 70 percent of the Battalion's heavy equipment, support weaponry, and supplies were lost before a single shot had been fired.

Despite the chaos, the well-trained paratroopers now began to assemble to carry on with their mission. Those who had landed away from the drop zone adapted to whatever unplanned situation unfolded. "I began to meet up with others and we made our way toward our objective," asserted Sergeant Denis Flynn, "Everyone knew what was required and we did whatever could be done under the circumstances." After all, Brigadier James Hill, their well-respected and beloved brigade commander, had warned them, "One must not be daunted if chaos reigned [because] it undoubtedly will!"[38] The brigadier's words provided some degree of reassurance to the paratroopers. "I think most of us anticipated that we could go into battle by dropping right onto our objective — right into battle," confessed Private de Vries. "Nonetheless, Brigadier Hill warned us that chaos would reign."[39]

As such, the paratroopers now, as individuals and small groups, began to fulfill their tasks. "C" Company was part of the 3 Para Bde's advance party and landed before the main group. They exited their Albemarle aircraft between 0020 hours and 0029 hours, 6 June 1944, and were some of the first Allied soldiers to invade occupied Europe. While most of the men of the first aircraft landed on or near DZ "V," northwest of Varaville, those in the following aircraft were dropped between eight and 10 kilometres from the intended point.[40]

Shortly after landing on their designated drop zone, the Canadians, as well as the members of the 3 Para Bde pathfinder teams, experienced serious difficulties.[41] Many of their "Eureka" beacons required to guide the main body to the DZ had been either damaged or lost.[42] This would have dramatic consequences. The paratroopers of "C" Company also experienced their fair share of problems. Less than 50 had reached the rendevous (RV) assembly point.[43] Regardless, an impatient company commander, Major H.M. McLeod, refused to wait. With the impending arrival of the main body of 3 Para Bde, including the remainder of 1 Cdn Para Bn, it was imperative that "C" Company accomplish its initial task — securing the DZ.[44]

Once the area was secured, McLeod split up his skeletal force and dispatched one group to seize and hold the Varaville bridge. These paratroopers were instructed to defend the structure at all costs until the arrival of the airborne engineers who were tasked to destroy it. Then, McLeod and the remaining men would proceed to their next objective — the capture of a series of defensive positions located on the grounds of Le Grand Château in Varaville. McLeod knew that speed under the cover of darkness, combined with bold, aggressive action and surprise would offset the temporary lack of manpower. Upon arrival they located, captured, and disabled a German communication centre. McLeod then organized his men into small groups to seize the remaining positions that consisted of a bunker, a series of trenches, and an anti-tank gun position. However, as the paratroopers deployed and inched their way towards these positions, the defenders opened up with a withering fire.

Throughout the next few hours the ongoing battle at the Varaville Château and surrounding area attracted small groups of paratroopers who had been dropped off course. All moved to the sound of battle. Private Cliff Funston was among a group of paratroopers who had finally made their way to Varaville before dawn. "It was rather confusing to tell you the truth," related Funston. "There was a lot of uncertainty as well as a lack of heavy weapons and men."[45] Nevertheless, these welcomed reinforcements were immediately fed into the battle. One British airborne captain, who landed in the outskirts of Varaville, described the intense fighting. "Complete chaos seemed to reign in the village," he reported. "Against a background of Brens, Spandaus and grenades could be heard shouts in British and Canadian, German and Russian."[46]

Initially, the German defenders pinned down the paratroopers with heavy machine-gun and anti-tank fire. However, once the enemy's range and positions were confirmed, the paratroopers replied with well-directed anti-tank, mortar, and Bren gunfire of their own. Around 0300 hours, a German anti-tank shell crashed through the Château's Gatehouse where Major MacLeod and six other paratroopers had set up their anti-tank gun. Upon impact, the projectile ignited the paratroopers' anti-tank shells and grenades. A terrible explosion ripped through the group and resulted in the death of four paratroopers. Of the original six-man group, only Privates H.B. Swim and G.A. Thompson survived, but even they sustained serious injuries.[47]

Despite this terrible blow, the battle raged on. As additional paratroopers joined the fray they successfully cordoned off the German defenders. Nevertheless, the enemy was not prepared to surrender. Private Esko Makela, who had been separated from "B" Company, showed up in Varaville as the darkness began to fade. He was ordered to take up a position in the gatehouse and engage the anti-tank gun position with his Bren gun. The intensity of the increased firepower forced the German gun crew to pull back. As the sun rose over the horizon, the Canadians could now observe the layout of the enemy's positions and troop movements. "I was then given a rifle," explained Private Makela, "and I sniped at quite a few heads."[48]

By 1030 hours that morning, the German garrison of Varaville surrendered. A total of 80 prisoners and walking wounded were corralled. As the prisoners were marched off, the airborne soldiers were surprised by the number of defenders captured. "Two enemy soldiers," tallied Corporal Dan Hartigan, "for every Canadian paratrooper who fought in Varaville."[49] Corporal John Ross, a signalman attached to "C" Company, recalled, "The Germans were mad when they saw that they had been captured by a small group of lightly armed paratroopers."[50]

"C" Company was then ordered to pull out, regroup and take up a series of defensive positions to guard the roads going through Varaville.[51] By 1500 hours, the first elements of the British 6th Commando Cycle Troop arrived and relieved the company.[52] The Canadian paratroopers now commenced the final phase of their D-Day mission. They marched to the Le Mesnil crossroads and took up new defensive positions within the Battalion perimeter.

But "C" Company was not the only sub-unit to be afflicted by a scattered drop. By 0600 hours only two officers and 20 paratroopers from

"A" Company, as well as a handful of airborne soldiers from other units, had reached their RV. Severely undermanned and behind schedule, Lieutenant J.A. Clancy assembled his small group and headed to the Merville Battery to join the 9th Parachute Battalion (9 Para Bn). The drop had also severely hampered 9 Para Bn, who had been give the critical task of destroying the battery. Of the 650 paratroopers earmarked for the assault, only 150 had managed to reach the RV.[53] Nevertheless, anxious to get on with this important task, Lieutenant-Colonel T.H. Otway, the commanding officer, organized his men into two assault teams. They quickly cleared two paths across the minefield surrounding the battery. As they painstakingly inched their way towards their final objective, the German defenders positioned in adjoining casemates opened fire with three heavy machine guns. It quickly turned into a bloodbath.[54] Seventy British paratroopers were killed in the short, savage battle. Heavy losses notwithstanding, Otway and his men succeeded in capturing the battery by approximately 0500 hours.[55] Yellow signal flares were sent up shortly after to confirm that the battery had been captured and, more importantly, to cancel a naval bombardment from HMS *Arethusa* that was planned for that morning.[56]

Upon entering the main structure, the British paratroopers were surprised by the type and calibre of the guns positioned at Merville Battery. Due to the size of battery's outer structure Allied planners assumed that it could possibly contain four 150 mm guns capable of firing 96-pound shells every 15 to 20 seconds, with a maximum eight-mile range.[57] They concluded that if this battery opened fire it could cause great mayhem on the beaches. Therefore, it was crucial that it be neutralized at all costs before the troops disembarked on the beachhead. But, instead of the anticipated 150 mm guns, the paratroopers found only four 100 mm 1916 Skoda Works Czechoslovakian howitzers. Regardless, these had to be destroyed in the event that the Germans mounted a counterattack and recaptured the battery. But since the airborne engineers attached to the Battalion had been dropped off course it was now up to the paratroopers to neutralize these guns themselves. Gathering their Gammon bombs, they proceeded to destroy two guns and disable the others.[58]

Lieutenant Clancy's group finally reached the battery as Otway's men were in the process of securing the perimeter, tending to the wounded, and assembling the prisoners. Their trek had been delayed at Gonneville-sur-Merville because of a heavy Royal Air Force (RAF) bombardment. As the British paratroopers assembled and prepared to move out, Clancy briefed his men. They were to lead the way and protect Otway's march to their final assembly point, the high ground of Le Plein in Amfrèville.

As the survivors and walking wounded of 9 Para Bn headed towards Le Plein, they suddenly came under fire from a heavy German machine gun located in a nearby chateau. The Canadians quickly spread out and neutralized this enemy position. Following this short engagement, Clancy reorganized his group so that they formed an all-around protective shield for the members of 9 Para Bn during their withdrawal to their new positions in Le Plein.[59] Despite being severely undermanned, the members of "A" Company had nevertheless successfully completed all their D-Day missions. By 0900 hours, they left their British comrades and rejoined the Battalion at the Le Mesnil crossroads.

"B" Company's personnel fared no better than the other companies. A total of only 30 all ranks had managed to regroup at the designated RV. Lieutenant Normand Toseland moved the group towards their objective, the Robehomme bridge. During their advance they unexpectedly came across a young French girl who volunteered to guide them. Once at the bridge, they met up with two other Battalion officers, Major C.E. Fuller and Captain Peter Griffin, and a mixed group of British and Canadian paratroopers. The small force took up a defensive posture and waited patiently until 0300 hours for the arrival of a team of British airborne engineers.[60]

Growing restless and unsure if the engineers would actually arrive, the group decided to blow up the bridge themselves. Toseland collected all of the available high explosives. A charge was prepared and subsequently detonated. Regrettably, it proved insufficient. Even though the structure had been weakened, it could still be used by enemy infantry. Knowing that this blast would surely attract the enemy's attention, Major Fuller ordered his group to form a defensive perimeter once again to repel any German patrols. As the paratroopers were digging in, a small group of British airborne engineers, led by Lieutenant Jack Inman, finally arrived. They proceeded to rig a second charge. It was successfully detonated and sent the structure crashing into the river.[61] With the mission accomplished the group moved off to the Le Mesnil crossroads.

The route to the Battalion's position, however, was now active with enemy troops. Without any means of communications, and uncertain as of the fate of the other companies, Major Fuller preferred to use patience and caution. He opted to travel by night and use to the fullest the terrain to cover his movements. During the next day and a half, Major Fuller's group increased to 150 Canadian and British paratroopers. While pleased in assembling such a large force it nevertheless complicated his mobility behind enemy lines. He ordered that all contact with the enemy be avoided so as not to compromise their position. If contact could not be averted, they were to attack and pull out quickly. Fuller ordered a group of 30 paratroopers to act as an advance force to protect the main group and the wounded. Sergeant Roland Larose was part of this band. "As we advanced silently up the road towards Le Mesnil we came across a parked German half-track. We froze instantly. A German officer stepped out and said something to us," recalled Larose. "My friend Russell Harrison yelled back at him, 'I beg your pardon.' Then we opened up and threw grenades into the vehicle." Within seconds 11 enemy soldiers had been killed. An hour later, the group was called back to provide rear area protection. A German jeep drove up. Before the driver could get his vehicle into reverse a volley of automatic fire killed all the occupants.[62] The ad hoc company group finally reached Le Mesnil at 0330 hours on 8 June.[63]

Notwithstanding the numerous unforseen complications and the loss of most of their heavy support weaponry during and immediately following the dispersed drop, the stamina and composure of the paratroopers enabled the Battalion to successfully accomplish all its assigned D-Day tasks.[64] The enemy was fully aware that they were not facing a conventional ground force. The commander of the 711th Infantry Division was impressed by the fighting qualities of the Canadian paratroopers. "The portion which were employed in the bridgehead to the east of the Orne," observed Lieutenant-General Joseph Reichert, "fought in an excellent manner both during the attack and the defense."[65]

This is high praise, after all, considering that the strain due to the bad drops, fatigue, stress, and combat was immense. However, the rigorous training and physical conditioning enabled the Canadian paratroopers to endure and, more importantly, to overcome the great physical and mental hardships encountered during D-Day, as well as the remainder of the Normandy campaign. In hindsight, Lieutenant-Colonel Bradbrooke

Lance-Corporal John Ross attempts to grab a moment's rest. The fatigue is clearly visible on his face.

Courtesy 1 Canadian Parachute Battalion Association.

attested that the Battalion's D-Day successes could not have been achieved if the unit had not undergone such a demanding airborne training regime. "Dropping at night, several hours before the seaborne assault, in strange and hostile territory, all added up to confusion and an appreciation of the reasons why prior training of such severity was necessary," remarked Bradbrooke.[66]

Brigadier Hill agreed. "All this training," he later acknowledged, "gave us an invaluable asset — endurance." Hill added, "I think after D-Day without it we would have had difficulty in producing the stamina required to stick to our ridge for ten whole days of intensive fighting at close range after a tough initial parachute operation and with the casualties suffered." Hill underlined that "Physical fitness saves lives in battle and enables men to better survive their wounds."[67] The young paratroopers now also realized the benefits of such a demanding training regimen. "The training you got, the people you trained with, the people that trained you," explained Sergeant John Feduck, "you might have hated them, but that is why you were there and that is why you were alive."[68]

Nevertheless, the Battalion's initiation to airborne operations was achieved at a very heavy price. After the first 24 hours, out of the 541 paratroopers who had jumped into Normandy, a total of 116 were killed, wounded, or taken prisoner.[69] And a great number of paratroopers were still missing. Others were hunted down and captured. Those who had landed far from the DZ and sustained serious injuries during their landings or had been wounded in subsequent firefights, died alone. During the course of the following days, the lucky ones eventually made their way back to Le Mesnil.

As the troops arrived on the high ground of Le Mesnil they were immediately directed to their respective company defensive positions. Morale was good, however, the paratroopers were tired and hungry. The first priority was to consolidate the perimeter and dig in. The initial defensive positions were very crude. "We dug holes in a large ditch about one hundred yards from the crossroads," remembered Major Hilborn. "They provided good protection against mortar fire."[70] Setting up and defending the assigned Battalion perimeter proved to be a challenging task for the under-strength companies. "We did not have the manpower. We were pretty thinned out," noted Feduck. "Many times, I wish the hell that I was back home."[71]

Others, such as Corporal John Ross, were becoming frustrated because positions were being changed regularly. "We were told to dig a defensive position, which we did. The area that I was in consisted of gravel. We had

Photographer D.A. Reynolds, PA-130154.

Members of 1 Canadian Parachute Battalion dig in at Le Mesnil crossroads, 8 June 1944.

to work very hard to dig this hole," explained Ross. "By the time we were finished we were told that we weren't in the right spot. We were ordered to move further down and start all over again."[72] Nonetheless, as dusk fell over the Orne bridgehead the 1st Canadian Parachute Battalion's Le Mesnil positions were occupied.

Undermanned, and with very few support weapons and no radio communications between the Battalion headquarters and the companies, the surviving paratroopers braced themselves for the imminent German counterattacks. Regardless, Lieutenant-Colonel Bradbrooke was pleased with his men's fighting spirit and the Battalion's defensive perimeter. "The country around Le Mesnil was very close with its ditches and hedges," described the CO, "and it was a perfect position for determined boys like ours." However, Bradbrooke did not like the fact that his men were isolated from the main invasion force. Nevertheless, a contemplative Bradbrooke resigned himself to the fact that during the following days his unit would be "just one little pocket on the end of nowhere."[73]

In the end, the night of 6 June 1944 was seared into the minds and souls of the Canadian paratroopers. "No soldier involved," wrote one veteran, "could ask for more: exciting challenges, tests of ingenuity,

This composite photograph taken from Lance-Corporal Ross's trench in front of the gate house at Varaville captures the surrender of German forces and their subsequent disarming.

Courtesy 1 Canadian Parachute Battalion Association.

matching of wits with a clever and dedicated enemy. More adventure in one night than most men live in a lifetime."[74] Private Melvin Jones agreed, but was slightly more cautious. "I am proud and very glad I was part of the 1st Canadian Parachute Battalion airborne invasion of France," he confided. "But I would never, never do it again … jumping out of an airplane into black space towards a land full of the enemy …. There are no front lines at a time like this; there were Germans all over the place … you could be among any number of them."[75]

His sentiments are understandable. They had jumped in the dead of night into chaotic conditions. As individuals, small groups, and severely depleted sub-units, they overcame the bedlam and successfully attained *all* of their assigned objectives. And so, the Canadian paratroopers of the 1st Canadian Parachute Battalion, as part of the British 3rd Parachute Brigade of the 6th Airborne Division, played a vital part in ensuring the protection of the eastern flank of the invasion force's D-Day landing.[76] Their jump into chaos was truly a daring action.

Courtesy 1 Canadian Parachute Battalion Association.

Canadian paratroopers take a brief rest after the battle of Varaville.

NOTES

1. The 1st Canadian Parachute Battalion (1 Cdn Para Bn) was established by government decree on 1 July 1942. Although initially nominally slated for home defence, its purpose in the mind of the army leadership was always for offensive action and overseas duty. Recruiting began immediately and volunteers from units across Canada were put through a rigorous selection process. Those who passed were sent to Fort Benning, Georgia, for training from October 1942 until March 1943, when Canadian facilities, designated as the S-14 Canadian

Parachute Training School at Camp Shilo, Manitoba, had been constructed. In March 1943, although the unit had not yet completed its collective training, it was offered up for inclusion into the newly formed British 6th Airborne Division (6 AB Div) in the UK. As such, the Battalion arrived in Bulford, England, in early August 1943 and underwent an intensive training regime as part of the 3rd Parachute Brigade under the battle-tested Brigadier James Hill in preparation for the invasion of Normandy.

2. Interview with Harry Reid. 24 January 2002. Oral History Project. 1st Canadian Parachute Battalion Association Archives.

3. Interview with Jan de Vries, 18 January 2001.

4. David Owen, "A Portrait of a Parachutist," unpublished manuscript, 1 Cdn Para Bn Assn Archives, David Owen fonds.

5. Terry Copp, "The Airborne on D-Day," *Legion Magazine*, May–June 1998, 46.

6. Stephen E. Ambrose, *Pegasus Bridge* (London: Touchstone Books, 1985), 109.

7. Interview with John Feduck. 19 December 2001. Oral History Project. 1 Cdn Para Bn Assn Archives.

8. Interviews with 1 Cdn Para Bn veterans.

9. Interview with Anthony Skalicky. 10 January 2002. Oral History Project. 1 Cdn Para Bn Assn Archives.

10. Interview with William Talbot, 28 December 2002. *Ibid.*

11. Interview with John Simpson, 13 December 2002. *Ibid.*

12. Interview with Ernie Jeans, 22 January 2002. *Ibid.*

13. Boyd Anderson, *Grass Roots* (Wood Mountain: Windspeak Press, 1996), 269–270.

14. *Ibid.*, 269–270.

15. "Recollections of a Canadian Parachuting Medical Officer in World War II," 6. Brian Nolan fonds, Colin Brebner file, 1 Cdn Para Bn Assn Archives.

16. *Ibid.*, 6.

17. Michael Hanlon, "Paratroopers Landed at Night," *Toronto Star*, Special Section on the Normandy Landing, 6 June 1944, Section D, D2 .

18. Interview with Doug Morrison, 2 February 2002.

19. Letter from Ted Kalicki to Brian Nolan, Warsaw, New York, 7 February 1994. Brian Nolan fonds, Ted Kalicki file, 1 Cdn Para Bn Assn Archives.

20. Dan Hartigan, *A Rising of Courage* (Calgary: Drop Zone Publishers, 2000), 113.

21. Interview with H.R. Holloway, 4 November 1998.

22. Jan de Vries, written submission to authors, 9 January 2001.

23. Interview with Dan Hartigan, 30 October 2000.

24. Letter from John Feduck to Dan Hartigan, non-dated. 1 Cdn Para Bn Assn Archives, Dan Hartigan, file 23-7.

25. Letter from D.S. Parlee to Dan Hartigan, 24 March 1990. *Ibid.*

26. Interview with Denis Flynn, 18 April 2001.

27. Colonel C.P. Stacey, Historical Officer, Canadian Military Headquarters, *Report No. 19, The 1st Canadian Parachute Battalion In France, 6 June–6 September 1944*, 13.

28. Interview with Anthony Skalicky, 10 January 2002. Oral History Project. 1 Cdn Para Bn Assn Archives.

29. Private M. Zakulak, Vickers Section, "Eighty Days Behind Enemy Lines, 1944." 1 Cdn Para Bn. 1 Cdn Para Bn Assn Archives, file 8-7, Gavinski, Thomas.

30. Ross Munro, "Nicklin's Feat, Lands In Nazi-Held Town," *Winnipeg Free Press*, 26 June 1944, Vol. 50, No. 232, 1, 8. NL, microfilm N-24564.

31. Lieutenant-General Richard N. Gale, *With The 6th Airborne Division in Normandy* (London: Sampson, Low, Martson & Co. Ltd., 1948), 80–81, 83.

32. Letter from Lieutenant-Colonel G.F.P. Bradbrooke (ret'd) to David Owen, 6 March 1985. David Owen fonds, Series 1: Correspondence, File G.F.P. Bradbrooke, 1 Cdn Para Bn Assn Archives.

33. Letter from Lieutenant-Colonel G.F.P. Bradbrooke (ret'd) to Brian Nolan, Ramsey, Isle of Man, 19 August 1985. Brian Nolan fond, Lieutenant-Colonel G.F.P. Bradbrooke file, 1 Cdn Para Bn Assn Archives.

34. *Ibid.*

35. Ralph Allen, "Canadian Paratroops Create Proud History," *Globe and Mail*, No. 29,495, 26 June 1944, 1 and 3, microfilm N-20057.

36. Interview with Richard Hilborn, February 2002, Oral History Project, 1 Cdn Para Bn Assn Archives.

37. Interview with Ernie Jeans, 22 January 2002. *Ibid.*

38. Jean E. Portugal, *We Were There: The Army*. A Record for Canada, Volume #2 of Seven (Toronto: The Royal Canadian Military Institute, 1998), 943–944.

39. Interview with Jan de Vries, 18 January 2001.

40. RAF Station, daily entry, 5 June 1944. Public Record Office (PRO), AIR 28/343 Air Ministry and Minister of Defense: Operations Record Book, Royal Air Force Station, Harwell; Hartigan, *A Rising of Courage*, 108–109.

41. A total of three advance parties with pathfinders were dropped to protect and mark three Drop Zones between the Orne and Dives Rivers. The units of the main body that jumped onto them were: Drop Zone "N," 5th Para Bde Gp; Drop Zone "V," 3rd Para Bde Gp; and Drop Zone "K," 8th Para Bn. Peter Harclerode, *"Go To It!" The Illustrated History of The 6th Airborne Division* (London: Caxton Edition, 2000), 88; The Drop Zone "V" pathfinder group consisted of two sticks. Stick No. 1 dropped directly onto the DZ. Regrettably, this stick's DZ marking equipment was either damaged or lost in the marshes. Stick No. 2 landed 1,000 yards north of the DZ. They finally reached the DZ as the main body was jumping. The DZ markings that were set up for the main body consisted of two green lights set up prior to the main drop. An additional two lights were installed by the paratroopers of the second stick during the main body's jump, 6 Airborne Division, Report on Operations in Normandy, 6 June–27 August 1944, Part III, Conclusions, Appendix "H," Details of Pathfinder Drop. Library and Archives of Canada [hereafter LAC], RG 24, Vol. 10955, file 225.B6.013 (D1), 6 AB Div report; Simultaneously, two small forces of "D" Company Group 2 Oxford and Buckinghamshire Light Infantry were glider inserted to carry out a *coup de main*

that resulted in the capture of the bridges over the Caen Canal and the River Orne. Harclerode, 88.

42. The "Rebecca/Eureka" was a two-part homing devise. The first part, the "Eureka," was a beacon housed in a small rectangular box with a collapsible aerial. The "Eurekas" were operated by pathfinder units to assist the pilots transporting the main bodies to locate their DZs. This beacon was designed to receive on one frequency and transmit on another. The second part, the "Rebecca," was installed in the aircraft. It was designed to transmit and receive on the same transmitter frequency as the "Eureka." When receiving an impulse signal from the "Rebecca," the "Eureka" responded by sending a signal. This enabled the pilot to confirm his approach and distance to the DZ, Otway, Appendix D, Radar Homing Devices, 405-406. *Circumstances attending dispersion of the 6th Airborne Division on D-Day* from "The Liberation of North West Europe. Volume III: The Landings in Normandy." The Varaville Dropping Zone "V," 2–3. LAC, RG 24, Vol. 10955, file 2255B6.013(D3), Circumstances attending dispersion of the 6th AB Div on D-Day.

43. Hartigan, *A Rising of Courage*, 109.

44. Allied Airborne Missions For D-Day: The Allied command understood that within the first 24 hours they had to ensure the unimpeded sea landing and ensuing breakout from the constrictive beaches of more than 20,000 vehicles and 176,000 men. As a result, the Allies elected to use their airborne forces to guard the vulnerable flanks of the invading force. As such, before first light, on 6 June 1944, three airborne divisions — two American and one British — were to be inserted by parachute and glider behind enemy lines. The American, British, and Canadian paratroopers would occupy, defend, and protect the eastern and western flanks of the invasion force throughout the initial days of the landing. The two American Airborne Divisions were assigned to protect the western flank. The U.S. 82nd "All Americans" Airborne Division, commanded by Major-General Matthew B. Ridgway, was comprised of 6,000 paratroopers and 4,000 glider infantry and was allocated three drop zones (DZ). Ridgway's mission consisted of capturing Sainte-Mère-Église, which represented a vital communication and transportation hub, as well as all causeway exits from Utah Beach. In addition, the road systems traversing the flooded area within their boundaries were to be taken and defended. This included the seizure and control of the bridges spanning the Douvre and Merderet rivers. Once these objectives were secured, defensive positions were to be set up to repel German counterattacks that were anticipated from the Pont l'Abbé-St-Sauveur le Vicomte sector. Concurrently, the U.S. 101st "Screaming Eagles" Airborne Division, led by Major-General Maxwell Taylor, would fight on the flank of the 82nd Airborne Division. Taylor's 6,600 men were to be transported in 1,432 C-47 Dakota aircraft and were also allocated three DZs. Their first responsibility was to capture and hold the causeways and bridges within their designated area of responsibility, spanning the Douvre and Mederet Rivers for the arrival of the American 4th Infantry Division. Once these objectives were seized, they were to gain control of all the major roadways leading to Utah

Beach in their area. More importantly, they had to secure the designated Landing Zones (LZ) for the glider troops who were scheduled to land later in the day. The protection of the eastern flank was the responsibility of Major-General R.N. Gale, commander of the British 6th Airborne Division (6 AB Div). His division was composed of the 3rd and 5th Parachute Brigades and the 6th Air Landing Brigade. Also attached to the division was Lord Lovat's 1st Special Service Brigade. This unit was designated to land by sea and link up with Gale's troops early on the first day of the invasion. The mission of 6 AB Div was to secure, establish, and hold a bridgehead on the high ground between the Caen Canal, the Orne, and Dives Rivers. The control of this important elevated feature was vital because it would enable units of the British 1st Corps, commanded by Lieutenant-General John Crocker, to land and quickly move out from Sword Beach, so that they could seize and consolidate a bridgehead south of the Orne River. Each of the Brigades was given specific tasks and areas of operation. The 3rd Parachute Brigade, which included the 1st Canadian Parachute Battalion, was ordered to capture the Merville Battery and destroy its guns. In addition, the bridges over the Dives and Divette rivers were to be destroyed to prevent German reinforcements and counterattacks from reaching the beaches. Lastly, all roads in the Troarn-Sannerville, Troan-Escoville, Robehomme-LeMesnil, Merril-Bréville, and the Franceville-Sallenelles areas were to be held and defended. The 5th Parachute Brigade, under the command of Brigadier J.H.N. Poett, was to seize by "coup de main," using glider-borne troops, two bridges spanning the Orne, Ranville, and Bénouville canals. Furthermore, Poett's troops were to clear landing zones of obstructions and defend them for subsequent glider landings. Concurrently, the brigade was to occupy and defend the Bénouville-Ranville-Bas sector. The third brigade, the 6th Air Landing Brigade, was commanded by Brigadier H. Kindersley. It consisted of the 12th Battalion Devonshire Regiment, the 2nd Battalion Oxfordshire, the Buckinghamshire Light Infantry, and the 1st Battalion Royal Ulster Rifles. These three battalions and other specialized airborne units were to land by glider on two LZs at 2100 hours on 6 June 1944. Their task was to occupy and hold and the Longueval, Honorine, La Chardonerette, Escouville, and Le Bas De Ranville area. Moreover, the glider troops were to deny all approaches to the crossings of the Orne River and the Caen Canal to the enemy. Additionally, they were to provide a firm base from which the 6th Airborne Division could operate offensively in the area between the Orne and Dives Rivers.

45. Interview with Cliff Funston. 25 January 2002. Oral History Project. 1 Cdn Para Bn Assn Archives.

46. *By Air To Battle, The Official Account of The British First and Sixth Airborne Divisions* (London: The Whitefriars Press Ltd., 1945), 87.

47. Hartigan, *A Rising of Courage,* 114–115.

48. Taped recollections of Esko Makela. Non-dated. Dan Hartigan fonds, Makela file, 1 Cdn Para Bn Assn Archives.

49. *Ibid.,* 132.

50. Interview with John Ross. 14 February 2002. Oral History Project. 1 Cdn Para Bn Assn Archives.

51. 1 Cdn Para Bn War Diary, 6 June 1944, Varaville, "C" Company. LAC, RG 24, Vol. 15299, June 1944. 1st Canadian Parachute Battalion, Operational Order No.1, Method, 4. "C" Company, Phases 1-5. *Ibid.*, May 1944, Appendix 6.

52. 1 Cdn Para Bn War Diary, 6 June 1944, Varaville, "C" Company. *Ibid.*

53. Carl Shilleto, *Pegasus Bridge & Merville Battery: British 6th Airborne Division Landing in Normandy D-Day, 6 June 1944* (South Yorkshire: Battlefield Series Club Pen & Sword Books Ltd., 2001), 81, 93.

54. 1 Cdn Para Bn War Diary, 6 June 1944, Protection of left Flank of 9 Para Bn, "A" Company. LAC, RG 24, Vol. 15299, June 1944. 1st Canadian Parachute Battalion, Operational Order No.1, Method, 5, "A" Company, Phases 1–3. *Ibid.*, May 1944, Appendix 6.

55. Shilleto, 104.

56. *Ibid.*, 87; Hilary St. George Saunders, *The Red Beret: The Story Of the Parachute Regiment at War 1940-1945* (London: Michael Joseph Ltd., 1950), 185; "Silent Guns," *Red Berets '44, The Illustrated London News*, 1994, 38.

57. Shilleto, 77; "Silent Guns," *Red Berets '44, The Illustrated London News* 1994, 36–40.

58. Gregor Ferguson, *The Paras, 1940–1984*, Elite Series No. 1 (London: Osprey Military, 1996), 29.

59. 1 Cdn Para Bn War Diary, 6 June 1944, Protection of left Flank of 9 Para Bn, "A" Company. LAC, RG 24, Vol. 15299, June 1944.

60. Napier Crookenden, *Dropzone Normandy: The Story of the American and British Airborne Assault on D-Day 1944* (New York: Charles Scribner's Sons, 1976), 210.

61. There are conflicting accounts from both British and Canadian sources as to how this bridge was destroyed. Canadian sources: Lieutenant N. Toseland recalled that "We attempted to blow the bridge with the plastic explosives each man carried in his helmet. We did not succeed in destroying the bridge as our charges were insufficient. Finally, the British Para Engineers appointed to do the job arrived and expertly dropped the bridge into the river." Interview of Normand Toseland, "Out Of The Clouds: The Story Of The First Canadian Parachute Battalion," *The Legion Bugle*, Vol. 2, Issue 11 (July/August 1988): 1; The Battalion's war diary entry reads, "Captain Griffin waited until 0630 hours for the R.E.'s who were to blow the bridge. As they failed to arrive explosives were collected from the men and the bridge successfully demolished." 1 Cdn Para Bn War Diary, 6 June 1944, "B" Company. LAC, RG 24, Vol. 15299, June 1944; Captain Peter Griffin writes, "In the first two days I had fun blowing up two bridges … So finally we pooled all the explosives we normally carry and no one knowing anything about engineering, we slapped it up against the bridge hoping against hope. Sure enough when I touched it off the bridge split in the center and fell in the river — big thrill!" Letter from Captain Peter Griffin to his sister Margeret, Normandy, 20 June 1944. NA, MG 30, E 538, William M.R. Griffin and Peter R. Griffin fonds. British sources: Lieutenant

Inman states that he arrived at the bridge at 0900 hours where he met Sergeant William Poole. The sergeant stated that he had dropped nearby and collected 30 pounds of explosives from the paratroopers and "destroyed the span with a clean cut." Appendix C, Report on Operations Re. 6th AB Div D-Day + 1, Part 1, D-Day, 3 Parachute Squadron, Royal Engineers. LAC, RG 24 Vol. 10956, file 2556.018 (D2+3), War Diary 6AB Div, June–July 1944. Crookenden concurred with Inman's recollections, but added that Lieutenant Inman used his explosives, "to create a worse obstacle by preparing two carters on the near side abutment, 210; and Peter Harclerode wrote, "However, Sergeant Bill Poole of No.3 Troop of 3rd Parachute Squadron RE, who was one of the sappers who had joined up withe Lieutenant Toseland, collected all the plastic explosives carried by infantrymen to make Gammon bombs. This amounted to some 30 pounds in all. Sergeant Poole attempted to blow the bridge but, with the limited amount of explosive available to him, only managed to weaken it. At about 0600 hours, however, Lieutenant Jack Inman and five sappers of No. 3 Troop arrived with 200 pounds of explosive charges and the bridge was duly destroyed," 72. It is most likely that during the course of the night two charges had been set off. The first charge prepared with the explosives collected from the paratroopers only weakened the structure. The second larger charge rigged by the British engineers destroyed the bridge.

62.   Interview with Roland Larose, David Owen fonds, Larose file, 1 Cdn Para Bn Assn Archives.

63.   1 Cdn Para Bn War Diary, 6 June 1944, Protection of left Flank of 9 Para Bn, "A" Company. LAC, RG 24, Vol. 15299, June 1944. As the group made its way to Le Mesnil they met up with Lieutenant I. Wilson, a Battalion intelligence officer. Wilson guided the paratroopers back to the Battalion's defensive positions.

64.   The members of the Vickers platoon had packed their machine guns, spare parts, and ammunition in their leg kit bags. This was the first time that they had used these kit bags to jump with their weapons. This method of transporting weaponry into combat proved totally unsatisfactory. When the paratroopers released the bags, the shock generated by the full extension of the 20-foot rope was so severe that the bottoms ripped. Within seconds, the contents fell out, scattered, and crashed to the ground. Mortar platoon personnel also experienced a similar problem with their leg kit bags. Since most of these platoons members were mostly dropped over marshy and flooded areas, the conditions were such that it was impossible for the paratroopers to locate their heavy weapons. 1 Cdn Para Bn War Diary, 6 June 1944. LAC, RG 24, Vol. 15299, June 1944. The signalers fared no better. All the radios had been lost. Interview with John Simpson, 13 December 2001.

65.   David C. Isby, ed., *Fighting The Invasion: The German Army at D-Day* (London: Greenhill Books, 2000), 145, 179.

66.   Letter from Lieutenant-Colonel G.F.P. Bradbrooke (Ret'd) to David Owen, Ramsey, Isle of Man, 6 March 1985. David Owen fonds. Series 1, Correspondence, G.F.P. Bradbrooke, file. 1 Cdn Para Bn Assn Archives.

67. Brigadier James Hill's speaking notes on the training and briefing of the 6th Airborne Division for their role in Operation "Overlord". Talk given to Staff College, Camberley, 7 June 1968. Brigadier James Hill's speaking notes, November 1993. Brian Nolan fonds, file Brigadier Hill, 1 Cdn Para Bn Assn Archives; Ross Munro, "Canadian 'Chutists Held Crossroads In 11 Days and Nights of Fighting," *The Evening Citizen*, No. 321, 26 June 1944, 8. LAC, microfilm N-18015.

68. Interview with John Feduck, 19 December 2001. Oral History Project. 1 Cdn Para Bn Assn Archives.

69. On 6 June 1944, the casualties sustained by the 1st Canadian Parachute Battalion were: 3 Officers and 18 ORs killed or died of wounds; 1 officer and 8 ORs wounded; 3 officers and 83 ORs captured. Colonel C.P. Stacey, Director, Historical Section (G.S.). The 1st Canadian Parachute Battalion in France, 6 June–6 September 1944. DHH, Report No.26 Historical Section (G.S), Army Headquarters, 23 August 1949, 21.

70. Interview with Richard Hilborn. February 2002. Oral History Project. 1 Cdn Para Bn Assn Archives.

71. Interview with John Feduck. 19 December 2001. Oral History Project. 1 Cdn Para Bn Assn Archives.

72. Interview with John Ross. 14 February 2001. Oral History Project. 1 Cdn Para Bn Assn Archives.

73. Ross Munro, "Canadian 'Chutists Held Crossroads In 11 Day and Nights of Fighting," *The Evening Citizen*, No. 321, 26 June 1944, 8. LAC, microfilm N-18015; Ross Munro, "Invasion's East Flank Canada 'Chutists' Job," *Toronto Daily Star*, 26 June 1944. LAC, microfilm N-28589.

74. Dan Hartigan, *A Rising of Courage*, 160.

75. Portugal, 951.

76. Despite heavy casualties the Canadian paratroopers doggedly held at the Le Mesnil crossroads against determined German attacks until the Allied break out of the Normandy pocket in mid-August. At this time, 1 Cdn Para Bn, as part of the 6 AB Div, chased the retreating German Army to the Seine River. In early September 1944, it was pulled from the line and returned to England. Once back at Bulford, the unit was reinforced and re-equipped. It also underwent training to prepare for it next airborne operation. However, a crisis interceded. On Christmas Day 1944, the Battalion was ferried to Belgium with the remainder of the 6 AB Div to assist with crushing the surprise German offensive in the Ardennes. As such, 1 Cdn Para Bn was the only Canadian unit to fight in the Battle of the Bulge. By the end of January, the Germans had been once again forced to retreat and the Battalion was deployed into a defensive position across from a German parachute division along the Maas River in Holland. By the end of February 1945, the unit returned to England and prepared for its last airborne operation. On 24 March 1945, the Canadian paratroopers participated in the largest concentrated airborne operation of the war — Operation VARSITY — the crossing of the Rhine River. After a very short but bloody battle, the Battalion, as part of 6 AB Div, embarked on six-week,

300-mile race across Germany to Wismar, on the Baltic Sea. As a precursor to the Cold War, British prime minister Winston Churchill had personally ordered the 6 AB Div to beat the Russians to that port city. On 2 May 1945, the Canadians led the division into Wismar, mere hours before the arrival of the first Russian troops.

The war in Europe was declared over on 8 May 1945. The Battalion was returned to England later that month. On 31 May, it was repatriated to Canada — the first complete unit to return home after the war. On arrival in Halifax, it received a hero's welcome. The paratroopers then took some well-deserved leave and returned to Niagara-on-the-Lake where the unit was disbanded in September 1945.

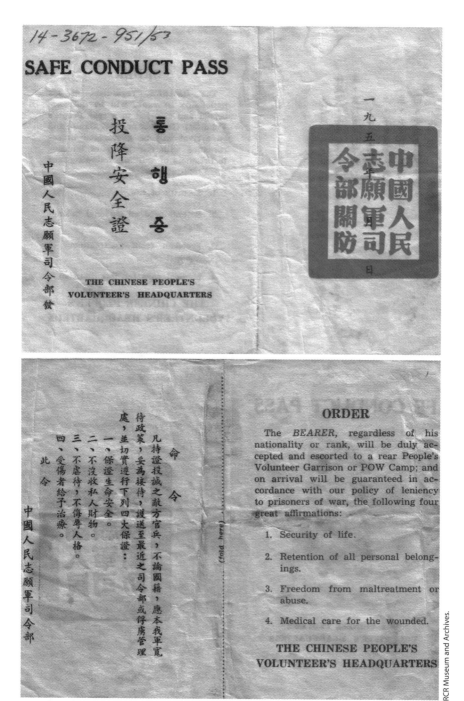

Chinese Safe Conduct Pass (front and back).

CHAPTER 10

"A Specially Daring Raid":
Toe to Toe with the Chinese, 31 May 1952

BERND HORN

The night air was still stale and hot as the group of 23 soldiers with blackened faces and dressed in an assortment of sweaters, camouflage smocks, and balaclavas huddled close to the ground. Overhead, although they could not see the jet aircraft, they could certainly hear them as they roared passed on their way to bomb the Chinese on Hill 113. The muted thuds of the explosions in the distance heartened the waiting troops. Anything to increase their odds was a bonus. Once again, they found themselves tempting fate in another tense game of "cat and mouse" with the Chinese. They were not just venturing into no man's land, rather, they were doing a fighting patrol right into the lion's den. Although the war was in its second year, it seemed that not much had changed. It was a bitter struggle in the trenches, more for personal survival than for national conquest.

It had all started in the inky darkness of early morning, on 25 June 1950, when approximately 135,000 North Korean soldiers, supported by Soviet-supplied T-35 tanks, washed over the South Korean border like a tsunami. Against the poorly equipped and ill-trained Republic of Korea (ROK) defences and military forces, the Communist onslaught swept right up to the Korean capital of Seoul. Within three days of its initiation, the North Korean People's Army (NKPA) offensive had captured the capital.[1]

International condemnation was swift. On the afternoon of 25 June, the UN Security Council met and demanded an immediate halt to the aggression and the withdrawal of all NKPA forces from South Korea. Fortuitously, the Soviet Union had boycotted the Security Council session and therefore did not exercise its veto. This Soviet oversight allowed the UN Security Council to act. Five days later, President Harry S. Truman authorized American forces to intervene. On 5 July 1950, one U.S. division deployed from Japan and made contact with the enemy. Other nations offered assistance and two days later the Security Council recommended all forces be placed under a single commander. As a result, a UN Command was established in Tokyo under General Douglas MacArthur.

The Canadian government was reluctant to get embroiled in another ground war. The spectre of the conscription crisis in the dying days of the Second World War still haunted the Liberal government. Initially, in July 1950, three destroyers and a transport squadron were sent to Korea to assist in operations but this commitment was quickly dismissed by the Americans as a token effort. As a result, pressure mounted on Canada to deploy ground combat forces. On 7 August 1950, with UN forces hemmed in around the Port of Pusan, the Canadian government finally authorized the recruitment of the Canadian Army Special Force (CASF). Canada was at war once again.

However, it took months to raise and train the CASF. In the interim, the war had taken a number of dramatic turns. Initially, the UN forces had been pushed into the tiny "Pusan Perimeter," but in mid-September 1951 a daring amphibious assault was launched at Inchon, the port of Seoul. Quickly overcoming NKPA resistance, the South Korean capital was recaptured by 26 September and by the first week of October MacArthur's forces were driving a battered enemy back across the 38th Parallel. Sensing victory, the UN forces continued their advance, crossed the North Korean border and seized the capital of Pyongyang. Fatefully, MacArthur ordered his forces to advance towards the Yalu River, the boundary between North Korea and China.

With the fortunes of war apparently turned, the Canadian government cut back its commitment of an entire brigade group, the 25th Canadian Infantry Brigade (25 CIB), and dispatched only one battalion, the 2nd Battalion, the Princess Patricia's Canadian Light Infantry (2 PPCLI), to Korea. After all, with the war almost won, there did not seem to be any need for additional troops. As a result, 2 PPCLI sailed for Korea on 25 November 1950.

However, unbeknownst to the UN command, by the end of October six Chinese armies, numbering approximately 300,000 troops, had already crossed the Yalu River and were concentrating in the path of the now over-confident UN forces.[2] On 26 November the UN forces ran up against the main enemy defensive line between Pyongyang and the Yalu River. The Chinese unleashed their ambush on MacArthur's overextended forces. The UN advance became a rout, which was finally stopped at the Imjin River. It was into this atmosphere of crisis that 2 PPCLI arrived in December.

However, the situation would worsen. The Chinese launched another crushing offensive early in the New Year and by 4 January 1951, Seoul was once again in the hands of the Communists. By 21 February 1951, the Canadian government announced it would send an entire infantry brigade to Korea as originally intended. At about the same time, 2 PPCLI entered the line and on 24–25 April fought its famous battle of Kap'yong. On the night of 24–25 April 1951, the advancing Chinese attacked the hilltop defences of the PPCLI and the Royal Australian Regiment. The Australians were forced to withdraw, but the PPCLI held their positions at great cost and stopped the enemy advance. As a result, they were awarded a U.S. Presidential Unit Citation. By 1 May the enemy offensive had come to an end and the UN forces held an irregular line some 30 kilometres south of the 38th Parallel forming an arc north of Seoul. By 1 May the enemy offensive had come to an end and the UN forces held an irregular line some 30 kilometres south of the 38th Parallel, forming an arc north of Seoul.

This was the general situation that faced The Royal Canadian Regiment upon their arrival in Korea at the beginning of May 1951. Some were foolishly worried that the war would be over before they had a chance to fully experience the adventure, since the American government, at the end of the month, instructed General Matthew Ridgeway, who had replaced the sacked Douglas MacArthur, to invite the Chinese and North Koreans to discuss a ceasefire. The next day both sides agreed to meet on 8 July in a small village on the 38th Parallel, called Kaesong. Unfortunately, nothing came of the talks with the exception of decreased activity for a short period. As a result of the parley, the UN forces halted offensive action and adopted a heavy program of patrolling throughout the summer.

The remainder of the summer epitomized conflict in general. "Fighting alternated between boredom and danger, intense physical effort and completely lazy days," wrote one veteran.[3] The heavy patrolling continued with each side trying to dominate the ground. With the fall approaching and any hope of a lasting peace now but wishful thinking, the UN decided to advance once again.

By early October 1951, the front line stabilized. The Canadians (25 CIB) attained their objectives, positions overlooking the Nabu-ri Valley, which represented no man's land between the UN forward positions and those of the Chinese. These positions represented roughly the ground the Canadians would hold for close to the next two years of fighting.

A reverse slope RCR position overlooking the Nabu-ri Valley. This picture provides an idea of the underground existence experienced by the front-line troops.

The RCR now dug in once again and set about making their positions defensible. The Battalion now settled in to a routine of patrolling, small-scale skirmishing, repelling Chinese raids, and fighting the tedium of boredom. Frequently prisoners were captured either through patrols, failed enemy attacks, or simply through desertion.

The attritional warfare continued. The Chinese moved a large number of heavy artillery pieces close to the front line and continually

Photographer Paul E. Tomelin, LAC, PA-128850.

Private Heath Matthews awaits medical attention after a night patrol.

hammered the UN forward positions in conjunction with limited attacks by infantry. In return, the UN forces would also strike back, but normally with sub-unit or smaller-sized forces with limited objectives.

At the end of the month, on 25 October 1951, UN command representatives and Chinese and North Korean delegates met at Panmunjom to resume peace talks. As a result the war entered its static phase. Political consideration, namely fear of provoking enemy retaliation, resulted in restrictions on offensive operations. In essence, nothing greater than a company size raid was authorized. This became a hugely unpopular directive as it did not allow UN forces to disrupt Chinese intentions if a buildup of forces or material was detected prior to a suspected enemy offensive.

In many ways, it became a war of patrols. In early May 1952, the 1st Battalion, The RCR (1 RCR) rotated into theatre to replace 2 RCR who had completed their year-long tour. By the end of the month, activity on both the UN and Chinese increased dramatically. Each night 1 RCR had approximately 40–60 all ranks engaged in myriad standing, fighting and reconnaissance (recce) patrols. The "Royals" also introduced the "jitters" patrol that was intended to keep the enemy in a state of anxiety. To achieve this, equipment such as bugles, whistles, tin cans, and any other noise-making instrument was employed.[4]

The Battalion's active patrol regimen was in conformity with the 1st U.S. Corps HQ policy. Each forward battalion within the Commonwealth Division was ordered to conduct one fighting patrol a week against enemy positions and capture one prisoner every three days. The policy was very costly, however, as troops were forced to penetrate enemy defences to find their prey.

Patrols ranged from 20 men to entire companies and were supported by heavy supporting fire from tanks and artillery. Patrols passed through their own wire and defensive minefields through existing gaps and crossed the floor of the valley and worked their way to the hills opposite them. The RCR staged the most raids in the brigade. In fact, the 25 CIB commander ordered the Battalion "to cut down on patrols so other units can catch up."[5] The "Royals" concentrated on Hills 75 and 113, which lay across the valley of the Sami-ch'on tributary with Hill 166 immediately to the rear.

And so, on the night of 31 May 1952, 23 men from "A" Coy, 1 RCR, comprising one officer and 22 men, tempted fate once again and launched yet another patrol against the enemy. This night the patrol would prove to be particularly challenging — what Major-General Jim Cassels, the commander of 1 Commonwealth Division later described as a "specially daring raid against a strong enemy position."[6]

The objective was a familiar one, Hill 113. The patrol was given a simple task — "kill or capture the enemy."[7] As the smoke from the air strike delivered by eight jet aircraft drifted lazily off the objective, the patrol left friendly lines and stealthily entered no man's land. The troops quickly crossed the valley floor and closed in on the burned-out village of Chinch'on, which was approximately 100 yards (300 metres) from the forward enemy defences. Lieutenant A.A.S. Peterson, the patrol commander, then called in the fire plan. As artillery shells began to pummel Hill 113, Peterson led his men to the first line of trenches. These proved to be "deserted and in a state of disrepair."[8] The walls were broken in and there was brush in the trenches. At this location, Peterson left Sergeant H.J.D. Shore, seven men, and a two-inch mortar to form a firm base to provide security for the patrol's eventual withdrawal.

LAC, PA-184740.

RCR troops man a front-line trench and bunker, March 1952.

The patrol commander now called off the artillery fire, leaving only the tanks to continue to fire onto the objective. Under cover of this timed supporting fire program delivered by the tanks, the patrol then proceeded to the second line of trenches higher up the feature. These too were abandoned. Here, Peterson left Corporal Stinson and six men to clear the bunkers while he pressed on with the remainder of his patrol to the crest of the hill.

Stinson and his group worked their way down the trench line clearing bunkers with phosphorous grenades. Each patrol member carried three high-explosive (HE) grenades. Four soldiers were designated "bombers" and they carried 11 HE and five phosphorous grenades. At each bunker they yelled "*Chu-la*" (come out) before tossing in the grenades. All of a sudden, "one Chinaman appeared from a bunker with hands raised and said 'me officer.'"[9] He was subsequently taken prisoner, "subdued [hit on the head] and his head covered with a blanket."[10] However, things quickly heated up. Stinson's squad observed some enemy troops moving up the south side of Hill 113, defying the artillery, mortar, and machine-gun fire currently pounding the objective area. As the enemy neared Stinson's location a gunfight broke out as grenades and small-arms fire were exchanged. Private M.J. Fitzgerald, a Bren gunner, opened fire and a number of enemy dropped but others tenaciously continued to crawl forward. Soon he was bombarded by a barrage of potato-masher type Chinese grenades that proved to be ineffective. In addition, they were easy to see because of their flash and smoke. Nonetheless, one hit Fitzgerald on the head, bounced off, and burst harmlessly at his feet. Others failed to detonate.[11]

A RCR patrol commander conducts a final inspection of his patrol members prior to leaving the relative safety of his company position.

As the melee broke out Private J.M. McNeil, who was guarding the prisoner, was wounded in the arm. The Chinese prisoner quickly seized the opportunity and scrambled off but Private P. Mullet "stopped him with about 20 rounds."[12] Throughout the firefight the soldiers cursed their Sten sub-machine guns as they repeatedly jammed when needed most.

Meanwhile, Peterson and the seven remaining soldiers worked their way along trench on the crest of Hill 113, clearing the defences with phosphorous grenades. They quickly noted that there was a series of tunnels underneath the communication trench they were in and they could actually see the enemy scurrying around below them. The discovery was no real surprise. By March 1952, intelligence on the Chinese tactics, techniques, and procedures had identified:

> The Chinese have shown themselves to be masters in the preparation of defensive works. The report noted that "their defensive positions are a maze of bunkers, bays, weapon pits, storage and sleeping quarters. All these positions are connected by deep communication trenches. They made use of outposts located at the foot of occupied terrain features to warn of the approach of UN forces. Enemy held locations were a series of elaborately prepared defensive positions echeloned up the sides of the occupied terrain features and connected by communication trenches."[13]

The Chinese rapidly recovered from their initial surprise and the intense pounding they had taken by the supporting fire. The Chinese now appeared from bunkers and foxholes from all directions. A virtual hornet's nest erupted as the enemy swarmed over the position. Peterson ordered Corporal Stinson's group to pull back to the firm base and withdrew his own group immediately as well. He did not hear Corporal Stinson's warning, "Don't come this way!" and so began to withdraw by the same route they had come. However, he quickly abandoned the idea when he was showered by grenades. Realizing that the enemy had weaseled their way between the elements of his patrol he now retreated straight down the feature.[14]

In the interim, Stinson's group came under increasing pressure. Additional Chinese reinforcement braved the cauldron of fire and advanced on the patrol over the open ground, tossing grenades as they approached. As the firefight intensified, at least four Chinese soldiers were killed, but two more of Stinson's men, as well as himself, were now wounded. Upon receiving the order to withdraw, Corporal Stinson led his group back down the crawl trench they had come up, however, not before searching the dead Chinese officer. Stinson himself personally covered the withdrawal and personally killed three enemy at a distance of 5–10 feet (1.5–3 metres).

As the entire patrol was extricating themselves from the chaos they had created, Peterson called down another heavy-artillery bombardment. The firm base also lent a hand to support the withdrawal. They pumped small arms and two-inch mortar bombs (fired at low trajectory and close range) into the pursuing enemy. Under the curtain of fire, the patrol was able to break clean and make their way back to friendly lines.

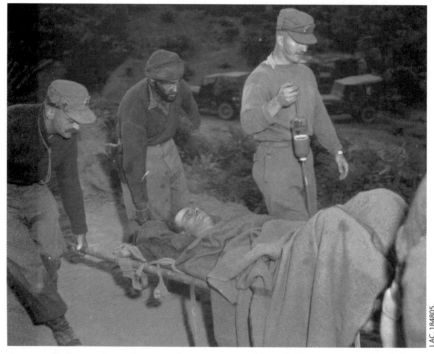

A wounded member of a patrol on return to friendly lines is evacuated for further medical attention.

Upon return, Corporal Stinson, who had just finished his 25th patrol, made no attempt to have his wounds dressed, and in fact did not even disclose he was wounded until he had finished his patrol debrief.[15] Based on the documentation gathered, the Chinese "officer" actually turned out to be Private Ho Chee Fah and no valuable information was retrieved.[16] Although no prisoners were taken, the patrol had met the other requirement. They counted five enemy killed and at least five wounded. Their own casualties amounted to four wounded.

NOTES

1. When the Japanese surrendered in 1945, the U.S. occupied the southern half of Korea and the Soviet Union moved into the northern half. The 38th Parallel was used as a boundary. The intent was a temporary occupation pending steps to establish a unified independent country. However, as the Cold War developed, the divided country became part of the growing conflict between former allies. The Americans created a democratic state under Syngman Rhee. On 10 May 1948, elections were held in South Korea and on 15 August the Republic of Korea was established and subsequently recognized by the UN General Assembly. The Soviet Union immediately countered and established and armed a Communist state, the Democratic People's Republic of Korea, under the control of wartime guerilla leader Kim Il Sung. Moreover, by December they announced that they had withdrawn all their forces from the peninsula and thus forced the Americans to do the same. Shortly thereafter, trouble began to brew as North Korean patrols began to penetrate into South Korea. With the withdrawal of the Americans the ROK army, armed with only small arms and mortars, was left to face a hostile well-armed neighbour.

2. William Johnston, *A War of Patrols* (Vancouver: UBC Press, 2003), 37.

3. "2nd Bn. The Royal Canadian Regiment," *The Connecting File*, Fall–Winter 1951–52, 12.

4. "Battalion Notes," *The Connecting File*, Spring–Summer 1952, 31.

5. "Commanding Officers Conference," 080930 Jun 52. Appendix C, War Diary, 1 RCR 1 Jun 52–30 Jun 52. RCR Museum Archives.

6. Wood, 189.

7. "Preliminary Report on 1 RCR Fighting Patrol, Night 31 May/1 Jun 52," Appendix X, War Diary, 1 RCR 1 Jun 52–30 Jun 52. RCR Museum Archives.

8. "Preliminary Report on 1 RCR Fighting Patrol, Night 31 May/1 Jun 52."

9. *Ibid.*

10. *Ibid.*; and "RCR Fighting Patrol on Point 113, 31 May 52. Account of Interview with 14 participants, by Major F.G.B. Maskell and Capt F.R. McGuire, in Paekhang-myon Area on 5 June 52," Directorate of History and Heritage (DHH), File 145.2R13.013 (D6).

11. "RCR Fighting Patrol on Point 113, 31 May 52."

12. "Further Information Supplied by NCO IC No. 2 Section," Appendix B to "RCR Fighting Patrol on Point 113, 31 May 52."

13. "Intelligence Brief (based on info available up to 25 Mar 52) Prepared by: General Staff (Intelligence) HQ 1 Commonwealth Division," 12. War Diary, 2 RCR 1 Mar 52- 31 Mar 52. RCR Museum Archives.

14. "RCR Fighting Patrol on Point 113, 31 May 52."

15. "Award of Military Medal to SG 9631 Corporal Arthur Irvine Stinson, Royal Canadian Infantry Corps." RCR Korea Awards & Citations, RCR Museum Archives.

16. "Preliminary Report on 1 RCR Fighting Patrol, Night 31 May/1 Jun 52."

CHAPTER 11

The Defence of Strong Point Centre: 14 August 2006

BERND HORN

The day started out as all the others, under a blue cloudless sky. Although still early in the morning, the relentless sun began to bake the soldiers of "Charles" Company ("C" Coy), of the 1st Battalion, The Royal Canadian Regiment Battle Group (1 RCR BG), also known as Task Force 3-06. The Canadian soldiers from Petawawa, based in northern Ontario, took the heat in stride. More irritating was the constant dust churned up by any movement, whether vehicle, human, or wind. The fine talcum powder-like sand covered everything and it was impossible to keep anything clean. To add to the misery were the unremitting sand fleas and flies that tortured the soldiers without pause.

"Charles" Company was deployed in fortified outposts along a stretch of new road that was being constructed in the Pashmul area of Kandahar Province in Southern Afghanistan in the aftermath of NATO's Operation MEDUSA. This offensive operation was designed to root out and destroy the Taliban, who had made this area a stronghold. In fact, Kandahar province, and this area specifically, was the birthplace and heartland of the Taliban movement. In early September 2006, the International Security Assistance Force's (ISAF) Multi-National Brigade, centred on the combat power of Task Force 3-06, engaged the militants, killing hundreds and forcing the remainder to withdraw.

The war, however, was far from over. Hard-core Taliban forces infiltrated back into the area. They simply blended back into the countryside and among the local population. They adopted guerrilla and terrorist tactics — intimidating locals and coercing them to provide support to the Taliban; planting improvised explosive devises and mines; deploying suicide bombers in vehicles, on bicycles and on foot; and conducting hit-and-run attacks against Coalition forces throughout the area. The enemy was skilled and extremely clever. They quickly learned the limitations of the Coalition's capabilities and constraints of their rules of engagement (ROE). As such, the Taliban struck back swiftly and with some effect. The security situation once again quickly deteriorated and Canadian casualties began to mount.

Despite this renewed activity by the Taliban in the wake of the destruction wrought by Operation MEDUSA, there was considerable pressure brought to bear by ISAF headquarters (HQ) to press on with reconstruction in order to show progress was being made. Although still engaged in a deadly struggle with Taliban forces, Task Force 3-06 did what it could.

The construction of the road seemed a good place to start. Indeed, the road would serve a twofold function. First, it fulfilled a security requirement. The only existing route through the area was a narrow dirt road that snaked its way through close canalizing terrain that cut through built-up areas and a complex array of compounds. It was impossible to secure and a nightmare to traverse. Most of the armoured vehicles were simply too large. Moreover, improvised explosive devices (IEDs) and ambushes were a constant threat in an environment that clearly favoured the Taliban.

The new road cut a 100-metre-wide swath straight through the marijuana fields and grape vineyards. Its wide berth and straight trajectory provided easy observation, control, and security. More importantly, this easily accessible road, which would eventually be paved, would furnish local farmers with an excellent route that would allow produce and trade to transit quickly from the fertile Arghandab River valley to Highway 1 — the major artery leading to Kandahar City and elsewhere.

But before these two major benefits could be reaped the road had to be completed. The 1 RCR BG soldiers faced a formidable task. With a very active area of operations (AO) spanning approximately 60,000 square kilometres, the Battle Group was stretched thin. Exacerbating this challenge was the fact that in less than two months TF 3-06 already suffered roughly 15 killed and 85 wounded. Very few of the replacements had yet arrived and the leave plan had now also kicked in and troops were being rotated out of theatre for the three weeks of leave that they were entitled to during the six-month tour. Moreover, the Taliban

Photo by B. Horn.

A LAV III from 7 Platoon provides security for Route Summit, which was under construction.

harassed the thinly stretched troops persistently. During the night they would stealthily plant IEDs and mines in the sandy furrow that currently represented the road. In addition, the Taliban deployed small teams that would attempt to surprise and ambush the Canadian troops. They had already immobilized two bulldozers and several other vehicles through IED and mine strikes.

To compound the problems of the Battle Group even more, the terrain in the area was a soldier's worst nightmare. Marijuana fields as high as nine feet tall obscured visibility, even when observing from a turret of a Light Armoured Vehicle (LAV) III. The plants absorbed energy and heat so readily that it was extremely difficult to penetrate the forests of "pot" with thermal surveillance equipment. Burning the fields with white phosphorous and diesel fuel also failed because the plants were still too full of water. Therefore, the Taliban had a high degree of freedom of movement.

To add to the difficulties, the rest of the landscape was covered by grape vineyards, which consisted of an array of one-metre-high dirt walls approximately a metre apart, upon which the vines grew. These provided additional protection from which to fire from, or to move across the battlefield undetected. And then there were the large array of buildings and compounds and other walls, as well as 10-metre-high grape-drying huts with firing ports already built in throughout the area. These structures, along with many of the others in the area, were virtually impregnable strongholds, as their walls were anywhere from 0.5–1.5 metres thick. They were constructed of a mix of mud, thatch, and straw. Once they had dried and baked in the heat of the sun they were as solid as concrete and could only be penetrated by powerful munitions. In addition, the entire area was interconnected with a canal system that allowed concealed high-speed dismounted approaches throughout much of the battlefield.

To assist "C" Coy in securing the road construction, Afghan National Security Forces (ANSF) were finally, after weeks of cajoling the National government, sent to the area. However, although welcomed, they were of limited value. Although the Afghan National Army (ANA) troops that arrived were fairly professional, adequately trained, and ready to enter battle — if they had Canadians along — there were just too few of them. Instead of the 300 troops promised, only a small group of approximately 40 actually arrived to help.

Conversely, the Afghan National Police (ANP) were qualitatively on the exact opposite extreme of the spectrum. Young, untrained, and answerable to the Governor of the Province, they resembled and behaved more like common thugs than police. They wore no uniforms, and were notoriously corrupt and unreliable. Significantly, large elements therein were suspected of being sympathetic to, if not in league with, the Taliban.

Within this context, "Charles" Company began yet another normal day in what can arguably be called the "Wild West." As the experienced and hardened commanding officer (CO) of the Battle Group, Lieutenant-Colonel Omer Lavoie rolled down the new road, which was still under construction, with his four-vehicle convoy to coordinate with his sub-units and verify defences and progress being made, he came across call sign (C/S) 33A (i.e. 1 Section, of 9 Platoon, of "C" Coy). Their LAV III, which was located halfway between the 7 and 9 Platoons' positions, had backed over an IED and the vehicle had become a mobility kill. Luckily, no one was injured. Unfortunately, the Task Force had just lost another precious vehicle that would be hard to replace.

Significantly, the IED had been placed in the middle of the unfinished road about 400 metres from 7 Platoon's defensive position, which was co-located with a small ANA detachment. Everyone was mystified as to how this had transpired. How had the "ghosts of Panjwayi" planted it without being seen? But, an IED strike was not an uncommon occurrence and efforts soon turned to recovering the vehicle back to Patrol Base Wilson (PBW).

As the morning wore on, members of 7 Platoon continued with their surveillance duty in the growing heat. Those not on duty within the LAV III or sentry positions sheltered themselves under a tarp behind the protection of a low wall that was situated between two buildings that had been partially destroyed in recent fighting during Operation MEDUSA. On the opposite side of the wall ran a canal in which an ANA detachment had taken residence. The ANA manned several observation posts (OPs) that were constructed to control the old road and the terrain to the west.

The members of the platoon had been in the field in this threat environment for 23 days straight. They slept, ate, and tried to relax in the filth that surrounded them. They slept on thermarest mattresses on the ground with their body armour at their side. Water in short supply, and facilities lacking — washing clothes was unheard of and even personal hygiene was limited. The incessant dust covered everything and made maintenance of weapons and vehicles a constant concern. Conditions were primitive, to say the least.

At approximately 1100 hours, a radio message arrived stating that a group of three Taliban had been seen to the West of 7 Platoon's position. Warrant Officer (WO) Ray McFarlane, the Platoon Warrant/second-in-command (2IC), and Sergeant (Sgt) Donovan Crawford quickly coordinated with the ANA detachment. After patiently trying to convey the message to the ANA leader, who understood some English, and with a large degree of innovative sign language, the message was passed and the ANA mobilized. With members of 7 Platoon close by, with their 60 mm mortar ready to engage in the fight, the ANA sent a small patrol out several hundred metres from the position to investigate the sighting.

A short time later excited voices could be heard close by, followed by the "whoosshh" and explosion of an RPG 7 rocket and the crack of some small-arms fire. Within minutes the ANA soldiers returned with great

Photo by B. Horn.

Warrant Officer Ray McFarlane discusses course of action with ANA detachment commander and his own troops during a report of enemy activity in the vicinity during the morning of 14 August 2006.

big smiles gesturing with a wave of the hand and a simple "Taliban gone." WO McFarlane was unable to ascertain whether the Taliban had been killed or simply scattered. Each question elicited the same grunts and nodding of heads from the ANA patrol. Nonetheless, the threat seemed to have dissipated for the moment.

Meanwhile, several kilometres down the road to the south, 9 Platoon (C/S 33) manned their position. It was given the designation "Strong Point Centre," aptly named since it was the middle position within the Battle Group's defensive network that followed the path of the new road from PBW on Highway 1 to the imposing Ma'Sūm Ghar mountain feature where "A" Company, which had been seconded from the 2nd Battalion, Princess Patricia's Light Infantry, was constructing the new Forward Operating Base (FOB) Zettlemeyer. Strong Point Centre was a formidable position that was based around an imposing mud structure and built on a small outcropping that dominated the road and the surrounding area.

Photo by B. Horn.

The centre of Strong Point Centre prior to the attack. C/S 33C covers the Southwestern portion of Route Summit.

The platoon used the natural lay of the land to anchor their defence. Two LAV IIIs flanked the position and covered the western approach and the road. To their front lay a 100-metre swath of sand and beyond that, marijuana fields, grape vineyards, and an array of mud compounds and grape-drying huts. Visibility was limited. Sheltered behind the large mud building that was the centre point of the defensive position and protected by a natural wall to its other side, another LAV III aimed its deadly 25 mm cannon to the north covering the road approach. Finally, dug into the raised island that was Strong Point Centre were two machine-gun pits. One faced south to control the road, while the other faced east to cover the close terrain, mainly grape vineyards, which bordered right up to the defensive position. The platoon had augmented the natural fortress with a series of sandbagged walls.

Much like 7 Platoon, the soldiers rotated between sentry duty in the LAVs or in the machine-gun posts and catching up on sleep or a meal. Manpower was especially tight since the section in the IED strike in the morning were back at PBW getting checked out medically for any injuries sustained during the blast. The platoon also played host to a number of visitors. A local district chief, his ANP bodyguard, and civil-military affairs (CIMIC) personnel conducted an on-site meeting to discuss the progress of the road. In addition, a combat cameraman and a senior officer on a technical assistance visit were also present. The incidents of the morning seemed to harbour no sinister omen and were largely forgotten. After all, those types of events were virtually everyday occurrences.

Back at 7 Platoon, at approximately 1430 hours the gunner in the turret of the LAV covering south along the road and the vast fields to the east summoned WO McFarlane. Out in the grape vineyards, approximately 200–300 metres away, six men, ostensibly "farmers" as they carried no weapons, calmly walked south through the fields in single file towards a large grape-drying hut located approximately 400 metres from 7 Platoon's position. ROEs forbade firing on unarmed civilians regardless of how suspicious they appeared. The Taliban were aware of this and utilized their ability to blend in with the normal farmers to their advantage. Identifying friend from foe was one of the greatest challenges in this environment. The Task Force soldiers observed fighting-age males in the fields on many occasions, but whether they were legitimate farmers or Taliban posing as such was difficult to ascertain. With cached weapons throughout the area, the enemy could transform from one to the other and back again very quickly. Determining who was the enemy, as well as being able to physically dominate the ground and sweep it for weapons was almost impossible due to the shortage of personnel.

Lacking manpower to send a patrol to investigate, WO McFarlane attempted to convince the ANA to follow up; however, the ANA claimed they too lacked the troops to wander out into the fields to scrutinize the suspicious party. Quite simply, without direct Canadian participation, they would not venture out. As a result, McFarlane was forced to try and keep surveillance on the individuals as long as possible since he was unable to take any other action. Not surprisingly, the "farmers" quickly melted away into the maze of walls, buildings, and vegetation.

At approximately 1450 hours, the visitors started to congregate at the front of the position to await the CO's convoy. Lieutenant Ray Corby, the 9 Platoon Commander, had taken over the platoon three weeks prior when the casualties incurred in the early days of Operation MEDUSA triggered a reshuffling of personnel. Corby was proud of his platoon and all they had already endured and was confident of their current position, which was well sited and very defensible.

While waiting for the vehicles to arrive, Corby made an effort to speak to the district chief but was brushed off. He turned his attention to the CIMIC detachment commander, Chief Warrant Officer Fred Gratton. However, he was interrupted three times in a span of less than 10 minutes by the district chief who persistently asked when his ride would be arriving. During that same period the district chief received two phone calls on his cellphone and placed another call himself. He seemed desperately eager to leave.

The CO arrived at Strong Point Centre at approximately 1455 hours and dismounted to briefly discuss details of the earlier IED incident with Lieutenant Corby while the visiting personnel at the location loaded onto the vehicles that made up the CO's tactical HQ (or 9er Tac). Just as the vehicles were in the midst of loading, a threat warning came over the air — "a Canadian position was in imminent threat of attack." The grid given was uncomfortably close to their current position. The soldiers had learned to dread these threat warnings — they were usually accurate. Inside Strong Point Centre, the warning was relayed verbally

Photographer Sergeant Lou Penney, DND Combat Camera.

9er Tac arriving to Strong Point Centre minutes before the attack. C/S 33B, which bore the brunt of the enemy's initial barrage of fire, is in the forefront.

to Lieutenant Corby. As he formulated his next course of action, the initiative was wrested away from him. Less than a minute passed from the time he was given the notice to all hell breaking loose.

The initial barrage of enemy fire caught the soldiers of "C" Coy by surprise. The attack commenced with multiple RPGs being fired at the position. A minimum of three RPGs were fired in close succession, targeting C/S 33B, which was manning the southwest perimeter of the position, an empty trench on the western flank of the strongpoint and the OP on the southeast of the defensive that contained a C-6 general-purpose machine gun (GPMG). A high volume of small-arms fire also hit the position, some rounds impacted short and kicked up the dust on the new road while others cracked over the heads of the "C" Coy troops.

Lieutenant Corby was in the midst of discussing the platoon's course of action with Sergeant Jamie Walsh. As the RPG rockets and small-arms fire rained in, the reaction was immediate. Corby and Walsh dove for cover behind a small berm located behind C/S 33C, which was the

Photo by B. Horn.

Temporary shaded rest area for members of 7 Platoon. The ANA detachment was located on the other side of the mud wall to the left of the photograph. This position was one of the five targets that came under enemy attack at 1500 hours on 14 August 2006.

LAV in the centre of the position. From this vantage point, looking towards the southwest, they could see smoke coming from the treeline and marijuana fields, as well as rounds splashing across the sand of the new road towards them. Visibility was quickly obscured as the dust was kicked up by the fire. Nevertheless, it seemed the concentration of the enemy attack was coming from the west. As such, they had the bright sun to mask their movement and blind the defenders.

Those on sentry duty responded with alacrity. The 25 mm cannons on the LAVs, aided by their thermal sights that could see through the dust, thundered in reply, supported by light machine guns (LMGs) and GPMGs while the others quickly manned their fighting positions.

When the storm struck, Private Jess Larochelle was in the south-most machine-gun pit. The enemy attack washed over him like a rogue wave. His position erupted in explosions, as bullets and shrapnel hissed through the air around him. Larochelle thought he was hallucinating as he saw seemingly mini-explosions go off above his outpost. Little did he realize at the time that the enemy was using RPG munitions that emitted mini cluster rounds from its 75 mm warhead, which in turn exploded, spraying deadly shrapnel much like an air-burst round. Despite the weight of fire he continued to fire at his invisible antagonists who were cloaked by the treeline.[1]

Close by, the CO's tactical HQ had just started to roll when a RPG rocket swished to the rear and exploded in a ball of flame approximately 80 metres behind the convoy, where mere minutes prior the CO, platoon commander, and others had been standing. The three LAVs and the RG-31 Nyala armoured vehicle, which made up the tactical HQ, quickly swung around and immediately began to engage the enemy, adding an enormous amount of fire into the fields and buildings to the west from where the enemy assault was originating.

Unfortunately, it was a bit too late. As the "pum-pum-pum" of the 25 mm cannons echoed across the battlefield, the first situation report (sitrep) cut through the noise of the battlefield and hit everyone as if they had been struck through the heart with a spike — "two VSA [vital signs absent], three wounded." Stark reality once again set in. The Taliban are little match for the Western forces in either equipment or firepower. As a result, they rely on surprise, either through IEDs, mines, or ambushes. And they depend on achieving success in the first 30 seconds of the engagement before they become engulfed in return fire. Once again they got lucky.

The crew and section of C/S 33B were resting when the attack commenced. Private Jesse Kezar was in the driver's hatch and Corporal Jeremy Penney was in the gunner's seat when the initial barrage of fire hit. Corporal Penney attempted to fire the 25 mm gun, but the cannon jammed. Corporal Darryl Jones was in the process of moving into the turret from the rear of the LAV when the RPG round struck around the vehicle's laser warning tower. The resultant explosion showered the area with shrapnel, as lethal shards of metal and blast washed down through the rear air sentry hatch and over the back deck, killing one soldier who had been seated on the left bench and wounding another who was seated on the right bench. The same round also killed the section commander and wounded two others who were at the back of the LAV.

At exactly the same time, at 1500 hours, 7 Platoon was also hit. RPK machine-gun fire and RPGs engulfed the surprised troops. Bullets stitched their way along the wall that soldiers earlier had rested against, kicking up dirt and forcing all to find cover. The fire emanated from the grape-drying hut where the six "farmers" were seen heading to earlier. The platoon replied in rapid succession, bringing all its firepower, as well as that of the neighbouring ANA, to bear. During the contact as many as 20–30 enemy were sighted in this area alone. Notwithstanding the enemy's strength, the situation was brought under control.

Back at 9 Platoon, Sergeant Walsh organized his section to better engage the enemy in their location. He placed Corporal Nick Damchuk, Private Jay Royer, and Private Garret Achneepineskum behind a small berm directly behind his LAV, C/S 33C, where they laid down suppressing fire to the area west of the stronghold. Sergeant Walsh then deployed Corporal Chris Saumure and Private Ed Runyon-Lloyd at the front of the LAV to observe for enemy activity to the east of the position. Corporal Mike Lisk was in the turret of C/S 33C and he was soon joined by Master-Corporal Rob Murphy, who used the small escape hatch on the side of the LAV to crawl up into the turret. Due to the lack of enemy activity in their primary arcs to the northeast of the position, Master-Corporal Murphy traversed the turret over the back deck of the LAV so that the cannon could be fired to the southwest. He then used the height of the pintle-mounted machine gun to fire over the high feature to their front to add extra firepower to the fight. All the while, Corporal Jeff Morin began redistributing ammunition to the section as the scale of the combat quickly depleted the immediate supply.

Simultaneously, Lieutenant Corby quickly moved to his HQ LAV that was sited on the north side of the position to ensure that a contact report had been sent out. As he neared his vehicle he could see they were busy engaging a large number of enemy directly to the west. Corporal Morgan Gonci had been in the driver's hatch prior to the attack. As the first few rockets exploded nearby he could feel the LAV shake. Corporal James White, observing from the gunner's seat, also felt C/S 33 reel as a RPG rocket hit the front right side of the LAV, ripping off some of its up-armour plating. With the onset of the attack, Sergeant Craig Dinsmore crawled up through the rear of the vehicle into the crew commander's seat and Corporal Gonci immediately began to provide target indication from the driver's hatch. At the same time, Corporal Shane Robertson and Corporal Joey Paolini jumped into the back of LAV and raised the ramp. When Lieutenant Corby arrived he banged repeatedly on the back door until it was opened. He then instructed Robertson and Paolini to provide security to the north of C/S 33 to ensure the enemy did not outflank their position.

Corby now took a headset and sent a supplementary contact report on the company net. He also requested a fire mission, sending his exact location, the distance to the enemy, and the bearing of 4800 mils. Fortuitously, Major Greg Ivey, G29 the CO's affiliated battery commander who travelled in the 9er Tac convoy, was already in the process of calling in artillery support. Within 10 minutes of the start of the engagement, 155 mm rounds exploded with an earth-shaking "krummpp" 400 metres away, danger close, from Strong Point Centre. In addition, word was passed over the net that "AH" (Apache attack helicopters) were on their way.

Satisfied that the call for fire was taken care of, Corby now tried to raise his sections on the radio to get a more accurate read on the battle. He began with the OP with the GPMG as it had the highest vantage point. He became concerned when he received no reply. His second call went to C/S 33B to the south of the position. Corby received a sitrep from Corporal Jones, who was in the turret of the 2 Section LAV. Jones informed the platoon commander that they had two casualties who were vital signs absent. He also requested a medic to look after the other three wounded soldiers. Corby questioned Jones on the extent of the other injuries and determined that they were not critical. Luckily there was an advanced qualified soldier, Master-Corporal Jeremy Leblanc, to administer first aid. However, he was in dire need of additional medical supplies. As a result, Corby decided not to risk his only medic by sending her across exposed terrain in light of the heavy volume of enemy fire. Instead, Corby grabbed the medical bag and made his way to 2 Section's location himself.

Meanwhile, Corporals Paolini and Robertson, on the outside of the HQ vehicle, were busy engaging the enemy. Between the two soldiers they saw two separate groups, five individuals in total, with small arms and RPGs engaging their position.

Out on the road, the CO's convoy continued to pour fire into the buildings, wood line, and marijuana fields. C/S 9B2, commanded by Captain Chris French, the forward deployed operations officer, developed a malfunction with their 25 mm cannon. As a result, when the call came from 9 Platoon HQ that they were in desperate need of ammunition, Captain French rushed his vehicle over to Strong Point Centre. Dropping the ramp, Corporal Nick Friesen and one of the passengers grabbed heavy cans of ammunition and dashed across the open ground, ducking into C/S 33 to drop the badly needed supplies. They were immediately joined by Corporal Robertson, who assisted in the hauling of ammo. The original two would later make a similar dash to pick up casualties only to learn that the issue had already been settled — such is the confusion of combat.

At about this time, Lieutenant Corby moved back to C/S 33C, which occupied the centre of the platoon position. He looked across at C/S 33B and could see that the turret was still firing. He quickly informed Sergeant Walsh of his plan to run the medical bag first to the OP and then to C/S 33B's location. Corporal Damchuk and Private Achneepineskum proceeded to lay down a wall of suppressive fire as Corby made his mad dash.

To get to 2 Section's LAV he first had to pass by the southernmost OP. Corby did not expect to find anyone alive. As he arrived at the bowl in the centre of the strongpoint position, which was also the casualty collection point, he was able to get eyes on the OP. At first glance it had appeared that the OP had been struck hard. He could not see anyone and the tarp that had been hung above the outpost to provide shade had been torn away by the fire and now hung in tattered rags. Close by he could see the empty casings of four M72 launchers.

Corby called out twice to the OP. He finally got a response. Private Larochelle poked his head up with his C-6 and confirmed he was "okay" and "by himself." The platoon commander then directed Larochelle to provide covering fire so he could enter the OP. Larochelle then pointed out where he had been engaging the enemy with his C-9 LMG, the C-6 GPMG, and the M72s. The firefight had been so brisk that Larochelle was down to his last half belt of 7.62 mm GPMG ammunition. He had weathered the storm and continued to fire at any movement or weapon signature he could see. He also maintained his discipline and continued to observe his arcs of fire to ensure no enemy was approaching from the east, even though he was taking heavy fire from the west.

Corby was humbled by the young soldier's valiant efforts. However, he had no time to reflect on Larochelle's courage — there was work to be done. Corby now instructed Larochelle to lay down more fire so he could make his final way to 2 Section's (C/S 33B) LAV. Corby promised that when he returned he would bring additional ammo.

After the first deadly RPG strike, Corporal Jones had remedied the gun malfunction and started to return fire. A second RPG round then hit C/S 33B, setting off the automatic fire-extinguishing system in the LAV. When Lieutenant Corby arrived, he quickly recognized that they had in fact suffered two killed. Master-Corporal Leblanc, who himself was wounded, had bandaged up the casualties, while the rest of the section were on the line busy returning fire from a sandbagged wall they had constructed adjacent to the LAV position. Once patched up, Corporals Chris Dowhan and Chris Meace joined their section on the firing line.

By this time the "C" Coy soldiers were about 15–20 minutes into the fight. Corby now sent another sitrep to his company HQ. He learned that the company second-in-command was on the scene with numerous other LAVs to lend a hand. Corby then recommended that they form a firing line north of his position and orientate themselves to the southwest so that they could assist in suppressing the enemy's heavy fire into Strong Point Centre.

As the battle dispositions were discussed, Corporal Jones reported a second stoppage of the cannon. Master-Corporal Leblanc, despite his wounds, switched places with Corporal Jones in an attempt to rectify the stoppage. However, becoming faint and weak from loss of blood, he was pulled from the turret and Corporal Jones returned to do what he could.

Once Lieutenant Corby learned that 1 Section, who had hit the IED in the morning, were on their way back out with a replacement LAV, which was just off the assembly line, and that the Bison ambulance was now disabled, he decided to use C/S 33B to evacuate the dead and wounded to PBW. This would get his men back to PBW for medical attention quickly and C/S 33A could provide the necessary reinforcements and added firepower.

By now the Taliban were largely suppressed. The weight of fire and dreaded artillery, which impeded their movement, swung the battle to the advantage of the Task Force soldiers. But, this was of no surprise to the Taliban. They were very aware of Coalition tactics, techniques, and procedures (TTPs) and knew exactly how long it would take Coalition resources to be fed into the battle. To further complicate the response, the Taliban often coordinated attacks to buy themselves more time. Today, they hit simultaneously at five different locations throughout the AO.

The sense of purpose that prevailed throughout the fight was not surprising, but the resounding calmness was. The small engagement was compounded by additional problems, or the "friction" of war. As the 9er Tac convoy jockeyed for firing positions during the fight, one LAV became hung up in a small ditch and required a quick tug to make it mobile again. A more serious concern was that the Bison armoured ambulance, on its way to pick up the casualties, hit a small wall that broke its right front tire. The driver tried to valiantly limp his vehicle into Strong Point Centre, however, the rough terrain just exacerbated the damage and the vehicle was abandoned. The personnel were cross-loaded into C/S 33A and delivered to 9 Platoon. But it was now just another burden for "C" Coy to observe and protect.

By 1530 hours, Corby moved back to the OP in order to link up with Private Larochelle. From there he used the radio to speak with company HQ. At the same time, he noticed that the company quarter master sergeant (CQMS), Warrant Officer Keith Olstad, who was also the acting company sergeant-major (CSM), had arrived with the 7 Pl commander Captain Wessan in order to recover the wounded and provide a re-supply of ammunition. By this time the Platoon 2IC warrant officer, Scott Robinson, had also arrived. He was back at PBW with the damaged LAV from the morning's IED hit, and the moment Robinson heard his platoon was under attack he gathered up 1 Section and a new LAV and rushed to the position. About 100 metres out from the strongpoint, he realized he could not bring the LAV in closer because of the heavy outgoing fire. He dismounted and covered the last part on foot, leaving C/S 33A to join the ring of steel outside the strongpoint to pour fire into the Taliban positions.

Upon entering the 9 Platoon position, Robinson was quickly briefed by the platoon commander on the plan and events quickly unfolded. Warrant Officer Olstad completed the re-supply of 2 Section and the dead and wounded were loaded into the back of C/S 33B. Although Master-Corporal Leblanc insisted on staying on the position, Corby ordered him out. However, the tenacious Leblanc would render one more service. So short on the ground was Corby that he needed the wounded Leblanc to crew command the vehicle back to PBW. As the replacement LAV, C/S 33A, worked its way into position, C/S 33B tore off, and C/S 33A took up its position in the defensive line. With the added reinforcements, Corby now augmented the OP with additional personnel who provided Private Larochelle with some badly needed support and a re-supply of ammunition.

As C/S 33B tore off, Captain French quickly took off in pursuit. The security situation necessitated that vehicles travel as a minimum in pairs so that there was local security and assistance should a vehicle hit a mine, IED, or get ambushed. Moreover, the heavy fighting had depleted stocks of ammunition and, despite the CQMS's re-supply, additional ammunition was desperately needed. C/S 9B2, part of the CO's Tac HQ, was one of the only available vehicles to do the job. As it was, the CO himself remained in the firing line to provide badly needed fire support. Manpower and vehicles were stretched so thin that the unheard of became necessary. The CO was involved intimately in the actual fight.

With the enemy suppressed and the dead and wounded evacuated, Lieutenant Corby now put his thoughts to securing the position for the night. He quickly briefed Sergeant Joe Power, the 1 Section commander whose vehicle replaced C/S 33B on the southern flank of the strongpoint, to get himself organized to hold the position for the night.

Several kilometres away, the two LAVs that had left the strongpoint exploded through the gates of PBW. The entire garrison, at least those not on sentry duty, were waiting to respond. Warrant Officer Steve Konyenburg and the medical team quickly took control of the dead and wounded and arranged the medical evacuation. An American Blackhawk helicopter was already en route and would arrive within minutes. At the same time Warrant Officer Richard Melo had a work party standing by to load ammo and combat supplies. As C/S 9B2 pulled up and lowered the ramp, cans of ammunition were quickly passed forward. The interior of the LAV was literally stuffed with ammunition, taking up every available space right to the roof. Only a small area was left open in the rear so that the rear sentries could man the back hatches. Someone commented, "This will sure ruin our day if we get hit."

Corporal Friesen retorted dryly, "Well, at least we won't feel a thing."

Once uploaded, arrangements were made to bring a 10-ton wrecker to recover the disabled Bison ambulance. The key concern, however, was finding the second escort vehicle. With PBW already depleted of manpower, Captain French approached the surviving crew of C/S 33B. "I need you," he simply stated to a man, and without hesitation they quickly manned their LAV and fell into the three-vehicle convoy.

As the convoy crept through the gates of PBW, darkness descended. It was pitch black as the small packet of vehicles inched its way over the sandy terrain that represented the new road under construction. The sound of fighter aircraft streaking over the route and defensive position was reassuring. F-18 and F-16 fighter aircraft remained on station the entire night, providing observation and fire when required. At one point an air strike lit up the darkness with a bright orange wall of flame — a beautiful sight in a macabre sort of way.

And then battlefield "friction" kicked in once again. Losing the roadway in the dark, the 10-ton wrecker became stuck and, in the process of trying to get out, blew the driveshaft. The weight of the wrecker and the soft, sandy soil negated the LAVs as a means of extraction. There were now two vehicles disabled. And then the second escort LAV, C/S 33B, which had sustained some damage to its turret earlier, began to "red-line." With two vehicles down, stopped in close country with a LAV full of ammunition, C/S 9B2 was in a potentially precarious situation.

Once again, the CO shuffled his scarce resources to accomplish the mission. Two engineer LAVs towed the Bison ambulance to 9 Platoon's position for security for the night. They then proceeded to C/S 9B2's location where one LAV remained as security while the other acted as an escort so that the ammunition could be delivered to Strong Point Centre.

Once the ammunition was downloaded, and to ensure the position was secure for the night, the CO directed reinforcements from "B" Coy, specifically 2 Section, 4 Platoon (C/S 21B), be dispatched to support 9 Platoon. This provided a fourth LAV, as well as dismounted infantry that allowed Lieutenant Corby to solidify his northern flank.

As further testimony to the strain the large AO places on the Battle Group, once the CO was convinced Strong Point Centre was secure, he shifted into a recovery/escort role. The engineer bulldozer used to carve out the road and driven by Master-Corporal Lance Hooper, who had two 'dozers blown up under him already, was now employed to tow the 10-wrecker back to PBW under the security umbrella of the CO's tactical HQ convoy.

During this time an updated threat warning was received that indicated the enemy was still planning on pressing attacks throughout the night, however, they would do so as individuals to avoid further risk to themselves. Their attacks earlier had been coordinated efforts that resulted in five simultaneous attacks in the BG's AO. The attack against Strong Point Centre was one of the larger strikes. In any case, the continued threat meant that for 9 Platoon, from the time darkness descended on the battlefield at approximately 1845 hours until sunrise at 0600 hours, the platoon remained at 100 percent stand-to.

Throughout the night soldiers spelled each other off. While some remained vigilant, others cleaned their weapons in preparation for the battle's continuation. In addition, water and food was brought to their fighting positions and soldiers took turns eating and grabbing a few moments of sleep. Throughout the night Lieutenant Corby and his Platoon 2IC, Warrant Officer Robinson, remained awake and moved throughout the position to ensure it was secure.

At 0700 hours, 4 Platoon arrived to relieve the exhausted 9 Platoon. The relief in place went smoothly. 4 Platoon already had a section in place and the entire platoon had already done a stint of duty at Strong Point Centre several weeks earlier. For 9 Platoon it was a bittersweet moment. They had weathered the storm well and shown resilience and courage. Tragically, they lost two of their comrades.

The pain of such loss ran deep, even with hardened men who had already lost so much. Nowhere was the sadness more evident than in the unspoken actions of two individuals. On return to PBW after the action, the CO, the regimental sergeant major (RSM), and a few others sat around exhausted. Little was said — yet, the silence spoke volumes. Quietly, Warrant Officer Olstad, the CQMS, walked up to the RSM, Chief Warrant Officer Bob Girouard, with a very sombre, painful look on his face and a clenched fist. He then took the RSM's hand in his own and placed two "dog-tag" (identification disc) stubs into Girouard's palm. The RSM closed his hand immediately with a firm grasp.[2] Both men looked at each other and nodded. There were no words, yet, more could not have been said. The powerful message expressed in this simple ceremony conveyed the bonds of warriors, yet the sadness of men. As the American General William Tecumseh Sherman said so long ago, "War is hell."

NOTES

1. Private Larochelle was awarded the Star of Valour for his actions.
2. Chief Warrant Officer Bob Girouard was killed weeks later when his Bison AVGP was hit by a suicide vehicle.

CONTRIBUTORS

Major Tony Balasevicius is an infantry officer and member of The Royal Canadian Regiment (RCR). He has served in numerous command positions in The RCR as well as in the Canadian Airborne Regiment. He served as the deputy commanding officer of the 1st Battalion, The RCR, in 2002. He is currently on staff at the Department of Applied Military Science at the Royal Military College of Canada.

John Bell is a senior archivist at Library and Archives Canada. A member of the Canadian Nautical Research Society, he has written extensively on various aspects of Canadian history. His most recent book publications are *Against the Raging Sea: Stories from the Golden Age* (Pottersfield, 2002), *Confederate Seadog: John Taylor Wood in War and Exile* (McFarland, 2002), and *Invaders from the North* (Dundurn, 2006).

(Major) Dr. Andrew Godefroy is head of academic research, outreach, and publications for the Director General Land Capability Development, Canadian Army, as well as the editor of the *Canadian Army Journal*. He holds an MA and PhD in War Studies from the Royal Military College of Canada. He is currently completing a monograph on the conceptual and doctrinal evolution of the Canadian Army since the Second World War.

Major John R. Grodzinski teaches history at the Royal Military College of Canada, where he is also a doctoral candidate in the War Studies program. His areas of interest include North American wars and warfare from 1608 to 1815, particularly the War of 1812. His other academic fields of interests are the Napoleonic Wars, specializing in British operations in the Iberian Peninsula, and the development of smoothbore weaponry.

John also regularly leads battlefield tours to Seven Years' War and War of 1812 sites and is also editor of the online *War of 1812 Magazine*, available through the Napoleon Series website.

(COLONEL) DR. BERND HORN is an experienced infantry officer who is currently serving as the deputy commander of Special Operations Forces Command. He has command experience at the sub-unit and unit level and was the officer commanding 3 Commando, the Canadian Airborne Regiment, from 1993 to 1995 and the commanding officer of the 1st Battalion, The Royal Canadian Regiment, from 2001 to 2003. He is also an adjunct associate professor of history at The Royal Military College of Canada. He has authored, co-authored, edited, and co-edited 20 books and numerous articles on military affairs and military history.

MICHAEL WYCZYNSKI is a senior archivist at Library and Archives Canada. He has authored and co-authored numerous books and articles on Canadian military history and is an acknowledged expert on the Canadian Airborne experience.

INDEX

Marquis Book Printing Inc.

Québec, Canada
2008